ACCOUNTABILITY FOR COLLECTIVE WRONGDOING

Ideas of collective responsibility challenge the doctrine of individual responsibility that is the dominant paradigm in law and liberal political theory. However, little attention is given to the consequences of holding groups accountable for wrongdoing. Groups are not amenable to punishment in the way that individuals are. Can they be punished – and if so, how – or are other remedies available? The topic crosses the borders of law, philosophy, and political science, and in this book, specialists in all three areas contribute their perspectives. They examine the limits of individual criminal liability in addressing atrocity, the meanings of punishment and responsibility, the distribution of group punishment to a group's members, and the means through which collective accountability can be expressed. In doing so, they reflect on the legacy of the Nuremberg Trials, the philosophical understanding of collective responsibility, and the place of collective accountability in international political relations.

Tracy Isaacs is Associate Professor in the Department of Philosophy and the Department of Women's Studies and Feminist Research (which she also chairs) at The University of Western Ontario. She is coeditor, with Samantha Brennan and Michael Milde, of *New Canadian Perspectives in Ethics and Value Theory* (2011) and has published articles in a number of philosophical journals, including *Ethics, Criminal Justice Ethics*, and *The American Philosophical Quarterly*. She has a forthcoming monograph titled *Moral Responsibility in Collective Contexts*.

Richard Vernon is Distinguished University Professor in the Department of Political Science at The University of Western Ontario. His publications include *The Career of Toleration* (winner of the C. B. Macpherson Prize in 1998); *Political Morality: A Theory of Liberal Democracy* (2001); *Friends, Citizens, Strangers: Essays on Where We Belong* (2005); and *Cosmopolitan Regard: Political Membership and Global Justice* (2010). His current work in progress includes a monograph on historical redress.

Accountability for Collective Wrongdoing

Edited by

Tracy Isaacs

The University of Western Ontario

Richard Vernon

The University of Western Ontario

CAMBRIDGE UNIVERSITY PRESS
Cambridge, New York, Melbourne, Madrid, Cape Town, Singapore,
São Paulo, Delhi, Dubai, Tokyo, Mexico City

Cambridge University Press
32 Avenue of the Americas, New York, NY 10013-2473, USA

www.cambridge.org
Information on this title: www.cambridge.org/9780521176118

First published 2011

Printed in the United States of America

A catalog record for this publication is available from the British Library.

Library of Congress Cataloging in Publication data

Accountability for collective wrongdoing / edited by Tracy Isaacs, Richard Vernon.
  p.   cm.
Includes bibliographical references and index.
ISBN 978-1-107-00289-0 (hardback)
1. Criminal liability (International law)   2. Crimes against humanity.
3. Government liability.   I. Isaacs, Tracy Lynn.   II. Vernon, Richard, 1945–
K5301.A923   2011
345'.04–dc22   2010035955

ISBN 978-1-107-00289-0 Hardback
ISBN 978-0-521-17611-8 Paperback

Contents

Contributors

Mark A. Drumbl is the Class of 1975 Alumni Professor at the School of Law, Washington and Lee University.

Toni Erskine is a Professor in the Department of International Relations at the University of Aberystwyth.

Tracy Isaacs is Associate Professor of Philosophy and Women's Studies and Feminist Research and Chair of the Department of Women's Studies and Feminist Research at The University of Western Ontario.

Erin I. Kelly is Associate Professor of Philosophy at Tufts University.

Anthony F. Lang, Jr., is Senior Lecturer in International Relations at the University of St. Andrews.

David Luban is University Professor and Frederick J. Haas Professor of Law and Philosophy at Georgetown University.

Larry May is W. Alton Jones Chair of Philosophy at Vanderbilt University and Professorial Fellow, Centre for Applied Philosophy and Public Ethics, Charles Sturt and Australian National Universities.

Avia Pasternak is Lecturer in political theory at the University of Essex.

Michael P. Scharf is Professor of Law and Director of the Frederick K. Cox International Law Center at Case Western Reserve University School of Law.

Sara L. Seck is Assistant Professor in the Faculty of Law at The University of Western Ontario.

Amy Sepinwall is Assistant Professor in the Department of Legal Studies and Business Ethics at The Wharton School, University of Pennsylvania.

Richard Vernon is Distinguished University Professor in the Department of Political Science at The University of Western Ontario.

Acknowledgments

This book has its origin in a workshop organized by (the former) Nationalism and Ethnic Conflict Research Group at The University of Western Ontario in April 2009. The organizers, Richard Vernon and Tracy Isaacs, are grateful to the Faculty of Social Science (The University of Western Ontario) for the funding that made the group's program of workshops and conferences possible.

An earlier version of Toni Erskine's contribution to this book appeared in *Ethics & International Affairs* 24, no. 3 (2010) and is reprinted with permission of the publisher.

Introduction

Accountability for Collective Wrongdoing

Tracy Isaacs

The contributions to this volume address a range of questions that arise when we start to consider legitimate ways to respond to collective wrongdoing and collective guilt. The chapters that follow cover an array of topics, from the effectiveness of international courts and tribunals, especially atrocity trials, in achieving postconflict justice to home state responsibility for the conduct of transnational corporations. Many of the contributors engage either directly or indirectly with questions of collective punishment and what justified means, if any, there are to punish collectives. Although the notion of collective responsibility is not the central focus of debate in this volume, the authors attend extensively to what collective responsibility consists in and how it distributes, particularly but not exclusively, in the context of justified forms of collective punishment. The issue of distribution raises questions about the nature of membership and the responsibilities, obligations, and even risks to which membership in a collective such as a state or nation gives rise, particularly if that collective is engaged in wrongdoing.

The chapters address the issues from the multiple disciplinary perspectives of law, political science, and philosophy. The volume is divided into two parts. Part I focuses on collective accountability in international law. Part II focuses on distributing accountability. In truth, many of the chapters fit well into both sections, but those in Part I engage more directly with the international legal structures – such as international criminal tribunals, the International Court of Justice (ICJ), and the International Criminal Court (ICC) – and some of the challenges and limitations that those entities have in addressing collective justice.

In this introduction, I take up two tasks. First, I provide a basic historical and scholarly context for the topics that arise in the chapters that follow. Second, using these contexts as a starting point, I draw attention to three main themes that arise throughout the chapters: (1) the limits of individual criminal trials for addressing atrocity; (2) issues about responsibility, punishment, distribution, and group membership; and (3) collective punishment and alternatives.

HISTORICAL CONTEXT

In the aftermath of World War II, two major events occurred that had a profound influence on contemporary thinking about accountability for collective wrongdoing. The first of these events was the establishment of International Military Tribunals to address war crimes committed in World War II. The most famous of these, the Nuremberg Tribunal, was established in 1945 to try high-ranking Nazis accused of war crimes. The Tokyo Tribunal (1946) prosecuted Japanese war criminals. The second event is a more scholarly turn – namely, the publication of Karl Jasper's *The Question of German Guilt* (1947).[1] In the series of lectures that produced this text, Jaspers confronts the question of the guilt of German citizens for the Nazi atrocities of World War II, most notably the Holocaust. Jasper's book stands as a classic text in the large body of scholarship on collective responsibility generated in the latter half of the twentieth century up to the present.

Nuremberg introduced the idea of individual legal guilt and punishment for political crimes. This approach found its way into the United Nations Convention on the Prevention and Punishment of the Crime of Genocide (1947).[2] Between 1949 and 1954, the International Law Commission (ILC) drafted several statutes for an international criminal court, but none was adopted.[3] No agreement could be reached concerning the definition of aggression, and then the Cold War put a stop to further efforts for the next three decades.[4] The possibility of an international criminal court was revisited beginning in 1989, when Trinidad and

---

[1] Karl Jaspers, *The Question of German Guilt*, trans. E. B. Ashton (Dial Press, 1947) from the German *Die Schuldfrage* (1946).

[2] Convention on the Prevention and Punishment of the Crime of Genocide. Resolution 260 (III) A of the U.N. General Assembly on 9 December 1948. Entry into force: January 12, 1951.

[3] "Chronology of the International Criminal Court," n.d. Available at http://www.icc-cpi .int/Menus/ICC/Home.

[4] Joanna Harrington, Michael Milde, and Richard Vernon, "Introduction," *Bringing Power to Justice? The Prospects of the International Criminal Court*, ed. Joanna Harrington, Michael Milde, and Richard Vernon (Montreal: McGill-Queen's University Press, 2006), p. 5.

Tobago asked the United Nations to expand the jurisdiction of international law to include drug trafficking. Although this expansion did not happen, it prompted the UN General Assembly to mandate the ILC to renew its efforts to develop a draft statute for an international criminal court.[5]

During the period leading up to the establishment of the ICC in 2002, the International Criminal Tribunal for the Former Yugoslavia (ICTY)[6] and the International Criminal Tribunal for Rwanda (ICTR)[7] were established by a UN Security Council resolution in 1993 and 1995, respectively, to address ethnic cleansing during the war in the former Yugoslavia and genocide in Rwanda. As at Nuremberg, these tribunals tried individuals, not states. The approach to addressing international crime by trying and prosecuting individuals continues in the ICC in The Hague. The ICC Statute was adopted in 1998 at the United Nations Conference of Plenipotentiaries in Rome. The Statute came into force on July 1, 2002, after receiving the requisite sixty ratifications.[8]

Mark Drumbl has described the approach of the legal prosecution and punishment of individuals for international crimes as following the model of the *liberal criminal trial*.[9] He has also subjected it to great scrutiny and criticism, as have other contributors to this volume. In the second part of this Introduction, I identify some of the key concerns that the authors raise regarding the effectiveness of this approach to international criminal justice. First, I turn briefly to the scholarly context out of which these discussions arise.

The scholarly conversation about collective responsibility that followed Jaspers's examination of German guilt has had as much influence on the subject matter and direction of discussion in this volume as the developments in international criminal law just outlined. Jaspers's lectures raise philosophical questions about the reach, extension, and mechanisms of collective guilt. He draws important distinctions between four types of guilt: criminal guilt, political guilt, moral guilt, and metaphysical guilt.[10]

---

[5] Ibid.

[6] "About the ICTY," the United Nations International Criminal Tribunal for the Former Yugoslavia, n.d. Available at http://www.icty.org/sections/AbouttheICTY.

[7] For an extensive and informative website about the International Criminal Tribunal for Rwanda, see the United Nations International Criminal Tribunal for Rwanda. Available at http://www.ictr.org/.

[8] "Chronology of the International Criminal Court."

[9] See Mark A. Drumbl, *Atrocity, Punishment, and International Law* (Cambridge: Cambridge University Press), as well as Drumbl's contribution to this volume.

[10] Jaspers, *The Question of German Guilt*, p. 31.

His philosophical analysis of the way in which the German people – not just those who participated but the people as a group and as a nation – might bear some guilt for the war crimes of their government and military, generated a scholarly discussion that still takes place today among philosophers, legal scholars, and political scientists. Jaspers points out that "the restriction of the Nuremberg trial to criminals serves to exonerate the German people. Not, however, so as to free them of all guilt – on the contrary. The nature of our real guilt only appears the more clearly."[11] In Jasper's taxonomy of guilt, the sense in which all Germans are guilty is the political sense, in so far as "[w]e were German nationals at the time when the crimes were committed by the regime which called itself German, which claimed to be Germany and seemed to have the right to do so, since the power of the state was in its hands and until 1943 it found no dangerous opposition."[12] In 1963, Hannah Arendt's *Eichmann in Jerusalem: A Report on the Banality of Evil*, a detailed account of Eichmann's trial for crimes against the Jewish people, crimes against humanity, and war crimes, introduced the idea that evil is not the exclusive property of sociopaths.[13] On the contrary, she argues, Eichmann's testimony demonstrates the workaday commitment of a man whose main objective was to discharge the duties of his job as efficiently as possible.

In the decades between the end of World War II and the present, the point of focus has understandably moved away from the specific historical example of the German people in World War II to more general questions about the nature of collective agency and responsibility, including collective intention and collective action. There has been lively debate about the possibility and nature of collective responsibility.[14] Further, although some of the "applied" discussion addresses responsibility for war and war crimes,[15] much of the work has focused on corporate responsibility. Among the most frequently cited works in both the applied and theoretical literature is Peter French's article, "The Corporation as a Moral Person."[16] In it, French argues that corporate structures and

---

[11] Ibid., p. 61.   [12] Ibid., p. 61.

[13] Hannah Arendt, *Eichmann in Jerusalem: A Report on the Banality of Evil* (New York: Viking Press, 1963).

[14] See, for example, Stacey Hoffman and Larry May, eds., *Collective Responsibility: Five Decades of Debate in Theoretical and Applied Ethics* (Savage, MD: Rowman and Littlefield, 1991).

[15] Richard Wasserstrom, "The Relevance of Nuremberg," *Philosophy and Public Affairs* 1, no. 1 (Autumn 1971): 22–46.

[16] Peter French, "The Corporation as a Moral Person," *American Philosophical Quarterly* 16, no. 4 (July 1979): 207–15.

decision-making mechanisms are the basis for intentional corporate action and support the idea that collectivities with sufficient organizational structure fulfill the conditions for moral personhood. When they satisfy the relevant criteria, they may justifiably be held collectively responsible for their actions in a way that is independent of the responsibility of any individual member.

As influential as French's argument has been, the concept of collective responsibility has many detractors. Some object on the grounds that collective entities do not have the requisite qualities for moral agency and that we do better to focus on the moral responsibilities of individual members, whose agency is less contested.[17] The most frequently cited reason against collective responsibility, voiced even before French argued for the corporation as a moral person, is that it holds some people responsible for the actions of others, a state of affairs that smacks of injustice.[18] In response, a number of authors have emphasized that if an attribution of moral responsibility is truly collective, then no individual member of the collective is necessarily implicated.[19] As Jaspers notes, there are a number of ways a person may be guilty, and without an exploration of what collective responsibility is and how it might hold some individuals responsible for the actions of others, the objection underdescribes its complex target. For example, Larry May picks up on Jaspers's notion of metaphysical guilt to explore the means through which membership in a guilty collective might subject a person to *moral taint,* a condition that does not always involve responsibility but, as the word "taint" suggests, also does not leave a person morally spotless.[20]

The concern about moral responsibility implicating or condemning innocent individuals is most urgent when we extend the discussion to the realm of punishment. When we begin to consider collective liability for international crimes, the impact of the actions of some on the lives of

---

[17] Seumas Miller, *Social Action: A Teleological Account* (Cambridge: Cambridge University Press, 2001); Christopher Kutz, *Complicity* (Cambridge: Cambridge University Press, 1999).

[18] See H. D. Lewis, "Collective Responsibility," in *Collective Responsibility,* ed. Stacey Hoffman and Larry May, op. cit., pp. 17–33, and more recently, Jan Narveson, "Collective Responsibility," *The Journal of Ethics* 6, no. 2 (2002): 179–98.

[19] Peter French, "The Corporation as a Moral Person," op. cit.; Tracy Isaacs, "Collective Intention and Collective Moral Responsibility," *Midwest Studies in Philosophy (Shared Intentions and Collective Responsibility)* XXX (2006): 59–73; Toni Erskine, this volume, Chapter 10.

[20] Larry May, "Metaphysical Guilt and Moral Taint," in *Collective Responsibility,* eds. Stacey Hoffman and Larry May, op. cit., pp. 239–54.

others is no longer an abstract concept but a concrete reality. If collective sanctions befall a nation's citizens because of the war crimes of some subset of them, innocent individuals suffer the consequences of others' transgressions. In the wake of the atrocities committed in the former Yugoslavia and Rwanda, recent scholarly work has engaged closely with the prosecution and punishment of criminals in international tribunals and courts, examining the merits, shortcomings, and justice of trying and punishing individuals for collective crimes.[21]

The contributors to this volume advance the discussion about collective punishment in significant ways, taking a careful look at the possibilities for and justice of collective forms of punishment that address wrongdoing at the level of collective entities such as states. In what follows, I articulate the contribution that this volume makes to three themes in particular. First, a number of authors question the emphasis on individual accountability that has emerged as the dominant approach to the prosecution of international crime since Nuremberg and argue that a broader base of responsibility, including the responsibility of states, would more effectively achieve the goals of justice. Second, a host of moral challenges ensue when we consider collective sanctions and the way in which their impact distributes among potentially innocent members of collectives. Here, the discussion addresses not only distribution but also the nature of membership and the extent to which it implicates. Third, the authors examine and propose possibilities for collective punishment as well as alternatives to it. These contributions help us gain practical and theoretical purchase on the problems and debates outlined throughout the volume.

THE "LIBERAL CRIMINAL TRIAL" APPROACH
TO PROSECUTING ATROCITY: CHALLENGES AND LIMITS

Despite mass crimes such as genocide generating interest in collective responsibility, the brief historical overview in the previous section demonstrates that from Nuremberg to the contemporary ICC, the purpose of international criminal trials has been to prosecute individuals.[22] Apart from being extremely resource-intensive, this approach to atrocity

---

[21] Larry May, *Crimes against Humanity: A Normative Account* (Cambridge: Cambridge University Press, 2005); Mark Drumbl, *Atrocity, Punishment, and International Law*, op. cit.

[22] Drumbl, Ibid.

arguably falls short in a number of ways that are taken up in this collection by Drumbl, Lang, and Luban.

In "Collective Responsibility and Postconflict Justice," Drumbl argues that the international criminal courts are ineffective at achieving justice because the liberal criminal trial model is limiting and inconclusive, precisely because it fails to attend to collective responsibility in exactly the sorts of cases in which collective responsibility is most appropriate. Atrocity, maintains Drumbl, is the product of collective violence. Individual participation is "deeply conformist" and simply would not occur outside of the collective undertaking. Thus, maintains Drumbl, the prosecution of individuals through the mechanisms of the ICC simply does not do justice to the nature of the atrocities committed. If, instead of pursuing individual criminal prosecutions and traditional legal punishment such as incarceration, emphasis were placed on collective responsibility, justice might be sought through different mechanisms of accountability. These results could be more satisfying. The prosecution of individual criminals at high-profile atrocity trials not only fails to address the collective nature of the violence committed but is also enormously-resource intensive and leaves as an open question whether convicted perpetrators can ever receive their just deserts, given the nature of the crimes.

In "State Criminality and the Ambition of International Criminal Law," David Luban argues that one of the primary reasons international criminal law focuses on individuals is because of its "fetishization" of the state. This tendency to fetishize states means that officially recognizing a category of state criminality would be heretical. Luban cites the notion of head-of-state immunity as part of the evidence for this claim; until recently, heads of state have enjoyed immunity because they personified the state. International tribunals, however, do not recognize head-of-state immunity; but neither do they prosecute states. Instead, notes Luban, in attributing international crimes to individuals, these tribunals reduce atrocity to "mere crime." This focus sidesteps an important fact: states can be the worst criminals. Moreover, those individuals who do stand trial are not ordinary criminals, even if their brand of evil is of the banal variety. Drumbl points out that war criminals reintegrate well into society and are extremely unlikely to reoffend. Luban maintains that their particular criminality requires not individual evil, but the context of a criminal state. Again, the individual criminal trial does not adequately address this feature of the transgressions in question.

In "Punishing Genocide: A Critical Reading of the International Court of Justice," Anthony Lang suggests that international crimes such as genocide have a "dual criminal nature" in so far as they are crimes of individuals and of states. At present, the recent international tribunals and the ICC are equipped to handle the individual criminal nature of these crimes. The International Court of Justice addresses complaints against states but does not prosecute them as criminals. Thus, the current international legal order cannot sufficiently address state criminality. An explicit statement of the possibility of states being held responsible for the crime of genocide comes from the ICJ in its consideration of the responsibility of Serbia for genocide in Bosnia and Herzegovina. Although the ICJ judgment does not find Serbia responsible for genocide in Bosnia and Herzegovina, it explicitly asserts that states can be held responsible for genocide.

What solutions do we find for the shortcomings of prosecuting individuals for extraordinary crimes such as genocide, war crimes, and crimes against humanity? The authors in this volume make a number of suggestions.

In response to the unsatisfying and limited nature of atrocity trials that follow the liberal criminal trial model, Drumbl suggests that an approach he calls "cosmopolitan pluralism" would more effectively integrate multiple sites of justice at the local, national, and international levels instead of favoring the high-profile international trial. In addition to reclaiming the significance of local and national judicial bodies, this approach would allow for extralegal accountability mechanisms with the primary goals of reconciliation and repair. Such mechanisms might include truth commissions, public inquiries, reparative funds, the politics of commemoration, redistributing wealth, and fostering constitutional guarantees that structurally curb the concentration of power. Such an approach would maintain the integrity and functioning of indigenous institutions of justice instead of forcing them to "judicialize" by conforming to the liberal model if they are to have respect and funding.

As we have seen, Drumbl sees this point as a reason for expanding beyond criminal trials into the broader category of collective responsibility. In so doing, the mass participation and broad complicity does not drift out of sight. Luban urges that state criminality be added to legal doctrine. This latter solution leads to additional questions, which he recognizes must be addressed if his proposal is to have teeth. First, some will question whether a state, being an artificial person, can commit a crime. Luban gestures toward the legal model of agency as one means of addressing this challenge. He notes further that there are promising directions for ascribing acts of humans to states articulated in the International

Law Commission's 2001 "Draft Articles on Responsibility of States for Internationally Wrongful Acts." Corporate criminality provides a legal model of how extending the application of the Draft Article from civil to criminal law might work.

Lang urges a restructuring of the international legal order to capture the duality of international crimes. He maintains that in order to recognize the state and individual dimensions of the crime of genocide, a new relationship between the ICJ and the ICC must be established. The ICJ statement in the Bosnia and Herzegovina genocide case helps to support the argument that, by viewing states as corporate agents, the ICJ might work in a more integrated fashion with the ICC to address the dual nature of international crime.

So far, the main criticism of current judicial means of addressing atrocity we have seen is that the emphasis on the prosecution of individuals inadequately captures the collective element of such crimes. Intermediate between the accountability of states and the accountability of individuals lies the potential accountability of regimes, or of groups of individuals in authoritative positions, who jointly engage in atrocious acts.[23] Michael Scharf's chapter, "Joint Criminal Enterprise, the Nuremberg Precedent, and the Concept of 'Grotian Moment,'" addresses a concept that offers to fill this intermediate space, thus introducing a collective element of criminality into what would ordinarily be individual criminal trials: the concept of "joint criminal enterprise." Scharf's chapter discusses and defends the proposed use of this category in proceedings of the tribunal before which, at the time of writing, some alleged perpetrators of Cambodian atrocities face prosecution. Scharf makes the case that the concept of joint criminal enterprise is supported by precedents dating back to the prosecution of war crimes in World War II. The originating precedents do not, indeed, concern regimes; they concern groups of combatants whose actions resulted in war crimes (the murder of prisoners) in circumstances in which it was impossible to isolate individual culpability – to stand guard while a comrade pulls the trigger is not to commit murder, but it is to be complicit in a murderous "enterprise." However, the relevance of the idea to the case of regimes is clear. Regimes do not pull triggers, but they collectively create circumstances in which triggers get to be murderously pulled, and so should attract accountability. If the idea of "joint criminal enterprise" can be sustained, then we would have

---

[23] See Luban's and Vernon's chapters in this volume (Chapters 2 and 11, respectively) for a discussion of the distinction between a state and a regime.

something important to contribute to solving the problem of individual criminal prosecution for atrocity: we could show that criminal prosecution can extend its reach significantly beyond strict individual culpability. Its potential, in so far as it extends the reach of accountability, is that it may capture just those degrees of culpability that attach to members of a regime whose actions are jointly necessary for atrocity, although none of them individually commits atrocious acts.

The chapters discussed thus far suggest that some revisions to the individual crime and punishment approach of the "liberal criminal trial" are in order. All of the suggestions point in the direction of a model that takes collective responsibility, and in some cases even collective criminality, more seriously. The idea of putting more emphasis on collective responsibility brings us squarely up against skeptical worries about the impact attributions of collective responsibility might have on innocents. The next section takes up this worry, which is primarily about the distribution of responsibility and punishment among members of guilty collectives.

RESPONSIBILITY, PUNISHMENT, DISTRIBUTION, AND MEMBERSHIP

Much of the skepticism directed against collective responsibility turns on the concern that it unjustly distributes punishments to innocents. A number of authors take a close look at the possibilities for collective punishment, and in so doing, they examine questions of distribution and justice. These issues relate closely to the way collective responsibility (not just collective punishment) might distribute, which in turn presses us to clarify our understanding of membership and its implications. Finally, as we have seen in Drumbl's cosmopolitan pluralism and shall see in other chapters as well, punishment is not the only response to collective responsibility. There could be other ways of holding collectives accountable, and these warrant our attention as well.

In "The Distributive Effect of Collective Punishment" (Chapter 8), Avia Pasternak examines the impact collective punishment might have on group members by drawing attention to three bases for distribution: proportional, equal, and random. Recognizing that it is almost inevitable that collective punishment will pose burdens on individuals simply by virtue of their group's wrongdoing, she argues that the way the burden is distributed ought to be taken into account when assessing the legitimacy of collective punishment. Her discussion begins with the example of the proposed academic boycott of Israeli universities, advocated by a number of British academic associations, as a punitive measure against the state of Israel.

Some people (e.g., Peter French) maintain that the harm individuals suffer as a consequence of collective punishment is not to be considered *punishment,* because they are not the intended recipients of the burden. Instead, they experience a derivative harm, in much the same way that the financial hardship the family of a convicted criminal faces is a derivative harm if the criminal goes to prison. Nonetheless, argues Pasternak, derivative harm is not normatively neutral. Considerations of how harm distributes among those who are not the intended recipients of the punitive measure ought to play a role in decisions about a particular punishment's appropriateness.

She considers and evaluates three possibilities for the distribution of the burdens of collective punishment: proportional distributions, in proportion to personal involvement in bringing about the collective harm; equal distributions, distributed equally among all members of the collective; and random distributions, not guided by any systematic principle but randomly befalling people.

Pasternak draws attention to our normative intuitions about fairness. These intuitions tend to be based in our sense of what individuals do and do not deserve. The possibility that someone may bear the burden or cost of punishment although she or he is not individually responsible for the transgression is in conflict with retributive views about desert. The normative considerations in her discussion of the three ways that collective punishment might distribute pick up a thread of the retributive intuition that a person should only suffer punishment to the extent that she or he is responsible. The primacy of retributivism is tempered by Pasternak's claim that equal distribution might be understood as an expression of the value of the common bond of citizenship. Although equal distribution might at first seem to fly in the face of fairness, Pasternak suggests that Michael Walzer's notion of "common destiny" can support equal distribution on normative grounds in so far as "each citizen is tied to outcomes of the political community's shared political goals and institutions in a way that does not depend on his or her personal contributions to it" (p. 226).

Amy Sepinwall invokes a similar idea – co-citizenship – to broaden the reach of accountability in her chapter, "Citizen Responsibility and the Reactive Attitudes: Blaming Americans for War Crimes in Iraq," (Chapter 9). Using American war crimes in Iraq as her running example, she argues that even when not individually culpable, individuals may still bear responsibility for group transgressions. Although she discusses responsibility more than punishment, her conclusion clearly legitimates the *blaming* – that is, the holding responsible – of U.S. citizens for the war crimes of their military. Citizens may be morally responsible without being causally responsible, and they may be blameworthy without considering themselves to be blameworthy. This is not to say that all citizens bear the same relationship to the wrongdoing. Sepinwall recognizes distinctions between dissidents, complacent bystanders, and perpetrators with respect to the magnitude of their responsibility. Dissidents, bystanders, and perpetrators might not share all the same grounds for responsibility, but with respect to war crimes, they share the ground of commitment to the nation itself. This commitment is very like Pasternak's idea of citizenship as common destiny, in which citizens recognize their political activity as a joint venture with other citizens. Sepinwall's emphasis is somewhat different, insofar as she sees the commitment in terms of the value of loyalty to one's fellows. Membership generates an obligation of loyalty: "citizens have an obligation . . . to operate with a certain regard for the ways in which their acts reflect on or contribute to the nation-state" (p. 240). Similar points about membership arise in Richard Vernon's discussion of the risks of citizenship and in Erin Kelly's view, it would stand as a good reason for "cautious thinking ahead to how things might go wrong" (p. 209).

One might worry that if everyone is responsible as co-citizen, then the distinction between perpetrators and nonperpetrators dissipates. However, claims Sepinwall, a perpetrator will bear further responsibility, not just as citizen, but also as perpetrator. In this way, Sepinwall's view makes space for the claim that perpetrators bear more responsibility than bystanders or dissidents, while being able to claim that all citizens bear some responsibility.

In her contribution, "Kicking Bodies and Damning Souls: The Danger of Harming 'Innocent' Individuals while Punishing 'Delinquent' States," Toni Erskine draws attention to the distributive risks of collective punishment. Although the main aim of collective punishment is to punish collectives, she recognizes, as do many others, that this form of punishment has an impact on individuals in a number of ways. First, it might render them vicariously responsible, in the sense that all are held responsible for the misdeeds of some. Second, it might result in misdirected harm, such that individuals are punished instead of the state, for the simple reason that "lacking a soul to be damned and a body to be kicked," the collective cannot really be punished. Third, institutional punishment might result in "overspill" or collateral damage, through which individuals indirectly suffer the burden of institutional punishment. In the case of overspill, because the punitive action is neither intended nor directed against these people as targets, it does not automatically undermine collective punishment, although the overspill ought to be minimized. With respect to vicarious responsibility and misdirected harm, however, innocent individuals are specifically implicated and targeted, thus rendering these consequences unjust. Erskine maintains that punishment may only distribute if responsibility for the action or omission to which it is a response also justly distributes. This conclusion places a fairly stringent restriction on legitimate uses of collective punishment in cases where it distributes. Once again, however, it is worth noting that overspill or collateral damage is not the same thing as punishment, and if that is the only consequence, then collective punishment might be justly imposed.

Thinking about the way collective responsibility and punishment distribute down to individual group members turns significantly on our understanding of group membership. Drumbl, introducing a helpful distinction, suggests that group membership be defined in a "crude–careful" manner for the purposes of liability. To define membership crudely is to base it wholly on one crude feature of a group, that is, nationality, ethnicity, religion, or inhabited territory. To define it carefully is to work on the basis of individual causal responsibility, according to which one is a member of a culpable group for liability purposes only if one's action or inaction causally implicates one in the wrongdoing. Drumbl's moderate position defines group membership crudely but provides individuals with an opportunity to demonstrate that they should be excluded from the liable group. This crude–careful approach to group membership moderates the concern about wrongfully implicating innocent group members. When Sepinwall and Pasternak invoke the values of co-citizenship and of a common destiny to justify more broadly implicating compatriots in the transgressions of their states, they are closer to the crude than the careful side of Drumbl's continuum. An "opt-out" option would compromise the values they use to ground their conclusions. In some ways, Erskine's approach is more careful. Where distribution of punishment is concerned, those who are punished must be individually responsible as well. With respect to the way the *harm* might distribute, however, she is closer to the crude side of the spectrum, recognizing harm to innocents as potentially unavoidable. We can see that cruder and less careful approaches to group membership legitimate broader implications and leave less space for individuals to escape bearing the costs of membership legitimately. As Richard Vernon notes in his chapter, "Punishing Collectives: States or Nations?" (Chapter 11), group membership has its risks. This is especially true if membership is defined crudely.

Vernon maintains that whether individuals might bear a personal share of punishment in virtue of their membership depends on their relationship to the collective entity – are they co-citizens of a state or conationals of a nation? We are to understand states as essentially politically organized entities and nations as essentially historically abiding entities. The dividing of Germany at the end of World War II, for example, might be understood as a sanction directed against the German state or at the German national identity. The subject of the sanction (state or nation) has a moral bearing, argues Vernon, on the justice of a downward distribution of the punishment to the members. Vernon believes that it is as a state rather than as a nation that the collective liability of what he calls a "sociopolitical entity" (SPE) makes the most sense. More than nations, states have the sorts of deliberative structures that French and others, including Erskine, Lang, and Seck, argue are requisite for corporate or institutional agency. They also endure over time, even surviving regime change. Although some might be inclined to identify states with the regimes that rule them, and nations with a shared public culture that appears to have more inherent continuity, Vernon maintains that the political character of a state provides "an abiding 'shape' that underwrites continuity despite change" (p. 295).

We have seen other authors – Drumbl, Sepinwall, Erskine, Pasternak, Kelly – talk about, although not in all cases defend, the view that being a member of an SPE brings with it benefits but also, as a trade-off, burdens in the form of responsibilities, obligations, and sometimes suffering the consequences of the state's blameworthy acts and omissions. In Vernon's terms, members of SPEs "share in a complex and unpredictable mix of advantages and risks" (p. 299). Individual liability for the acts of the SPE is based in participation in the scheme, and the scheme presents each participant with the possibility of loss. All are subject to the risk of loss, so all are bound to contribute to the reduction of the risk as far as they can. They share in the liability insofar as their actions as members amount to support. Among the many risks imposed on the members of an SPE by virtue of their membership is the risk that their SPE will use coercive force against the members of another SPE in a manner that constitutes international crime. What, however, could justify the extension of this risk to suffering punishment meted out as a retributive response to the crimes of their SPE? Here Vernon invokes the notion of political membership; exit options are costly, and participation in the political process does not give ordinary members much control over the actual ends their SPE will adopt and pursue. This uncertainty is the great risk of political society, with the potential to render citizens complicit in decisions and policies with which they disapprove. We see this very idea at play in Sepinwall's analysis of citizen responsibility. Even the dissident who strongly and vocally disapproves of the U.S. conduct in Iraq bears some responsibility for it qua citizen, simpliciter. No excuse can relieve that burden of responsibility. Although Vernon believes, as does Sepinwall, that political society requires membership to be characterized in the crude way, not admitting of excuses on the basis of personal disagreement with state policy, he believes also that this crudeness supports restraint in punishment. Punishment must aim as far as possible to strike collectives in their political dimensions.

Collective punishment and alternatives to it constitute the third central theme with which many of the chapters engage. The next section examines the ways in which this theme is taken up in the volume.

COLLECTIVE PUNISHMENT AND ALTERNATIVES

Historically, one of the more common types of collective punishment leveled against states has been war. Another form of collective punishment that we have seen and that has gained attention in recent years is the collective detention of people who might be security threats. The prisoners at Guantanamo Bay are an example; stateless individuals being detained in refugee camps, such as those displaced by civil war in Sudan, are another example. In "Collective Punishment and Mass Confinement," Larry May considers the justification for collective punishment in the form of war or collective detention. His discussion takes place in the context of international law and just war theory and concludes that war is not a legitimate form of collective punishment and that collective detention is only justified in the rarest of cases. His argument draws explicit attention to issues of distribution that arise when we move from a finding of blameworthy collective responsibility to collective punishment.

War as collective punishment is hard to justify because of the inexact nature of its target and because of the severity of the conditions to which it exposes innocent individuals. May's concern extends beyond prisoners in Guantanamo Bay to detainees in refugee camps and camps for displaced persons. These camps hold stateless individuals who have fled their home countries and are not accepted by the host countries. They must remain in the camps not because of any qualities they have as individuals, but because of their relationship to a collective identity. For this reason, these kinds of detention centers constitute collective punishment. May maintains that they are condemnable because they render people "outlaws" in the sense that their rights are protected by neither domestic nor international law. May challenges them on equity grounds, in so far as they fail to distinguish innocents from criminals, thus treating them all equally. Moreover, May argues, it is by virtue of being a member of the human community, not a citizen of a particular state, that individuals should have their basic human rights protected. The mere fact of being stateless is not a legitimate reason to have rights ignored. May's argument takes place in the context of some fundamental principles inscribed in the Magna Carta, most notably those concerning "arbitrary imprisonment, outlawry, or exile" (p. 186).

Erskine shares the concern that war and other forms of collective punishment might miss their target – namely, the state. However, she leaves it an open question worthy of further exploration whether military engagement such as war might ever constitute a legitimate form of punishment. Although this conclusion might appear to depart significantly from May's claim that war is an unjust response to state wrongdoing on the grounds that it imposes unacceptable burdens on innocent populations, Erskine, too, thinks that this distributive feature of war means that it is not the most appropriate form of *collective* punishment. If, however, the responsibility for the acts or omissions that are being punished is legitimately distributed among individuals as individuals, then war might be a coherent response. She would agree with May that if war is directed against the state, the broadness and severity of its impact calls it into question.

The real challenge of collective punishment is to find a way of doing it that strikes at the right level. Only then do we recognize it as a just response to the wrongdoing. If a state warrants punishment for its delinquent behavior, then the state should suffer, not the individual citizens. Vernon addresses the challenge of collective punishment hitting its mark, particularly in the case of states or nations, arguing in favor of what he calls "political punishments," that is, punishments that strike at political capacity.

Vernon proposes a number of means of punishing a collective in its political aspect: eliminate its political identity by absorbing it into a larger state or dividing it into pieces; impose a regime change; limit its political capacity, perhaps by restricting its military; restrict sovereignty (enforced no-fly zones, monitored guarantees to minorities, international inspection regimes). The political aims of these punishments make them collective in the right sort of way. Reparations are not as straightforward because they will inevitably be paid from tax revenue. In one way, this makes them political because collecting and spending tax revenue is an important function of SPEs. Yet if an SPE must pay reparations from tax revenue instead of using it in ways that would reduce consumer expenses, reparations might be understood as ultimately being punitive to the citizens. Vernon suggests moderating the latter conclusion by noting that if reparations are necessary, arguments can be made to support favoring the innocent over those whose political membership aligns them with the guilty collective.

In addition to offering candidates for collective punishment, as Vernon does, the authors in this volume also offer alternatives to it. Whereas Vernon considers reparations and compensation as a kind of punishment, others (Kelly, Drumbl, Pasternak, Erskine) propose them as alternatives. Other alternatives include truth commissions as well as reconciliation schemes (Drumbl, Erskine), boycotts (Pasternak), and public inquiries (Drumbl). The merit of many of these approaches is that, being less severe than war, they do not require the same strict standards of culpability to be justified. Moreover, in most cases, except perhaps boycotts, these measures do not have retributive goals. As a result, any distributive shortcomings they might have are less concerning. In fact, in some instances, the broader impact of such measures might be a merit. Both Drumbl and Sepinwall point out that in collective transgressions, a broad base of responsibility implicates many through their complicity. For this reason, Drumbl suggests that we expand our sights beyond criminal prosecutions and think instead in terms of collective responsibility, which does not necessarily require criminality.

In "Collective Responsibility and Transnational Corporate Conduct," Sara Seck takes the notion of state responsibility under international law into a different application than the extreme of international criminal conduct. The framework for her discussion is the issue of state responsibility for the actions of transnational corporations (TNCs) – in particular, with respect to human rights violations. Her investigation of the relationship as found in international law between a home state's duty to protect human rights and a TNC's human rights violations sheds light on how the state may be understood as a collective agent. As do Lang and Erskine, Seck applies the model of corporate agency, with its origins in the work of Peter French, to states. On this basis, she concludes that home states have a duty to regulate. If they have this duty, then they also can violate this duty. They are not responsible for the violations of TNCs per se, however. As do the views of Lang, Drumbl, and Luban, Seck's conclusions challenge existing international legal doctrine, which limits the jurisdictional scope of home states. By drawing attention to the broader category of collective responsibility – a category that transcends the law and makes space in international law for noncriminal sanctions – her view allows for home states to play proactive preventive roles in regulating the conduct of transnational corporations abroad. Her analysis offers ways for states, as corporate agents, to exercise their agency in positive ways in the protection of human rights.

In "Reparative Justice," Erin Kelly turns to reparative justice, which, she argues, yields a lower threshold of fault and is more forward-looking than backward-looking in its aims. A case for reparative justice might be viable when a justification for a retributive response is not.

Kelly extends this urge in the direction of reparative justice to collective responsibility contexts through Karl Jaspers's idea of metaphysical guilt, the concept of moral luck, and the forward-looking notion of *taking responsibility*. Because reparative justice is less stringently tied to individual responsibility from the beginning, it is a good match for collective action scenarios; it does not seek to attach blame to particular individuals to provide a reason for their obligation to participate in reparative schemes. To take responsibility is to acknowledge and to respond appropriately to one's part in a morally objectionable outcome. Jasper's notion of metaphysical guilt articulates one instance in which a direct individual causal role is not a prerequisite for taking responsibility. Taking responsibility for wrongdoing provides an opportunity for agents to redirect future behavior in accordance with new values. This redirecting opens the door to reparative obligations. Collective agency, argues Kelly, expands "our understanding of what participants do to include what they do together" (p. 204). For this reason, when an individual has misgivings about the collective actions of her group, she may *take responsibility* as a group member even if her own contribution to the misdeed is marginal.

Note that Kelly does not understand reparative schemes as forms of punishment. Indeed, she does not believe that complicity is a sufficient basis for either individual or collective punishment. Reparative justice as she understands it calls for measures that follow from taking responsibility, such as acknowledging the wrong done, compensating those who are wronged, or directly repairing the wrong. When participants acknowledge their roles as group members, they open up possibilities for "a collective commitment to taking responsibility for social injustice" (p. 209). One way to fulfill this commitment is to engage in schemes of reparative justice. Because the reasons for participating in such reparative schemes are, in Kelly's view, forward-looking in nature rather than punitive, she would not follow Vernon in reserving it for only the extreme case.

As this brief survey of collective punishment and the alternatives to it that are discussed in the pages that follow shows, when retributive punitive measures are deemed necessary, the manner in which the punishments distribute need careful attention. At the same time, retribution is not the only response to collective wrongdoing that makes sense. Approaches that provide opportunities for repair and rebuilding also make sense, and these opportunities might be available at both the collective and individual levels.

CONCLUSION

Although this collection does not solve the issues of state responsibility, state criminality, effective means of punishing collectives or otherwise making them accountable for their transgressions, and the challenging questions surrounding the almost inevitable downward distribution of collective punishment to the members, it nevertheless raises the level of discussion to a new level of complexity. No longer can we simply say that corporate entities, lacking souls to be damned and bodies to be kicked, cannot be held responsible or suitably punished. Nor can we end the discussion of distribution by noting only that any impact collective punishment might have on individuals as a result of distribution is justified because it is a mere side effect, not to be understood as punishment at all. The discussion in the chapters that follow highlights a rich territory of interdisciplinary discussion about accountability for collective wrongdoing, in which the perspectives of legal scholars, philosophers, and political scientists mutually inform one another and advance our thinking on this increasingly urgent issue.

PART I

Collective Accountability
in International Law

Collective Responsibility and Postconflict Justice

Mark A. Drumbl

International lawmakers largely associate justice for atrocity with court-rooms and jailhouses, and therefore with international criminal law. These associations have captured the imagination of important con-stituencies, such as foreign-aid donors, not-for-profit advocacy networks, and transnational human rights entrepreneurs. Coincident with the emer-gence of international criminal law as the preferred ideal type of justice for atrocity is an understanding that individuals are responsible for mass crimes such as genocide and, accordingly, that individual criminal cul-pability is the optimal form of accountability – the "first-best" practice. This paradigm effectively emerged at Nuremberg, where the International Military Tribunal (IMT) intoned that the crimes in question were not the crimes of abstract entities but the "crimes of men" and, what is more, that "*only* by punishing individuals who commit such crimes can the pro-visions of international law be enforced."[1] After lying fallow for several

---

This chapter is adapted and updated from portions of chapters 1, 2, 6, and 7 of Mark A. Drumbl, *Atrocity, Punishment, and International Law* (Cambridge: Cambridge University Press, 2007). I extend my gratitude to Michael Baudinet, Mark Sullivan, and Kara Coen for research assistance and to two anonymous reviewers for their instructive comments.

[1] *The Trial of Major War Criminals: Proceedings of the International Military Tribunal Sitting at Nuremberg Germany*, pt. 22 (London: H.M. Stationery Office, 1950), 447 (emphasis mine). The IMT judges underscored that these crimes were those of individu-als in an attempt to avoid a situation in which the responsibility of an abstract collective precludes the identification of individual guilt, which was in fact an argument raised by the defense. That said, in the many years since Nuremberg, this sentence has come to stand (and be relied on) for a much more independent proposition – namely, that only by prosecuting individuals can justice be served, thereby obscuring the responsibility of collectives.

decades, this paradigm has recently bloomed with the creation of several international and internationalized criminal tribunals.[2]

Because of the iconic (others use the term "dominant")[3] status of the atrocity trial, international criminal tribunals attract a vastly disproportionate amount of resources, intellectual effort, hope, and faith – even though such tribunals represent only one among many possible modalities of justice.[4] The iconography of the atrocity trial pulls our gaze away from these other justice modalities, such as truth and reconciliation commissions, indigenous forms of dispute resolution, and group-based sanctions that may implicate state, corporate, organizational, or collective responsibility. Assuredly, these other justice modalities exist and operate, but they live in the shadow of, and are subaltern to, the liberal criminal trial.

I contend that there are limits to the ability of judicialized determinations of individual criminal culpability to attain postconflict and transitional justice. Many of these limits derive from the reality that atrocity is the product of collective violence, in which individual participation is often deeply conformist. The collective nature of the violence sits queasily with international criminal law's predicate of individual agency, action, and authorship. In the end, the justice pursued by international criminal tribunals, although tangible, is also strikingly underinclusive. These limitations suggest that adequately redressing collective violence requires a discursive shift to other accountability mechanisms, including *collective forms of responsibility*. Any such discussion cannot be complete without

---

[2] International (and internationalized) institutions include the International Criminal Court (ICC, 2002, now with 110 states as parties), ad hoc tribunals for Rwanda (International Criminal Tribunal for Rwanda, ICTR, 1994) and the former Yugoslavia (International Criminal Tribunal for the Former Yugoslavia, ICTY, 1993), the Special Court for Sierra Leone (SCSL, 2000), the Special Tribunal for Lebanon (STL, 2007), and hybrid panels or chambers that operate, or have recently operated, in Cambodia, Timor-Leste, and Kosovo.

[3] André Nollkaemper, "Introduction," in *System Criminality in International Law*, eds. André Nollkaemper and Hermen van der Wilt (Cambridge: Cambridge University Press, 2009), 3.

[4] See prosecutor's opening statement in the Milošević trial: "The accused in this case, as in all cases before the [ICTY], is charged as an individual. He is prosecuted on the basis of his individual criminal responsibility. No state or organisation is on trial here today. The indictments do not accuse an entire people of being collectively guilty of the crimes, even the crime of genocide." *Prosecutor v. Milošević*, Case No. IT-02-54-T, Prosecution Opening Statement, 4 (February 12, 2002). See also Special Court for Sierra Leone Trial Chamber's Summary of Judgment in the case against Sesay, Kallon, and Gbao: "[T]he Chamber emphasizes that this is a case against particular individual members of the RUF and not a trial against the RUF organization." *Prosecutor v. Sesay, Kallon, and Gbao*, Case No. SCSL-04-15-T, Judgment Summary, par. 1 (February 25, 2009).

challenging the idealized nature of the Nuremberg principle. My goal in undertaking this challenge is to achieve a more robust instantiation of justice in the aftermath of terrible atrocity. In this vein, I believe that there is a need to canvas carefully the legal, political, and philosophical implications of collective responsibility.

Collective responsibility means something quite different from collective guilt or collective punishment. I believe that collective determinations of criminal guilt, in which individuals whose conduct did not affirmatively contribute to the crime are indiscriminately imprisoned, executed, or otherwise denied their liberty, run afoul of customary international law.[5] States or collective entities simply cannot commit crimes under international law as currently formulated. This does not imply that conversations about the merits of collective criminal punishment or state crimes cannot or should not be had. It does mean, however, that in terms of pragmatics, those conversations contemplate sanctions that, at present, are not just disfavored but in some cases are actually viewed as illegal by the international community. Consequently, reinserting collective punishment in the dialogue entails scaling a steep uphill slope.

Collective responsibility implies noncriminal sanctions that attach to groups whose misfeasance or nonfeasance is supportive of, acquiescent in, causally connected to, or necessary for serious violations of international criminal law to occur. The terms "collective punishment," "collective guilt," and "collective responsibility" are not interchangeable. My proposal to consider collective responsibility frameworks aims to move us away from the current dependence on criminal law. Although sanctions such as civil liability, community service, and public reintegrative shaming are powerful measures, they are not the equivalent of incarceration or execution.

I anchor my thoughts within a philosophical construction of postconflict justice that is animated by "cosmopolitan pluralism." In my book *Atrocity, Punishment, and International Law* (2007), I examine what I understand cosmopolitan pluralism to mean, and, more specifically, I propose vertical and horizontal reforms to the extant architecture of international criminal law that could advance a cosmopolitan pluralist vision of justice. In this chapter, I briefly reprise some of this argumentation in favor of a horizontal expansion of the justice narrative that actualizes collective responsibility. I examine how to constitute responsible groups,

---

[5] Kenneth S. Gallant, *The Principle of Legality in International and Comparative Criminal Law* (New York: Cambridge University Press, 2009), 395.

drawing from the *Bosnia v. Serbia* litigation at the International Court of Justice (ICJ), and propose a crude–careful way. I then examine reactions to the collective responsibility proposal as raised in some published reviews of *Atrocity, Punishment, and International Law*.[6] Finally, and in turn, I offer a preliminary response to these reactions.

Regardless of the direction that the conversation about collective responsibility takes, I believe it is important to have such a conversation. At present, collective responsibility, tainted by its association with collective punishment and saddled with the legacy of the Treaty of Versailles, has become a bête noire. It would be disappointing if international lawyers' understandable fear of collective punishment were to preclude a dispassionate conversation about collective responsibility. Moreover, now that international criminal tribunals have become firmly anchored in the fabric of international relations, assessing other modalities of justice does not present an existential challenge to these tribunals. My goal is to plumb the discursive space to explore alternative justice modalities to diversify and enrich synergistically a more fulsome instantiation of justice to the many victims of atrocity. By victims, I contemplate both direct victims in afflicted places and indirect victims – namely, us all – haunted by atrocity simply owing to our common membership in humanity.

Let me also situate my work within the broader framework of the chapters presented in this edited collection. These contributions can be grouped into two baskets. The first basket focuses on what, exactly, is the collective, whereas a second basket focuses on what, exactly, it is that the collective does wrong and for which sanction is appropriate. Assuredly, these baskets intersect. David Luban, for example, focuses on state criminality,[7] whereas Richard Vernon focuses on the state as the

---

[6] The following journals have published reviews: *Buffalo Law Review, Jura Gentium, Michigan Law Review, Journal of International Criminal Justice, American Journal of International Law, Journal of Criminal Law and Criminology, Chinese Journal of International Law, International Journal on World Peace, International Journal of Transitional Justice, Leiden Journal of International Law, Melbourne Journal of International Law, Peace and Change, Human Rights Quarterly, New York University Journal of International Law and Politics, Journal of Conflict and Security Law*, and *H-Net Book Review*. There are briefer reviews in the human rights and political science literature. These reviews, when taken together, address nearly all of the arguments raised in this book; for the purposes of this chapter, I explore those reviews that contemplate my proposed turn to collective responsibility.

[7] David Luban, "State Criminality and the Ambition of International Criminal Law" (Chapter 2). "[T]he test of state criminality includes some combination of the following: pervasive wrongdoing; a bad political culture; active involvement of a significant part

responsible agent but views sanction in a more restrained sense.[8] Larry May discusses war as punishment.[9]

My proposal is more modest. I encourage us to consider collective responsibility schemes, which I limit to sanctions other than mass imprisonment, execution, or destruction of personal or real property. In contradistinction to Avia Pasternak's equal distribution within the group justified by associative obligations (in particular, solidary action)[10] and Amy Sepinwall's crude liability justified on the basis of citizenship,[11] I defend a crude–careful approach in which the responsible group may be defined crudely, but individual members are given an opportunity to exclude themselves from membership in the designated group.

Chapters in the first basket largely focus on the state as the responsible collective. My proposal is to consider the state but also to look beyond to other kinds of entities and groups (including, as Sara Seck's work emphasizes, the corporation).[12] My proposal pushes beyond international institutions as a reflexive place in which to house collective responsibility schemes and examines how national and local methods of collective accountability can be fostered. I chart the topography of the claims advanced in this edited collection to emphasize that whereas my envisioned schematic of collective responsibility departs from the ethos of liberal criminal law, other contributors propound greater departures on the one hand, and narrower departures on the other.

---

of the state's leadership; and the complicity of at least some significant portion of the people."

[8] Richard Vernon, "Punishing Collectives: States or Nations?" (Chapter 11), 20. Vernon sets out "reasons for limiting the consequences of political liability. Accepting the 'crude' characterization, I propose that the crudeness of attribution demands restraint in punishment." In terms of sanctions, Vernon mentions eliminating the political identity of the state (by incorporating it within a larger state or by dividing it into several pieces); imposing regime change; imposing strict limits on a state's political capacity, particularly military capacity; restrictions on sovereignty such as enforced no-fly zones, monitored guarantees to minorities, or international inspection regimes; and reparations.

[9] Larry May, "Collective Punishment and Mass Confinement" (Chapter 6).

[10] Avia Pasternak, "The Distributive Effect of Collective Punishment" (Chapter 8). Pasternak develops a normative defense of equal distribution among group members grounded in the notion of associative obligations rather than proportional or random distribution.

[11] Sepinwall contends that "citizenship itself can ground responsibility for the crimes of one's nation-state." Amy Sepinwall, "Citizen Responsibility and the Reactive Attitudes" (Chapter 9).

[12] Sara Seck, "Collective Responsibility and Transnational Corporate Conduct" (Chapter 5).

COLLECTIVE VIOLENCE, MASS ATROCITY,
AND INDIVIDUAL PUNISHMENT

In this section, I advance three interconnected claims: (1) atrocity crimes are group crimes characterized more by collective obedience than by individual transgression; (2) nonetheless, individual criminal responsibility premised on deviant or pathological conduct has ascended as the first-best form of accountability for collectively committed and collectively inflicted atrocity, thereby bestowing on the atrocity trial iconic status as *the* vehicle to deliver justice; and (3) the atrocity trial falls short of its goals, which include retribution, deterrence, expressive storytelling, rehabilitation, and reconciliation, in part because of the structural disconnect between claims (1) and (2). I elaborate these arguments in much greater length in *Atrocity, Punishment, and International Law*. In the interest of brevity, I do not revisit these arguments here. I instead signal that many distinguished scholars – Hannah Arendt,[13] Daniel Jonah Goldhagen,[14] Steve Heder,[15] Peter French,[16] and David Luban[17] – have explored the systemic nature of widespread atrocity crimes – in particular, genocide and crimes against humanity. Experiments by Stanley Milgram[18] and Jerry Burger[19] examine the human penchant to commit harm while

---

[13] Hannah Arendt, *Eichmann in Jerusalem: A Report of the Banality of Evil* (New York: Viking Press, 1963).

[14] Daniel Jonah Goldhagen, *Hitler's Willing Executioners: Ordinary Germans and the Holocaust* (New York: Knopf, 1996).

[15] Steve Heder notes that in Cambodia, much of the violence arose from the exercise of discretionary zeal on the part of low- and midlevel cadres; this violence was not the result of specific applications of top–down pressure. Steve Heder, "Reassessing the Role of Senior Leaders and Local Officials in Democratic Kampuchea Crimes: Cambodian Accountability in Comparative Perspective," in *Bringing the Khmer Rouge to Justice: Prosecuting Mass Violence before the Cambodian Courts*, ed. Jaya Ramji and Beth Van Schaak (Lewiston, NY: Edwin Mellen Press, 2005), 382, 384–85, 393.

[16] Peter A. French, "Unchosen Evil and Moral Responsibility," in *War Crimes and Collective Wrongdoing*, ed. Aleksandar Jokić (Malden, MA: Blackwell, 2001), 32–34.

[17] David Luban, "Intervention and Civilization: Some Unhappy Lessons of the Kosovo War," in *Global Justice and Transnational Politics*, ed. Pablo de Greiff and Ciaran P. Cronin (Cambridge, MA: Massachusetts Institute of Technology Press, 2002).

[18] Stanley Milgram, "Behavioral Study of Obedience," *Journal of Abnormal and Social Psychology* 67, no. 4 (1963): 371–78; Milgram, *Obedience to Authority: An Experimental View* (New York: Harper and Row, 1974).

[19] In 2008, Jerry Burger, a researcher at Santa Clara University, replicated the Milgram experiment. The replication was not exact in that he made some allowance for ethical requirements for research subjects, which have changed since the 1960s. Berger, who published his findings in *American Psychologist* in 2008, found that 70 percent of his participants administered a 150-Volt shock (the highest on his scale) and had to be stopped. Adam Cohen, "Just following orders," *New York Times* (December 29,

following orders; so, too, does a televised game show modeled on the Milgram experiment – namely, France's *Game of Death*, which aired in 2010 – in which 80 percent of participants, egged on by a sadistic hostess and a chanting audience, administered electric volts to a victim until he appeared to die.

Liberal criminal law determinations proceed through adversarial third-party adjudication under due process norms, premised on a construction of the individual as the central unit of action. A number of select guilty individuals are blamed for systemic levels of group violence. Although at Nuremberg some of the guilty were executed, today punishment predominantly takes the form of incarceration in accordance with the classic penitentiary model in which convicts are incapacitated in accordance with international human rights standards. The enemy of humankind effectively is punished no differently from a car thief or armed robber. That said, the *génocidaire* is not like the common criminal. As atrocity becomes more wide scale in nature, and more popular, it becomes more difficult to construct participation therein as deviant. Simply put: most perpetrators, as Alette Smeulers writes, are "ordinary people in extraordinary circumstances."[20] In some cases, states themselves may perpetrate crimes instead of serving as the authorities who prevent and punish crimes – a phenomenon that Smeulers and Holá note "turns the theoretical framework of criminologists upside down."[21] James Waller flatly remarks that "the most outstanding common characteristic of perpetrators of extraordinary evil is their normality, not their abnormality."[22] Even less deviant is the complicity and acquiescence of the bystander. This complicity and acquiescence fall outside of the criminal law paradigm but constitute an essential prerequisite for violence to become truly massive in scale. Part of the riddle of purposively responding to and preventing mass atrocity is to assess how law can implicate the complicit and acquiescent masses

---

2008). Although this percentage was less than in the original Milgram experiment, the difference was not significant. To this end, notwithstanding the many sociopolitical changes in the United States since the time of the 1963 Milgram experiment, the basic behavioral implications of obedience to authority, the agentic state, and diffusion of responsibility persist.

[20] Alette Smeulers, "Punishing the Enemies of All Mankind," *Leiden Journal of International Law* 21, no. 4 (2008): 973.

[21] Alette Smeulers and Barbora Holá, "Criminology Discovers International Criminal Law" (draft paper, International Studies Association Conference, New York, February 15, 2009), 2. Available online at http://www.allacademic.com/meta/p_mla _apa_research_citation/3/1/1/5/8/p311584_index.html.

[22] James Waller, *Becoming Evil: How Ordinary People Commit Genocide and Mass Killing* (New York: Oxford University Press, 2002), 87.

who are responsible, even if not formally guilty. The criminal law does not reach bystanders, so how could it ever deter them, stigmatize their involvement, or accord them their just deserts?

The ascendancy of the criminal trial, courtroom, and jailhouse to promote justice for atrocity is moored in a particular worldview that derives from the intersection of two influential philosophical currents. The first of these currents is legalism; the second is liberalism.

All choices trigger externalities and opportunity costs. In this case, the preference for criminalization has triggered skepticism toward other justice mechanisms. However, evidence on the ground reveals that many afflicted populations actually prefer these other modalities or, at least, prefer for them to be included in the mix. Alternative justice mechanisms often must compete with liberal criminal law, to which they remain subordinate and against which they become measured, thereby crimping their status and independence.

Among the justificatory rationales advanced by international criminal law are retribution, deterrence, expressive storytelling, rehabilitation, and reconciliation. Do atrocity trials and concomitant correctional preferences (overwhelmingly, incarceration) attain these goals? As I have argued elsewhere, there is cause for skepticism in this regard. These shortfalls, which trace to liberal criminal law's awkward interface with crimes of obedience, present an additional reason why the international community ought to consider alternative forms of accountability, including collective responsibility.

Although retributive theory has many shades, these share in common the precept that the criminal deserves punishment proportionate to the gravity of the offense. Liberal legalist institutions that punish extraordinary international crimes place retribution high on the list of the goals of punishment. The question, then, follows: do the sentences issued to perpetrators of extraordinary international crimes attain their self-avowed retributive goals? Can an architect or tool of mass atrocity ever receive just deserts?

Available data reveal that at both the national and international levels, punishment for multiple international crimes is generally not more severe than what national jurisdictions award for a single serious ordinary crime.[23] This is in part due to the reality that human rights standards limit

---

[23] "In war crimes trials the sentences may be shorter than those imposed in an equivalent domestic context." Iain Bonomy, "The Reality of Conducting a War Crimes Trial," *Journal of International Criminal Justice* 5, no. 2 (May 2007): 351. See also Mark B.

the amount of pain that institutions can inflict on convicts and preclude the massive nature of atrocity from being reflected in retributive punishment. How can a perpetrator like Adolf Eichmann receive his just deserts? Or Athanase Seromba, the Rwandan priest who ordered the demolition of his own church in which 1,500 Tutsi refugees were trapped? Moving beyond theory to actual institutional behavior, despite well over a decade of sentencing practice and growing predictability in this regard, inconsistencies still emerge at the international level in terms of the quantum of punishment meted out to similarly situated offenders *within* institutions and, more graphically, *among* institutions.[24] I believe that these

Harmon and Fergal Gaynor, "Ordinary Sentences for Extraordinary Crimes," *Journal of International Criminal Justice* 5, no. 3 (July 2007): 684. The authors conclude that at the ICTY "extraordinary crimes have attracted ordinary sentences"; Silvia D'Ascoli, "Sentencing in International Criminal Law: The Approach of the Two UN Ad Hoc Tribunals and Future Perspectives for the International Criminal Court" (doctoral thesis, Department of Law, European University Institute, May 2008), 329. Available online at http://cadmus.iue.it/dspace/handle/1814/9861. D'Ascoli notes that "as regards sentence length, it is clear that sentences imposed by the ad hoc Tribunals are more 'lenient' if compared to national sentencing, where harsh penalties such as life imprisonment are frequently imposed for one murder alone"; Mark Drumbl, *Atrocity, Punishment, and International Law* (New York: Cambridge University Press, 2007), 57–58.

[24] There is also "considerable discrepancy" among the length of sentences meted out by the ICTY and the ICTR, with the former having sentenced 1.8 percent of convicts to life and the latter having sentenced 37 percent of convicts to life; what is more, at the ICTY 35 percent have received sentences of less than ten years, whereas only 11 percent of the ICTR convicts fall into this category. Harmon and Gaynor, "Ordinary Sentences for Extraordinary Crimes," 684–85 (see n. 23); see also *Prosecutor v. Kvočka et al.*, Case No. IT-98-30/1-A, ICTY Appeals Chamber Judgment, par. 669 (February 28, 2005). The court stated: "Sentencing is essentially a discretionary process on the part of a Trial Chamber." Recent empirical work on ICTR and ICTY practice suggests that some predictability and detectability regarding quantum of sentence has emerged in the sentencing jurisprudence. D'Ascoli, "Sentencing" (see n. 23); Barbora Holá, Alette Smeulers, and Catrien Bijleveld, "Is ICTY Sentencing Predictable? An Empirical Analysis of ICTY Sentencing Practice," *Leiden Journal of International Law* 22, no. 1 (2009): 79–97. D'Ascoli found significant and high correlations between length of sentences and (1) leadership level, in particular, leaders who also were direct perpetrators; (2) a number of aggravating factors (gravity, premeditation, willingness, superior position, and abuse of authority/trust); and (3) a number of mitigating circumstances (family status, remorse, surrender, and guilty plea). D'Ascoli found insignificant and low correlations between length of sentences and (1) modes of liability (e.g., aiding and abetting, instigating, ordering, and command responsibility); (2) ostensibly other than for the top leaders, between direct and indirect perpetrators; (3) sentencing factor of age; and (4) composition of the judicial bench. Holá, Smeulers, and Bijleveld conclude, in work on the ICTY alone, that sentences can be predicted by legal criteria. Number of offenses and the rank of the offender are the strongest predictors of sentence length in the model. The emergence of predictability suggests that concerns regarding inconsistency in sentencing may be waning, which would be a salutary development, or, in the least, that

inconsistencies arise from a variety of factors, including the broad discretion that is accorded to international judges and the lack of a sentencing heuristic. On another note, tension arises between national institutions that may sentence perpetrators of extraordinary international crimes and international institutions that may do the same. Sometimes international institutions sentence more leniently than national institutions. The fact that national institutions may punish offenders more harshly than international institutions or subject them to more onerous conditions of imprisonment is problematic for the retributivist insofar as international institutions tend to assert jurisdiction over the leaders and planners of atrocity who, according to conventional wisdom, are more responsible and, hence, ostensibly more deserving of harsher punishment.

A further challenge to the retributive value of punishment at both the national and international levels is the procedural incorporation of plea bargains in cases of extraordinary international crime. Holá, Bijleveld, and Smeulers found that at the International Criminal Tribunal for the Former Yugoslavia (ICTY), where the median sentence is approximately 15 years, those who plead guilty receive sentences that are 2.5 years shorter than those who go to trial.[25] Plea bargains disconnect punishment

there is reason for the intensity of criticism of the ICTY's sentencing practice to diminish over time. However, there are discrepancies between D'Ascoli and Holá et al.'s recent empirical findings, although in part these might be accounted for by methodological differences (multiple regression analysis instead of simple regression analysis) and also differences in sample size. Although empirical analysis may identify some factors that correlate with the severity of sentence, these correlations are not necessarily stated as such by the judges, and other stated factors have no correlation, nor are the correlations necessarily in accordance with penal theory. To this end, any emergent predictability may not be matched with transparency. Although we benefit from the fact that scientists can locate some correlative variables through regression analysis, it troubles me that the jurisprudence fails to state openly that Person X is being sentenced to Term Y for the reasons unearthed by the empirical research. Moreover, whether a system is predictable does not mean that the sentencing is effective or that it is connected to valid criminological/penological aspirations or the etiology of atrocity. Although Holá et al. conclude that "These findings can offer empirically based counter-arguments to all the criticism raised against the ICTY sentencing regime as to its disprateness and inconsistency," I have a nagging feeling that this conclusion seems a bit optimistic and extends beyond the empirics (Holá et al., "Is ICTY Sentencing Predictable?," 96) In some instances, in coming to this conclusion, Holá et al. adopt a low threshold of legitimacy. For example, they conclude that "sentence length is reduced if factors in mitigation are present" (ibid., 95). On one hand, it may be comforting that proof of mitigating factors correlates to a lower sentence; on the other hand, this correlation truly constitutes the moral minimum of any punitive system – if there were no correlation with mitigating factors as a whole, or if mitigating factors actually correlated with an increased sentence, then the ICTY sentencing practice would flout any moral minimum of legitimacy.

[25] Holá et al., "Is ICTY Sentencing Predictable?" (see n. 24).

from desert or gravity and often render it contingent on what the convict knows and who else the convict is willing to implicate. The fact that plea bargains are readily available for atrocity crimes but are not available in many jurisdictions for serious ordinary crimes weakens the purportedly enhanced retributive value of punishing atrocity crimes. To be sure, many other reasons favor plea bargaining for atrocity crimes. However, plea bargains intersect clumsily with retributive aspirations.

Although there is some scattered reference to the merits of specific deterrence in the transsystemic jurisprudence, general deterrence largely remains the focus. General deterrence, however, is perhaps even more problematic than retribution as a goal for the sentencing of extraordinary international criminals. General deterrence posits that if one person is punished, this punishment will reduce the likelihood that another person in that same place or elsewhere will offend in the future. To this end, it makes sense to consider empirical evidence regarding whether potential extraordinary international criminals would be deterred by the punishment of others following criminal trials. There are scattered anecdotal reports (i.e., anecdata) of deterrence.[26] However, no systematized or conclusive evidence of discernible deterrent effect has yet been proffered. In fact, atrocity has continued to occur in places (e.g., the former Yugoslavia) following the creation of criminal tribunals to punish perpetrators. Assuredly, we simply cannot know how much worse atrocity would have been in the absence of judicial institutions. We can have faith that deterrence occurs. However, I posit two challenges to this faith. The first is the reality that there is a low probability that perpetrators will actually be taken into the custody of criminal courts. According to Cherif Bassiouni, less than a fraction of 1 percent of perpetrators of international crimes have been brought to justice.[27] The second challenge is the assumption of at least a certain degree of perpetrator rationality amid the cataclysm of mass atrocity. Rationality is central to deterrence theory insofar as the theory assumes that perpetrators make some kind of cost–benefit

---

[26] See, e.g., William W. Burke-White, "Complementarity in Practice: The International Criminal Court as Part of a System of Multi-level Global Governance in the Democratic Republic of Congo," *Leiden Journal of International Law* 18, no. 3 (2005): 557–90. But see contra Julian Ku and Jide Nzelibe, "Do International Criminal Tribunals Deter or Exacerbate Humanitarian Atrocities?" *Washington University Law Review* 84 (2006): 777–833.

[27] M. Cherif Bassiouni, ed., *The Pursuit of International Criminal Justice: A World Study on Conflicts, Victimization, and Post-Conflict Justice* (Antwerp: Intersentia, 2010). Discussion online at http://www.insidejustice.com/law/index.php/intl/2010/03/31/cherif_bassiouni_international_criminal.

analysis and thereby control their behavior. The work of anthropologists and the research of journalists in conflict zones suggest that individuals often commit atrocities because they believe they are doing good or because they simply wish to survive to tomorrow.[28] In these instances, it is fanciful to believe that individuals would refuse to act out of fear that they may be hauled before a court in The Hague many years down the line. Finally, given that the passive acquiescence of group members rarely – if ever – is implicated by a system based on individualized criminal law, it is unclear how this system can deter this fundamental prerequisite to mass atrocity.

Expressivism is a third rationale for punishment that conceptually emerges in cases of extraordinary international crime. It occupies a less influential place than either retribution or deterrence. Expressivist theories look at the messaging effect of trials, verdict, and punishment. Expressivists maintain that trials and punishment affirm the value of law, strengthen social solidarity, and incubate a moral consensus among the public. Trials narrate events – publicly – and then impose punishment on the guilty in a manner that can shame and stigmatize. The result is an intensely dramaturgical process that tells a story. The performance aspect is particularly elevated for leaders and propagandists of atrocity – public figures known to many and before whom many have trembled. Performativity can, however, also arise through the prosecution of the small fry, insofar as atrocity also involves many local narratives. In some cases, the expressive value of storytelling is enhanced when it takes the form of judicial pronouncement, which is cloaked in a mantle of authority and occurs through rules of evidence, which can convey an aura of reliable impartiality. Although it seems a reach for liberal legalist punishment to exact retribution or deter individuals through fear of getting caught, punishment could educate future generations about the effects of extreme evil and edify a moral consensus that repudiates discrimination-based violence and those who peddle in it. To this end, I believe expressivism has

---

[28] "Warlords and foot soldiers in Darfur or Congo are probably more likely to fear death at the hands of their enemies or rivals than prosecution at a court in The Hague. And no sentence will deter a crazed ultranationalist from committing atrocities under the misapprehension that he [is] defending his people from extermination." Harmon and Gaynor, "Ordinary Sentences for Extraordinary Crimes," 695 (see n. 23). Philip Gourevitch interviewed a genocide perpetrator in Rwanda who described the genocide "like a festival [. . .] [w]e celebrated." Philip Gourevitch, "The Life After," *The New Yorker* (May 4, 2009): 41.

greater viability than deterrence or retribution as a basis for a penology of extraordinary international crime.

That said, the expressive goals of punishment are fragile. Their attainment is jeopardized by the selectivity and formalism of the legal process. The historical narrative can become crimped by prosecutorial strategizing and plea bargaining. Gaps between the international criminal process and expectations of local populations – in particular, non-Western populations – may externalize justice, thereby diminishing the prophylactic value of verdict and punishment. Although due process may authenticate a historical record, it may also distort it.[29]

It is difficult to predict which sorts of microscopic truths trials actually produce. Looking beyond law and peering into literature, Bernhard Schlink's *The Reader* unpacks the limits of the truth-telling function of atrocity trials.[30] Schlink's book examines the relationship between an adolescent, Michael Berg, and a former Nazi concentration camp guard, Hannah Schmitz. The two part ways when Hannah abruptly leaves town. They are reacquainted years later, however, when Michael, then a law student, attends a trial where, to his surprise, Hannah faces war crime charges. Hannah is desperate to hide the truth of her illiteracy, so at the trial, she tells purported truths that in fact are false. These purported truths erroneously implicate her as a leader of the killings that form the basis of the charges and, ironically, as the author of a report that was faulted for falsely exonerating responsibility for the crime. The narrative emerging from Hannah's trial is incorrect and consciously fabricated, largely because Hannah prefers to hide a truth that is more painful to her than a conviction for atrocity.

Rehabilitation was mentioned en passant in the 2006 *Orić* trial judgment, in which a light sentence (two years) was imposed at trial (Naser Orić subsequently was acquitted by the ICTY Appeals Chamber on the ground that the prosecutor had not discharged the burden of proof on the issue of command responsibility, and the Appeals Chamber did not address the issue of rehabilitation as a sentencing goal).[31]

---

[29] Mirjan Damaska, "What Is the Point of International Criminal Justice?" *Chicago-Kent Law Review* 83 (2008): 336.

[30] Bernhard Schlink, *The Reader*, trans. Carol Brown Janeway (New York: Random House, 1997).

[31] *Prosecutor v. Orić*, Case No. IT-03-68-T, Judgment, par. 721 (June 30, 2006). The Trial Chamber also mentioned social defense and restoration (ibid.). The Trial Chamber had given considerable weight as a mitigating factor to the "abysmal conditions" in which Orić, a local Bosnian Muslim police chief, had to operate, noting in particular the "total

Rehabilitation, however, is particularly problematic in the context of extraordinary international criminals because these offenders typically are not maladjusted. As Harmon and Gaynor note, with reference to the ICTY: "[D]etainees are an unusual group of offenders. Compared to offenders in domestic prisons, many of whom may be highly violent individuals . . . ICTY detainees are characterized by . . . good social skills. They . . . do not clearly pose a criminal threat to society."[32] This leads Harmon and Gaynor, with considerable experience as ICTY prosecutors, to conclude that "at the ICTY, the aims of rehabilitation or re-socialization should not be one of the fundamental objectives of sentencing: the offenders are already re-socialized."[33] Harmon and Gaynor's experiences with ICTY defendants resonate in the examples of Nazis who fled Germany following World War II to take up residence elsewhere in Europe or the Americas. Many of these fugitives, who engaged in acts of unfathomable barbarity during wartime, were able to conform easily and live unobtrusively as normal citizens for the remainder of their lives. This ability to fit in suggests something curious, and deeply disquieting, about atrocity perpetrators – namely, their lack of subsequent delinquency or recidivism and their easy integration into a new set of social norms.

A final goal, reconciliation, also arises in the rhetoric of international criminal law. To this, Tim Waters responds:

> The personalization of guilt is supposed to move societies subjected to atrocity beyond collective, ethnic formulations of conflict and make reconciliation possible. As with any point of pride, the belief that this is both true and right is largely unquestioned by mainstream ICL [International Criminal Law] practitioners and scholars; the [ICTY] trumpets this accomplishment prominently on its website, despite an almost total lack of evidence of this effect in the former Yugoslavia.[34]

Similarly, in my research in postconflict Rwanda, I found that trials did not serve reconciliatory purposes. Part of the problem, of course, is that we do not have a satisfactory method to measure reconciliation.

---

breakdown of society in Srebrenica including a collapse of law and order" (ibid., par. 768).

[32] Harmon and Gaynor, "Ordinary Sentences for Extraordinary Crimes," 693–94 (see n. 23).

[33] Ibid., 694.

[34] Timothy William Waters, "Killing Globally, Punishing Locally? The Still-Unmapped Ecology of Atrocity," review of *Atrocity, Punishment, and International Law*, by Mark A. Drumbl, *Buffalo Law Review* 55 (January 2008): 1351–52.

In conclusion, the courtroom and the jailhouse make modest gains in terms of actualizing retributive, rehabilitative, reconciliatory, and deterrent goals following atrocity; they do somewhat better at actualizing expressive goals. In the aggregate, however, these modalities fall short of their penological objectives. This may be because these objectives are too ambitious. It may also be because the criminal law, standing alone, simply is not enough – nor can it ever be enough.

What is more, the individuation of guilt occasioned by criminal trials has a shadow side. Focusing only on the most notorious killers and senior leaders may falsely, although conveniently, bestow collective innocence on lower-level cadres. Individuation may mask structural and systemic responsibility for atrocity. Action or inaction by states, for example, may be scrubbed from the historic record when only select brutal killers are implicated in the dock. As Damaska notes: "In explaining what happened in Rwanda or the former Yugoslavia . . . legal relevancy restrains judges from embarking on an exploration of the role played by the U.N. and foreign states in these tragic events – even if causal links between foreign conduct and triable offenses are probable."[35] It is perhaps for this reason that states and international organizations may gravitate toward individual criminal culpability, and support institutions that proceed this way, insofar as equating justice with the atrocious acts of a few individuals masks much more discomfiting questions. The atrocity trial does not embarrass too much or too many.

CONSIDERING COLLECTIVE RESPONSIBILITY

In *Atrocity, Punishment, and International Law*, I advocate for a cosmopolitan pluralist approach to international justice. Accountability for atrocity is a shared universal value that forms part of our set of cosmopolitan values. However, certain substantive universals, including accountability for extreme evil, can best be attained through diverse and pluralized procedural mechanisms. Both legal pluralism and cosmopolitan theory recognize that, in certain instances, the local, national, or parochial may convey tangible meaning, relevance, and legitimacy.

A cosmopolitan pluralist vision of international justice animates two synergistic reforms to the architecture of international criminal tribunals. These reforms would wean the pursuit of accountability for perpetrators of extreme evil from a selective, and ill-fitting, liberal criminal law model.

[35] Damaska, "What Is the Point," 336 (see n. 29).

The first reform is *vertical*. I propose to recalibrate the application of authority among criminal justice institutions at multiple regulatory sites (the international, national, and local). Currently, these applications of authority radiate downward from the international. Instead, I propose reform to better welcome bottom–up approaches to procedure and sanction. Insofar as local and national accountability mechanisms are potentially abusive, corrupt, illegitimate, and susceptible to machination, there is a need for gatekeeping. Accordingly, I propose that national or local justice modalities be accorded a presumption of *deference* but that this presumption be *qualified*. I outline six criteria to qualify the presumption of deference and thereby fulfill this gatekeeping function. These are as follows: (1) good faith, (2) the democratic legitimacy of the procedural rules in question, (3) the specific characteristics of the violence and of the current political context, (4) the avoidance of gratuitous or iterated punishment, (5) the effect of the procedure on the universal substance, and (6) the preclusion of the infliction of great evils on others. Although a liability scheme would retain its entitlement to qualified deference even if it did not emulate liberal approaches to fault and liability, qualified deference would operate to diminish the hazards of abusive communitarian punishment.

The second reform is *horizontal*. Here, I propose loosening the grip of the criminal law paradigm on the accountability process: initially, by integrating approaches to accountability offered by law generally (such as judicialized civil sanctions, lustration, or group-based public service) and, subsequently, by involving quasi-legal or fully extralegal accountability mechanisms such as truth commissions, legislative reparations, public inquiries, transparency, arbitral claims commissions, and the politics of commemoration. The goal of horizontal reform is to advance *from law to justice*: initially, by moving international criminal law to a capacious law of atrocity and, ultimately, to an enterprise that constructively incorporates extrajudicial initiatives. If operationalized, these reforms evoke the possibility that a larger number of individuals could become implicated in the justice process, thereby inviting a broader conversation regarding the viability of collective responsibility for collective criminality. Assessing the place of collective responsibility in international justice should be a cause for contemplation and optimism, not embarrassment or annoyance.

Private law and extrajudicial mechanisms already form part of the practice of states in response to atrocity. At national levels, for example, extrajudicial mechanisms are commonly invoked in the aftermath of mass atrocity. However, the internationalized paradigm generally views these mechanisms as separate from, subaltern to, and in competition with criminal trials. International tribunals operate in some cases with primacy over national institutions and, in the case of the ICC, as prima facie complementary to national institutions. As I have argued elsewhere,[36] however, the result in both cases poorly harnesses the potential of extrajudicial initiatives. Cosmopolitan pluralism would welcome and recognize these initiatives and thereby better reflect bottom–up aspirations as to what the practice of postconflict justice might look like.

In particular, tort and restitution might serve valuable goals. Tort and restitution implicate involved masses by permitting more carefully calibrated measurements of degrees of responsibility beyond the scarlet letter of guilt. These alternative sources of regulation offer a more textured understanding of the key roles played by many otherwise neglected actors. Tort and restitution can promote different goals – such as restoration and reparation – that are underarticulated by liberal criminal law.

Tort permits declaratory or monetary relief for violations of state responsibility and, potentially, for organizational or group liability outside the structures of the state. This relief might provide an additional layer of justice insofar as the criminal law does not directly reach the state or organization as an actor. The law of restitution could integrate private reparations, instantiated through community service, which could be fitting for situations in which much of the violence is committed locally by perpetrators known to victims and by neighbors on neighbors. Community service is a complex and delicate remedy. Directly restitutionary community service projects would require the murderer to return to the land of the family whose members he murdered and make up for his crime through, for example, farmwork. Not all survivors may be comfortable with this. Supervision and remedy in the case of subsequent breach are also tricky and expensive. These are among several reasons why community service in the Rwandan *gacaca* system has incorporated reparative community service through which perpetrators work on larger state projects instead of directly restituting their victims through their labor.

Going further, I propose a broader integration of extrajudicial and extralegal modalities, such as truth commissions, reparative funds,[37] public inquiries, the politics of commemoration, redistributing wealth, and fostering constitutional guarantees that structurally curb the

---

[36] Drumbl, *Atrocity, Punishment, and International Law*, chap. 5 (see n. 23).
[37] For discussion of reparative justice, see Erin Kelly's contribution to this volume (Chapter 7).

concentration of power. The impulse to broaden the response to mass atrocity must extend beyond legal proceedings and should welcome communal sociolegal institutions – in particular, indigenous institutions – thereby expanding the template of policy options.

Collective responsibility mechanisms may promote a number of goals. Frank Haldemann ascribes considerable value to "giving public recognition to the victims of collective violence and, thereby, to their moral worth and dignity as fellow citizens."[38] He observes:

> If an entire community or group – such as a state or government – plans, permits, or condones acts that are terribly unjust or humiliating, the individual victim is made to look inferior or wanting in the eyes of the public: she is publicly told that her life simply does not matter, that her presence counts for nothing in the society's scheme of things.[39]

Collective forms of responsibility can right this structural wrong. Collective responsibility schemes can permit a much larger number of victims, as Haldemann puts it, to be "validat[ed] and vindict[ed] [as] . . . victim[s] of wrongdoing. The purpose of punishment, so understood, is to correct the perpetrator's implied message that it is fine for his victim to be treated in this way. After wrongdoing, the truth of the victim's value must be publicly reasserted, and punishment is an especially powerful way of communicating that reassertion."[40]

Collective responsibility also may favor utilitarian goals. Many atrocities begin with the devious kindling of conflict entrepreneurs, who seek to inflame and exacerbate communal tensions. Community responses to this kindling are not predestined. How the community – in particular, bystanders – responds is the central determinant regarding whether violence subsequently erupts and, if so, of its necropolitical amplitude. If community members ignore these flames and look past attempts to habituate them into violence and hatred, then the conflict entrepreneur remains marginal. If community members are attracted to the flames and identify with violence and hatred, then the wheels of atrocity start to turn. Once set in motion, these wheels quickly become unstoppable by anything other than the use of countervailing force.

Criminal punishment goes some way toward developing expressive values that edify a moral consensus regarding the manifest illegality of discrimination-based violence. This consensus might serve as a bulwark

---

[38] Frank Haldemann, "Another Kind of Justice: Transitional Justice as Recognition," *Cornell International Law Journal* 41 (Fall 2008): 722.
[39] Ibid., 715.   [40] Ibid., 713.

against exhortations by conflict entrepreneurs in favor of such violence. The threat of criminal punishment, however, will not deter committed individuals acculturated into hatred from implementing their own final solutions. Criminal law does little to deter eliminationist killers. However, collective responsibility might go some way to diminish the mainstreaming of conflict entrepreneurship and the festering of cultures of hatred.

Group members, including bystanders, are in an advantageous position to identify and monitor the behavior of conflict entrepreneurs. Group members may have the ability to ignore the behavior or quash it before it metastasizes. Because the criminal law paradigm does not reach group members, it provides them no incentive to cabin or control the behavior of conflict entrepreneurs. Collective responsibility might do more to encourage group members to control conflict entrepreneurs early on, and hence serve as gatekeepers, because they could be called to task afterward. Group members would, as Mark Osiel suggests, begin to police each other's activities and responses.[41] The threat of collective sanctions may activate group members to marginalize the conduct of conflict entrepreneurs or, in the best-case scenario, snuff it out.

Collective responsibility frameworks can affix a cost to an individual's drawing the blinds, receiving a promotion at work because the "other" got fired, moving into a suddenly vacated apartment, and acquiescing in the hijacking of the state by extremists. It is well-nigh impossible to deter a suicide bomber or crazed ideologue. Once an individual has passed a threshold of habituation to or affection for violence, has deeply imbibed hatred, or needs to kill to survive, the law can offer little in deterrence. However, the law may more plausibly reach the much larger group of people that passively allows the conflict entrepreneur to assume office, procure weapons, and build a power base of habituated killers. Any structure that incentivizes the masses to root out the conflict entrepreneur before that individual can indoctrinate and brainwash will diminish the depth of perpetrator moral disengagement that is a condition precedent to mass atrocity. Such a structure thereby inhibits early on, when inhibition still remains possible, the "escalating commitments" that psychologist James Waller believes demarcate the "road to extraordinary evil."[42] The social death of the victims – a precondition to their actual deaths – may thereby be impeded. Capturing all individuals in a responsible collective

---

[41] Mark Osiel, "The Banality of Good: Aligning Incentives against Mass Atrocity," *Columbia Law Review* 105 (October 2005): 1839–40. Osiel is one of the few scholars to explore the role of incentives, monitoring, and policing in contexts of mass atrocity.

[42] Waller, *Becoming Evil*, 205 (see n. 22).

might make it much more difficult for individuals to hide within the collective, seek exoneration in its anonymity, benefit from the diffusion of responsibility, and proffer excuses in Milgram's agentic state of transposed responsibility.

Monitoring could also extend to corporate entities, thereby implicating relevant actors who currently fall outside the reach of international criminal law. Corporate entities are major facilitators of genocide, insofar as they produce the tools with which genocide is executed and often provide the means to industrialize atrocity. Litigation under the U.S. Alien Tort Claims Act, in which corporate entities have contestedly been held civilly liable for *jus cogens* violations on theories of aiding and abetting, envisions this broader form of responsibility. Tony Lang's recent book argues in favor of creating a new international criminal court for groups, which would include both nonstate political groups (NGOs, terrorist organizations) and multinational corporations, which could adjudicate international political crimes.[43] Clearly, there are significant institutional, jurisdictional, and operational hurdles to such a proposal, but by challenging our thinking, Lang does us a great service.

Collective responsibility does not have to limit itself to agents of the perpetrator group. Would international institutions and foreign states have responded with the same nonfeasance to genocide in Rwanda or Srebrenica were they to be subject to the reach of collective sanctions? This is a particularly poignant question given empirical research indicating that mass violence, particularly state-centered violence, can be decelerated by military interventions, led by the international community or foreign states, that directly challenge the perpetrator or aid the target of the policy.[44]

Collective responsibility frameworks also might augment the quality of political decision making. Although states have duties to their citizens, I also believe that citizens have certain duties to the state. One of these is to prevent the state from actualizing extraordinary international crimes. This duty becomes all the more onerous to the extent that citizens actually have input into decision-making. Citizens should be put on notice that they cannot stand by while hate mongering becomes normalized.

That said, this is a discussion of what might be, not, obviously, what is. Collective responsibility frameworks may well disappoint. It is not

[43] Anthony F. Lang, Jr., *Punishment, Justice and International Relations: Ethics and Order after the Cold War* (Abingdon, UK: Routledge, 2008).

[44] See Matthew Krain, "International Intervention and the Severity of Genocides and Politicides," *International Studies Quarterly* 49, no. 3 (2005): 383.

implausible that the existence of a collective sanctions framework would induce group members to permit atrocity and then simply devote their energies to covering it up. Group-based remedies might entrench the very group identities that require dissolution or attenuation to create meaningful space for postconflict transition. Perhaps benefiting bystanders are not rational thinkers; perhaps they are no different than Rwandan Hutu *Interahamwe* militia or al-Qaeda suicide bombers. It may be that mobilized direct perpetrators are less bound by ethnic, national, or religious solidarity than I may assume; perhaps they are equally motivated by economic gain. Or perhaps fear is a central motivation; were this to be the case, however, the inference remains that ordinary people who participate in atrocity do so to conform to a social norm instead of rebel against it. Whatever the mix of disposition and situation in any given instance, it remains that the criminality of mass atrocity is, at a minimum, much more collective in nature than ordinary common crime.

In any event, we will never be able to evaluate the potential or limitations of a horizontally expanded law of atrocity that contemplates group-based sanction unless we shed our fears and dispassionately engage with collective responsibility as a regulatory mechanism and as a possible tool in the justice toolbox. My point here is to spark renewed discussion and research.

WHAT IS THE COLLECTIVE? REVISITING
THE *BOSNIA V. SERBIA* LITIGATION

How, exactly, to define the responsible group? As a starting point, I propose that the responsible group can be defined either *crudely* or *carefully*.

The crude way structures the responsible group along its most evident characteristic or combinations thereof – for example, nationality, ethnicity, inhabited territory, or religion. So, for example, it renders all German nationals responsible for the Holocaust. It renders all Lord's Resistance Army members responsible for crimes against humanity in northern Uganda regardless of their age, their conduct, or the manner of their conscription. The crude way assigns responsibility to the group in whose name atrocity was undertaken independently of the actions of its individual members. So long as the atrocity was committed in their collective name, responsibility could be assigned to group members, including those who were incompetent, who were unable to resist, or who did resist.

In cases in which atrocity is committed at the behest of a state, the crude way includes within the group all those individuals living within the jurisdiction of that state. This can have particularly harsh consequences. Levying sanctions against a collectivity when that collectivity contains both perpetrators and victims certainly would hinder the victims' recovery efforts. This is the case with Rwanda. Holding all Rwandan citizens responsible for the genocide perpetrated by the Rwandan state means that Tutsi survivors have to pay up. In this regard, crude designations of responsibility based on citizenship (Sepinwall) or associative obligations (Pasternak) fit awkwardly with the transitional equities of postconflict societies. Although it may arguably be fair for all Americans, for example, to be held responsible for crimes committed in the name of America elsewhere (Sepinwall's argument) or for members of a democracy who elected a genocidal leader to be held responsible, it seems deeply inequitable to hold *all* Cambodians, Rwandans, or Sudanese responsible on the basis of citizenship for the crimes the state committed internally. Although prosecuting a small number of criminal defendants undercaptures the public complicity that makes atrocity truly massive, sanctioning an entire state may lead to significant overcapture in that individuals who resisted or were themselves victimized are found responsible. Saddling a well-intentioned successor state with the tortious liability and obligations of its abusive predecessor may undermine political transition. Consequently, there is much to be said in favor of pardoning "odious debt."[45]

In sum, the crude way does not limit the group to the aggregate of those individuals whose action or inaction culminated in atrocity. Damages ultimately pass through to and are borne by all group members, regardless of how bravely they resisted, how servilely they complied, how eagerly they killed, or how much hurt they endured. At first blush, the crude way of group designation is anathema to liberalists.

The *careful* way, on the other hand, pays attention to individual agency. It limits the group to those individuals who, by virtue of their action or inaction, are causally responsible for atrocity. The careful way requires a more fine-grained analysis and thereby abides by certain Western legalist assumptions of individual agency. In cases of civil responsibility, the careful way would condition group membership on some sort of demonstrable linkage between action (or nonfeasance) and the great evil. Individuals or entities for whom no connection affirmatively could be delineated would avoid membership in the sanctioned group. Ironically,

---

[45] For a contrary proposition, see David Gray, "Devilry, Complicity and Greed: Transitional Justice and Odious Debt," *Law and Contemporary Problems* 70 (Summer 2007): 137.

this renders the careful way dependent on similar modalities that limit the effectiveness of criminal trials. To be sure, insofar as the context is not one of penal culpability, the required causality would not involve the currently dominant notion of a "beyond a reasonable doubt" standard.[46] Pursuit of the careful way would enable finer-grained assessments of the group that is actually responsible (and, separately, of the group entitled to damages) beyond the confines of the state as a whole. In such a scenario, civil damages or declaratory denunciation would perhaps only be awarded against ministries of the state government, members of associations with control over the apparatus of the state, corporate entities who funded and equipped genocide, or militia groups. The careful way would prevent liability from necessarily trickling down to *all* citizens of the state.

Although it does problematize them considerably, the ascendancy of individual criminal culpability as an iconographic ideal type of accountability has not precluded international justice claims based on the crude way. One self-evident case study is state responsibility for violations of international criminal law. International law forecloses the concept of state crimes but does permit states to be held responsible for breaches of their international obligations, including their obligations not to commit, or to prevent and punish, breaches of international criminal law.

Litigation before the ICJ is instructive. The ICJ was established in 1946 as the principal judicial organ of the United Nations. It has jurisdiction only over states.[47] The ICJ's docket includes cases that involve boundary disputes, treaty interpretation, and the responsibility of states for international wrongs. States afflicted by atrocity – for example, Bosnia and Herzegovina (BiH or Bosnia), Croatia,[48] and the Democratic Republic of

---

[46] The United Nations Security Council has invoked some of the harshest kinds of collective sanctions – for example, the imposition of economic sanctions on a state and monitoring of a state's activities.

[47] Article 36 of the Statute of the ICJ establishes the bases for the ICJ's jurisdiction to adjudicate contentious disputes among states. These bases are largely grounded in consent, although a state can become subject to jurisdiction against its will in a particular case based on an a priori grant of jurisdiction it may have provided by its ratification of a treaty that contains a dispute resolution clause that refers disputes to the ICJ, or through the state's a priori grant of compulsory jurisdiction. The ICJ also renders advisory opinions, although these are not binding on states. Statute of the International Court of Justice art. 36 (1945). Available at http://www.icj-cij.org/documents/index.php?p1=4&p2=2&p3=0.

[48] See Application of the Convention on the Prevention and Punishment of the Crime of Genocide (*Croat. v. Yugo.*), I.C.J. Application (July 2, 1999). The application alleged that Serbia and Montenegro was liable for infringements of the Genocide Convention by virtue of the activities of Federal Republic of Yugoslavia armed forces and paramilitary

Congo (DRC)[49] – have filed claims with the ICJ that allege that other states bear legal responsibility for serious violations of international humanitarian law and, in the case of Bosnia and Croatia, genocide.

Although international criminal trials proceed on the assumption that stakeholders in the justice process know and care about the outcomes, which they well do, it also must be underscored that stakeholders also really care about ICJ judgments, perhaps even more so. Lara Nettelfield's work emphasizes how families of the victims of the Srebrenica genocide took the litigation at the ICJ very seriously – the widows had high expectations and, when the judgment was delivered, shared their disappointment through the circulated protest image of a gavel thrust into a heart like a stake.[50] Jelena Subotić chimes in more generally, concluding that the ICJ lawsuit "truly captured the imagination of the Bosnian people."[51]

In its claim, BiH asserted that Serbia and Montenegro, the state into which the Federal Republic of Yugoslavia (FRY) was transformed in 2003, violated its obligations under the Genocide Convention. The Confederation of Serbia and Montenegro was dissolved in May 2006 when, following a plebiscite, Montenegro narrowly voted for independence.

---

detachments on the territory of Croatia from 1991 to 1995. According to Croatia, 20,000 people were killed in Croatia and 55,000 wounded as a result of these atrocities (ibid., 8). On November 18, 2008, the ICJ determined that it has jurisdiction in this case. Application of the Convention on the Prevention and Punishment of the Crime of Genocide (*Croat. v. Yugo.*), I.C.J. Summary of the Judgment, par. 146 (November 18, 2008).

[49] The ICJ issued a state responsibility award in *DRC v. Uganda* that primarily involved the unlawful use of force, although the case also implicated violations of international criminal and humanitarian law (albeit not genocide). See Armed Activities on the Territory of the Congo (*Democratic Republic of the Congo v. Uganda*), I.C.J. Judgment (December 19, 2005). The ICJ ordered Uganda to pay reparations in light of its responsibility for armed activity, plundering, and massive human rights violations in the DRC. Specifically, the ICJ located Uganda's responsibility for inter alia killing, torture, training of child soldiers, incitement of ethnic conflict, and other forms of inhumane treatment (ibid., par. 345). The ICJ effectively engaged in a form of avoidance doctrine when it came to ignoring the DRC's claim that Uganda committed aggression and should therefore be responsible. On February 3, 2006, the ICJ dismissed on jurisdictional grounds a claim brought to it by the DRC against Rwanda regarding violence on Congolese territory that might have overlapped with the ICC's investigations. ICJ "Armed Activities on the Territory of the Congo (New Application: 2002) (*Democratic Republic of the Congo v. Rwanda*)" Press Release 2006/4, February 3, 2006.

[50] Lara Nettelfield, "Srebrenica: Special Status for a Special Crime" (draft paper presented to the workshop "Collective Punishment," The University of Western Ontario, April 17–19, 2009).

[51] Jelena Subotić, *Hijacked Justice: Dealing with the Past in the Balkans* (Ithaca, NY: Cornell University Press, 2009), 138.

Serbia became the successor state to Serbia and Montenegro. On February 26, 2007, the ICJ held that although Serbia was not directly responsible for committing genocide in BiH, it was responsible for having failed to prevent genocide at Srebrenica, where seven thousand Bosnian Muslim men and boys were massacred by Bosnian Serb military forces in July 1995.[52] The ICJ found that only acts committed at Srebrenica in July 1995 qualified as acts of genocide but that other atrocities complained of by Bosnia in its application did not constitute genocide.[53] The ICJ concluded that the Srebrenica atrocities could not be attributed to Serbia directly through acts committed by its dependent organs or persons or by parties under its direction or control.[54] In other words, Bosnian Serb forces at Srebrenica were not acting under Serbia's direction or effective control and, therefore, Serbia could not be directly responsible for genocide. However, Serbia's responsibility was incurred in that it did not meet its obligation to prevent genocide. Failure to meet the obligation to prevent genocide can be incurred by omission and can be incurred when a state is merely aware that genocide might be committed. This is a lower standard than that required for complicity, which is one of a positive act in which there is knowledge that a genocide is incipient or under way. The ICJ also found Serbia responsible for its failure to prevent genocide at Srebrenica, as well as for breaching the Genocide Convention because of its failure to cooperate fully with the ICTY (in particular, its failure to bring notorious suspects into custody).[55] The ICJ did not

[52] Application of the Convention on the Prevention and Punishment of the Crime of Genocide (*BiH v. Serbia and Montenegro*), I.C.J. Judgment (February 26, 2007) (hereafter cited as *Bosnia v. Serbia*). As an aside, Bosnia had brought its claim against Serbia in 1993; Serbia was found responsible for failure to prevent a genocide that occurred at Srebrenica in 1995, *after* the claim was brought against it.

[53] *Bosnia v. Serbia,* par. 291–97, 471.

[54] *Bosnia v. Serbia,* par. 395, 412. The ICJ found that Serbia did not have effective control over the VRS (the army of Republika Srpska) and that the VRS and other entities were not organs of Serbia, meaning that Serbia's responsibility for direct commission of genocide, conspiracy to commit genocide, incitement to commit genocide, or complicity in genocide could not be established. Four judges disagreed on the complicity point. See, e.g., Judge Bennouna, who held that: "[L]e *mens rea* exigé du complice n'est pas le même que celui qui incombe à l'auteur principal, soit l'intention spécifique (*dolus specialis*) de commettre le genocide, et il ne peut pas en être autrement, car exiger cette intention reviendrait à assimiler le complice au coauteur." *Bosnia v. Serbia*, Déclaration de M. le juge Bennouna, 2. Available online at http://www.icj-cij.org/docket/files/91/13702 .pdf.

[55] The ICJ took note of evidence signifying that Serb authorities failed to make reasonable efforts to apprehend General Mladić, indicted by the ICTY for genocide. *Bosnia v. Serbia*, par. 447–49. The ICJ also noted Serbia's failure to fulfill its obligations regarding

award damages against Serbia. It ruled that the issuance of the judgment alone constituted satisfaction for Bosnia. Looking at the question from the Bosnian perspective, a successful claim would inure to the benefit of all its citizens. Included among the beneficiaries are individuals who were victimized, those who were not, and those who were complicit in the violence or actually committed it. Tracking problems abound. Although Srebrenica's Bosnian Muslims were the target of genocide, not each of Srebrenica's Bosnian Muslims was equally a victim. In the end, had BiH's claim attracted a damage award, it would restitute some individuals while unjustly enriching others.

As a matter of jurisprudence, the ICJ ruled that state responsibility can issue from a breach of the Genocide Convention: states can be responsible for genocide, and individual culpability does not extinguish collective state responsibility. The ICJ held that "*duality* of responsibility continues to be a constant feature under international law,"[56] citing an International Law Commission Commentary that notes a "State is not exempted from its own responsibility for internationally wrongful conduct by the prosecution and punishment of the State officials who carried it out."[57] The ICJ cited to the Rome Statute, Article 25(4) of which states that "no provision in this Statute relating to individual criminal responsibility shall affect the responsibility of States under international law."[58] State responsibility could arise under the Genocide Convention regardless of whether individuals are criminally convicted or acquitted on charges of genocide.

Despite the friendly language of duality, the interface of international criminal tribunals with the ICJ remains jittery in matters related to accountability for the great evils. Although ultimately finding it had jurisdiction over the contentious dispute, the ICJ's handling of the jurisdictional question (adjudicated in 1996) in *Bosnia v. Serbia* belied a sense

the ICJ's provisional measures award issued in 1993 (ibid. par. 451–58). Following the 2007 ICJ judgment, one particularly notorious indictee, Radovan Karadžić, was in fact taken into custody and transferred to the ICTY in The Hague, where he is undergoing trial. International Criminal Tribunal for the former Yugoslavia, "Radovan Karadžić Trial to Resume on 13 April 2010" Press Advisory, April 1, 2010.

[56] *Bosnia v. Serbia*, par. 173 (emphasis mine).

[57] Ibid. Article 58 of the International Law Commission Articles on State Responsibility stipulates: "These articles are without prejudice to any question of the individual responsibility under international law of any person acting on behalf of a State." International Law Commission, *Articles on State Responsibility*, art. 58 (2001). Available at http://untreaty.un.org/ilc/texts/instruments/english/draft%20articles/9_6_2001.pdf.

[58] Ibid.

of unease.[59] Similar unease persists in the views of some judges who dissented from the 2007 judgment or who issued separate declarations.[60] For example, Judges Shi and Koroma in a joint declaration held that the Genocide Convention serves to punish individuals and not place collective liability on states.[61] According to Judges Shi and Koroma, the obligation to punish individuals who perpetrate genocide was embedded in the Convention so as to avoid attributing genocide to the state itself.[62] Not all judges shared these reservations, however: Judges Bennouna (appending a separate declaration) and Mahiou (dissenting) expressed comfort with the notion of state responsibility for genocide.[63] That said, it seems

[59] Application of the Convention on the Prevention and Punishment of the Crime of Genocide (*Bosnia v. Serbia*), I.C.J. Judgment: Preliminary Objections (July 11, 1996). One of the preliminary jurisdictional objections was that the allegations of state responsibility brought by BiH simply fell outside the scope of the Genocide Convention. The majority of ICJ judges dismissed this preliminary objection. This group tersely found that the plain language of the Convention, in particular the compromissory clause, did not exclude any form of state responsibility (ibid., par. 32). Four judges, however, disagreed. Two of these four judges – Judges Shi and Vereshchetin – ultimately ruled that the ICJ had jurisdiction over the Bosnian claim, but they appended a separate joint declaration to the ICJ preliminary objection judgment. In this declaration, they expressed their "disquiet" with the holding that the Genocide Convention does not exclude state responsibility. Application of the Convention on the Prevention and Punishment of the Crime of Genocide (*Bosnia v. Serbia*), I.C.J. Joint Declaration of Judges Shi and Vereshchetin (July 11, 1996). Available at http://www.icj-cij.org/docket/files/91/7355.pdf.

[60] In the 2007 judgment, five judges dissented on the jurisdictional finding (see n. 52).

[61] *Bosnia v. Serbia*, Joint declaration of Judges Shi and Koroma, par. 1. Available online at http://www.icj-cij.org/docket/files/91/13695.pdf?PHPSESSID=4035476c6c7926d1026c168e28d194cc.

[62] Ibid., par. 4.

[63] In his declaration, Judge Bennouna commented on the interplay between individual penal responsibility and state responsibility for genocide. Judge Bennouna found a close relationship between the two and noted that the proof of penal responsibility of those who lead the state ("au travers du comportement de ceux qui engagent l'Etat et de leur mise en jugement") can lead to state responsibility. *Bosnia v. Serbia*, Déclaration de M. le juge Bennouna, 3. Available at http://www.icj-cij.org/docket/files/91/13702.pdf. Judge Bennouna also took an optimistic understanding of the importance of civil sanction and justice. He noted that state or governmental succession is not a basis to negate state responsibility and, in fact, acceptance of the truth of the past, and the request for forgiveness for the inflicted suffering, was the only way to reconstruct a shared future (ibid., 5). Judge Mahiou, like Judge Bennouna, would have gone further than the majority in holding Serbia responsible for genocide. Writing in dissent, he found that the Genocide Convention introduces direct responsibility of states in matters of genocide: "Il ne peut en être autrement car une entreprise génocidaire est difficilement envisageable sans la participation ou la complicité d'un Etat," *Bosnia v. Serbia*, Opinion dissidente de M. le juge Mahiou, par. 45. Available at http://www.icj-cij.org/docket/files/91/13706.pdf. For Judge Mahiou, the majority judgment had some incoherence in that it found

problematic to conclude that these jitters had no bearing whatsoever on the ICJ majority's reluctance actually to award damages.

I posit that despite the ICJ's identification of the purported *duality* of responsibility between individual culpability and state responsibility, in practice this duality operates much like *subalternity*.

One probative example of the subalternity of the ICJ toward the ICTY involves the production and use of evidence in the *Bosnia* v. *Serbia* litigation. The ICJ relied on evidence presented to the ICTY, along with certain ICTY findings, in its analysis of Serbia's involvement in the alleged acts of genocide.[64] However, salient portions of the documentary evidence presented to the ICTY were redacted. Specifically, the redacted portions involve the minutes of meetings of the FRY Supreme Defense Council. The Serb government sent these redacted documents to the ICTY in 2003. ICTY Chief Prosecutor Carla Del Ponte had requested them for use in the Milošević prosecution. Serbia, however, claiming national security interests, would only share the documents on the condition that they remain redacted and shielded from public view. After two years of negotiations, Prosecutor Del Ponte agreed and assured such confidentiality.[65] She presented a letter to ICTY judges when Serbian lawyers pressed for the secrecy of the archives. ICTY judges then approved the request for protective status for these documents under a broad reading of Serbia's national security interests.[66]

that the Serbian government was not complicit in genocide because it lacked a certain level of knowledge, but that it was still responsible for a failure to prevent genocide and had the requisite level of knowledge to that end (ibid., par. 128).

[64] See *Bosnia* v. *Serbia*, par. 206, 211–12.

[65] "[D]uring the trial of Slobodan Milošević, hundreds of documents arrived at the war crimes tribunal in The Hague marked 'Defense. State Secret. Strictly Confidential.' . . . Serbia, the heir to Yugoslavia, obtained the tribunal's permission to keep parts of the archives out of the public eye. Citing national security, its lawyers blacked out many sensitive – those who have seen them say incriminating – pages. Judges and lawyers at the war crimes tribunal could see the censored material, but it was barred from the tribunal's public records." Marlise Simons, "Genocide Court Ruled for Serbia without Seeing Full War Archive," *New York Times*, April 9, 2007. See also: "The unredacted documents were not available to Bosnia and Herzegovina from the ICTY because of a confidentiality order imposed by the [ICTY] at Serbia's request." Richard J. Goldstone and Rebecca J. Hamilton, "*Bosnia* v. *Serbia*: Lessons from the Encounter of the International Court of Justice with the International Criminal Tribunal for the Former Yugoslavia," *Leiden Journal of International Law* 21, no. 1 (2008): 108.

[66] Protective measures were granted in 2003 in two decisions by the ICTY Trial Chamber in the Milošević proceedings. Andrea Gattini, "Evidentiary Issues in the ICJ's Genocide Judgment," *Journal of International Criminal Justice* 5 (September 2007): 892 n. 10. Rule 54*bis* of the ICTY Rules of Procedure and Evidence permits protective measures,

On the eve of oral hearings in the ICJ litigation, Bosnia requested production of the unredacted documents, which it felt were germane to its case. Even though the ICJ has the authority to do so pursuant to its *proprio motu* powers, the ICJ did not grant Bosnia's request and hence never requested unredacted versions of the documents.[67] What is more, the ICJ also refused to draw a negative inference from Serbia's failure to provide the unredacted documents.[68]

The full unredacted evidence, news reports cite lawyers as stating anonymously, may have indicated that officers and soldiers from the Yugoslav army were serving in the Bosnian Serb army; that they were deployed, paid, promoted, or retired by Serbia; that Serbia financed and supplied fighting in Bosnia; and that Serbian forces and secret police were involved in the takeover and lead-up to the Srebrenica massacre.[69] If some or all of these facts indeed were established, the full evidence may have influenced the subsequent legal question whether the Bosnia Serb forces acted under Serbia's effective control.[70] These reports claim that Serbia's motivation in initially presenting the ICTY only with redacted documents was one of foresight – namely, to protect itself from the ICJ litigation by obscuring key facts. News reports also indicate that Serbia was not reticent to state this intention at the same time it advanced a national security privilege claim.[71]

Although the ICTY and ICJ are only located one mile apart in The Hague, there is a wide informational gap between the two. The ICJ and ICTY coexist in some sort of duality but one that apparently requires bargains that compromise the overall justice narrative to the detriment of collective civil responsibility and in favor of individual criminal responsibility. Pressures to obtain a blockbuster conviction against Milošević led to a bargain between the ICTY and Serbia regarding the production of evidence. Milošević then died during the course of a languid and

including redaction, to be awarded by the judges and Rule 77 makes the disclosure of information in knowing violation of a Trial Chamber order an act of contempt (ibid.).

[67] Goldstone and Hamilton, "*Bosnia v. Serbia*: Lessons," 108 (see n. 65). Two ICJ judges dissented from the majority's failure to order the documents to be produced.

[68] Ibid., 97. Ironically, uncensored portions of that evidence were apparently available from other sources. Simons, "Genocide Court Ruled for Serbia" (see n. 65).

[69] Simons, "Genocide Court Ruled for Serbia" (see n. 65).

[70] Ibid.

[71] "[L]awyers and others who were involved in Serbia's bid for secrecy say that, at the time, Belgrade made its true objective clear: to keep the full military archives from the International Court of Justice, where Bosnia was suing Serbia for genocide. And they say Belgrade's goal was achieved ... when the [ICJ] declared Serbia not guilty of genocide, and absolved it from paying potentially enormous damages" (ibid.).

obstructed prosecution. One of the results of this bargain, several years later, is a perceived impoverishment of the ICJ litigation. Serbia was more concerned with the ICJ judgment, which may have bankrupted the state and inextricably bound it to genocide, than with the fate of a handful of former leaders and their more notorious underlings and killers.[72] It consequently sought to insulate itself from state responsibility and, to some degree, was able to hamstring the ICJ by co-opting the ICTY. The ICJ had a chance to authenticate a detailed, complete, and factually grounded record of the Bosnian genocide as a whole and of Serbia's involvement therein. Connections between the Serb government and Bosnian Serb forces who committed atrocities were not presented publicly; what is more, if the redacted portions of the evidence suggested there were no such connections, then the failure to transparently share this information is also distorting. In short, the institutional pursuit by the ICTY of its mandate and political purpose – to prosecute Milošević and others – led it to enter into bargains that may have undercut the ability of another court with concurrent jurisdiction over genocide in the Balkans to do its job effectively.

Although the ICJ held that as a matter of law it would be possible to determine that a state committed genocide in the absence of individuals who controlled the state being found criminally liable for genocide,[73] Goldstone and Hamilton point out that the meekness of the ICJ's fact-finding in *Bosnia v. Serbia* "raises doubts as to whether, in practice, a state will ever be held responsible for genocide outside the parameters of the prior convictions of individual perpetrators."[74] Goldstone and Hamilton further note that although it refused to draw negative inferences from Serbia's unwillingness to provide evidence, the ICJ appeared to do so from the ICTY's paucity of genocide convictions (only one to date) as well as the small number of genocide charges actually brought to trial by the ICTY prosecutor. The ICJ based its conclusion that "specific intent was lacking in all situations other than Srebrenica," at least in part on these negative inferences.[75] Goldstone and Hamilton note that in this

---

[72] Luban confirms much of this and adds that another motivation among certain Serbs was that an ICJ judgment against Serbia might have toppled the moderate government and embolden reactionaries and right-wing extremists. Luban, "State Criminality," 34–5 (see n. 7).

[73] *Bosnia v. Serbia*, par. 180. "The Court accordingly concludes that state responsibility can arise under the Convention for genocide or complicity, without an individual being convicted of the crime or an associated one" (ibid., par. 182).

[74] Goldstone and Hamilton, "*Bosnia v. Serbia*: Lessons," 103 (see n. 65).

[75] Ibid., 106.

latter regard, the ICJ was uncritically deferential to the ICTY and too dependent on the ICTY's fact-finding.[76] In practice, then, this constitutes another example of how the purported duality turns into subalternity:

> If its fact-finding approach in *Bosnia* v. *Serbia* is to set any precedent for how the ICJ will adjudicate future cases under the Genocide Convention, it is hard to see how the Court will ever make a positive genocide determination in the absence of a criminal court having already convicted individual perpetrators of genocide.... If this is correct, then the *Bosnia* v. *Serbia* judgment may have taken away with one hand what it has offered with the other – promising an international legal system that can hold states accountable for the commission of genocide, while simultaneously ensuring that in practice that promise will only rarely be fulfilled.[77]

The burden of proof required by the ICJ constitutes yet another example of how purported duality morphs into subalternity. Gattini notes that, in substance, the ICJ upheld Serbia's argument that questions of affirmative state responsibility for genocide are to be determined by the standard of beyond a reasonable doubt that prevails for individual defendants in international criminal law.[78]

The question then arises as to how a different structural conception of justice might better coordinate these two justice institutions along lines of genuine duality instead of suborning the ICJ to the ICTY. One starting point is to reassess the crude designation of the responsible collective as the state.

My proposal for horizontal cosmopolitan pluralism, which I label the *crude–careful* way, is a humanistic one that supports collective claims but endeavors to straddle the gap between crude and careful group demarcation. *I believe the group can be defined crudely, with the subsequent opportunity for group members to demonstrate affirmatively why they should be excluded from the liable group.* Reasons for exclusion would include members' activities before or during the atrocity or proof of their own victimization. In the event genocide were attributable to a state, I would proffer a liability framework in which the state could be

---

[76] Ibid., 106, 109.

[77] Ibid., 112. See also Amabelle C. Asuncion, "Pulling the Stops on Genocide: The State or the Individual," *European Journal of International Law* 20, no. 4 (November 2009): 1196. Asuncion concludes: "The legal architecture for genocide prosecution, however, is designed for individual convictions and state acquittal." She argues that states are more likely to be deterred from committing genocide by virtue of reputational concerns than would individuals with genocidal intent.

[78] Gattini, "Evidentiary Issues," 889–904 (see n. 66).

sanctioned but in which individual or institutional members of society could be permitted to avoid footing the bill, or foot less of the bill than others, by affirmatively demonstrating what they did to prevent genocide or to oppose the state. Such a process could open up a wide discursive space about who did what during times of atrocity, thereby serving powerful didactic and expressive purposes. The crude–careful way is a modality of distribution within the group that tends more to the proportional distribution end of Pasternak's allocative spectrum and also permits the impugned collectivity some say in how responsibility ought to be internally attributed. This allocation of distributive discretion might well permit the impugned group to develop some autonomy and dignity in the postconflict transition, thereby countering one of the major critiques of collective responsibility schemes (namely, that they incapacitate the group as a whole). The crude–careful way also permits the collectivity to have some say in the process.

Looking at the other side of the coin, I believe the claimant group can be defined crudely if this is how it elects to define itself. Victims should be entitled to constitute themselves as they see fit for the purpose of filing claims and should be given qualified deference in the event that not every individual member of the group meets exacting standing rules. I am less concerned over unjust enrichment for some members of victim communities than I am over sanction for some members of perpetrator communities who actively resisted.

I also believe the crude–careful way harmonizes with proposals, such as Lang's, to create new juridical institutions internationally, to amend existing institutions, or to encourage modalities such as the Alien Tort Claims Act nationally that may envision responsible groups other than the state. There is no reason why slightly less crude designations of responsible entities cannot be accompanied with careful safety valves for certain individuals to exclude themselves from imputed membership in the responsible group.

CRITIQUES OF THE CRUDE–CAREFUL WAY AND MY RESPONSES

In a thoughtful and lengthy review, Kevin Jon Heller concludes that *Atrocity, Punishment, and International Law* "provides a damning critique of the transformative potential of international criminal law. It is hard to imagine that anyone who reads the book will still be able to believe that liberal-legalist criminal trials, however well-intentioned, are capable of dealing with the collective nature of mass atrocity. Drumbl is absolutely right: a 'richly multivalent approach' to transitional justice is needed – one in which international criminal law plays a far more modest role than it has hitherto. His call to experiment with new kinds of transitional-justice institutions is thus both long overdue and most welcome."[79] Heller is more circumspect, however, regarding the prospect of collective sanctions. Collective sanctions present two "basic problems" for Heller:

[1] in order to be retributively just, sanctions would have to be imposed using the same liberal-legalist procedures that paralyze international criminal trials; [and]

[2] only retributively unjust collective sanctions can effectively deter mass atrocity.[80]

Heller faults the crude way for being retributively unjust. In particular, the crude way might be overinclusive but also underinclusive in that it excludes individuals "who were personally responsible for atrocities but did not possess the defining characteristic of the sanctioned group."[81] Crude designations of liability also risk obscuring the guilt of those individuals most responsible for atrocity. I would offer a reply to this latter criticism that there is no reason criminal trials cannot be held for the most responsible members while the group as a whole is also sanctioned. For Heller, the careful way would be more retributively just, but "the individualized hearings [the careful way] requires would be procedurally indistinguishable from liberal-legalist criminal trials."[82] In fact, for Heller, the "careful way would be completely impractical."[83]

With regard to the crude–careful way that I propose, Heller finds it "no more workable than the careful way."[84] He notes: "Although perhaps not requiring quite as much liberal legalist procedure, an individualized hearing in which the burden of proof is on the defendant is still an individualized hearing."[85] Heller then argues that the crude–careful way would be more likely to be retributively unjust than the careful way:

There is an important but deceptive asymmetry between normal and reversed burdens of proof in situations involving mass atrocity: when the prosecution bears the burden of proof, it would need to prove only that

---

[79] Kevin Jon Heller, "Deconstructing International Criminal Law," *Michigan Law Review* 106 (April 2008): 998.

[80] Ibid., 992.

[81] Ibid., 993.

[82] Ibid., 994–95.

[83] Ibid., 995.

[84] Ibid.

[85] Ibid.

the defendant was involved in one act of group atrocity [to include him in collective sanctions]; but when the defendant bears the burden of proof, he would have to prove that he did not commit any of the group atrocities [to be excluded from collective sanctions].[86]

In the end, Heller fears it will be difficult for the individual to rebut the presumption of sanction. According to Heller, my proposal simply imposes too much pain on too many people.

In response, the reverse burden of proof envisioned by the crude–careful way would not have to operate on a beyond a reasonable doubt standard. I do not envision a criminal trial. In fact, the goal would be to move *away* from liberal criminal trials. Therefore, one permutation might be for group members to demonstrate affirmatively what they did during the conflict that may, on a balance of probabilities, justify excluding them from the sanctioned group. In any event, the spirit of my proposal would be for the exceptional individual – the one who actively resisted, who had no capacity, or who is in the group but for clear equity reasons should not be sanctioned (i.e., a Muslim living in Serbia who did not collaborate in the ethnic cleansing of other Muslims but who is a Serb citizen) – to be excluded.

Whatever retributive excesses might arise from application of the crude–careful way are considerably narrower than the retributive short-falls that currently plague the dominant narrative of postconflict justice. International criminal law is retributively unjust because sanction is, on the one hand, too lenient in comparison to ordinary criminal law and, on the other and much more important hand, because it reaches far too few.

Heller's other critique involves workability.[87] In response, workability concerns could be leveled against all deep-reaching justice mechanisms – they are complex, implicate large numbers of people, and are messy. This is unsurprising, given that transitional justice is a huge undertaking. That said, it is also prudent not to overstate the workability of international criminal trials. Although trials may be workable in the sense that they usually target a small number of defendants, they are unworkable in another regard: they are extremely expensive, especially when assessed from a per capita basis. Each ICTR conviction has cost tens of millions of

---

[86] Ibid., 996.

[87] Although she does not reference crude–careful modalities of distribution, Pasternak alludes to workability concerns with proportional distribution and, given the parallels between the crude–careful method and proportional distribution, these concerns could well extend to my proposal. Pasternak, "The Distributive Effect of Collective Punishment," Chapter 9 (see n. 10).

U.S. dollars. On the other hand, Helena Cobban reports that it cost US$1,075 to demobilize and reintegrate, often through traditional ceremonial rituals, former fighters (many of whom committed grievous war crimes) in Mozambique's internecine conflict.[88] Proceedings that contest group membership conducted under the crude–careful way, although potentially large in number, would be modest in per capita cost. It is not required that these proceedings be conducted within the framework of a judicialized hearing. In fact, processes that involve traditional mechanisms or truth commissions would be particularly welcome.

Moreover, notwithstanding the possibility that retributive unfairness might ensue, these proceedings would serve important expressive functions and would relate a far more accurate story of who did what and a far more comprehensive account of who is responsible for what during times of atrocity. In this regard, proceedings under the crude–careful way would promote a variety of other goals, in particular truth telling and norm-generation. Heller also argues that only retributively unjust sanctions could serve deterrent purposes and that for him the crude–careful way is in fact retributively unjust. Hence, for Heller the crude–careful way would have near maximum deterrent value. He then adds, however, that, to deter, sanctions "would have to be sufficiently onerous to encourage bystanders not only to avoid participating in atrocities . . . but also to actively try to prevent them."[89] He raises "bulldozing all of the houses in a town that produced a suicide bomber" as an example.[90] Bulldozing all the houses in a town that produced a single offender, which would trigger homelessness, property destruction, and forced migration, falls outside the kinds of sanctions that I envision. Bulldozing, in fact, may be harsher than the imprisonment of an entire town for a short period of time – and hence falls well within the collective punishment side of the continuum. To this end, Heller faults the crude–careful way for excessive sanctions when it does not even call for such sanctions. In any event, I believe that less onerous sanctions could reach bystanders and impede the mainstreaming of eliminationism. At present, bystanders and other members of the collective whose acquiescence, condonation, or quiet support eludes the criminal law avoid any assignation of responsibility and thereby are rendered collectively innocent. Extending even the

---

[88] Helena Cobban, *Amnesty after Atrocity? Healing Nations after Genocide and War Crimes* (Boulder, CO: Paradigm, 2007), 209, table 6.1.
[89] Heller, "Deconstructing International Criminal Law," 997 (see n. 79).
[90] Ibid.

slightest sanction to the group as a whole injects some accountability into a situation where at present there is none.

In the end, the discussion returns to the common thread in Heller's critique – namely, that the crude–careful way, to be effective or workable, would have to be retributively unjust. Heller writes:

> [N]othing in [my] analysis indicates that it would be impossible for the crude way or the crude–careful way to coerce bystanders into trying to prevent mass atrocity. But it would not be just – particularly given that neither the crude way nor the careful crude way could justly determine who was a member of the collectively sanctioned group....
>
> ... Collective sanctions maybe effective, but they cannot be just if they sever the relationship between an individual's responsibility and the magnitude of his crime.[91]

Attaining retributive goals in the context of atrocity is problematic. As I have argued elsewhere, there is no way for liberal correctional preferences ever to give the *génocidaire* his just deserts. Consequently, it seems perplexing to singularly judge my reform proposal by a metric of retribution and then fault it for being too harsh. Whether Heller is correct on the supposed retributive unfairness of the crude–careful way, he may simply be placing my proposal against a template that should not be used or that is unusable. In my opinion, whether the crude–careful way is inexorably retributively unjust remains an open question given the magnitude of the crimes in question.

Other scholars contest whether my proposal would in fact serve deterrent purposes. Smeulers states that she "doubt[s] whether this would really play a role," but does not say why.[92] Smeulers, however, adds that it is important to match the collective nature of the crime with collectivized forms of responsibility and that, by logical extension, proposals for collective responsibility more accurately reflect the actual etiology of the crimes. Smeulers concludes by noting that "[I]f the establishment of individual criminal responsibility inherently entails a rejection of collective responsibility and thus creates a myth of collective innocence, then international criminal law misses its point."[93]

Another thoughtful reviewer, Tim Waters, casts my proposal as a "turn to collective punishment" that "is in effect a headlong assault on one of ICL's points of pride and principal justifications: the claim that by

---

[91] Ibid., 998–99.
[92] Smeulers, "Punishing the Enemies of All Mankind," 983 (see n. 20).
[93] Ibid.

advocating individualized criminal process, it is ridding the world of dangerous notions of collective guilt ... Drumbl's argument goes well beyond critique to an affirmative embrace of the very thing ICL abhors."[94] By way of initial caveat, I would once again note that my proposal is not one for collective punishment. Instead, it is for collective responsibility. As I have consistently maintained, there are important differences between the two. The terms "collective punishment" and "collective responsibility" are simply not interchangeable. Waters takes up a similar critique as Smeulers with regard to the deterrent value of collective responsibility:

> I am not sure I find the utilitarian rationale persuasive – it makes a big assumption about the rationality of actors, despite Drumbl's having already persuasively demonstrated just how different the standard assumptions about rationality, deviance, and conformity are under differing conditions, and presumably therefore, how different the calculations individuals make in those differing environments are too.[95]

Squarely unlike Heller, however, Waters is open to supporting collective responsibility on retributive grounds.[96]

In the end, little is known about the deterrent value of collective sanctions. This knowledge gap arises because the international community has neglected collective sanctions as accountability mechanisms for atrocity – in particular, along crude–careful lines. This neglect arises in part because international criminal law simply has occupied much of the imaginative space of postconflict justice. Is it necessary for proponents of collective sanctions first to prove that collective sanctions deter before they can be taken seriously? Obviously, it would be preferable to discharge this burden of proof *ex ante*. But this is not yet possible.

International criminal law largely has been established on faith. Now that several institutions have punished perpetrators – in some cases, for over a decade – a body of legal practice arises that suggests serious grounds to question whether the individual incarceration of a few offenders necessarily deters others from committing genocide or crimes against humanity. It is unknown whether collective sanctions would fare any better on this metric. Heller thinks they might. I think they might as well and have suggested some reasons why, all the while believing that they might not be too offensive to retributivist sensibilities. However, so long as collective responsibility remains a bête noire and exists in subalternity

---

[94] Waters, "Killing Globally," 1351–52 (see n. 34).
[95] Ibid., 1353.   [96] Ibid., 1353–54.

to the atrocity trial, meaningful opportunities to learn more about the modalities of collective sanction simply will not arise.

CONCLUSION

The cosmopolitan pluralism I envision would permit criminal trials and punishment to stake a claim in the justice matrix and hence potentially be a participant in the justice process. It would, however, cast this claim as procedurally deferential (with qualifications) to the local and as conceptually porous to alternate private law and extrajudicial modalities. In both cases, the result is that the universal norm of accountability for great evil enters into dialogue with local procedure *and* the richness of the legal landscape beyond the narrowness of ordinary criminal law.

In the end, an independent theoretical understanding of the organic and myriad sources of mass atrocity shall not come from a process of reduction animated by a strong preference for deviance-based criminal law. Rather, it more readily emerges from a process of accretion that recognizes that mass atrocity arises when, collectively, groups fail to respect fundamental obligations owed to humanity, and individuals within those groups either actively or passively facilitate that failure.

As an immediate starting point, conversations about collective responsibility will remain but theoretical until extant power dynamics within the field of postconflict justice are altered. At present, liberal criminal law dominates. Until the grip of liberal criminal law on the justice narrative is relaxed and the architecture retooled, collective responsibility schemes simply will not step outside the realm of theory or subalternity. As such, an important first step is to implement a different incentive structure for modalities of justice that differ from the liberal criminal trial. The challenge is to view individual and collective responsibility as genuinely complementary to the justice narrative, not in tension such that the instantiation of the former comes at the cost of the suborning of the latter.

2

State Criminality and the Ambition of International Criminal Law

David Luban

THE BANALITY OF EVIL AND THE CRIMINALITY OF STATES

In the discussion of mass atrocity, no phrase is more familiar than Hannah Arendt's "banality of evil" – one of the few coinages by political theorists that has entered the moral vocabulary of the wider world. The phrase has often been misunderstood, but Arendt assigned it a well-defined meaning: "the phenomenon of evil deeds, committed on a gigantic scale, which could not be traced to any particularity of wickedness, pathology, or ideological conviction in the doer."[1] Arendt formulated the banality of evil idea to describe the personality of Adolf Eichmann, and we can most readily understand it as a concept within moral psychology, describing a certain type of wrongdoer.[2] As Arendt diagnoses Eichmann, he is a kind of chameleon who takes on the moral coloration of those surrounding

This chapter was originally written for an April 2009 conference at The Western Ontario University on collective punishment, at which this volume originated. I am grateful to the participants in the conference, as well as participants in faculty seminars at the Harvard, University of Saskatchewan, and University of Texas law schools, for their comments. I owe special thanks to Diane Marie Amann for her comments on the first draft and to Gabriella Blum and Paul Kahn for comments on the second.

[1] "Thinking and Moral Considerations," in Hannah Arendt, *Responsibility and Judgment*, ed. Jerome Kohn (New York: Schocken Books, 2003), p. 159. The phrase "banality of evil" comes from *Eichmann in Jerusalem: A Report on the Banality of Evil*, rev. ed. (New York: Penguin, 1964), which I henceforth refer to as EJ.

[2] Years before the Eichmann trial, Arendt had identified none other than Heinrich Himmler as a similar personality type: "neither a Bohemian like Goebbels, nor a sex criminal like Streicher, nor a perverted fanatic like Hitler, nor an adventurer like Goering. He is a 'bourgeois' with all the outer aspect of respectability, all the habits of a good *paterfamilias* who does not betray his wife and anxiously seeks to secure a decent future for his children." Hannah Arendt, "Organized Guilt and Universal Responsibility" (1945), in *Essays in Understanding 1930–1954*, ed. Jerome Kohn (New York: Harcourt, Brace & Co., 1994), p. 128.

him and adapts his conscience to the situation he is in. Arendt's observations and speculations mesh well with the powerful line of experimental social psychology associated with cognitive dissonance theory and the "situationist" school – a line represented most vividly by the famous Milgram and Zimbardo experiments.[3]

But describing a specific pattern of moral psychology is only half the story Arendt tells. To understand why a chameleon is a specific color at a given time, you must know the color of its surroundings. Arendt zeros in on the social conditions that induce the "banal" wrongdoer to discount the monstrosity of the crimes he commits: it is a political regime in which exceptions and rules, deviance and normality, criminality and lawfulness, have become inverted. Precisely because those around Eichmann treated mass murder as though it were an ordinary function of government and regarded common human decency as a crime against the state, "this new type of criminal, who is in actual fact *hostis generis humani*, commits his crimes under circumstances that make it well-nigh impossible for him to know or to feel that he is doing wrong" (EJ, p. 276). In an ordinary regime, gross criminality flies "like a black flag" above atrocious misdeeds, and murderous orders are "manifestly illegal." (Arendt lifts the quoted phrases from an Israeli court decision about war crimes, and "manifest illegality" marks the worldwide legal test for military orders that may not be obeyed: no defense of superior orders avails soldiers who commit crimes in obedience to manifestly illegal orders.) Arendt comments: "in a criminal regime this 'black flag' with its 'warning sign'

---

[3] I discuss these and other experiments in detail, and connect them with Arendt's view, in "The Ethics of Wrongful Obedience" and "Integrity: Its Causes and Cures," both revised and reprinted in Luban, *Legal Ethics and Human Dignity* (Cambridge: Cambridge University Press, 2007); on the connection between the Milgram experiments and Arendt's diagnosis of Eichmann, see pages 250–52. The most significant difference between the situationist analysis and Arendt's is that where she uses the banality of evil idea to describe one particular kind of person, situationists contend that what she observed in Eichmann is true of all people: situations influence behavior far more than personality does, and thus we are all chameleons. For situationists, theories of personality types commit the "fundamental attribution error" of ascribing behavior to character rather than situation. In the works cited here, I express hesitation about interpreting the experiments as the situationists do: it is difficult for their theory to explain why a significant number of people in (for example) the Milgram experiments do not comply. See *Legal Ethics and Human Dignity*, pp. 247, 282–85. Arendt's less global version of the banality of evil thesis seems more in line with the fact that, as she said, "most people will comply but *some people will not*.... Humanly speaking, no more is required, and no more can reasonably be asked, for this planet to remain a place fit for human habitation." EJ, p. 233.

flies as 'manifestly' above what normally is a lawful order – for instance, not to kill innocent people just because they happen to be Jews – as it flies above a criminal order under normal circumstances" (EJ, p. 148). Mark Drumbl, discussing the Rwanda genocide, likewise observes that many of the *génocidaires* were just the opposite of deviants: they were dutiful citizens murdering in fulfillment of civic obligation.[4] Perversely, to spare or save Tutsis at a time when all governmental offices were doing their utmost to enlist the population in massacring them in a supposed war of self-defense, a person had to be a deviant.

Arendt's explanation, like Drumbl's, rests on an important premise: that the Nazi state, like the Hutu Power state half a century later, was in a literal sense criminal to the core. Notice that Arendt begins her remark about the black flag of illegality with the words "in a criminal regime." A state that turns the world upside down and makes the monstrous the centerpiece of civic obligation is a criminal state.[5] The concept "banality of evil" – a fragment of personality theory and moral psychology – travels in tandem with the concept "criminal state" – a fragment of legal theory and political philosophy. Rightly understood, they are cognate concepts within a single theory of radical evil. Both of them pose deep challenges to an understanding of criminal law that centers on the personal responsibility of individuals and that concedes the legal immunity of states. Yet although endless debate and discussion have surrounded the banality of evil, the idea of state criminality has received far less attention. I suggest that part of the reason is that international law fetishizes and idolizes states, so that recognizing a category of state criminality would be as heretical as a religion labeling its own gods criminals. As Drumbl puts it, "International law is deeply paradoxical: it courageously operates in opposition to state interests while stubbornly protecting state interests" by focusing solely on individual perpetrators (APIL, p. 173).

International criminal law is the legal discipline that comes closest to recognizing the category of state criminality, but it never quite gets there: with the exception of one slightly aberrant Nuremberg doctrine that international law never took on board, its framers have insisted that only natural, flesh-and-blood human beings can be tried for crimes against humanity, war crimes, genocide, and aggression – the so-called core international

---

[4] Mark Drumbl, *Atrocity, Punishment, and International Law* (New York: Cambridge University Press, 2007), pp. 25–26, 173. Henceforth, I refer to Drumbl's book as APIL.
[5] For the moment, I use the terms "state" and "regime" more or less interchangeably. Later in this chapter, it proves essential to distinguish between them.

crimes.[6] It nevertheless comes closer to the truth than any other system of jurisprudence, because it strips away from state officials the defenses of "act of state," "superior orders," and "domestic legality."[7] International criminal law represents a major, if incomplete, effort toward deflating the state-worship that defines public international law as a subject. Deflating the state, even incompletely, is perhaps the most radical ambition of international criminal justice. Its enemies are not wrong to perceive this ambition and the threat it poses to state sovereignty. In its institutional design, the International Criminal Court (ICC) is in fact highly protective of sovereignty, perhaps more than it should be; but the fears of its enemies have little to do with the actual mechanics of the Rome Statute. Statists smell a rat, and the rat is the innuendo that states, far from ultimate objects of dignity "beyond law and lawlessness," can be the world's supreme criminals. As I have suggested elsewhere, this is heresy akin to labeling Abraham's sacrifice of Isaac, which the Bible depicts as a nation-founding act of faith, as nothing more than attempted murder.[8] A full-fledged doctrine of state criminality would similarly blaspheme the sacred order of public international law, in which states are like gods.

THE STATE BEYOND GOOD AND EVIL

Among legal philosophers, Paul Kahn has been foremost in insisting on the religious (I would say idolatrous) character of citizens' connection with their states. Lest this seem like hyperbole, he reminds us that throughout the Cold War, both the United States and the Soviet Union were prepared to annihilate each other rather than let the other impinge on their sovereignty; if the mark of religion is human sacrifice, it is no mere figure of speech to describe states as jealous gods. No state, including

---

[6] The doctrine allowed groups or organizations to be declared criminal (Nuremberg Charter, Article 9); it was applied to specific organizations of the German state, but not to the state as such. I discuss it later.

[7] Article 7 of the Nuremberg Charter removes immunity from the head of state and other government officials; Article 8 removes the superior orders defense; and the definition of crimes against humanity in Article 6(c) criminalizes the specified misdeeds "whether or not in violation of the domestic law of the country where perpetrated."

[8] David Luban, "Fairness to Rightness: Jurisdiction, Legality, and the Legitimacy of International Criminal Law," in *The Philosophy of International Law*, eds. Samantha Besson and John Tasioulas (Oxford University Press, 2010), pp. 577–78.

liberal states that currently have no draft, has ever disavowed its authority to conscript its citizens to die and kill on its behalf.[9]

Tribal rulers had manna, and Egyptian and Roman emperors became gods.[10] European monarchs ruled by divine right, and Chinese emperors enjoyed the mandate of heaven. As Ernst Kantorowicz showed, English lawyers in the early modern period distinguished the king's "body natural" from his "body politic" – a legal fiction derived from the theological distinction between Christ's physical and mystical bodies.[11] The king's body natural is born, becomes decrepit, and perishes; his body politic is immortal. In modern democracies and republics, people like us live and die, but "we the people" perdures outside of ordinary time.

Obviously, divine right has vanished as a political ideology, and the social contract tradition of political theory since Hobbes proclaims that the state is a human, not a divine, construction. Historians of political theory sometimes trace this humanization of the state back to Marsilius of Padua's 1324 *Defensor Pacis*. Siding with the emperor against the pope in a political showdown, Marsilius argued that the state is a human artifact, and "Christ Himself did not come into the world to have dominance over men, nor to judge them with judgement in the third signification [i.e., civil judgment], nor to be a temporal prince, but rather to be subject in respect of the status of this present world."[12]

Although at first glance it may seem that humanizing the state deflates it, political history instead suggests that charisma simply migrated from the mandate of heaven to a fetishized conception of state sovereignty. Hobbes himself called the commonwealth a "mortal god."[13] We find the

---

[9] Paul W. Kahn, *Putting Liberalism in Its Place* (Princeton: Princeton University Press, 2005), p. 228; Kahn, "Nuclear Weapons and the Rule of Law," *New York University Journal of International Law and Politics* 31 (1999): pp. 379–81.

[10] On the religious status of tribal chieftains and emperors, see Martin van Creveld, *The Rise and Decline of the State* (Cambridge University Press, 1999), pp. 15, 38–39.

[11] Ernst H. Kantorowicz, *The King's Two Bodies: A Study in Medieval Political Theology* (Princeton: Princeton University Press, 1957), pp. 193–223.

[12] Marsilius of Padua, *The Defender of the Peace*, ed. and trans. Annabel Brett (Cambridge: Cambridge University Press, 1324/2005), pp. 160–61. Marsilius concedes that all principates derive "from God as the remote cause"; but "in most cases and almost everywhere he established these principates through the medium of human minds, to which he granted the freedom to establish them in this way." Ibid., p. 44.

[13] Thomas Hobbes, *Leviathan*, ed., Michael Oakeshot (Oxford: Basil Blackwell, 1957), p. 112 (ch. 17). Hobbes says that the social contract "is the generation of that great LEVIATHAN, or rather, to speak more reverently, of that *mortal god* to which we owe, under the *immortal God*, our peace and defence." Diane Marie Amann has reminded

fetishism of the state reflected in innumerable features of contemporary international law, both large and small. The largest, of course, is the very nature of international law. The positivist and consensualist theory that became dominant by the early twentieth century holds that the sole and absolute source of international law is the will of states manifested in custom and agreements.[14] Even *jus cogens* is, in standard doctrine, merely super-custom that "can be modified... by a subsequent norm of general international law having the same character."[15]

Because international law can, on the consensualist view, have no source outside the will of states as reflected in their customary practices and the agreements they reach, states take on the charisma formerly reserved for kings. A Kantian might say that sovereign states are the transcendental condition for the possibility of international law. This situation has hardly changed in the United Nations era; arguably, the UN system formalizes and augments the *corpus mysticum* of states. Article 2(1) of the UN Charter recognizes the "sovereign equality" of states; Article 51 reserves for states the right of self-defense, and on the basis of Article 51 the International Court of Justice (ICJ) found that it could not even "conclude definitively whether the threat or use of nuclear weapons would be lawful or unlawful in an extreme circumstance of self-defence, in which the very survival of a State would be at stake."[16] That's how important states are: important enough that the law cannot forbid them from blowing up the world if their survival is threatened. This is a far cry from the pragmatic idea that states are merely forms of organization

---

me that the frontispiece to the first edition of *Leviathan* depicts the sovereign garbed in chain mail made of his subjects' bodies. Of course what is interesting about this image is that chain mail absorbs blows and defends the sovereign, not the other way around.

[14] Martti Koskenniemi has demonstrated that the main line of international lawyers from the 1870s on has been less enamored of positivism than later writers, like Oppenheim, asserted. Koskenniemi, *The Gentle Civilizer of Nations: The Rise and Fall of International Law 1870–1960* (Cambridge: Cambridge University Press, 2002), p. 92. Koskenniemi's history shows that the triumph of positivism over "Grotian" natural law is hard to date precisely, and indeed it may be a twentieth-century creative misreading to push it back to the nineteenth century. I ignore this complication, which I do not think undermines the story I am telling. It seems clear that consensualism prevailed by 1927, when *Lotus* proclaimed that "rules of law binding upon States... emanate from their own free will as expressed in conventions or by usages generally accepted as expressing principles of law." The Case of the S.S. Lotus (*France v. Turkey*), 1927 P.C.I.J. (ser. A) No. 10 (Sept. 7). Available at http://www.worldcourts.com/pcij/eng/decisions/1927.09.07_lotus, p. 14.

[15] Vienna Convention on the Law of Treaties, Article 53.

[16] *Legality of the Threat or Use of Nuclear Weapons, Advisory Opinion, I.C.J. Reports 1996*, p. 263, ¶97. Available at http://www.icj-cij.org/docket/files/95/7495.pdf.

meeting the human need for government given that we are not angels. The UN's member states resemble the Homeric gods on Olympus – quarrelsome, mutually self-congratulatory, and often taking sides in bloody wars waged by mere mortals in which the most powerful Olympians intervene if peace threatens to break out.

International lawyers and political theorists are likely to bridle at the assertion that state sovereignty retains its exalted status in the contemporary system: in obvious respects, legal developments since the end of World War II have qualified and eroded the classical model of Westphalian sovereignty.[17] Small states ceded power to the Security Council by accepting its Chapter VII powers; European states have devolved at least bits of their sovereignty to Brussels and Strasbourg; the World Trade Organization represents a further departure from Westphalia. Yet nationalism persists nearly everywhere, and European electorates rejected the European constitution.[18] For understandable reasons, former colonies jealously cherish their sovereignty and harbor deep suspicions that internationalism is a Trojan horse for Westerners with neo-colonial ambitions. Consensualism remains untouched as the dominant theory of international law. In short, if the deified state is dead, it still casts a longer shadow than cosmopolitans might think or hope.[19]

STATE FETISHISM AND IMMUNITY

In international and transnational law, the state fetishism that I am describing comes out most vividly in doctrines of state immunity from the jurisdiction of other states' courts, a doctrine of considerable significance for international criminal enforcement. As Lord Millett explained in his *Pinochet* speech, the classical theory of international law "taught that states were the only actors on the international plane.... States were sovereign and equal: it followed that one state could not be impleaded in the national courts of another; *par in parem non habet*

---

[17] For useful discussion, see John H. Jackson, *Sovereignty, the WTO and Changing Fundamentals of International Law* (Cambridge: Cambridge University Press, 2006).

[18] See Ulrich Haltern, "On Finality," in *Principles of European Constitutional Law*, eds. Jürgen Bast and Armin von Bogdandy (Oxford Hart Publishing, 2006), pp. 727–64.

[19] "After Buddha was dead, his shadow was still shown for centuries in a cave – a tremendous, gruesome shadow. God is dead; but given the way of men, there may still be caves for thousands of years in which his shadow will be shown. – And we – we still have to vanquish his shadow too." Nietzsche, *The Gay Science*, §108, trans. Walter Kaufmann (New York: Vintage, 1974), p. 167.

imperium."[20] For that reason, a head of state enjoys immunity *ratione personae*: "He is regarded as the personal embodiment of the state itself. It would be an affront to the dignity and sovereignty of the state which he personifies and a denial of the equality of sovereign states to subject him to the jurisdiction of the municipal courts of another state."[21] Contemporary heads of state are immune, according to this personification theory of immunity, by a legal metonymy: *l'état c'est moi.* A head of state cannot be prosecuted for crime because that would involve one state prosecuting another in violation of *par in parem.* Notably, although Lord Millett believes that the classical theory "no longer prevails in its unadulterated form," he never doubts that the head of state's immunity *ratione personae* remains a valid rule of customary international law.

Notwithstanding the Latin maxim *par in parem,* the key to this personification theory is not the equality of states but their sovereignty. A rule permitting any state to implead any other in its courts would satisfy equality just as surely as the rule forbidding states to do so. Only because states are not only equal but sovereign would it affront the dignity of a state to be called to account for its acts in another state's courts. State immunity, which for a moment seemed threatened by the *Pinochet* case, has come roaring back in the new century. In its 2001 *Al-Adsani* opinion, the European Court of Human Rights found on the basis of *par in parem non habet imperium* that Kuwait's immunity from judicial process in other states' courts outweighs the *jus cogens* prohibition on torture.[22] In its 2006 *Jones* decision,[23] the U.K. Law Lords backtracked significantly from *Pinochet* and found that official torture is indeed a state act – they had held in *Pinochet* that it is not – and therefore that Saudi Arabian officials are immune from being sued in British courts for torture because of sovereign immunity.

The personification theory according to which the head of state enjoys immunity *ratione personae* because he or she personifies the state in its majesty is not the only possible basis for the immunity. The immunity can be placed on a less occult and more practical basis – namely, the

---

[20] *Regina v. Bow Street Stipendiary Magistrate, ex rel. Pinochet Ugarte (No. 3),* United Kingdom House of Lords [2000] 1 A.C. 147 (1999), 2 W.L.R. 827 (H.L.), reprinted in 38 I.L.M. 581, 644 (1999) (speech of Lord Millett). The Latin slogan means "equals have no dominion over equals."

[21] Ibid.

[22] *Al-Adsani v. Kingdom,* [2001] ECHR 35763/97, ¶61.

[23] *Jones v. Ministry of the Interior Al-Mamlaka Al-Arabiya AS Saudiya (The Kingdom of Saudi Arabia) and others* [2006] UKHL 26.

functional requirements of international diplomacy. This was the theory the ICJ relied on in the *Arrest Warrant* case; but even there, the Court concluded that Belgium's arrest warrant for Congo's foreign minister constitutes a "moral injury" to Congo,[24] a phrase with a distinct aroma of *lèse majesté* theology about it.

THE RADICAL AMBITION OF INTERNATIONAL CRIMINAL LAW

Notably, the immunity of heads of state has been abolished in international tribunals. In theory, this abolition is consistent with *ratione personae* immunity in state courts: states are each other's equals, whereas international tribunals are a product of the entire international community. Therefore (the argument goes), *par in parem* has no application to international tribunals and therefore stripping immunity from heads of state and acts of state in international tribunals leaves the customary international law of immunity intact.

However, there remains some conceptual tension, particularly vivid in the ICC. Created by a multilateral treaty rather than by the UN Security Council, the ICC has jurisdiction over specified crimes committed in the territory or by the nationals of its member states. Presumably, it derives this jurisdiction from its member states proxying their own territorial or nationality jurisdiction to it. However, because none of the member states has jurisdiction over rulers of other states, it is not theirs to proxy, and so it is unclear under what theory the ICC can abrogate head-of-state immunity. The answer cannot be that ICC members tacitly waive the immunities of their own rulers. That would explain why member states' rulers have no immunity before the ICC, but it does not explain why the ICC has jurisdiction over the rulers of non-states parties responsible for crimes in the territory of member states.

It seems to me that the termination of head-of-state immunity and abolition of the act-of-state defense before international tribunals are clues

---

[24] *Arrest Warrant of 11 April 2000 (Democratic Republic of the Congo v. Belgium)*, *Judgment, I.C.J. Reports 2002, p. 31*, ¶75. Available at http://www.icj-cij.org/docket/files/121/8126.pdf. See also *Prosecutor v. Blaškić*, which holds that state officials "are mere instruments of a State and their official action can only be attributed to the State. They cannot be the subject of sanctions or penalties for conduct that is not private but undertaken on behalf of a State. In other words, State officials cannot suffer the consequences of wrongful acts which are not attributable to them personally but to the State on whose behalf they act." ICTY Appeals Chamber (1997), 110 ILR 607, 707, ¶38.

that international criminal justice, rather than being a consistent extension of existing international law, actually mounts a dramatic challenge
to the prevailing idolatry of the state. An even clearer sign is the actual
spectacle of a Slobodan Milošević or Charles Taylor in the dock. There,
strikingly, they stand revealed as bodies natural, not bodies politic, just
as Charles Stuart and Citizen Louis Capet did in the seventeenth and
eighteenth centuries.[25]

Obviously, not all defendants in international proceedings are state
officials. They include warlords, militia chiefs, adventurers, rebels, and
their underlings. However, defendants also include state officials who
used their troops to perpetrate the same atrocities as the barbarians at
the gate. In an obvious way, the fact that high state officials are tried for
the same crimes, before the same courts, as unofficial thugs makes the
proceedings even more deflationary of the dignity of the state. Charles
Taylor is accused of crimes equivalent to those of Foday Sankoh; Biljana
Plavšić and Jean Kambanda stood in the same dock as Duško Tadić
and Hassan Ngeze. This is precisely the phenomenon I noted earlier:
deflating official acts to mere criminality is the equivalent gestalt shift
to labeling the sacrifice of Isaac mere attempted murder. Bringing about
such a gestalt shift is the radical ambition of international criminal law.
It aims to reconceptualize political violence, justified in other ages as
raison d'état or *Kriegsraison* – therefore beyond good and evil – as mere
crime.

THE EXPRESSIVE FUNCTIONS OF INTERNATIONAL CRIMINAL PROCEEDINGS

I am offering an answer to the question "what is the point of international
criminal proceedings?" that focuses on the message its trials and punishments convey – specifically, the message that political violence, mystified
by states, is nothing but crime. In its form, this is an *expressivist* answer,
that is, an answer that focuses not on the tangible consequences of a
social practice (like international criminal proceedings) but on the collective attitudes it expresses. Obviously, this is not the only way to answer
the question. Instead, one could explain the point of international criminal proceedings consequentially: they are meant to deter atrocities, or to
incapacitate dangerous murderers and torturers, or to create an authoritative record of political cataclysms as a bulwark against future liars

---

[25] See Michael Walzer, *Regicide and Revolution* (Cambridge: Cambridge University Press,
1974).

and deniers. When the UN Security Council established the International Criminal Tribunal for the Former Yugoslavia (ICTY) and International Criminal Tribunal for Rwanda (ICTR), it invoked its Chapter VII powers and thus implicitly claimed that the tribunals were created to help "maintain or restore international peace and security."[26] Some theorists claim, on the basis of questionable psychological assumptions, that the aim of the proceedings is to provide closure and healing to victims, or closure and healing to posttraumatic societies. The ICTY's *Blaškić* decision, drawing on the German criminological theory of "positive prevention," has stated that an aim of sentencing is to reassure the world "that the legal system is being implemented and enforced," which enhances compliance.[27] All of these are tangible, consequential aims.

Notoriously, there are grounds for skepticism about all these aims.[28] We simply have little reason to believe that international proceedings achieve any of these goals. Incapacitation is the only one of them that imprisonment surely does accomplish; yet even that seems to rest on a false premise – namely, that most international criminals remain dangerous even though the conditions that turned them from good citizens into murderers have disappeared. (This is not to deny that some political leaders should be incapacitated because of their proven talents as conflict entrepreneurs.)

Expressive theories focus on less tangible goals. They rest on the premise that actions can express attitudes and send messages, quite apart from their consequences. A clear example of an expressive aim of international criminal conviction is one of those itemized in the *Blaškić* decision: "public reprobation and stigmatisation by the international community."[29] Even retribution can be understood along expressivist lines, and in my opinion that is the best way to understand it. On Jean Hampton's well-known account of the retributive idea, crimes committed by one person against another have expressive content: they express the moral falsehood that I, the perpetrator, am "high" and you, the victim, are "low" – that I am the sort of person who gets to do things like that to others, or you are the sort of person to whom others get to do it, or both. The aim of retribution, Hampton argues, is to "plant the flag of moral

---

[26] UN Charter, Article 39.
[27] *Prosecutor v. Blaškić*, ICTY Case No. IT-95-14-A, Judgement (July 29, 2004), ¶678. Theoretically, it does so by treating laws as what game theorists call an "assurance game."
[28] Drumbl, p. 184; Martti Koskenniemi, "Between Impunity and Show Trials," *Max Planck Yearbook of International Law* 6 (2002): 1–35.
[29] *Blaškić*, note 27, ¶678.

truth" by humbling the perpetrator. In Hampton's phrase, the retributive aim of punishment is to inflict an "expressive defeat" on the wrongdoer to reaffirm the equal moral worth of the victim that the wrongdoer has implicitly or explicitly denied.[30]

Expressive theories are not committed to the idea that perpetrators intend their actions to communicate their expressive messages, in which case expressivism would be quite implausible. Expressivists can admit that a mugger's conscious intention and purpose may be simply to steal the victim's wallet and iPod, not to say "I am high up and you are low down." The robber's contemptuous attitude toward the victim is built into the action regardless of whether the robber consciously thinks contemptuous thoughts or means to communicate them.[31] The imperative to take retribution can also be explained in expressivist terms: a society that leaves palpable crimes unpunished or punished with a slap on the wrist has in effect expressed that it accepts the wrongdoer's "I am high up and you are low down." Thus, for example, a university that systematically hushes up rapes committed by star athletes has, like it or not, confirmed the rapist's message that he gets to do stuff like that and undergraduate women have to take it.

I have used the phrase "international criminal proceedings" to refer to a process that includes both trials and punishments. The expressivist accounts of international trials and punishments need not be the same, and I think they are not.

Punishment

In the case of international tribunals addressing mass atrocities, it seems to me that the most plausible among the standard rationales for punishment is retribution (in which I include the "public reprobation" that the *Blaškić* decision lists separately from retribution). When I expressed skepticism earlier about the various consequentialist aims of international punishment, I did not include retribution, because it is not consequentialist, and it seems utterly obvious that at bottom these tribunals exist because

---

[30] Jean Hampton, "The Retributive Idea," in *Forgiveness and Mercy*, Jean Hampton and Jeffrie Murphy (Cambridge University Press, 1990), especially pp. 122–30.

[31] On this point, see Elizabeth S. Anderson and Richard H. Pildes, "Expressive Theories of Law: A General Restatement," *University of Pennsylvania Law Review* 148 (2000): 1529–30. I do not address the difficult philosophical question of whether the expressive content of practices rests on a network of conventions, or whether some actions express certain attitudes intrinsically.

we believe that atrocities deserve to be punished – or, in an equivalent negative formulation, that letting them go unpunished is a morally deficient response.[32]

Trials

In domestic criminal law, we generally think of the trial as a means to an end – namely, ascertaining whether the defendant should be convicted and punished. The punishment, not the trial, occupies the center of our attention. Matters seem rather different in international and transnational trials of atrocity crimes. Here, it seems to me that the center of gravity lies in the trial, far more than the punishment.[33] That was certainly true in the two iconic trials of the twentieth century, Nuremberg and the Eichmann trial (despite the fact that by all accounts Nuremberg was excruciatingly boring, as prosecutors spent hour after hour reading documents into the record). The trials lie at the heart of the proceeding because the full

---

[32] In APIL (p. 130) Drumbl points out that the actual sentencing schemes used in the ICTY and ICTR are hard to square with the retributive idea of desert, and I agree. However, I do not think that undermines the claims that retribution lies at the heart of the tribunals or that it plays a role in sentencing. Not the former, because imperfections in sentencing – notably, the totally discretionary sentencing of the ad hoc tribunals – don't speak to whether the purpose of the tribunal is retribution or something else. Not the latter, for two reasons. First, retribution is not the only aim of criminal sentencing, as *Blaškić* makes clear, and therefore we should not expect to find strict correspondence between desert and actual sentence. Second, there is no such thing as a "natural" sentence. Sentences make sense only within systems. See Michael Davis, "How to Make the Punishment Fit the Crime," *Ethics* 93 (1983): 726–52, especially 736–37. There is another reason as well for why retributivists might accept sentences for enormous atrocities that are no greater than those for some lesser crimes. In the case of mass atrocities, proportionate sentences may well be so harsh, cruel, and degrading that morality does not permit them to be inflicted. Hampton argues that the same respect for human dignity that provides the strongest argument for retributive punishment also imposes limits on how harsh the punishment can be. "The Retributive Idea," pp. 135–37. If so, permissible punishments will "max out" long before judgments of heinousness max out. Moreover, precisely because mass atrocities are crimes of a different order than ordinary domestic criminal offenses, the system of punishments for the former may be compelled to shift the scale away from the system of the latter, leaving incongruities when we view them side by side. For example, if a lead defendant in a war crime trial receives a sentence of twenty-five years, it may be justifiable to sentence an accomplice to something less – say, ten years – even though a conventional murderer who killed fewer people than the accomplice could receive more than ten years in the domestic legal system. This result does not mean that the punishment scheme is irrational as a form of retribution. It means only that two punishment schemes, scaled differently because of differences in the nature and context of the crime, have been superimposed one on the other.

[33] Luban, "Fairness to Rightness," pp. 575–77.

dimensions of the human catastrophe are displayed to the world patiently, step by step, for all to see. The facts are not merely laid out in plain sight, however. They are, in the prosecutor's retelling and the tribunal's judgment, labeled as crimes against humanity, war crimes, or genocide. The defense challenges the evidence, of course, but it also challenges the labels. It is the acts of exposing the deeds, categorizing them as crimes, and naming exactly which crime they are that are the central point of the international proceeding.[34]

Of course, from the defendant's point of view, what matters most is the sentence and punishment. Am I going to prison for two years or twenty? For everyone else, the punishment is far less significant than the trial itself and its acts of renaming.[35] What the defendant called "defending the people," "reclaiming the heritage of our nation," "defeating the rebels," or "saving the country" is now stamped and sealed as genocide, torture, sexual enslavement, or forcible transfer of population. Political violence is no longer beyond good and evil, insulated as *raison d'état* or *Kriegsraison*. Now it is crime. The deeds have been translated from the realm of politics to the realm of law, and states are now subordinated to law. That subordination is illustrated by the trappings of the courtroom, with its fussy and exasperating little formalities. We should not let the blandness and boringness of legal process deceive us: the fact that "sacred violence" can be subjected to it is in its own tedious way a revolutionary development.

My view of the importance of the expressive power of the international trial as such is highly sympathetic to that of Mark Osiel, who argues that the mass atrocity tribunal is a "'theater of ideas,' where large questions of collective memory and even national identity are engaged."[36] Osiel observes that for the defense, the theatrical genre is tragedy; for the prosecutors, it is a morality play. In both cases, it is in a literal sense a "show trial." This label is dangerous, because one of its meanings is "sham trial" – an unfair trial designed to legitimize a prearranged outcome. That

---

[34] Drumbl also notes that the trial, rather than the punishment, is the central event of the international criminal proceeding (see APIL, p. 174) but correctly insists that we must not ignore the punishments.

[35] With one exception: an overlenient sentence may reinforce rather than defeat the expressive assault on the victims' worth.

[36] Mark Osiel, *Mass Atrocity, Collective Memory, and the Law* (Transaction Books, 1997), p. 3. I offered some thoughts on this function of trials in Luban, *Legal Modernism* (Ann Arbor: University of Michigan Press, 1994), pp. 379–91.

is not what Osiel means. He insists that a postdictatorship society aiming to establish liberalism must conduct scrupulously fair trials, because fair trials *are* one of the things that the proceeding means to dramatize. What he means by a show trial is rather, quite literally, a trial that is meant to show: a didactic trial, not a pretend trial.

Osiel focuses on trials conducted by a new democratic regime of the crimes committed by its predecessor – his examples were Latin American dictatorships coming to terms with their dirty wars. In Osiel's view, trials would allow a country with a guilty conscience and bloodstains on its collective identity to come to terms with itself and refashion that identity along liberal lines.

I am making a parallel point about the "theater of ideas" character of international tribunals. A pure international tribunal is not a vehicle for a country's self-examination; for self-examination, criminal justice must go local. The ideas an international trial expresses are therefore not vehicles for a state to refashion its own identity. Rather, the expressive character of the trials aims at something different: the projection to the wider world of new norms, norms under which political violence gets relabeled as crime.[37] Eventually, these norms can be incorporated into domestic criminal law as well, and into military policy and training. Hopefully, they will seize the moral imagination of larger societies as well, the way that abolitionist norms gradually replaced tolerance for human slavery. The fundamental message of international criminal norms is that the Great Game of politics, deeply embedded in the human condition, must never again cross moral lines that heretofore it has always crossed. That may be a preposterously utopian ideal, as fanciful as the injunction to beat swords into plowshares and study war no more. Utopian or not, that is the point – the sole point – of establishing courts to examine and punish war crimes, crimes against humanity, and genocide.

Scholars, activists, and diplomats are divided over whether this goal advances or retards peace and reconciliation in the land where the atrocities took place. Consider a recent controversy over sentencing in the Special Court of Sierra Leone (SCSL). The defendants, leaders of the Civil Defense Force (CDF) were convicted of war crimes, but the Trial

[37] Drumbl takes as a "premise . . . that one of the reasons international criminal law falls short is because it treats the extraordinary international criminal like the ordinary common criminal." P. 187. I am arguing that this is the whole point of international criminal proceedings, and if they fall short it is because they fail to drive the point home strongly enough.

Chamber mitigated their sentences because they were "defending a cause that is palpably just and defendable."[38] The CDF fought on the side of the government. Yet critics argued that war crimes are war crimes no matter who commits them, and selective mitigation sends the opposite message.[39] Eventually the Appeals Chamber agreed with the critics.[40] The case raises significant issues. The SCSL is a hybrid court, that is, a mixed national–international court, and in the Trial Chamber it was the Sierra Leonean judges who favored mitigation, reportedly echoing sentiment on the street. The critics tended to be internationalists from outside Sierra Leone. For those who believe that the primary audience must be the people of the afflicted country, this case might serve as an example of what is wrong with international criminal justice: it privileges the standpoint of the so-called international community over that of the victims of the horrific civil war.

The view I am defending sees matters differently. The expressivist emphasizes that war crimes even in defense of the state against a dire threat are, at bottom, war crimes. To mitigate sentences because the war criminals were defending the state would blur that message and shift it in the direction of reason-of-state, or "dirty hands," thinking.

The strength of the expressivist account is its iconoclasm, its smashing of political idols that drink rivers of human blood. The weakness of the expressivist account – and, if I am right, of the international criminal justice project – is a dangerous vagueness about who exactly belongs to the intended audience of its message. Hampton wants to "plant the flag of morality,"[41] but for whom? Is the message that war crimes are merely war crimes intended for the criminal, or his followers, or the victims, or the man and woman on the street in Freetown? Apparently not. Is it, then, a message for the diaphanous international community? Or for humanitarians within the like-minded countries? Is the audience ultimately the Angel of History, who (in Walter Benjamin's image) stands helplessly watching the rubble of history pile up, recording the crimes and

---

[38] *Prosecutor v. Fofana*, Case No. SCSL-04-14-T, Judgment on the Sentencing of Moinina Fofana and Allieu Kondewa (Trial Chamber I, Oct. 9, 2007), ¶86.

[39] See, for example, Human Rights Watch, Political Considerations in Sentence Mitigation for Serious Violations of the Laws of War before International Criminal Tribunals (March 2008). Available at http://www.hrw.org/backgrounder/ij/sierraleone0308.

[40] *Prosecutor v. Fofana*, Case No. SCSL-04-14-A, Judgment (Appeals Chamber, May 28, 2008), ¶¶529–35.

[41] Hampton, "The Retributive Idea," p. 130.

infamies but unable to make repairs?[42] Is it a message in a bottle, thrown into the sea? Or will someone read it somewhere, someday, and turn a page in human history?

THE PRINCE OF DENMARK WITHOUT DENMARK

So far, I have argued that international law and the international order are founded on a fetishism of states, displaced but not wholly deflated in the early modern era. Because states are fetishized, the category of state criminality has been conspicuously lacking from international law. Branding states criminals would violate their dignity, an argument that receives expression in the immunity *ratione personae* of heads of state. International criminal proceedings have the radical aim to further deflate states by putting acts of political violence, including state violence, on trial to relabel these acts as crimes. However, international proceedings have been deliberately limited to flesh-and-blood defendants. We then confront a curious drama: not *Hamlet* without the Prince of Denmark, but rather the Prince without Denmark.

Dropping the metaphor: a Milošević or al-Bashir is not simply a ruthless man giving orders. Although it is untrue that the entire state apparatus is implicated in the crimes that brought them international indictments, a significant portion of the state apparatus is. Further, although many Serbs and Sudanese people simply want to get on with their lives, no political leader can work his will on such a large and violent scale without the support of a party and a significant portion of the country. This is what it means to speak of a criminal state and not simply a criminal leader. To tell the story of their crimes without attributing them in any way to the state or its people is, simply, to falsify the story.[43] That is precisely Hannah Arendt's point: to demonize Adolf Eichmann's motives misunderstands him; to understand him means to understand that he could become a criminal only within a criminal state.

---

[42] Walter Benjamin, "Theses on the Philosophy of History," in *Illuminations*, ed. Hannah Arendt, trans. Harry Zohn (New York: Schocken Books, 1969), Thesis 9, pp. 259–60. See Luban, *Legal Modernism*, pp. 390–91.

[43] Martti Koskenniemi emphasizes the same point, but draws a diametrically different conclusion from mine. In his view, the falsity of prosecuting political atrocities as individual crimes is a reason not to have international criminal tribunals, not a reason to expand their reach to include states as I propose. Koskenniemi, "Between Impunity and Forgiveness," *Max Planck Yearbook of International Law* 6 (2002): 1–35.

The proposal to add state criminality to legal doctrine raises four questions that I address in the sections to follow. These are, first, what would it mean to describe a state as a criminal? Second, what are the conditions – the "test," as lawyers say – of state criminality? Third, is the proposal a good idea, or would it have destructive practical consequences? Fourth, how do you punish a state? The remainder of this chapter considers these questions in more detail.

HOW CAN A STATE BE A CRIMINAL?

To call a state a criminal sounds like a category mistake. States, one might say, don't murder people; people murder people. A state is an artificial person, and artificial persons cannot commit tangible crimes.

In law, however, long-established rules of agency allow the conduct of one person to be ascribed to another, and agency principles apply even if the latter is an artificial person. A corporate officer who signs a contract on behalf of the company binds the company. The same principles apply when the principal is a state: when the president of the United States signs a treaty, he or she does so on behalf of the United States, and in law, it is the United States that has signed. Conceptually, the agency model expands individual action to organizational action by steps. The first step is establishing conventions for when an agent's acts are ascribed to the principal. The second step expands the notion of principal from single natural persons to collectives of persons. The third step would show how a collective can be regarded as a single artificial person. Each of these raises philosophical puzzles – a point I return to shortly – but for the moment, the only point I wish to make is that if this three-step program can be carried out, the legal model of agency can explain the ascription of human acts to states.

Agency is not the only possible legal model of state criminality. International law contains at least a provisional doctrine on state responsibility for wrongful acts (acts that breach international legal obligations). This is the International Law Commission's 2001 "Draft Articles on Responsibility of States for Internationally Wrongful Acts."[44] It proposes several principles for ascribing acts of humans or groups of humans to states. The principles are straightforward applications of *respondeat superior*,

---

[44] General Assembly Resolution 56/83 of December 12, 2001, annex, and corrected by document A/56/49 (Vol. I)/Corr.4. Available at http://untreaty.un.org/ilc/texts/instruments/english/draft%20articles/9_6_2001.pdf.

rather than agency: conduct ascribed to the state includes that of all its "organs" (in any branch of government), including individuals holding official positions (Article 4); all people "empowered by the law of that State to exercise elements of the governmental authority" (Article 5); and the "conduct of an organ placed at the disposal of a State by another State" (Article 6). All this is true regardless of whether the person or entity is an agent of the state, and indeed even if "the person or entity . . . exceeds its authority or contravenes instructions" (Article 7).

These Draft Articles have to do primarily with civil breaches of international law, not crimes. They make no mention of criminal responsibility, and no other doctrine establishes state criminality. Interestingly, earlier drafts of the Articles did include state responsibility for "international crimes," a phrase that was replaced by "serious breaches" only in the final version. Nevertheless, even though the Draft Articles ultimately make no mention of criminality, a natural extension of their principles would include criminal as well as civil responsibility.

To see what this extension might look like, let us begin by examining an analogous legal concept, corporate criminality. No such doctrine exists in international law, and some domestic legal systems also do not recognize it. One that does is the United States, and I will use it as a template. In U.S. doctrine, corporations have legal personality, and corporate crime is defined in terms of crime by its employees. As in the Draft Articles, the doctrine is one of *respondeat superior*, and it is very simple: "a corporation is liable for the criminal misdeeds of its agents acting within the actual or apparent scope of their employment or authority if the agents intend, at least in part, to benefit the corporation, even though their actions may be contrary to corporate policy or express corporate order."[45] It follows that corporate crime simply tracks employee crime (in the actual or apparent scope of the employee's duties – a qualification that I henceforth omit, but which should be understood when I refer to employees' crimes). Any time the employee commits a crime intending to benefit the corporation, the corporation commits the crime as well; conversely, any time a corporation commits a crime, it must be that at least one employee has committed the same crime (or a group of employees has together committed the crime).

This means that a prosecutor always has a choice of three possibilities: charge the employee, charge the corporation, or both. In practice,

---

[45] Julie R. O'Sullivan, *Federal White Collar Crime: Cases and Materials*, 4th ed. (St. Paul, MN: West Publishing, 2009), p. 164.

prosecutors like easy-conviction legal doctrines because they can use them as leverage to elicit cooperation.[46] That makes easy-conviction doctrines useful, but utility does not make the *respondeat superior* doctrine fair or reasonable. For that, the U.S. Attorney's Manual sets out guidance on how prosecutors should make the choice:

> Charging a corporation for even minor misconduct may be appropriate where the wrongdoing was pervasive and was undertaken by a large number of employees, or by all the employees in a particular role within the corporation, or was condoned by upper management. On the other hand, it may not be appropriate to impose liability upon a corporation, particularly one with a robust compliance program in place, under a strict *respondeat superior* theory for the single isolated act of a rogue employee. There is, of course, a wide spectrum between these two extremes, and a prosecutor should exercise sound discretion in evaluating the pervasiveness of wrongdoing within a corporation.[47]

It is these criteria – the injunction to indict the corporation for pervasive wrongdoing but not for isolated misconduct by rogue individuals – that make the doctrine fair.

All the same things are true if you substitute "state apparatus" for "corporation" – not in existing doctrine but in principle. Governments are corporate organizations, and everything I have quoted from the U.S. Attorney's Manual about corporations could apply to states as well. If wrongdoing is pervasive and carried out by a large number of state functionaries, or all the functionaries in a given role, or condoned by higher officials, then the state is a criminal. This idea is a logical extension of the definitions of crimes in the Rome Statute of the ICC. A crime against humanity requires individual crimes committed "pursuant to or in furtherance of a State or organizational policy," and a war crime requires a plan or policy. In both definitions, the policy element is what makes the crime international.[48] If individuals pursue a state policy to commit widespread or systematic murders, then the state, not just the individuals, is a murderer.

There is one other historical model for the idea of state criminality, one that I mentioned earlier. Article 9 of the Nuremberg Charter states, "At the trial of any individual member of any group or organization the

---

[46] As the U.S. Attorney's Manual explicitly explains, § 9-28.700, cmt. (2008).

[47] U.S. Attorney's Manual, § 9-28.500 (2008).

[48] William Schabas, "State Policy as an Element of International Crimes," *Journal of Criminal Law and Criminology* 98 (2008): 953–82.

Tribunal may declare (in connection with any act of which the individual may be convicted) that the group or organization of which the individual was a member was a criminal organization." Under this article, the prosecutor indicted seven organizations: the Reich Cabinet, the Leadership Corps of the Nazi Party, the SS, the SD, the Gestapo, the SA, and the General Staff. The aim, clearly, was to pick out the subentities of the German state that were criminal to the core.[49] Article 9 might have paved the way to recognizing that a state as such can be a criminal.

Unfortunately, however, the Nuremberg Charter did one other thing as well: in Article 10, it provided that governments could try individual members of the criminal organizations, and "[i]n any such case the criminal nature of the group or organization is considered proved and shall not be questioned" if the group had been convicted under Article 9.

Using group criminality as a shortcut to individual criminal convictions proved to be more than the Tribunal could stomach. Even low-ranked members of the organization, who had little or no knowledge of or involvement in its crimes, could be convicted and, in theory, receive the death penalty. In its judgment, the Tribunal pared down the groups to "exclude persons who had no knowledge of the criminal purposes or acts of the organization and those who were drafted by the State for membership, unless they were personally implicated in the commission of [crimes]."[50] The Tribunal would not tolerate automatic transfer of the criminality of the group to individuals, and – stuck as it was with Articles 9 and 10 – used its discretion to redefine the group as an aggregate of guilty individuals. This in effect eliminates the notion of group criminality, and neither Article 9 nor 10 survived. They were excised when the UN General Assembly adopted the Nuremberg Principles in 1950.

In my view, the General Assembly threw out the baby (Article 9) with the bathwater (Article 10). Had Article 9's conception of criminal organs of the state survived in international law, it would have provided a model for declaring an entire state to be a criminal.

Notably missing from these doctrines are answers to vexing philosophical questions. What kind of a thing is an organization? How can it act? Is it the kind of thing to which acts can coherently be ascribed? Is its action some function of the acts of individuals within it? If the organization can act, can it act responsibly or irresponsibly, or would such

---

[49] However, the cabinet and General Staff were acquitted, as was the SA (Storm Troopers), which had ceased to exist years before the war.

[50] Judgment of the International Military Tribunal: The Accused Organizations. Available at http://avalon.law.yale.edu/imt/judorg.asp#general.

responsibility ascriptions be crude anthropomorphisms? Can it be judged morally? Is it an appropriate vehicle for reactive attitudes such as anger, indignation, or affection? If the organization is blameworthy, does that relieve the blameworthiness of individual employees or members?

These are intricate questions about which philosophers have had, and still have, a lot to say.[51] I propose to duck them all and simply assume it is possible to work out a coherent theory of organizational action and responsibility. For present purposes, we can settle for a crude version of the Turing Test: if, based on outcomes alone, you can't tell whether the decision maker was a single individual or a group of functionaries deliberating in the organization's name, that is good enough reason to suppose that some doctrine of organizational action and responsibility must make sense. Then the answer to our question "how can an organization be a criminal?" is that its functionaries commit crimes in a way that meets whatever the conditions are for ascribing their acts to the organization.

WHAT IS THE TEST OF STATE CRIMINALITY?

The U.S. Attorney's Manual gives plausible criteria for organizational criminality, but they can be further refined. Consider a provision of the Australian Criminal Code specifying that a culpable *mens rea* may be assigned to a "body corporate" if "a corporate culture existed within the body corporate that directed, encouraged, tolerated or led to non-compliance with the relevant provision" or "the body corporate failed to create and maintain a corporate culture that required compliance with the relevant provision."[52] This adds something important to the U.S. Attorney's Manual test of "pervasive" wrongdoing – namely, that pervasive

---

[51] For a sampling: Michael Bratman, "Shared Intention," *Ethics* 104 (1993): 97–113 and "Shared Cooperative Activity," *Philosophical Review* (1992): 327–41; Peter French, *Collective and Corporate Responsibility* (New York: Columbia University Press, 1984); Margaret Gilbert, *Sociality and Responsibility: New Essays in Plural Subject Theory* (Rowman & Littlefield, 2000); Christopher Kutz, *Complicity: Ethics and Law for a Collective Age* (Cambridge: Cambridge University Press, 2000); Larry May, *Sharing Responsibility* (Chicago: University of Chicago Press, 1993); John Dewey, "The Historic Background of Corporate Legal Personality," *Yale Law Journal* 35 (1926): 655–73; Frederick Hallis, *Corporate Personality: A Study in Jurisprudence* (London: Oxford University Press, 1930); Larry May and Stacey Hoffman, eds., *Collective Responsibility: Five Decades of Debate in Theoretical and Applied Ethics* (Savage, MD: Rowman & Littlefield, 1991).

[52] Australian Criminal Code §12.3(2)(c) and (d)(1995). Available at http://www.austlii .edu.au/au/legis/cth/consol_act/cca1995115/sch1.html. Corporate culture is defined as

wrongdoing results from organizational culture.[53] Organizations develop internal cultures – norms of interaction, articulated values, widely shared attitudes and emotions, canonical stories and histories that explain what the organization stands for. Returning to Arendt's insight that in some settings values become inverted and perverted, so that deviance and normality trade places, the bad corporate culture will turn conscientious employees into criminals.[54] It makes sense in that case to ascribe criminality to the organization. Bad organizational culture adds a qualitative dimension to the purely quantitative concept of pervasiveness of wrongdoing.

When we consider state criminality, I believe that two other conditions should be added as well. The first is the active involvement of upper levels of the state apparatus. Merely condoning wrongdoing is not enough to make a state peopled by criminals into a criminal state. To be a criminal state, the leadership itself must take an active rather than merely passive role.

I don't mean to argue against standards of individual command responsibility based on passive *mens rea* such as negligence, recklessness, or *dolus eventualis*.[55] These, however, are standards of individual criminal liability. My suggestion is that state criminal liability requires actively, not passively, complicit officials.

What about the state's people? As Drumbl tellingly and forcefully argues, innocent bystanders in a criminal state such as Rwanda in 1994 are not entirely innocent (APIL, pp. 25–26).[56] Bystanders who go about

"an attitude, policy, rule, course of conduct or practice existing within the body corporate generally or in the part of the body corporate in which the relevant activities takes place." Ibid., §12.3(6).

[53] For a proposal to add a similar test to U.S. law, see Pamela H. Bucy, "Corporate Ethos: A Standard for Imposing Corporate Criminal Liability," *Minnesota Law Review* 75 (1991): 1095–184.

[54] Perhaps the best study of this phenomenon in business corporations remains Robert Jackall, *Moral Mazes: Inside the World of Corporate Managers* (New York: Oxford University Press, 1989).

[55] See Amy J. Sepinwall, "Failure to Punish: Command Responsibility in Domestic and International Law," *Michigan Journal of International Law* 30 (2009), pp. 251–303.

[56] This is the theme of Karl Jaspers's *The Question of German Guilt*, as well as Raul Hilberg's *Perpetrators, Victims, Bystanders*; it is one of the issues at play in the debate between Christopher Browning, Daniel Goldhagen, and Goldhagen's critics and defenders. See, e.g., Omer Bartov, "Reception and Perception: Goldhagen's Holocaust and the World," in *The "Goldhagen Effect": History, Memory, Nazism Facing the German Past*, ed. Geoff Eley (Ann Arbor: Michigan University Press, 2000), pp. 33–87. See Laurel E. Fletcher, "From Indifference to Engagement: Bystanders and International Criminal Justice," *Michigan Journal of International Law* 26 (2005): 1013–95.

their ordinary business when they see evildoing and atrocity reinforce the sense of creepy normality that makes good into bad and bad into good. Some bystanders may actually be beneficiaries of the state crimes, taking over houses and property of the disappeared and the murdered. Even the most despotic political leaders always have a substantial number of loyalists – their fellow party members; their clan, tribe, or ethnicity; the clients in their patronage network; their retainers and guards and soldiers. In a criminal state, it is not only the officials who commit crimes pervasively; the evil infects at least some significant portion of the people.[57]

Thus, the test of state criminality I propose includes some combination of the following: pervasive wrongdoing, a bad political culture, active involvement of a significant part of the state's leadership, and the complicity of at least some significant portion of the people.

The analogy of state criminality with corporate criminality is imperfect, because the latter focuses on the organization and its employees. The equivalent in the context of state criminality is the *government* or *regime*, not the state itself. A state is more than a government: it is a government of a territory and its population.[58] The state itself, in law and in political theory, has legal personality – it is, in Hobbes's words, an artificial person – that survives changes in government and even in the form of government, so long as its territory stays more or less intact and its population more or less stable. Thus, we should distinguish the state, the regime (the government viewed collectively), and the particular personnel holding power within that regime. What the nature is of the political relationship binding together the elements of the state is a matter

---

[57] Jaspers famously distinguished different species of German guilt. In addition to criminal and moral guilt, Jaspers identifies categories of "metaphysical" and "political" guilt. The former is the guilt that attaches to the surviving bystanders simply by virtue of the fact that they survived – in other words, that they did not resist the atrocities unto death – and it is a notoriously speculative category. (I have discussed it in Luban, "Intervention and Civilization: Some Unhappy Lessons of the Kosovo War," in *Global Justice and Transnational Politics*, eds. Pablo de Greiff and Ciaran Cronin (Cambridge, MA: MIT Press, 2002), pp. 96–101). To be clear, the bystander guilt I discuss here is not "metaphysical," but rather something more tangible: passively acquiescing in an inversion of values. This is closer to Jaspers's "political guilt," which follows from his dictum that "Everybody is co-responsible for the way he is governed." *Question*, p. 31.

[58] "The state as a person of international law should possess the following qualifications: (a) a permanent population; (b) a defined territory; (c) government; and (d) capacity to enter into relations with the other states." Montevideo Convention on the Rights and Duties of States, 1933, 49 Stat. 3097, T.S. No. 881, 165 L.N.T.S., Article 1. This is more or less the definition of "state" adopted in the *Restatement (Third) of the Foreign Relations Law of the United States*, vol. 1, §201, p. 72.

of debate among philosophers. The state may be, as Hobbes thought of it, "one person, of whose acts a great multitude, by mutual covenants one with another, have made themselves every one the author";[59] it may be Burke's "partnership between those who are living, those who are dead, and those who are to be born";[60] or, as Hume argued, it may simply be the last warlord standing in a battle of warlords to consolidate rule over the territory, who maintains his rule by "obedience ... so familiar, that most men never make any enquiry about its origin or cause" – or else "by employing, sometimes violence, sometimes false pretences, to establish his dominion over a people a hundred times more numerous than his partizans."[61]

The test of state criminality proposed here rests on an understanding of the state according to which different states may embody different political relationships between the regime and the population. It is closest to Hume's. If Hobbes's definition were accepted, then every criminal regime would automatically be a criminal state, because the population "have made themselves every one the author" of the state's deeds. That would be a useless and unfair legal fiction. To be sure, even a police state starts and – usually – finishes with the political support of a significant part of its people. Otherwise it could never take power in the first place. However, after the police state takes power, it may continue to hold it through violence and terror long after it has lost popular support. Whether crimes should be attributed solely to individuals, or – as in the Nuremberg Article 9 model – to collective entities within the government, or to an entire regime, or, finally, to the state itself will depend on the specific political culture of the state, meaning here not only the organizational culture of the regime but also the level of support for the crimes within the population.

IS IT A BAD IDEA?

The previous three sections have described a legal model of state criminality without considering whether it is a good idea to implement it. Even sympathetic readers may find the prospect of declaring states criminals a mistake.

[59] Hobbes, p. 112.
[60] Edmund Burke, *Reflections on the Revolution in France* (Garden City, NY: Anchor Books, 1973), p. 110.
[61] David Hume, "Of the Original Contract," in *Essays Moral, Political, and Literary*, ed. Eugene F. Miller (Indianapolis, IN: Liberty Classics, 1985), pp. 470–72.

Since Nuremberg, one standard argument for restricting international criminal liability to natural persons has been that otherwise guilty individuals will hide behind the corporate veil of the state, ducking their own culpability by scapegoating the artificial person. Following this line of reasoning, it might be objected that a doctrine of state criminality will simply muddy the waters and provide a shield for flesh-and-blood bad guys.

Despite its surface plausibility, this argument strikes me as one-sided and mistaken. Scapegoating can go in both directions, and it might just as easily be said that guilty organizations hide their rotten culture by shifting all the blame to a fall guy and cutting him loose. The criminologist John Braithwaite, studying corporate crime in the pharmaceutical industry, interviewed executives who referred to themselves as "vice-presidents in charge of going to jail." They explained that if their company ever got caught, they would take the fall, expecting the company to take care of them financially.[62] Not that all organizations resort to this remarkable level of cynical conspiracy; but many will prefer to scapegoat employees rather than admitting the pervasiveness of the rot. After the Abu Ghraib scandal, General Janice Karpinski, who was in charge of U.S. prisons in Iraq, was the only high-level officer to take the fall (she was demoted to colonel), and she bitterly accused the army of scapegoating her; she later offered affidavit testimony implicating her superiors, including the U.S. secretary of defense.

These are familiar arguments from the literature on corporate crime, but it seems that only one side of the argument – the fear of guilty individuals scapegoating the state – has gotten traction in international criminal law; the other side, the argument that a rotten state might scapegoat individuals, has received no attention that I am aware of, presumably because the idea of state criminality is so alien to international law. In any event, state or regime criminality does not exclude individual criminality; both individual leaders and a state or regime as a whole can be indicted in tandem, just as under the *respondeat superior* theory of corporate criminality, both individual employees and corporations can be indicted.

A second argument against criminalizing states is that doing so would in effect blame their people. "We would also make clear that we have

---

[62] John Braithwaite, "Passing the Buck for Corporate Crime, *Australian Society* (1991): 3. See also Jackall, p. 85.

no purpose to incriminate the whole German people," Robert Jackson proclaimed in his opening address at Nuremberg. He went on:

> We know that the Nazi Party was not put in power by a majority of the German vote. We know it came to power by an evil alliance between the most extreme of the Nazi revolutionists, the most unrestrained of the German reactionaries, and the most aggressive of the German militarists. If the German populace had willingly accepted the Nazi programme, no Storm-troopers would have been needed in the early days of the Party, and there would have been no need for concentration camps or the Gestapo.[63]

This argument played to the German people's rage at the Nazis for the ruin of defeat, but thinking of the German people solely as innocent victims of a Nazi conspiracy was disingenuous. True, the Nazis won "only" 44 percent of the vote in 1933, but that was the largest of any of the parties. Jackson implies that Storm Troopers were necessary in the early days of the Nazi Party because the German public did not want Nazi rule. Even if he was right (and one can readily think of other explanations for the Storm Troopers), that was 1923, not 1933. Both of Jackson's assertions are true only in the most literal and technical sense. In fact, Hitler's popularity rose with his successes and fell only when the war began to fail. In Drumbl's terms, a great many Germans found themselves "beneficiaries" of Hitler's crimes and lost their faith in the Führer only when benefits turned to catastrophe.[64] The political culture of Germany was itself deeply implicated in the crimes of the regime, and on the tests I have proposed, Germany was indeed a criminal state.

This was precisely what Jackson wished to deny, however. Jackson had no purpose to incriminate the whole German people because the occupation aim was to win them over to democracy, and that required commiserating with them rather than alienating them. Apparently, the Allies consciously sought to scapegoat a few individuals because of the political inconvenience of proclaiming the guilt of many.[65] Here, I want

---

[63] The Trial of German Major War Criminals by the International Military Tribunal Sitting at Nuremberg, Germany, Nov. 21, 1945 (1946). The Avalon Project. http://avalon .law.yale.edu/subject_menus/fed.asp.

[64] See generally Friedrich Perzyval Rech-Malleczewen, *Diary of a Man in Despair*, trans. Paul Rubens (London: Macmillan, 1970), one of the most remarkable moral criticisms from within Germany, and one that greatly influenced Arendt.

[65] See, e.g., Diane Marie Amann, "Group Mentality, Expressivism, and Genocide," at p. 21.

to emphasize that culpability in mass atrocity is seldom simple. There are good reasons to restrict individual criminal liability to perpetrators and accomplices, perhaps with the categories suitably broadened.[66] Culpability and liability are not the same, however, and the "reprobation and stigmatization" of those who supported a state that comes from declaring their state to be an international criminal seems justified in the most elemental way: they deserve it.

This answer may not be sufficiently compelling. Alienating a people can simply make the transition from state criminality more difficult. Nationalism is a potent force, and nationalists will inevitably reject the charge of state criminality and attribute it to a political conspiracy of their enemies. This was, of course, Milošević's strategy at his trial. The issue arose again in 2007 when the ICJ decided the *Bosnia v. Serbia* genocide case, the closest thing international law has seen to putting a state on trial for an international crime.[67] (Technically, the case was "civil" – Bosnia accused Serbia of breaching its obligations under the Convention against Genocide and asked for monetary damages.) The ICJ found that the only provable act of genocide in the Balkan Wars was the Srebrenica massacre, that Serbia was insufficiently linked to that massacre to support a finding of state responsibility, and that Serbia was guilty only of sheltering Radovan Karadžić and Ratko Mladić.

As is now well known, the ICJ screened itself from damaging evidence of Serbian government involvement. It chose an especially demanding legal test of state responsibility; and its finding that Srebrenica was the only act of genocide in the Balkan Wars was not credible.[68]

One of the dissenting judges, Algeria's Mahmed Ahiou, speculated that the Court may have feared taking sides in a politically fraught historical

---

[66] I would include Category I and Category II Joint Criminal Enterprises (JCEs), but I accept the criticisms of Danner, Martinez, Osiel, and others that Category III JCEs are really illegitimate "just convict everybody" prosecutorial conveniences. Alison Marston Danner and Jenny S. Martinez, "Guilty Associations: Joint Criminal Enterprise, Command Responsibility, and the Development of International Criminal Law," *California Law Review* 93 (2005): 75–169; Mark Osiel, "The Banality of Good: Aligning Incentives against Mass Atrocity," *Columbia Law Review* 105 (2005): 1751–862.

[67] Case Concerning the Application of the Convention for the Prevention and Punishment of the Crime of Genocide (*Bosn. & Herz. v. Serb. & Mont.*), 2007 I.C.J. General List No. 91 (Judgment of Feb. 26) [henceforth: *Bosnia v. Serbia*].

[68] Marlise Simons, "Genocide Court Ruled for Serbia without Seeing Full War Archive," *New York Times* (April 9, 2007). After Serbia succeeded in persuading the ICJ to screen an archive of documents, "Vladimir Djeric, a member of the Serbian team, told lawyers there that 'we could not believe our luck.'" Ibid. See also Ruth Wedgwood, "Slobodan Milosevic's Last Waltz," *New York Times* (March 12, 2007).

debate or intruding on state sovereignty.[69] There is a far more obvious reason, however, which was laid out to me with great clarity by a Serbian lawyer a few months after the decision. Had the ICJ labeled the Serbian state a *génocidaire*, the nationalist backlash might have toppled the government, empowered the most right-wing nationalist parties, and derailed efforts to bring Serbia back into the fold of normal European states. The lawyer added, "You have no idea what we went through. I was living in Belgrade at the time, and could barely earn enough to eat." This lawyer, I might add, is no nationalist: a former law professor of cosmopolitan convictions who now works for one of the major humanitarian organizations in the world.

The phenomenon is familiar to criminologists who have studied shame sanctions. As John Braithwaite noted in connection with youthful offenders, shaming and stigmatizing them may simply push them deeper into a criminal subculture, such as gang life. Only when the aim is reintegrating the offender into the community can the sanctions actually help reduce crime rather than reproduce it.[70] Serbia was on a path to reintegration, and shaming its people might have driven it off that path.

I have no a priori response to this objection – obviously, there is nothing a priori to be said about a complex prediction of what might happen or might have happened. The lawyer with whom I was speaking may have been right or may (as I suspect) have been wildly overestimating the effect of a declaration in a lawsuit. Perhaps the ICJ's worry was that a finding of genocide would have required a hefty payment of compensation, which the regime may not have been willing to pay, defying the Court and revealing its weakness. (This was another speculation in Judge Ahiou's dissenting opinion.[71]) Perhaps it would have been resented like the Versailles-imposed reparations on Germany in the wake of World War I. On the other hand, it is worth recalling that at the time of the *Pinochet* case, many acute observers worried that it would destabilize the fragile Chilean democracy; instead, it seems to have fortified the resolve within Chile to end the amnesty and come to terms with the past.[72] Which

---

[69] *Bosnia v. Serbia*, Opinion Dissidente de M. le Juge Mahiou, ¶58. Available at http://www.icj-cij.org/docket/files/91/13706.pdf. Judge Mahiou was referring specifically to the Court's refusal to demand additional evidence from Serbia.

[70] John Braithwaite, *Crime, Shame, and Reintergration* (Cambridge: Cambridge University Press, 1989).

[71] *Bosnia v. Serbia*, Opinion Dissidente de M. le Juge Mahiou, ¶58.

[72] Naomi Roht-Arriaza, *The Pinochet Effect: Transnational Justice in the Age of Human Rights* (Philadelphia: University of Pennsylvania Press, 2005); Ellen Lutz and Kathryn

of these is more likely are political imponderables that I do not hope to address.

HOW DO YOU PUNISH A STATE?

Even supposing that states can be criminals and that the law should recognize that fact, how can a state be punished? Here, I mention some possibilities without addressing details. Again, the treatment of corporate crime can provide examples.

There is, first and most drastically, capital punishment for the state. In the context of corporate crime, capital punishment means ending the corporate charter or imposing a fine that reduces corporate assets to zero. In the context of state criminality, it means conquest and reconstruction, as in Germany and Japan after World War II. Both of these seem to have been successful examples of "reintegrative shaming," although few believe that the Nuremberg and Tokyo trials contributed to it. Germany's project of *Vergangenheitsbewältigung* (mastering the past) ultimately took three generations; Japan's is arguably still a work in progress.

Second, there are fines and reparations, both to outsiders and to victims within the state. It would obviously be perverse to demand internal reparations unless the criminal regime has been destroyed and the new regime is committed to reparations for the victims or their survivors. Compensating victims of atrocity can be a difficult process, particularly if it involves removing benefits from the beneficiaries of state crime. In many instances of transitional justice punishing individual criminals of the ancien régime has proven easier than restoring stolen property to which the thieves feel entitled by a past sense of grievance.[73] International tribunals are obviously not in a position to administer such microlevel reparation, but local institutions may be equipped to do so.

Fundamentally, however, the mechanism for recognizing state criminality is, as in Article 9 of the Nuremberg Charter, purely declaratory. This might be dismissed as a merely verbal flourish – unnecessary given that trying and sentencing the individual state leader implicitly puts the state on trial, and quite possibly a terribly destructive one for the reasons explored in the previous section. However, if we remember that the center of gravity in international criminal proceedings lies in the trial, not

Sikkink, "The Justice Cascade: The Evolution and Impact of Foreign Human Rights Trials in Latin America," *Chicago Journal of International Law* 2 (2001): 1–33.

73 See Jon Elster, *Closing the Books: Transitional Justice in Historical Perspective* (Cambridge: Cambridge University Press, 2004).

the punishment, then the point of putting the state in the dock becomes more apparent. As many commentators have noted, the criminal trial of an individual must focus on that individual, and bringing in pieces of history that cannot be directly tied to the defendant distorts the meaning of a criminal trial.

If, however, the state is on trial, the inquiry can meaningfully include the questions that Arendt raised. What were the mechanisms by which the state became criminal? How did it invert good and evil, and what were the values it appealed to in doing so? These are questions that strain the methods of a court of law, as the *Eichmann* opinion noted.[74] Such questions are nevertheless inevitable in the trial of highly placed defendants, as can readily be seen in the extensive background sections of ICTR judgments. Orienting the inquiry toward them by asking how the state operated is not beyond the capacity of a law court. Whether it is beyond the capacity of politics to establish or tolerate such an inquest is a question that I cannot answer.

[74] "The court does not have at its disposal the tools required for the investigation of general questions.... For example, in connection with the description of the historical background of the Holocaust, a great amount of material was brought before us in the form of documents and evidence, collected most painstakingly, and certainly in a genuine attempt to delineate as complete a picture as possible. Even so, all this material is but a tiny fraction of all that is extant on this subject. According to our legal system, the court is by its very nature 'passive,' for it does not itself initiate the bringing of proof before it, as is the custom with an enquiry commission. Accordingly, its ability to describe general events is inevitably limited. As for questions of principle which are outside the realm of law, no one has made us judges of them." *Prosecutor v. Eichmann*, Criminal Case No. 40/61, District Court of Jerusalem (1961), ¶2.

3

Punishing Genocide: A Critical Reading
of the International Court of Justice

Anthony F. Lang, Jr.

The crime of genocide deserves punishment, but should natural persons
be punished for a crime that requires an organized, political structure?
The Nuremberg legacy and creation of international criminal courts since
the 1990s suggests that people should be punished for genocide. Is this
legacy preventing the international community from considering alternative sanctions? Should states be sanctioned for the crime of genocide?
What institutional changes would be necessary to punish states for crimes
such as genocide? This chapter probes these questions through a critical
reading of the February 2007 judgment from the International Court of
Justice (ICJ) concerning the responsibility of Serbia for genocide in Bosnia
and Herzegovina.

My answer is that states should be subject to punishment for the crime
of genocide, but this necessitates understanding how states are corporate
agents and then recasting the international legal order such that these
agents can be formally tried and sentenced for the violations they commit. In the first part of the chapter, I review the distinction between
collectives and corporations through an engagement with other chapters
in this volume, arguing that the former cannot be punished in the way
that the latter can. The next section examines the logic underlying the ICJ
decision to support the point that states qua corporate entities should be
subject to punishment. Although the ICJ did not hold Serbia responsible
for genocide in this particular case, they did affirm that states can be held
responsible for genocide. This point stands in contrast to the generally
accepted legal view of genocide in which individuals commit the crime

Parts of the section on state responsibility is drawn from Anthony F. Lang, Jr., "Punishing States," in Toni Erskine, ed. *How Can We Respond to Delinquent Institutions?*
(London: Palgrave, forthcoming).

of genocide and should be punished for it. The Court's reasoning and use of the recently proposed Articles on State Responsibility provide an important legal resource for countering this assumption. The next section proposes a restructuring of the international legal order to capture the dual criminal nature of the crime of genocide. The changes I suggest rely on a conception of global constitutionalism in which various judicial authorities constitute a political space where norms can be enforced through sanction and punishment if necessary. The chapter concludes by pointing to how this alternative structure will not only allow for a new legal modality for countering genocide but will also provide political resources for resistance to such actions, particularly when courts are understood as political actors that can be subject to scrutiny by citizens. The current international order in which the enforcement of the norm against genocide is limited to an individual being tried before the ICC prevents a more robust enforcement structure. The goal of this chapter is to reinforce an order in which crimes such as genocide will be subject to sanction and political action at numerous levels, rather than simply at the level of the prosecution of individual natural persons.

COLLECTIVE VERSUS CORPORATE PUNISHMENT

The argument I wish to make in this section is that punishing states makes sense if we think of states as corporate entities and not collective entities.[1] Punishment is the infliction of harm in response to a violation of a norm. To punish an individual for such a violation assumes that the individual has legal and moral responsibility for the violation. Responsibility, in turn, requires that individual has the agency required to intend, plan, and execute the action that constitutes a violation. Generally, we assume that only natural persons have the agency and hence responsibility for the type of action that would constitute such a violation. As a result, we most commonly assume that only individuals can be subject to punishment

Yet this commonsense approach to ethics and law elides another way of talking and thinking about our common life, one that is perhaps better described as political. We normally say things such as "British Petroleum

---

[1] I have previously argued that states should be punished; Anthony F. Lang, Jr., "Crime and Punishment: Holding States Accountable," *Ethics & International Relations* 21, 2 (2007): 239–57. In this version, I did not rely on the distinction between collectives and corporations as I do here. It was only after attending the workshop that produced this volume and reading the papers presented there that I realized how important it is to make this distinction to justify punishing states.

has created an environmental disaster" or "Amnesty International tries to help prisoners of conscience." We even talk about groups as doing things in relation to their members; for instance, "General Motors is treating its workers unfairly" or "The United States fails to provide health care for its people." All these statements assume collective or corporate agents that intend, plan, and execute actions for which they are held responsible.

We might say that we have in the first instance an ethicolegal way of describing agency and responsibility and in the second instance a political way of describing responsibility. Some have tried to negotiate the space between these formulations of responsibility, seeking to locate the ethicolegal form in a political context.[2] For the purposes of this chapter, efforts that focus on the international realm are of most interest. In particular, attempts to think through the agency, responsibility, and potential liability to punishment of the nation-state and other global actors can contribute to how we might enforce norms such as those concerning crimes against humanity and genocide.

Two kinds of objections have been made to the idea that a corporate entity such as a state should be held responsible and punished. The first is that states are legal fictions that do not exist apart from their members. Harry Gould recently made a persuasive case for why states should not be subject to punishment on the grounds that the state is a historical artifact that cannot have the type of intentionality necessary for either responsibility or punishment.[3] Gould argues that the metaphor of the state as a legal person cannot support the imposition of actual sanctions, especially criminal ones. But Gould's argument fails to account for the fact that what he labels a fiction or metaphor constructs the world in which we live. The fiction of state agency and responsibility is not something that can be simply "unmasked" through a genealogy but provides the reality of our ethical, legal, and political universe.

A second objection to holding states responsible is that to impose punishment on them will actually harm those who cannot in any way be individually responsible for the violation. One of the clearest arguments for this position comes from Toni Erskine, who argues that harm inflicted

---

[2] The work of Larry May is exemplary here; see *The Morality of Groups* (Notre Dame, IN: University of Notre Dame Press, 1987) and *Sharing Responsibility* (Chicago: University of Chicago Press, 1992). For a range of debates about collective responsibility, see Larry May and Stacey Hoffman, eds., *Collective Responsibility: Five Decades of Debate in Theoretical and Applied Ethics* (Lanham, MD: Rowman and Littlefield, 1991).

[3] Harry Gould, "International Criminal Bodies," *Review of International Studies* 35 (2009): 701–21.

on states is really harm inflicted on persons.[4] Because states do not have "bodies to kick or souls to damn," they cannot be liable to any justifiable mode of punishment (although Erskine accepts that states can indeed be responsible agents, depending on the role of the state in the international order[5]). The response to this claim is that for a punishment to be just, it must be imposed on the state and not on the members. For this to be possible, punishment needs to focus on the corporate and not the collective character of the state.[6]

What is the distinction between the collective and corporate? A collective is a group of persons who may or may not be organized and capable of acting with intention. A corporation, in contrast, is a group that is recognized through a legal process and has a particular structure that allows it to intend, plan, and execute actions. Punishing collectives is not justified, but punishing corporations is and, as Sara Seck demonstrates in her chapter, is an important part of most legal systems.[7] Richard Vernon's argument that states and not nations can be held responsible and punished, an argument he poses in contrast to the famous attempt by Karl Jaspers to hold Germany responsible as a nation, could be fit into this distinction if he called a nation a collective and a state a corporation.[8]

Of course, when a corporation is punished, individuals will suffer. However, corporations are designed to locate agency and responsibility in a particular structure and the legal order that established them will include the assumption that they can be punished for violations of the norms of that order. Thus, the suffering that individuals experience when a corporation is punished can be justified because the individuals involved

---

[4] Toni Erskine, "Kicking Bodies and Damning Souls: The Danger of Harming 'Innocent' Individuals while Punishing Delinquent States," *Ethics & International Affairs* 24, 3 (Fall 2010): 261–86.

[5] Toni Erskine, "Assigning Responsibilities to Institutional Moral Agents: The Case of States and 'Quasi-States,'" *Ethics & International Affairs* 15, 2 (2001): 67–87.

[6] Other responses to this objection could include the way in which punishment is meted out such that its harm is more targeted at those responsible in the collective. This approach is found in Avia Pasternak, "The Distributive Effect of Collective Punishment," Chapter 8, this volume. Pasternak's account provides alternate ways of distributing punishment but assumes throughout that the agent to be punished is a collective, not a corporate, entity. If one accepts that agents are collectives and not corporations (which I do not necessarily accept in all cases), then Pasternak's alternatives provide ways to address the problem raised by Erskine.

[7] Sara Seck, "Collective Responsibility, Collective Punishment and Corporate Atrocities," Chapter 5 this volume. Although Seck provides evidence of how the law deals with corporate crime, the title of her chapter elides this important distinction between collectives and corporations.

[8] Richard Vernon, "Punishing Collectives: States or Nations?," Chapter 11, this volume.

understand that they are acting as a corporate entity recognized as such. Seck's chapter is helpful in understanding this point as well. In her review of corporations as subjects of liability for global harms, such as climate change, they are on one level certainly responsible. At a deeper level, however, it is the legal and political order that creates corporations that should also be responsible for the harms they commit. In other words, if states create corporations without regulatory frameworks or limits on their profit making, then the state should be considered somehow responsible.

Seck's argument points to how constitutional orders create responsible agents that may or may not be liable to punishment. In the course of this chapter, I will demonstrate that although the global constitutional order has created states that seemingly escape liability, that order can be restructured in such a way that it places more regulatory limits on what states can do. The regulatory and enforcement provisions available to the international community are much less clear than that open to the domestic political community. However, as Mark Drumbl demonstrates in his chapter in this volume and in his previous work, the assumption that only natural persons should be subject to punishment fails to ensure that international crimes are not committed.[9]

The remainder of this chapter demonstrates how the state is a product of the international constitutional order and, as such, should be understood as a corporate entity organized in a purposeful way such that it can intend, plan, and execute actions. If it is such an entity, and not simply a collective, then it can be justifiably punished. To make this case is not as easy as identifying the domestic legal norms by which a business becomes a corporation. Instead, to argue that states are corporations liable to punishment requires looking at how various political practices constitute the states as corporate agents. For the purposes of this chapter, I examine how one key part of that constitutional order – the ICJ – has contributed to our understanding of the state as a corporate entity liable to punishment. In making this argument, it will become clear that this is not the result of the ICJ acting on its own; rather, the ICJ is part of a widely dispersed set of practices that constitute states as agents that should be seen as responsible for their actions, responsibility that can justifiably lead to punishment.

---

[9] Mark Drumbl, "Collective Responsibility and Postconflict Justice," Chapter 1, this volume, and Mark Drumbl, *Atrocity, Punishment and International Law* (Cambridge: Cambridge University Press, 2007).

THE CONFLICT

Before reviewing the logic of the ICJ's decision, a brief description of the conflict in the Balkans is necessary. The case originally brought before the ICJ by Bosnia and Herzegovina in 1993 claimed that the state of Yugoslavia was in the process of committing genocide against the "People and State of Bosnia Herzegovina."[10] The application claimed that since the birth of the state of Bosnia and Herzegovina, the practice of ethnic cleansing being practiced by Yugoslavia was tantamount to genocide.[11] The evidence they cited included plans for a "Greater Serbia" in both historical documents and contemporary Yugoslav public policy, the destruction of Islamic sites, the killing and harming of Muslims and Croats, and a UN General Assembly resolution in which Yugoslavia is accused of ethnic cleansing, which the resolution states is "a form of genocide."[12] The response from Yugoslavia was that the ICJ had no jurisdiction in this matter because the conflict was primarily a civil war, one in which Yugoslavia was only supporting the beleaguered Serbs in Bosnia and Herzegovina.

As one author notes, the original submission by Bosnia and Herzegovina and the response from Yugoslavia were not only legal arguments but "a device though which both parties attempted to validate their broader, collective narratives as to the character of the Bosnian conflict, especially as to who were its heroes and who were its villains."[13] For instance, the Original Application includes sentences such as "Bosnia and Herzegovina is centuries old" (Paragraph 6). This use of the legal structures of the Court to construct a historical narrative of the conflict is not unusual, for such attempts often take place in contentious legal conflicts.

Briefly, conventional accounts of the conflicts among the different groups in the Balkans start in June 1991 when the republics of Croatia and Slovenia declared their independence from Yugoslavia (although, of course, a narrative on the conflict could stretch back much longer

---

[10] Application Instituting Proceedings filed in the Registry of the Court on March 20, 1993. Available at http://www.icj-cij.org/docket/files/91/7199.pdf. Hereafter referred to as Original Application.

[11] For a clarification on the distinction between ethnic cleansing and genocide, see Tim Dunne and Daniela Kroslak, "Genocide: Knowing What It Is That We Want to Remember, Forget, or Forgive," in *The Kosovo Tragedy: The Human Rights Dimension*, ed. Ken Booth (Portland, OR: Frank Cass, 2001), 27–46.

[12] UN GA Resolution 47/121, December 18, 1992, reprinted in Original Application, Paragraph 84.

[13] Vojin Dimitrijevic and Marko Milanovic, "The Strange Story of the Bosnian Genocide Case," *Leiden Journal of International Law* 21 (2008): 66.

than this).[14] Fighting between the new republics and the Serb-dominated Yugoslavia soon followed. The conflict changed when the Republic of Bosnia and Herzegovina was recognized as a sovereign state by Germany and the United States in April 1992. The ethnic diversity of Bosnia and Herzegovina soon degenerated into conflicts among Bosnian Muslims, Bosnian Serbs, and Bosnian Croats, with the latter two being covertly and overtly supported by their ethnic compatriots in the neighboring republics. In January 1993, the Vance-Owen plan was presented to the three Bosnian communities in an attempt to create a constitutional structure for the republic. Although it was only approved by the Croat community, it remained the model underlying much of the international community's future efforts.

Atrocities occurred on all sides of the conflict. As noted, the government of Bosnia and Herzegovina submitted its application in March 1993. Yet, the ICJ eventually ruled that genocide only took place in one location, Srebrenica, in July 1995, two years after the Original Application. This particular episode certainly captures elements of the broader conflict and does seem to provide the clearest evidence for genocide. Srebrenica is located in the east of Bosnia and Herzegovina, close to the border with Serbia. At the time of a 1991 census, the population of the city was roughly 37,000, of which 73 percent were Bosnian Muslims and 25 percent were Serbs. In early 1992, Serb military groups took control of Srebrenica, despite the fact that they were a minority. By May 1992, however, the Bosnian Muslims took back control, but with a disorganized military and political command structure. The conflicts among the Muslims in Srebrenica undercut their ability to resist Serb advances over the next three years. During this operation, there is some evidence that the Muslim forces "used techniques of ethnic cleansing similar to those used by the Serbs in other areas, burning houses and terrorizing the civilian population."[15]

By March 1993, the Serb forces had taken back Srebrenica and the surrounding areas. In that same month, Bosnia initiated its case against Yugoslavia for genocide, a genocide that did not yet include the actions

---

[14] For a critical reading of how the international community drew on contested narratives in both justifying and avoiding political and military actions, see David Campbell, *National Deconstruction: Violence, Identity and Justice in Bosnia* (Minneapolis: University of Minnesota Press, 1998).

[15] Report of the Secretary-General pursuant to General Assembly resolution 53/35: *The Fall of Srebrenica*, Document No. A/54/549 (New York: United Nations, 1999), Paragraph 35.

specific to Srebrenica but those more broadly throughout the Bosnian republic.[16] In August 1993, Serb forces improved their strategic position near Sarajevo, leading the Muslim leadership to pull out of peace negotiations with the Serbs and Croats. In February 1994, after a Sarajevo marketplace was bombed by the Serbs, the NATO leadership wanted to employ air strikes against the Serbs, but the UNPROFOR commander refused to authorize it. After a complex "dual-key" arrangement for using force was set up by NATO and the UN command, air strikes were authorized in April 1994 and in November 1994, but only after much wrangling between the parties. Debate within the UN and wider international community continued about the nature of the peacekeeping mission in the region and the ability to use military force to protect various parties.

At the same moment the new force was being debated, Serb forces made their move against the city of Srebrenica. In June and July 1995, there were approximately 300 Dutch infantry troops accompanied by 300 support troops in the vicinity of Srebrenica. The Serb forces in the area numbered about 2,000 while the Muslim forces were at about 3,000. The Muslims, however, were largely disarmed and had a weak command structure. There had been fighting between the Serbs and Muslims throughout the first six months of 1995, while the Dutch troops were positioned primarily to observe the ostensible cease-fire. The UN troops were located in seven-man observation posts at various locations surrounding the city of Srebrenica. On July 6, 1995, the Serb forces launched their attack on Srebrenica. Srebrenica fell to the Serb forces on July 11. Over the course of the next three days, the Serb forces, watched by the UNPROFOR troops, transported the population out of Srebrenica. In so doing, they separated out all males aged 16 to 65. Over the course of the next week, more than 10,000 of these men were systematically killed by Serb forces.

The attacks and following genocide were undertaken by the VRS, or the Army of the Republika Srpska, the self-proclaimed Bosnian Serb Republic within the state of Bosnia and Herzegovina, with Radovan Karadžić as the president and General Ratko Mladić as the head of the army. The then-Yugoslavian president Slobodan Milošević claimed that he had no control over the Bosnian Serbs, especially in the context of this attack. At the same time, in their pleadings before the court,

---

[16] *Case Concerning the Application of the Convention on the Prevention and Punishment of the Crime of Genocide (Bosnia and Herzegovina v. Serbia and Montenegro)*, Judgment of 26 February 2007 (hereafter referred to as Genocide Judgment): Paragraph 1.

the Yugoslav (and later Republic of Serbia) respondents argued that the attack on Srebrenica was a retaliatory response to attacks and atrocities being committed by the Muslim forces in the region.

THE JUDGMENT

The judgment by the ICJ issued on February 26, 2007 addressed a much wider range of issues than those concerning the attack on Srebrenica. The core of the judgment is that

1. genocide only took place in the town of Srebrenica,
2. states can be held responsible for committing genocide,
3. the Republic of Serbia was not responsible for committing genocide, and
4. the Republic of Serbia was responsible for failing to prevent and punish genocide.

In this chapter, I focus primarily on Conclusion 2, which is less about the facts of this particular case and more broadly about state responsibility for genocide. I of course refer to the judgment and the facts of the case when necessary. However, my primary interest is in whether a state can be held responsible for genocide. In this section, I examine two elements of the judgment: who counts as an agent and who can be held responsible for genocide.

The first section of the judgment (Paragraphs 1–141) addresses the history of the applications to the Court and the matter of its jurisdiction. This revolved largely around who were the two agents before the Court, especially because the two agents shifted and evolved as a result of the politics of the Balkans. These shifts and changes were put into a narrative by the Court in these opening sections in order that it could clarify which agent was being charged and which agent had been violated (although because it is not a criminal court, the ICJ does not put the issue in exactly this way). A reflection on how the Court took these shifts and turned them into a coherent narrative, one in which states end up being clearly identifiable as responsible agents, reveals how the ICJ produces certain kinds of agents, a process that constitutes not only the decision of this case but a wider international political structure.[17]

---

[17] In fact, the ICJ had addressed some of these questions in its 1996 judgment on the preliminary objections to the case raised by Yugoslavia, which included the question of whether Bosnia and Herzegovina was a sovereign state and whether the conflict was

The Original Application of Bosnia and Herzegovina on March 20, 1993 to the court included a large number of issues, not only those falling within the articles of the Genocide Convention; as one article points out, "What [Bosnia and Herzegovina] did, therefore, was to equate with genocide all the possible violations of international in relation to the then ongoing conflict, most notably the violations of the *jus ad bellum*."[18] In other words, the Bosnian government sought to redefine the conflict, particularly the actions of the Yugoslavian government, as genocide in its entirety. This move was rejected by the Court, however, which ended up ruling on the specific issue of whether the respondent had failed in its obligations concerning the Genocide Convention.

As the politics of the Balkans became more complicated, the parties before the court continued to change. Thus, the respondent was originally the Federal Republic of Yugoslavia but ended up being the Republic of Serbia. Because of the radical change in political structure that took place following the NATO bombing campaign in 1999, which included the eventual arrest of President Milošević, the respondent argued that it was no longer the same country and should not be held responsible for genocide. Indeed, it argued that because it entered the United Nations as a new state, it was no longer the same country that existed before 2000. The Court reviewed Yugoslavia/Serbia's interactions with the UN and with the ICJ in other matters and concluded that it was indeed the same state for the purposes of the case under consideration.

Although this seems logical, it is important to note that this decision effectively removed the leadership from responsibility for genocide and made the state as a whole responsible – the very issue before the court. By claiming that the state remained the same, it already assumed that acts committed by individuals in that state who may well have had very different political views from the ones defending themselves before the court were the same. This jurisdictional matter does not mean that the Court had already made its decision, but it does suggest that the structure of an international order in which states are responsible agents is necessary for the ICJ to function – but, it may not be an accurate reflection of the reality of the politics of a particular community and its interactions with the wider world. Here we have some evidence of the point made in the first section of the chapter: the construction of the state as a corporate

---

a civil war. This 1996 judgment was referred to in the 2007 final judgment, but it is worth reading on its own; see http://www.icj-cij.org/docket/files/91/7349.pdf.

[18] Dimitrijevic and Milanovic, "The Strange Story of the Bosnian Genocide Case," 68.

agent that is organized to accomplish particular outcomes is the result of the larger political order of which the ICJ is a central part.

Another version of this same dynamic happened with the applicant. Although the applicant did not change in the same way, its constitutional structure caused one of the strangest elements of the case. The government of Bosnia and Herzegovina was set up with a presidency that rotated among the three main ethnic groups, Muslim, Serb, and Croat. When the Bosnian Serb community took the presidency in 1999, its representative submitted a petition to the ICJ to withdraw its complaint against the respondent. The respondent quickly agreed, but before the Court could halt proceedings, the remaining parties to the shared presidency indicated that this application was not fully representative of them all.[19]

As noted earlier, both the applicant and the respondent sought to use the case to create their own narrative of the events in the Balkans. This process of constructing themselves in the court is an important part of making the case concerning responsibility. This process of narrating into existence the agents before the ICJ, however, did not take place only in the particular pleadings that the two parties brought to the case; importantly, the ICJ in its judgment also constructed the agents. Even more important, in a case about responsibility for genocide the judgment reflects a more widespread set of assumptions about who "counts" in international affairs. I have argued elsewhere that the stories states and international organizations tell about themselves constructs their agency in the international realm;[20] this case demonstrates how a court, especially a "constitutional court" like the ICJ, can play a role in this process as well. The simple recitation of the facts of the case that constitutes the opening of the judgment is not only about the responsibility of a particular state for a particular act of genocide; it is, in effect, part of the construction of state agency in the international political and legal order.

Furthermore, and in relation to the distinction between a collective and corporate entity, the ICJ did not officially state that any of the parties were "corporations" as that term is understood in domestic law. Rather, the point I am trying to make here is that by narrating into existence an agent with the ability to intend, plan, and execute actions, an entity that could not be reduced to its constituent members alone, the Court effectively incorporated the state. Of course, this is not simply the Court

---

[19] Ibid., 74.
[20] Anthony F. Lang, Jr., *Agency and Ethics: The Politics of Military Intervention* (Albany, NY: SUNY Press, 2002).

acting alone; it is part of a wider international legal discourse in which states are corporate agents capable of intending, planning, and acting. Gould's point that this process of constructing the state in this way relies on a historically contingent fiction remains true; what is important to recognize here is that this discourse gives us the reality of international law and politics, a reality in which states are responsible agents.

The next section of the judgment addresses the applicable law, or the Convention on the Prevention and Punishment of the Crime of Genocide and whether states can be held responsible for genocide according to that Convention (Paragraphs 142–201). It is here that the ICJ establishes that states can indeed be held responsible for genocide in a reading that has raised important questions concerning international law and genocide. A number of international legal scholars strongly disagreed with the Court's reading, both its use of the Articles on State Responsibility and its use of the Genocide Convention.[21] Article 4 of the Convention establishes clearly who can be punished for genocide: "Persons committing genocide or any of the other acts enumerated in Article III shall be punished, whether they are constitutionally responsible rulers, public officials or private individuals." It would seem that the ICJ has no business considering whether a state can be held responsible for committing genocide. The evolution of international criminal law since the 1990s further reinforces this reading. Individuals have been tried for and found guilty of genocide by both the International Criminal Tribunal for the Former Yugoslavia (ICTY) and the International Criminal Tribunal for Rwanda (ICTR).

However, the Convention includes an Article that complicates this issue, Article IX:

> Disputes between the contracting parties relating to the interpretation, application or fulfilment of the present Convention, including those relating to the responsibility of a State for genocide or any other acts enumerated in Article III, shall be submitted to the International Court of Justice at the request of any of the parties to the dispute.

Depending on one's reading, this Article gives the ICJ the ability to determine either the general question of whether states can be held responsible for genocide or whether a particular state in a particular case can be held responsible for genocide. This article arose in part from the efforts of the United Kingdom and Belgium to include states as agents responsible for

---

[21] See, for instance, Paola Gaeta, "On What Conditions Can a State Be Held Responsible for Genocide?" *The European Journal of International Law* 18, 4 (2007): 631–48.

genocide, an effort in which they were largely unsuccessful. The general consensus of those drafting the Convention was that it was a penal convention, and only individuals could be accused of crimes and punished for them.[22]

This article was not put to the test, however, until Bosnia brought its suit against Yugoslavia in 1993. The Court stated clearly that its jurisdiction in this case arises only from Article IX, not from any larger matters of customary law that might govern crimes such as genocide (Paragraph 147). A further clarification arose from a preliminary objection of the government of Yugoslavia. They argued in 1996 that the Court could only rule on whether or not the respondent was responsible for failing to prevent and punish genocide not whether or not the state itself had committed genocide. The Court responded that the Convention as a whole, beginning with Article I, is not simply about preventing and punishing but is about holding agents responsible for genocide:

> It would be paradoxical if States were thus under an obligation to prevent, so far as within their power, commission of genocide by persons over whom they have a certain influence, but were not forbidden to commit such acts through their own organs, or persons over whom they have such firm control that their conduct is attributable to the State concerned under international law. In short, the obligation to prevent genocide necessarily implies the prohibition of the commission of genocide. (Paragraph 166)

The Court goes on to argue that although it accepts that states are not capable of committing crimes, they can still be held responsible for the commission of genocide (Paragraphs 170–79). It also states that responsibility can be attributed both to individuals and states; "duality of responsibility continues to be a constant feature of international law" (Paragraph 173). I return to this point later, but one could ask whether it even makes sense. To distinguish between committing a crime and being responsible for committing something that is called a crime seems to be stretching the meaning of language beyond comprehension. I would suggest that the Court's verbal gymnastics here result from, on the one hand, living in a world in which states do commit actions (and crimes) and a world in which states cannot be labeled as criminals (for more on this, see the section below on state responsibility).

The Court then reviews other issues surrounding genocide, such as territorial limits on the crime of genocide, the nature of intention, and

---

[22] John Quigley, "International Court of Justice as a Forum for Genocide Cases," *Case Western Reserve Journal of International Law* 40 (2007–8): 259.

the question of proof. The judgment's next section examines the facts of the case in great detail, which leads it to conclude that genocide was only committed in one location, at the massacres of Srebrenica in July 1995. The Court found that genocide was committed by the VRS, which was not formally an organ of the State of Yugoslavia. To determine whether the acts of this military force could be attributed to Yugoslavia, the Court turns to two sources: the Articles on State Responsibility passed by the International Law Commission in 2001 and the Court's 1986 decision concerning U.S. support for the Contra forces in Nicaragua. The Court uses two kinds of tests of attribution, "complete dependence" and "effective control" (Paragraphs 385–415). Drawing on these two tests, the Court finds that the VRS was neither completely dependent nor under effective control of the respondent, and thus the latter cannot be held responsible for genocide. Finally, the Court finds that the respondent failed to prevent and punish genocide.

The judgment made a strong case that states can be held responsible for genocide, even if it did not find Serbia responsible for genocide in this specific case. This conclusion by the Court might seem odd, for why was it necessary to make the case that states can commit genocide if it did not find a state responsible for genocide in this case? Understanding why the Court chose to rule as it did would require a more thorough analysis of the justices who made the ruling and their decision making at various stages of the case (a full fourteen years from the Original Application to the final judgment). I have not undertaken this level of empirical research in this chapter, although it would be beneficial to see such research carried out. Rather, in what follows, I take up the logic embodied in the Articles on State Responsibility, coupled with some hypotheses about how the Court sees its role in the international order, to suggest a possible reason why the ICJ chose to make such a clear statement about state responsibility. In short, the ICJ ruled that states can be held responsible for genocide because they exist within a world of state agents where this is the only conclusion to which they could come. The constitutional order within which they make judgments necessitates that states be responsible corporate agents.

STATE RESPONSIBILITY

The ICJ turned to the Articles on State Responsibility as a source for its determination of whether states can be held responsible for genocide, mainly the sections concerning the question of attribution or how the actions of individuals or groups can be attributed to states. In particular, it drew on Articles 4 and 8 of the Articles on State Responsibility, which clarified what it means to say that an organ is either under complete control or effective control of a state. As noted earlier, coupled with the Court's 1986 judgment in the Nicaragua case, the ICJ established that a state can be held responsible under international law for actions undertaken by groups not formally in its political structure, although in this particular case, the facts did not allow such an attribution. The use of the Articles by the Court, and their use of the term "customary law" to describe the Articles, suggests that the idea of holding a state responsible for the crime of genocide is part of the international legal order. In this section, I turn to the drafting of the Articles to suggest that states can indeed be held responsible for committing crimes.[23]

The history of the drafting of the Articles on State Responsibility reveals that states were indeed thought capable of committing crimes. The notion of a state crime was, however, eventually removed from the final articles. When the International Law Commission (ILC) Committee on State Responsibility began work in 1956 its first rapporteur, F. V. Garcia Amador of Cuba, focused the discussions and his reports on injuries to aliens, leading to a civil law–like approach to the topic.[24] This approach was criticized by the Italian jurist, Robert Ago, who eventually replaced Amador in 1963. Ago argued that a civil law approach – one focused on repairing a contractual relationship that had been broken rather than criminal law which focuses on penalizing the guilty – would fail to capture many of the most egregious violations committed by states. Ago's work resulted in a draft of 35 articles in 1980, which were cited by both scholars and courts and which included, for the first time, an article describing "international crimes of state."[25] The remaining articles were drafted during the 1980s and early 1990s, resulting in a full draft in 1996.

These draft articles were then submitted to a full reading during the years 1997–2001. The commission, now led by Special Rapporteur James Crawford, had set for itself a goal of finalizing the draft articles by 2001.[26]

---

[23] For an alternative account of how states can be held responsible, see John M. Parrish, "Collective Responsibility and the State," *International Theory* 1, 1 (2009): 119–54.

[24] James Crawford, "Introduction," in *The International Law Commission's Articles on State Responsibility: Introduction, Text and Commentary*, ed. James Crawford (Cambridge: Cambridge University Press, 2001), 1.

[25] Ibid., 3.

[26] Two other rapporteurs served between Ago and Crawford: Willem Riphagen (1979–87) and Gaetano Arangio-Ruiz (1988–96).

The 1996 draft articles were divided into two parts, the first focusing on the "origins" of state responsibility and the second focusing on the consequences. The sixty articles raised a number of important issues, some of which resulted in major revisions.

The idea of an international crime is found in Article 19, which described international crimes and delicts:

> An act of a State which constitutes a breach of an international obligation is an internationally wrongful act, regardless of the subject-matter of the obligation breached.
>
> An international wrongful act which results from the breach by a State of an international obligation so essential for the protection of the fundamental interests of the international community that its breach is recognized as a crime by that community as a whole constitutes an international crime.
>
> Subject to paragraph 2, and on the basis of the rules of international law in force, an international crime may result, inter alia, from:
>
> A serious breach of an international obligation of essential importance for the maintenance of international peace and security, such as that prohibiting aggression;
>
> A serious breach of an international obligation of essential importance for safeguarding the right of self-determination of peoples, such as that prohibiting the establishment or maintenance by force of colonial domination;
>
> A serious breach on a widespread scale of an international obligation of essential importance for safeguarding the human being, such as those prohibiting slavery, genocide, and apartheid;
>
> A serious breach of an international obligation of essential importance for safeguarding and preservation of the human environment, such as those prohibiting massive pollution of the atmosphere or of the seas.
>
> Any internationally wrongful act which is not an international crime in accordance with paragraph 2 constitutes an international delict.[27]

This article did three controversial things: first, it defined certain acts of state as crimes, a concept that should result in punishment or at least punitive damages being imposed on the guilty state. Second, it differentiated between crimes and delicts, basing the distinction primarily on the severity of the violation. Third, although listed as examples only, it did

---

[27] Crawford, *The International Law Commission's Articles on State Responsibility*, 352–53.

spell out in some detail the types of actions that might be considered crimes.

State representatives were invited to comment on the drafts beginning in 1996. Reviewing the written submissions of states on Article 19 provides an important insight into how the concept of an international crime was understood.[28] The Czech Republic made a compelling case for keeping the idea of crimes in the text by avoiding the distinction between civil and criminal law: "The law of international responsibility is neither civil nor criminal, but is purely and simply international and therefore specific."[29] Denmark, presenting an argument on behalf of the Nordic countries, laid out the logic behind keeping in the idea of an international crime:

> If for instance, one looks at the crime of genocide or the crime of aggression, such crimes are, of course, perpetrated by individual human beings, but at the same time they may be imputable to the state insofar as they will normally be carried out by State organs implying a sort of "system criminality." The responsibility in such situations cannot in our view be limited to the individual human being acting on behalf of the State.[30]

Italy, Mongolia, Greece, and Uzbekistan also argued in favor of keeping in the concept of a crime.

The opposing view, that the concept of a crime should be deleted from the drafts, arose from a number of states. France, Ireland, Japan, the United Kingdom, and the United States submitted the fullest explanations as to why this provision should be deleted. The bulk of the arguments centered on the fact that crimes can only be committed by persons, with more than one quoting from the Nuremberg trials to this effect. The Irish Republic's statement gives the clearest version of this position:

> In our view, criminal liability is essentially about individual moral responsibility, and the best way forward in international law is to try to get universal agreement that particularly heinous behaviour on the part of individuals should be criminalized and to establish the necessary procedures and institutions at the international level to ensure that human beings are called to account for such behaviour. It seems to us that this is what the current

---

[28] For a legal analysis of the ILC's work, see Nina H. B. Jogensen, *The Responsibility of States for International Crimes* (Oxford: Oxford University Press, 2000).

[29] *State Responsibility Comments and Observations Received from Governments*. UN Doc. A/CN.4/488, March 25, 1998, 53. Available at http://ods-dds-ny.un.org/doc/UNDOC/GEN/N98/099/53/PDF/N9809953.pdf?OpenElement.

[30] Ibid., 53.

proposals for the establishment of an international criminal court are all about and that this is the best way of proceeding in the matter. As was said by the Nuremberg Tribunal crimes against international law are committed by men, not by abstract entities, and only by punishing individuals who commit such crimes can the provisions of international law be enforced.[31]

The British reiterated this position, adding a further argument that "By establishing the category of international crimes the danger of polarizing moral and political judgments into a crude choice between crimes and delicts is increased."[32]

These comments were taken by Crawford and included in his various reports to the ILC. In his report of May 11, 1998, Crawford agreed that the concept of an international crime makes sense when looking at the international system as a whole: "It would be odd if the State itself retained its immunity from guilt. It would be odd if the paradigmatic person of international law, the State, were treated as immune from committing the very crimes that international law characterizes as crimes in all cases whatsoever." However, although admitting this would be "odd," Crawford went on to argue that the draft articles do not spell out the institutional mechanisms of what would follow from defining certain actions as crimes. The articles say nothing of such issues as investigation, trial, proper sanctions, and "how a state could work its way out of the condemnation of criminality."[33] As a result, in his report to the commission in 1998, Crawford recommended that the idea of a crime be stricken from the draft articles, while suggesting that it may be worth pursuing the concept in a separate context.[34]

This recommendation and the objections of various state representatives resulted in a rather different article in the 2001 Draft Articles, which were eventually approved by the ILC at its 2002 meeting. Article 40 now states:

This Chapter applies to the international responsibility which is entailed by a serious breach by a State of an obligation arising under peremptory norm of general international law.

A breach of such an obligation is serious if it involves a gross or systematic failure by the responsible State to fulfil its obligation.

---

[31] Ibid., 58–59.   [32] Ibid., 61.

[33] Crawford, "Introduction" in *The International Law Commission's Articles on State Responsibility*: 18–19.

[34] Crawford, *First Report*: 10.

Crime has now been replaced by a serious breach of international law. The commentary on this article argues that it retains some of the older idea by employing the idea of a peremptory norm of general international law, or norms are those owed to the international community as a whole. Moreover, the commentary goes on to list many of the specifics that were cited in the previous Article 19, including aggression, self-determination, and human rights.[35]

Two points are important to note here. Crawford's concerns about Article 19 from the 1996 draft were largely based on the lack of an institutional structure that would allow states to be tried and sentenced; his objections were not based on a rejection of the idea of an international crime. As I have suggested elsewhere, an institutional structure could be constructed out of the current international system by redefining the role of the ICJ.[36] Second, the objections of the United States and other states concerning the relationship between individual responsibility and state responsibility are not insurmountable. The relationship between individual and state responsibility was addressed by the ILC, because another commission was in the process of drafting the articles that eventually became the ICC.

I would argue, therefore, that the failure of the ILC to include Article 19 in its final articles is not a conceptual one. In fact, when reading through the story of how Article 19 and the concept of an international crime was developed, one can better see the logic of state agency and responsibility and, more important, how those concepts should lead to punishment. In other words, perhaps the contribution of the ILC was not only the creation of a set of Articles on State Responsibility but the logic underlying even stronger claims about state crimes.

STATE PUNISHMENT

If it is possible to hold states responsible for crime, then what should result from this process?[37] I propose that there are four reasons to hold an agent responsible. First, to hold an agent responsible for something

---

[35] State Responsibility: Articles and Commentary, Article 40, paragraphs 1–9, in *The International Law Commission's Articles on State Responsibility*, 245–48.

[36] Anthony F. Lang, Jr. *Punishment, Justice and International Relations: Ethics and Order after the Cold War* (Routledge, 2008), 137–40.

[37] Responsibility can be both forward and backward looking. Forward responsibility is concerned with duties, whereas backward responsibility is considered with violations of norms, rules, and laws. This chapter is concerned with backward-looking responsibility, although this is related to forward looking, that is, if I am responsible for doing

is a statement that communicates a point, usually a point about the significance of the norm that has been violated. It signals not only to the agent held responsible but also to a wider community of agents, that this particular norm is important. If the point of responsibility is simply to communicate, than there needs to be no other purpose than simply stating that an agent is responsible.[38]

A second purpose is to stop the violation from happening. This can either be the case of the individual who continues to engage in the violation or as a deterrent function for the wider community of agents involved. To stop the individual agent from continuing the violation means that holding agents responsible must progress to something more like punishment, or at least detention.[39] To stop others from violating the same norm would mean that the communicative function of holding responsible is heard by other agents and internalized. If agents are inclined to be persuaded by words alone, then communication will be enough; if agents are not so inclined, then a more coercive consequence would seem necessary.

A third purpose would be to reestablish some level of justice by ensuring that the agent held responsible suffers in some way for the violation of the norm. This is an inexact answer, for it is unclear how imposing harm in response to a harm being inflicted is going to somehow "balance the scales." However, although it may be inexact, this is also one of the more commonplace notions of responsibility. In fact, this is where responsibility turns into punishment – retributive punishment in particular. An alternative version of this conception of justice could be labeled reparative. In civil law rather than criminal law cases, justice comes about not through an infliction of harm by the state but by forcing one agent to pay reparations to the other. This form of reparative justice is related to retributive, in that harm is inflicted, although it is inflicted by another agent rather than an overarching authority structure.[40]

---

something, I can be held responsible if I do not act in accordance with the relevant norm.

[38] David Luban makes a related point in his discussion of the "expressivist" logic behind collective punishment; see David Luban, "State Criminality and the Ambition of International Criminal Law," Chapter 2, this volume.

[39] For a discussion of the dangers of detention as they relate to the question of state responsibility, see Larry May's contribution to this volume, "Collective Punishment and Mass Confinement" (Chapter 6).

[40] I recognize that by combining retributive justice and what I am calling reparative justice, I am not necessarily following legal theory. Nevertheless, both seem related in that they are imposing harm in response to a violation of a norm so that there is a return to what

A fourth purpose would be to reform the agent that violated the norm in the first place so that he/she/it would not undertake such an action again. This is a form of punishment, although punishment designed merely to cause the agent to suffer, but harm designed to change the internal character of the agent. This might also be connected to restoring the relationship between the agent and other agents in the community, including the agent that was harmed by the violation. This can be either called rehabilitation or restoration.

From this review of four possible purposes behind holding an agent responsible, we can see how responsibility can lead to punishment. Before examining what state punishment might mean in the international realm, it is important to note that rather than punishment, contemporary international law refers to practices of enforcement as the most appropriate response to the violation of international rules and norms. Mary Ellen O'Connell has recently argued that enforcement in the international order comes in a wide range of individual and collective actions by states.[41] Although states cannot punish each other, enforcement actions give international law its teeth. For O'Connell and others who write about enforcement, often in response to critics of international law as lacking any capacity to truly provide responses to violations,[42] the difference between punishment and enforcement seems to rely on the question of authority; in the anarchic system of international relations, punishment is not a meaningful term, for punishment can only be issued from a sovereign authority. I have addressed this question elsewhere, but suffice it to say here that if punishment is defined as harm inflicted in response to a violation of a norm or rule, then it does not conceptually require a sovereign authority (a point made by Hugo Grotius and John Locke in the context of natural law).[43] The practices that O'Connell describes as enforcement (including collective security, reprisals, and sanctions) could just as easily be described as punishment if the necessity of a single authority structure in the theory of punishment is relaxed.

---

existed before the original violation took place – that is, both are attempts to achieve justice through imposing harm. For a nuanced discussion of reparative justice, see Erin Kelly, "Reparative Justice," Chapter 7, this volume. Kelly's argument is persuasive, although it applies more to collectives than to corporate agents.

[41] Mary Ellen O'Connell, *The Power and Purpose of International Law: Insights from the Theory and Practice of Enforcement* (New York: Oxford University Press, 2008).

[42] For a recent version of this critique, see Jack Goldsmith and Eric Posner, *The Limits of International Law* (Oxford: Oxford University Press, 2005). O'Connell admirably dismantles their arguments.

[43] Lang, *Punishment, Justice, and International Relations*: 25–44.

So, which of these purposes lies behind holding states responsible? What was the ICJ trying to do when it established the principle that states can be held responsible for committing genocide? This is difficult to determine in this case. When the ICJ agreed to consider the case (1993), the actions taking place in the Balkans were not the ones that eventually came to be called genocide, which according to the Court's judgment only took place in July 1995 at Srebrenica. It may have been, however, that the actions that were taking place at that time could be considered genocide, depending on how one interprets the facts. Thus, one reason might have been to stop a particular agent from committing genocide.

Second, when the Court finally issued its ruling, the genocide had stopped. Even more important, one might say that the "character" of the state of Serbia had been radically changed by this time. It was no longer Yugoslavia, or even the Republic of Serbia and Montenegro; instead, it was only the Republic of Serbia. Its leaders had given over Milošević to the ICC. It may be too strong to say that the state was "radically" changed, however, for the verdict of the ICJ was received in Serbia as a vindication that it was blameless in terms of genocide.[44] This raises the question of what actually constitutes the agent that is being held responsible; as Richard Vernon argues there is an immensely important difference between holding a state and a nation responsible.[45] The celebration of the verdict by newspapers and popular opinion points to the nation (unless all the news is controlled by the state), but to use this as evidence that there is a consistent "character" that can be held causally responsible for the genocide unfairly labels a community.[46]

It is important to emphasize, however, that the justices on the ICJ see that their role is not to necessarily stop actions taking place or to change the character of state agents who come before it. As a "constitutional court" in the international system, the ICJ's role is to provide clarity on the overarching rules governing the international order. Thus, its decision to take on this case must have been related to the emerging question of whether states can be held responsible for the crime of genocide.

[44] See Dimitrijevic and Milanovic, "The Strange Story of the Bosnian Genocide Case," and Lara Nettelfield "Srebrenica: Special Status for a Special Crime," in *Srebrenica in the Aftermath of Genocide*, eds., Lara J. Nettelfield and Sarah E. Wagner (New York: Cambridge University Press, forthcoming).

[45] Richard Vernon, "Punishing Collectives: States or Nations?," Chapter 11, in this volume.

[46] For a particularly egregious example of how a nation can be held responsible, see Daniel Goldhagen, *Hitler's Willing Executioners: Ordinary Germans and the Holocaust* (New York: Alfred A. Knopf, 1996).

Without access to the justices or more written material, I cannot say for certain why the justices made their decision. I can only conjecture on the basis of the logic of responsibility as I described earlier. My hypothesis is that the decision that states can be held responsible for genocide resulted from a combination of the first three purposes identified earlier: communicating the wrongness of genocide, deterring states from undertaking genocide, and ensuring some form of justice by giving satisfaction to those who have suffered genocide. The ICJ does not issue sentences or punishments, so to say that the justices intended to create a regime by which states can be punished may well stretch the logic of state responsibility too far. However, if it is the case that responsibility logically leads to the stated three purposes, then it would seem that the ICJ as an institution has created space not only for holding states responsible but for punishing them as well.

If it is the case that states can commit genocide, which the ICJ states, then it would seem to make sense that the next step is developing modes by which such rulings can be enforced. I have argued elsewhere that it is justifiable to punish states.[47] This argument includes a suggestion for revising international legal institutions so that the ICJ can punish states while the ICC can continue to punish individuals. Like the ICJ judgment, I agree that responsibility can be "dual" in the current international order, although I conclude with some questions about that structure in the next section of this chapter.

INTERNATIONAL CONSTITUTIONS AND THE CRIME OF GENOCIDE

The international legal order has progressively constructed a regime designed to hold individuals responsible for war crimes, crimes against humanity, and genocide.[48] This evolution crystallized in the creation of the ICC at the Rome negotiations in 1998 and the eventual ratification of the treaty creating the Court in 2002.[49] The ICC has yet to issue a judgment, but it currently has four cases under consideration: Uganda,

[47] Lang, "Crime and Punishment: Holding States Accountable."
[48] For a philosophical defense of this development, see Larry May, *Crimes against Humanity: A Normative Account* (Cambridge: Cambridge University Press, 2005), and Larry May, *War Crimes and Just War* (Cambridge: Cambridge University Press, 2007). For introductions to the legal issues, see M. Cherif Bassiouni, *Introduction to International Criminal Law* (Ardsley, NY: Transnational Publishers, 2003), and Antonio Cassese, *International Criminal Law*, 2nd ed. (Oxford: Oxford University Press, 2008).
[49] See William Schabas, *An Introduction to the International Criminal Court* (Cambridge: Cambridge University Press, 2001).

Democratic Republic of Congo, the Central African Republic, and the Sudan. The first three of these were brought to the Court by the states themselves, and the case of Sudan was brought to the Court at the initiative of the Security Council. Alongside of the ICC, the ICTY and the ICTR have received the most attention, although there are other tribunals, including the mixed one in Sierra Leone and the trials of the Khmer Rouge in Cambodia.

The ICC has not yet considered a case involving genocide, but the other courts have produced rulings on the matter that have informed the construction of an international legal order in which the "crime of all crimes" has been addressed. Individuals have not only been held responsible for genocide in these courts, they have also been sentenced and punished.[50] The attempt to capture genocide in the context of a legal court has been subject to various critiques. One comes from Hannah Arendt's examination of the trial of Adolf Eichmann.[51] Arendt's critique was not of international courts per se, but rather of trying to capture in the context of a trial a crime that seems to escape the confines of a courtroom.[52] For Arendt and others, the evil of genocide could not be comprehended through the mechanics of a courtroom.[53] Even more germane to the issues raised in this chapter, Arendt's critique of the trial was that it sought to place the crime of genocide on a specific person when such a large number of people were necessary to carrying out the plan, people who were just as "normal" as Eichmann. Indeed, the criticism of Arendt's book was largely from Jewish groups who disputed her account of how the Jewish Councils in European cities helped facilitate the genocide by providing bureaucratic assistance to the Nazi functionaries who had to move Jews from their homes to concentration camps.[54]

---

[50] For a perceptive treatment of these sentencing decisions, see Mark Drumbl, *Atrocity, Punishment and International Law* (Cambridge: Cambridge University Press, 2007).

[51] Hannah Arendt, *Eichmann in Jerusalem: A Report on the Banality of Evil* (New York: Penguin Books, 1965).

[52] Indeed, at the end of her book, which is more critical of Israel's use of the trial as a form of political theatre, Arendt gestures toward the importance of an international criminal court. For the standard account of how international law has responded to genocide, see William Schabas, *Genocide in International Law: The Crime of Crimes* (Cambridge: Cambridge University Press, 2000).

[53] However, Arendt's use of the term evil in both her critique of the Eichmann trial and her earlier *Origins of Totalitarianism* is often misunderstood. For a corrective to this misunderstanding and how her conception of evil has great relevance to global politics, see Patrick Hayden, *Political Evil in a Global Age: Hannah Arendt and International Theory* (London: Routledge, 2009).

[54] See Arendt's response to these critiques in the revised version of *Eichmann in Jerusalem*.

Larry May responds to Arendt's critique in his defense of individual prosecutions of genocide. His defense begins with a sentence that captures the overlapping structures of responsibility when it comes to genocide: "Understanding the collective dimension of individual responsibility for political crimes is crucial if individuals are to be justifiably prosecuted for genocide."[55] May develops his defense of the prosecution of individuals by exploring the interrelated nature of the *actus reus* and *mens rea* elements of genocide. In criminal law, the *actus reus* is the action(s) that constitutes the violation of the law, whereas the *mens rea* is the intention to commit the action. When it comes to genocide, considering the *actus reus* alone cannot suffice, for the types of actions that constitute genocide – killing people, primarily – can be committed even in large numbers without being considered genocide. As May notes, only when killing members of a particular group is linked to a larger plan for exterminating that group as a whole can it be considered genocide. As he points out, "The intent element in genocide is what makes the crime an international crime at all."[56]

May argues that individuals can be seen as having "shared responsibility" for political crimes such as genocide. Rather than relying on direct causal responsibility, political crimes are crimes "committed by a collectivity, typically by a State or by an organized group of people in some way acting systematically."[57] He argues that individuals who are in some way complicit in such crimes deserve punishment. At this point, May (like many others) shies away from holding the collectivity itself responsible, mainly because "many people's moral intuitions are offended by the thought of collective responsibility or collective punishment."[58] May's conclusion, in other words, suggests that although it may offend our moral sensibilities to hold collectives responsible, the very nature of genocide requires that there be some shared responsibility and, perhaps, shared punishment. That is, the crime of genocide cannot be reduced to individual evil persons but results from a widespread set of political practices. May's philosophical defense of individual prosecutions – a defense I believe is one of the clearest and most succinct – actually reveals that individual prosecutions should not be the only route through which genocide is countered.

It is here that the ICJ's judgment, considered alongside the ICC, gives us some grounds for considering alternative possibilities. The ICJ has, like

---

[55] Larry May, *Crimes against Humanity*, 157.   [56] Ibid., 165.
[57] Ibid., 171.   [58] Ibid., 175.

May, acknowledged that states commit genocide. Indeed, the very nature of genocide requires this conclusion. What this points to is the emergence (or perhaps simply the recognition) of two constitutional orders that both seek to address the problem of genocide. The international legal order within which the ICJ functions is that of the society of states. This society has long been focused primarily on the preservation of peace through the prevention of war. The other constitutional order is that of global society. This order is premised on the protection of human rights and the promotion of justice – specifically, international criminal justice. This constitutional order has the ICC at its apex.[59] These two orders constitute two kinds of agents as liable to prosecution. Rather than the *collective* agent that underlies May's account, I would suggest that the ICJ has constructed a *corporate* agent that can indeed be held responsible in that it is capable of intending, planning, and executing actions.

To understand these two orders and how they interact with each other would require another chapter. As Mark Drumbl points out, the interaction of the ICJ and ICTY in the context of the conflict in Balkans does not bode well for the construction of a unified international legal order.[60] The failure to properly share evidence and jealousies between the two institutions prevented an accurate account of the various perpetrators in the genocide. Drumbl concludes that this interaction demonstrates the subalternity, or the privileging of one structure above the other. As he suggests, "The ICJ and ICTY coexist in some sort of duality but one that apparently requires bargains that compromise the overall justice narrative to the detriment of collective civil responsibility and in favor of individual criminal responsibility."[61] This subalternity is most certainly a danger, one that provides a caution about the difficulties of constructing an alternative political–legal order. One response to this concern, however, would be to propose that the creation of an integrated legal order requires an attention to the political dimensions of a legal order.

---

[59] See Ian Clark's two works on legitimacy in international affairs for one attempt to capture how these two orders function and their differing conceptions of legitimacy. On the society of states, see Ian Clark, *Legitimacy in International Society* (Oxford: Oxford University Press, 2007); on global society, see Ian Clark, *International Legitimacy and World Society* (Oxford: Oxford University Press, 2007).

[60] Drumbl, "Collective Responsibility and Postconflict Justice," Chapter 1, this volume. See also Richard Goldstone and Rebecca J. Hamilton, "*Bosnia v. Serbia*: Lessons from the Encounter of the International Court of Justice with the International Criminal Tribunal for the Former Yugoslavia," *Leiden Journal of International Law* 21 (2008): 95–112.

[61] Drumbl, "Collective Responsibility and Postconflict Justice," 18.

In conclusion, let me make two points. First, the crime of genocide seems ideally situated to lead to the construction of an integrated legal order in which genocide can be prevented. As a crime that is committed by states but carried out by individuals, it demands an institutional response that can encompass agents in both orders. Related to this point, the almost universal condemnation of genocide within the international community suggests that this may be an ideal crime to use as a tool to construct such an order.

The second point concerns the relation of politics to law. Lara Nettelfield demonstrates how the ICJ's decision created a political response in Bosnia, leading her to conclude that "forms of punishment influence the mobilization of various social actors and perceived political solutions to problems confronted in the aftermath of mass atrocity."[62] The anger directed at the ICJ in response to the failure to hold Serbia responsible points to the possibility that judicial bodies can lead to political activism, a political activism that might be channeled into the construction of new constitutional structures. Nettelfield's argument draws on literature that suggests the potential for an "international law from below," which would connect global constitutional orders to local and national concerns such as those found in this context. Amy Sepinwall's contribution to this volume, although directed at the responsibility of the U.S. citizenry for war crimes in Iraq, points to a similar dynamic; that is, how can judicial deliberations point to political processes (or lack thereof) to reconstruct political orders?[63]

The construction of such orders is not easy. As Patrick Hayden suggests, a cosmopolitan realism points us to new beginnings, to alternative ways of approaching evils such as genocide: "One new beginning to be embraced by cosmopolitan realism, then, is to speak in favour of the juridification of extreme evil into the legally sanctionable acts of genocide and crimes against humanity."[64] Although Hayden's point here is addressed to how the ICC should be supported despite the difficulties of capturing genocide in a purely legal regime, I would suggest that an alternative beginning is to seek the juridification of genocide in more than one context. By finding mechanisms for the prevention and punishment of genocide in both the ICJ and ICC, we can come closer to reshaping the global political landscape in the pursuit of peace and justice.

[62] Lara Nettelfield, "Srebrenica: Special Status for a Special Crime."

[63] Amy Sepinwall, "Citizen Responsibility and the Reactive Attitudes," Chapter 9, this volume.

[64] Hayden, *Political Evil in a Global Age*, 22.

4

Joint Criminal Enterprise, the Nuremberg Precedent, and the Concept of "Grotian Moment"

Michael P. Scharf

During a sabbatical in the fall of 2008, I had the unique experience of serving as special assistant to the international prosecutor of the Extraordinary Chambers in the Courts of Cambodia (ECCC), the tribunal created by the United Nations and the government of Cambodia to prosecute the former leaders of the Khmer Rouge for the atrocities committed during its reign of terror (1975–79).[1] During the time I spent in Phnom Penh, my most important assignment was to draft the prosecutor's brief[2] in reply to the Defense Motion to Exclude "joint criminal enterprise" (JCE), and in particular the extended form of JCE known as JCE III, as a mode of liability from the trial of the five surviving leaders of the Khmer Rouge.[3]

---

[1] For background on the creation of the ECCC, see Michael P. Scharf, *Tainted Provenance: When, If Ever, Should Torture Evidence Be Admissible? Washington and Lee Law Review* 65 (2008): 129–172; Daniel Kemper Donovan, *Joint U.N.–Cambodia Efforts to Establish a Khmer Rouge Tribunal, Harvard International Law Journal* 44 (2003): 551, 553–564. The Tribunal's constituent instruments, including its Statute, Agreement with the United Nations, and Internal Rules, are available at its website: http://www.eccc.gov.kh.

[2] Co-Prosecutors' Supplementary Observations on Joint Criminal Enterprise, Case of Ieng Sary, No. 002/19-09-2007-ECCC/OCIJ, December 31, 2009. A year later, the co-investigating judges ruled in favor of the prosecution that the ECCC could employ JCE liability for the international crimes within its jurisdiction. See Order on the Application at the ECCC of the Form of Liability Known as Joint Criminal Enterprise, Case No. 002/19-09-2007-ECCC-OCIJ, December 8, 2009. The issue will not be completely settled until after final decision of the ECCC Appeals Chamber.

[3] Pursuant to the co-investigating judges' order of September 16, 2008, the co-prosecutors filed the brief to detail why the extended form of JCE liability, "JCE III," is applicable before the ECCC. The defense motion argued in part that JCE III as applied by the *Tadić* decision of the International Criminal Tribunal for the Former Yugoslavia (ICTY) Appeals Chamber is a judicial construct that does not exist in customary international law or, alternatively, did not exist in 1975–79. *Case of Ieng Sary*, Ieng Sary's Motion against the Application at the ECCC of the Form of Responsibility Known as

JCE III is a form of liability somewhat similar to the Anglo-American "felony murder rule"[4] in which a person who willingly participates in a criminal enterprise can be held criminally responsible for the reasonably foreseeable acts of other members of the criminal enterprise even if those acts were not part of the plan. Although few countries around the world apply principles of coperpetration similar to the felony murder rule or JCE III, since the decision of the Appeals Chamber of the International Criminal Tribunal for the Former Yugoslavia (ICTY) in the 1998 *Tadić* case,[5] it has been accepted that JCE III is a mode of liability applicable to international criminal trials. Dozens of cases before the ICTY,[6] the International Criminal Tribunal for Rwanda (ICTR),[7] the Special Court for Sierra Leone (SCSL),[8] and the Special Panels for the Trial of Serious

Joint Criminal Enterprise, Case No. 002/19-09-2007-ECCC/OCIJ, July 28, 2008, ERN 00208225–00208240, D97.

[4] For background about, and cases applying to, the felony murder rule, see David Crump and Susan Waite Crump, "In Defense of the Felony Murder Doctrine," *Harvard Journal of Law and Public Policy* 8 (1985): 359–398.

[5] *Prosecutor v. Tadić*, Judgment, Case No. IT-94-1-A, ICTY Appeals Chamber, July 15, 1999 [hereafter *Tadic* Appeals Chamber Judgment].

[6] *Prosecutor v. Milutinovic*, Decision on Dragoljub Ojdanic's Motion Challenging Jurisdiction – Joint Criminal Enterprise Liability, Case No. IT-99-37-AR72, ICTY Appeals Chamber, May 21, 2003 [hereafter *Milutinovic* Decision]; *Prosecutor v. Krnojelac*, Judgment, Case No. IT-97-25-A, ICTY Appeals Chamber, September 17, 2003, para. 96; *Prosecutor v. Simic*, Judgment, ICTY Trial Chamber, Case No. IT-95-9-T, October 17, 2003, para. 149; *Prosecutor v. Kvocka*, Judgment, Case No. IT-98-30/1-A, February 28, 2005, paras. 105, 309; *Prosecutor v. Krnojelac*, Judgment, Case No. IT-97-25-A, September 17, 2003, paras. 96, 100; *Prosecutor v. Brdjanin*, Judgment, Case No. IT-99-36-A, April 3, 2007, para. 395; *Prosecutor v. Brdjanin*, Decision on Interlocutory Appeal, Case No. IT-99-36-A, March 19, 2004; *Prosecutor v. Stakic*, Case No. IT-97-24-A, Judgment, March 22, 2006, paras. 101–4; *Prosecutor v. Krjaisnik*, Judgment, Case No. IT-00-39-T, September 27, 2006, para. 1082; *Prosecutor v. Milosevic*, Decision on Motion for Judgment of Acquittal, Case No. IT-02-54-T, June 16, 2004, para. 291; *Prosecutor v. Krstic*, Judgment, Case No. IT-98-33-A, ICTY Appeals Chamber, April 19, 2004, para. 144.

[7] *Prosecutor v. Ntakirutimana*, Judgment, Case Nos. ICTR-96-10-A and ICTR-96-17-A, ICTR Appeals Chamber, December 13, 2004, paras. 461–4; *Prosecutor v. Rwamakuba*, Decision on Interlocutory Appeal Regarding Application of Joint Criminal Enterprise to the Crime of Genocide, Case No. ICTR-98-44-AR72.4, October 22, 2004, paras. 14–30; *Prosecutor v. Kayishema and Ruzindanda*, Judgment, Case No. ICTR-95-1-A, ICTR Appeals Chamber, June 1, 2001, para 193; *Prosecutor v. Nchamihigo*, Decision on Defence Motion on Defects in the Form of the Indictment, Case No. ICTR-20010630R50, September 27, 2006, paras 14, 21.

[8] *Prosecutor v. Brima, Kamara and Kanue* (AFRC Case), Decision on Motions for Judgment of Acquittal Pursuant to Rule 98, Case No. SCSL-04-16-T, March 31, 2006, paras. 308–26; *Prosecutor v. Norman, Fofana and Kondewa* (CDF Case), Decision on Motions for Judgment of Acquittal Pursuant to Rule 98, Case No. 04-14-T, October 21, 2005, para. 130.

Crimes in East Timor[9] have recognized and applied JCE liability since 1998.

These modern precedents, however, were not directly relevant to the ECCC because the crimes under its jurisdiction had occurred some twenty years earlier. Under the international law principle of *nullum crimen sine lege* (the equivalent to the U.S. Constitution's *ex post facto* law prohibition), the Cambodia Tribunal can only apply the substantive law and associated modes of liability that existed as part of customary international law in 1975–79. Therefore, the question at the heart of the brief that I drafted was whether the Nuremberg Tribunal precedent and the United Nation's adoption of the Nuremberg principles were sufficient to establish JCE liability as part of customary international law following World War II.

The attorneys for the Khmer Rouge defendants argued that Nuremberg and its progeny provided too scant a sampling to constitute the widespread state practice and *opinio juris* required to establish JCE as a customary norm as of 1975.[10] In response, the Prosecution brief maintains that Nuremberg constituted what some commentators call "a Grotian Moment" – an instance in which there is such a fundamental change to the international system that a new principle of customary international law can arise with unusual rapidity. This was the first time in history that the term was used in a proceeding before an international court.

This chapter explores the concept of the Grotian Moment in the context of the validity of applying JCE to the Cambodia Tribunal's cases. It begins with a history of the concept of a Grotian Moment, comparing and contrasting it with the notion of "instant customary international law." It then examines whether the Nuremberg precedent fits within the profile of a legitimate Grotian Moment. Little has previously been written

---

[9] *Prosecutor v. Jose Cardoso Fereira*, Judgment, Case No. 04/2001, District Court of Dili, 5 April 2003, paras. 367–76 (finding the accused guilty under JCE theory, applying the *Tadić* Appeals Chamber Judgment and other ICTY judgments in interpreting UNTAET Regulation 2000/15); *Prosecutor v. De Deus*, Judgment, Case No. 2a/2004, District Court of Dili, April 12, 2005, p. 13 (holding that although the accused did not personally beat the victim, he was guilty "as part of a joint criminal enterprise" because he was part of an organized force intent on killing and contributed by carrying a gun, uttering threats, and intimidating unarmed people, thereby strengthening the resolve of the group).

[10] For the definition of customary international law, see *North Sea Continental Shelf* (*Federal Republic of Germany v. Denmark*; *Federal Republic of Germany v. Netherlands*), Merits, 20 February 1969, ICJ Rep. 3, para. 77.

about the concept of a Grotian Moment. Indeed, an extensive search of law review databases revealed only sixty-one previous references to the term, and few that use the term in the way it is being employed here. Although this chapter uses the lens of the Khmer Rouge trial to frame the discussion, the analysis and findings have implications far beyond the subfield of international criminal law.

ORIGINS OF THE TERM "GROTIAN MOMENT"

Dutch scholar and diplomat Hugo Grotius (1583–1645) is widely considered to be the father of modern international law as the law of nations and has been recognized for having "recorded the creation of order out of chaos in the great sphere of international relations."[11] In the mid-1600s, at the time that the nation-state was formally recognized as having crystallized into the fundamental political unit of Europe, Grotius "offered a new concept of international law designed to reflect that new reality."[12] In his masterpiece, *De Jure Belli ac Pacis* (The Law of War and Peace), Grotius addresses questions bearing on just war: who may be a belligerent; what causes of war are just, doubtful, or unjust; and what procedures must be followed in the inception, conduct, and conclusion of war.[13]

Although New York University Professor Benedict Kingsbury has convincingly argued that Grotius's actual contribution has been distorted through the ages, the prevailing view today is that his treatise had an extraordinary impact as the first formulation of a comprehensive legal order of interstate relations based on mutual respect and equality of sovereign states.[14] In semiotic terms,[15] "the Grotian tradition" has come to symbolize the advent of the modern international legal regime,

---

[11] *See* Charles S. Edwards, *Hugo Grotius, the Miracle of Holland* (Chicago: Nelson-Hall, 1981).

[12] John W. Head, "Throwing Eggs at Windows: Legal and Institutional Globalization in the 21st Century Economy," *Kansas Law Review* 50 (2002): 731, 771.

[13] Hugo Grotius, *De Jure Belli ac Pacis* (n.p. 1625).

[14] Benedict Kingsbury, "A Grotian Tradition of Theory and Practice? Grotius, Law, and Moral Skepticism in the Thought of Hedley Bull," *Quinnipiac Law Review* 17 (1997): 3, 10.

[15] Semiotics is the study of how meaning of signs, symbols, and language is constructed and understood. Semiotics explains that terms such as "The Peace of Westphalia" or "the Grotian tradition" are not historic artifacts with meanings that remain static over time. Rather, the meaning of such terms changes along with the interpretive community or communities. Michael P. Scharf, "International Law in Crisis: A Qualitative Empirical Contribution to the Compliance Debate," *Cardozo Law Review* 31 (2009): 45, 50 (citing Charles Sanders Peirce, *Collected Papers of Charles Sanders Peirce: Pragmatism and Pragmaticism*, eds. Charles Hartshorne & Paul Weiss) (1935).

characterized by positive law and state consent, which arose from the Peace of Westphalia.[16]

The term Grotian Moment, in contrast, is a relatively recent creation, coined by Princeton Professor Richard Falk in 1985.[17] Since then, scholars and even the UN Secretary-General have employed the term in a variety of ways,[18] but here I use it to denote a transformative development in which new rules and doctrines of customary international law emerge with unusual rapidity and acceptance.[19] Usually this happens during "a period in world history that seems analogous at least to the end of European feudalism... when new norms, procedures, and institutions had to be devised to cope with the then decline of the Church and the emergence of the secular state."[20] Commentators have opined

---

[16] Michael P. Scharf, "Earned Sovereignty: Juridical Underpinnings," *Denver Journal of International Law* 31 (2003): 373, n. 20. The Peace of Westphalia was composed of two separate agreements: (1) the Treaty of Osnabruck concluded between the Protestant queen of Sweden and her allies on one side and the Holy Roman Habsburg emperor and the German princes on the other and (2) the Treaty of Munster concluded between the Catholic king of France and his allies on one side and the Holy Roman Habsburg emperor and the German princes on the other. The conventional view of the Peace of Westphalia is that by recognizing the German Princes as sovereign, these treaties signaled the beginning of a new era, but in fact, the power to conclude alliances formally recognized at Westphalia was not unqualified and was a power that the German princes had already possessed for almost half a century. Furthermore, although the treaties eroded some of the authority of the Habsburg emperor, the empire remained a key actor according to the terms of the treaties. For example, the Imperial Diet retained the powers of legislation, warfare, and taxation, and it was through Imperial bodies, such as the Diet and the Courts, that religious safeguards mandated by the Treaty were imposed on the German princes.

[17] *The Grotian Moment in International Law: A Contemporary Perspective*, Richard Falk, et al., eds., (1985), 7, excerpt reprinted in Burns H. Weston et al., *International Law and World Order,* 2nd ed. (Eagan, MN: Thomson/West, 1990), 1087–92. See also *International Law and World Order,* 4th ed., eds. Burns H. Weston, Richard A. Falk, Hilary Charlesworth, and Andrew K. Strauss (Eagan, MN: Thomson/West, 2006). For the early seeds of this concept of a changing paradigm in Falk's work, see Richard A. Falk, "The Interplay of Westphalia and Charter Conceptions of International Legal Order," in *The Future of the International Legal Order*, eds. R. Falk and C. Black (1969), 32.

[18] Boutros Boutros-Ghali, "The Role of International Law in the Twenty-First Century: A Grotian Moment," *Fordham International Law Journal* 18 (1995): 1609, 1613 (referring to the establishment of the International Criminal Tribunal for the Former Yugoslavia as part of the process of building a new international system for the twenty-first century).

[19] Saul Mendlovitz and Marev Datan, "Judge Weeramantry's Grotian Quest," *Transnational Law & Contemporary Problems* 7 (1997): 401, 402 (defining the term "Grotian moment").

[20] Burns H. Weston, *International Law and World Order,* 3rd ed. (1997), 1369; B. S. Chimni, "The Eighth Annual Grotius Lecture: A Just World under Law: A View from the South," *American University International Law Review* 22 (2007): 199, 202.

that the creation of the Nuremberg Tribunal at the end of World War II constituted a classic Grotian Moment, on par with the negotiation of the Peace of Westphalia and the establishment of the UN Charter.[21]

Drawing from the writings of Professor Bruce Ackerman, who used the phrase "constitutional moment" to describe the New Deal transformation in American constitutional law,[22] some international law scholars have used the phrase "international constitutional moment" to convey the Grotian Moment concept. Professors Bardo Fassbender and Jenny Martinez, for example, have written that the drafting of the UN Charter was a "Constitutional moment" in the history of international law.[23] Professor Leila Sadat has described Nuremberg as a "constitutional moment for international law."[24] Professors Anne-Marie Slaughter and William Burke-White have used the term "constitutional moment" in making the case that the September 11 attacks on the United States evidence a change in the nature of the threats confronting the international community, thereby paving the way for rapid development of new rules of customary international law.[25] Although the phrase "international constitutional moment" might be useful with respect to paradigm-shifting developments within a particular international organization with a constitutive instrument that acts like a constitution, the term Grotian Moment makes more sense when speaking of a development that has an effect on international law at large.

[21] Ibrahim J. Gassama, "International Law at a Grotian Moment: The Invasion of Iraq in Context," *Emory International Law Review* 18 (2004): 1, 9 (describing history's Grotian moments, including the Peace of Westphalia, the Nuremberg Charter, and the UN Charter); Leila Nadya Sadat, "The New International Criminal Court: An Uneasy Revolution," *Georgetown Law Journal* 88 (2000): 381, 474, arguing that the Statute of the International Criminal Court constitutes the most recent Grotian moment.

[22] Bruce Ackerman, *Reconstructing American Law* (Cambridge, MA, and London: Harvard University Press, 1984).

[23] Bardo Fassbender, "The United Nations Charter as Constitution of the International Community," *Columbia Journal of Transnational Law* 36 (1998): 529–619; Jenny S. Martinez, "Towards an International Judicial System," *Stanford Law Review* 56 (2003): 429–529, at 463.

[24] Leila Nadya Sadat, "Enemy Combatants after *Hamdan v. Rumsfeld*: Extraordinary Rendition, Torture, and Other Nightmares from the War on Terror," *George Washington Law Review* 75 (2007): 1200, 1206–7.

[25] Anne-Marie Slaughter and William Burke-White, "An International Constitutional Moment," *Harvard International Law Journal* 43 (2002): 1–22, at 1, 2. See also Ian Johnstone, "The Plea of 'Necessity' in International Legal Discourse: Humanitarian Intervention and Counter-Terrorism," *Columbia Journal of Transnational Law* 43 (2005): 337, 370, arguing that 9/11 constituted a "constitutional moment" leading to recognition of a newly emergent right to use force in self-defense argued against nonstate actors operating with the support of third States.

COMPARING THE GROTIAN MOMENT CONCEPT TO THE
NOTION OF "INSTANT CUSTOMARY INTERNATIONAL LAW"

Normally, customary international law, which is just as binding on states as treaty law,[26] arises out of the slow accretion of widespread state practice evincing a sense of legal obligation (*opinio juris*).[27] Under traditional notions of customary international law, "deeds were what counted, not just words."[28] At the same time, a state's practice is not limited to its own acts; practice can consist of acquiescence, through failure to protest the acts of other states.[29]

Consistent with the traditional approach, the U.S. Supreme Court has recognized that the process of establishing customary international law can take decades or even centuries.[30] In the 1969 *North Sea Continental Shelf* cases, however, the International Court of Justice (ICJ) declared that customary norms can sometimes ripen quite rapidly and that a short period of time is not a bar to finding the existence of a new rule of customary international law, binding on all the countries of the world, save those that persistently objected during its formation.[31] As contemplated

---

[26] Although customary international law is binding on states internationally, not all states accord customary international law equal domestic effect. A growing number of states' constitutions automatically incorporate customary law as part of the law of the land and even accord it a ranking higher than domestic statutes. Bruno Simma, *International Human Rights and General International Law: A Comparative Analysis* (1995): 165, 213. In the United States, customary international law is deemed incorporated into the federal common law of the United States. Some courts, however, consider it controlling only where there is no contradictory treaty, statute, or executive act. See *Garcia-Mir v. Meese*, 788 F.2d 1446 (11th Circ. 1986), holding that the attorney general's decision to detain Mariel Cuban refugees indefinitely without a hearing trumped any contrary rules of customary international law.

[27] For the definition of customary international law, see *North Sea Continental Shelf (Federal Republic of Germany v. Denmark; Federal Republic of Germany v. Netherlands)*, Merits, 20 February 1969, ICJ Rep. 3, para. 77.

[28] Bruno Simma, *International Human Rights and General International Law*, n. 27, at 216.

[29] Akehurst, "Custom as a Source of International Law," *British Yearbook of International Law* 47 (1974–75): 1, 10, 23–24, 38–42.

[30] The Paquete Habana, 175 U.S. 677, 700 (1900).

[31] *North Sea Continental Shelf (Federal Republic of Germany v. Denmark; Federal Republic of Germany v. Netherlands)*, Merits, 20 February 1969, ICJ Rep. 3, paras. 71, 73, 74. The Court stated:

> Although the passage of only a short period of time is not necessarily . . . a bar to the formation of a new rule of customary international law . . . , an indispensable requirement would be that within the period in question, short though it might be, State practice, including that of States whose interests are specially

in the *North Sea Continental Shelf* cases, a Grotian Moment is a situation in which there is an acceleration of the custom-formation process due to the widespread and unequivocal response of states to a paradigm-changing event in international law, such as the unprecedented human suffering from the atrocities of World War II and the related recognition that there could be international criminal responsibility for violations of international law.

In an oft-cited 1965 article, Professor Bin Cheng argued that there could be such a thing as "instant customary international law."[32] Professor Cheng opined that it was not only unnecessary that state practice should be prolonged, but there need be no state practice at all provided that the *opinio juris* of the States concerned can be clearly established by, for example, their votes on UN General Assembly resolutions.[33] Legal scholars have been largely critical of Cheng's "instant custom" theory, at least to the extent that it does away with the need to demonstrate any state practice other than a country's vote in the U.N. General Assembly.[34]

There are three main problems with the "instant custom" theory when it is based solely on General Assembly resolutions. The first is that the UN Charter employs the language of "recommend" in referring to the powers and functions of the General Assembly, as distinct from the powers granted to the Security Council to issue-binding decisions.[35] The

affected, should have been both extensive and virtually uniform in the sense of the provision invoked; – and should moreover have occurred in such a way as to show a general recognition that a rule of law or legal obligation is involved.

Idem at para. 74. Although recognizing that some norms can quickly become customary international law, the ICJ held that the equidistance principle contained in Article 6 of the 1958 Convention on the Continental Shelf had not done so as of 1969 because so few states recognized and applied the principle.

[32] B. Cheng, "United Nations Resolutions on Outer Space: 'Instant' International Customary Law?" *Indian Journal of International Law* 5 (1965): 23–48. In contrast to Cheng's conception, the Grotian Moment concept contemplates accelerated formation of customary international law through widespread acquiescence or endorsement in response to state acts, rather than instant custom based solely on General Assembly resolutions.

[33] Idem at 36. Other scholars and commentators who have asserted the possibility of "instant customary international law" include Peter Malanczuk, *Akehurst's Modern Introduction to International Law*, 7th ed. (New York: Routledge 1997): 45–46; Jeremy Levitt, "Humanitarian Intervention by Regional Actors in Internal Conflicts: The Cases of ECOWAS in Liberia and Sierra Leone," *Temple International and Comparative Law Journal* 12 (1998): 333, 351; Benjamin Lengille, "It's 'Instant Custom': How the Bush Doctrine Became Law after the Terrorist Attacks of September 11, 2001," *Boston College International and Comparative Law Review* 26 (2003): 145.

[34] See G. J. H. Van Hoof, *Rethinking the Sources of International Law* (Deventer: Kluwer Publishing, 1983): 86.

[35] Charter of the United Nations, Articles 10 and 11, June 26, 1945, 59 Stat. 1031, T.S. No. 993.

negotiating record of the UN Charter confirms that the drafters intended for General Assembly resolutions to be merely nonbinding recommendations. In fact, at the San Francisco Conference in 1945, when the Philippines delegation proposed that the General Assembly be vested with legislative authority to enact rules of international law, the other delegations voted down the proposal by an overwhelming margin.[36]

The second problem is that states often vote for General Assembly resolutions to embellish their image or curry favor with other states, without the expectation that their votes will be deemed acceptance of a new rule of law. For example, the United States initially opposed the draft of General Assembly Resolution 1803, which mandated "appropriate compensation" following an expropriation because the United States felt that the correct standard should be "prompt, adequate, and effective" compensation. Yet the United States ultimately voted in favor of the resolution in a spirit of compromise.[37] ICJ Judge Stephen Schwebel has referred to this type of practice as "fake consensus."[38]

The third problem with an approach that focuses exclusively on words contained in nonbinding General Assembly Resolutions is "that it is grown like a flower in a hot-house and that it is anything but sure that such creatures will survive in the much rougher climate of actual state practice."[39] Elsewhere I have argued that outside of situations covered by treaties with a "prosecute or extradite" requirement, the so-called duty to prosecute crimes against humanity, recognized in nonbinding General Assembly resolutions, is a chimera.[40] A "rule" that is based only

---

[36] Gregory J. Kerwin, "The Role of United Nations General Assembly Resolutions in Determining Principles of International Law in United States Courts," *Duke Law Journal* (1983): 876, 879.

[37] *Banco Nacional de Cuba v. Chase Manhattan Bank*, 638 F.2d, 875, 890 (2d Cir. 1981), opining that General Assembly Resolutions "are of considerable interest" but they "do not have the force of law," the Court held that expropriation requires "prompt, adequate, and effective compensation" rather than the standard of "appropriate compensation" reflected in GA Res. 1803.

[38] Stephen Schwebel, "The Effect of Resolutions of the U.N. General Assembly on Customary International Law," *Proceedings of the American Society of International Law* 73 (1979): 301, 308. Schwebel has observed that members of the UN "often vote casually. . . . States often don't meaningful support what a resolution says and they almost always do not mean that the resolution is law. This may be as true or truer in the case of unanimously adopted resolutions as in the case of majority-adopted resolutions. It may be truer still of resolutions adopted by consensus." Idem at 302.

[39] Simma, *International Human Rights and General International Law*, n. 27, at 217.

[40] Michael P. Scharf, "Swapping Amnesty for Peace: Was There a Duty to Prosecute International Crimes in Haiti?," *Texas International Law Journal* 41 (1996): 1, citing examples of adverse state practice in which amnesty is traded for peace, thus disproving

on General Assembly resolutions is unlikely to achieve substantial compliance in the real world and therefore will end up undermining rather than strengthening the rule of law.

That is not to suggest that General Assembly resolutions are not relevant to the determination of the existence and content of customary international law. On the contrary, it is widely recognized that under certain circumstances, General Assembly resolutions can "declare existing customs [or] crystallize emerging customs."[41] As a 1975 U.S. Department of State pronouncement explained:

> General Assembly resolutions are regarded as recommendations to Member States of the United Nations. To the extent, which is exceptional, that such resolutions are meant to be declaratory of international law, are adopted with the support of all members, and are observed by the practice of States, such resolutions are evidence of customary international law on a particular subject matter.[42]

Consistent with this view, both U.S. domestic courts and international tribunals have relied on General Assembly resolutions as evidence of an emergent customary rule. Thus, in *Siderman de Blake v. Republic of Argentina*, the 9th Circuit confirmed that "a resolution of the General Assembly of the United Nations . . . is a powerful and authoritative statement of the customary international law of human rights."[43] On several occasions, the ICJ has affirmed that General Assembly resolutions have legal significance – not as an independent source of international law but as evidence of new customary international law.[44] In its advisory opinion on the *Construction of a Wall*, for example, the ICJ cited "relevant

the existence of a customary rule requiring prosecution in the absence of a treaty with a prosecute or extradite provision.

[41] Anthea Elizabeth Roberts, "Traditional and Modern Approaches to Customary International Law: A Reconciliation," *American Journal of International Law* 95 (2001): 757, 758.

[42] D. J. Harris, *Cases and Materials in International Law*, 5th ed. (London: Sweet and Maxwell, 1998): 62.

[43] *Siderman de Blake v. Republic of Argentina*, 965 F. 2.d 699, 719 (9th Circ. 1992).

[44] Examples include Military and Paramilitary Activities (*Nicar. v. U.S.*, 1986 I.C.J. 14 (June 27) (Merits); The Legality of the Threat or Use of Nuclear Weapons, 1996 I.C.J. 226, 254–55; Legal Consequences of the Construction of a Wall in the Occupied Palestinian Territory, Advisory Opinion, 2004 I.C.J. 136, 171 (July 9); Gabcikovo-Nagymaros Project (*Hung. v. Slovk.*), 1997 I.C.J. 7 (Sept. 25) (*Hungary v. Slovakia*); Armed Activities on the Territory of the Congo (*Dem. Rep. Congo v. Uganda*), 45 I.L.M. 271, 308–9, Dec. 19, 2005 (*DRC v. Uganda*); and Application of the Convention on the Prevention and Punishment of the Crime of Genocide (*Bosn. & Herz. v. Serb. and Mont.*), 46 I.L.M. 188, 190, February 26, 2007.

resolutions adopted pursuant to the U.N. Charter by the General Assembly" among the "rules and principles of international law" that were useful in assessing the legality of the measures taken by Israel.[45] In its judgment in the *Case Concerning the Application on the Convention on the Prevention and Punishment of the Crime of Genocide*, the ICJ cited General Assembly resolutions referring to ethnic cleansing as a "form of genocide" as evidence that ethnic cleansing could constitute acts of genocide in violation of the Genocide Convention.[46]

In deciding whether to treat a particular General Assembly resolution as evidence of a new rule of customary international law, the ICJ has stated that "it is necessary to look at its content and the conditions of its adoption."[47] In examining these factors, courts often consider the type of resolution to be significant. General Assembly resolutions fall within a spectrum, from mere "recommendations" (usually given little weight) to "Declarations" (used to impart increased solemnity) to "affirmations" (used to indicate codification or crystallization of law).[48] Courts also consider the words used in the resolution – for example, language of firm obligation versus aspiration.[49] Another consideration is the vote outcome. Resolutions passed unanimously or by sizable majorities are accorded more weight than those adopted over significant dissent or abstentions.[50] Moreover, the position of important players relative to the subject matter of the resolution is of particular significance.[51] Consensus resolutions (adopted without an actual vote) may be discounted because countries

---

[45] Legal Consequences of the Construction of a Wall in the Occupied Palestinian Territory, Advisory Opinion, 2004 I.C.J. 136, 171 (July 9).

[46] Application of the Convention on the Prevention and Punishment of the Crime of Genocide (*Bosn. & Herz. v. Serb. and Mont.*), 46 I.L.M. 188, 190 (Feb. 26).

[47] Legality of the Threat or Use of Nuclear Weapons, 1996 I.C.J. 226, 254–55.

[48] Office of International Standards and Legal Affairs, General Introduction to the Standard-Setting Instruments of UNESCO, Recommendations. Available at http://portal.unesco.org/en/ev.php-url_ID=237772&URL_DO=DO_Topic&URL_Sectrion±201.html#4. See also Noelle Lenoir, "Universal Declaration on the Human Genome and Human Rights: The First Legal and Ethical Framework at the Global Level," *Columbia Human Rights Law Review* 30 (1999): 537, 551; Major Robert A. Ramey, "Armed Conflict on the Final Frontier: The Law of War in Space," *Air Force Law Review* 48 (2000): 1, 110–485.

[49] Robert Rosenstock, "The Declaration of Principles of International Law Concerning Friendly Relations: A Survey," *American Journal of International Law* 65 (1971): 713, 715–16.

[50] Legality of the Threat or Use of Nuclear Weapons, 1996 I.C.J. 226, 255.

[51] *Nguyen Thang Loi v. Dow Chem. Co.* (In re Agent Orange Prod. Liab. Litig.), 373 F. Supp. 2d 7, 126–27 (E.D.N.Y. 2005).

are often pressured to remain silent so as not to break consensus.[52] The ICJ has also indicated that if a state expressly mentions, while voting for a particular General Assembly resolution, that it regards the text as being merely a political statement without legal content, then that resolution may not be invoked against it.[53]

In addition to these considerations, the Grotian Moment concept may be helpful to a court examining whether a particular General Assembly resolution should be deemed evidence of an embryonic rule of customary international law, especially for a case in which there is not the traditional level of widespread and repeated state practice. In periods of fundamental change, whether by technological advances, the commission of new forms of crimes against humanity, or the development of new means of warfare or terrorism, rapidly developing customary international law as crystallized in General Assembly resolutions may be necessary to keep up with the pace of developments. A few examples of some recent potential Grotian Moments may provide a helpful lens for examining the validity of the concept.

One such situation arose when the United States and Soviet Union first developed the ability to launch rockets into outer space and place satellites in Earth's orbit.[54] In response to this new technological development, the UN General Assembly adopted the *Declaration of Legal Principles Governing the Activities of States in the Exploration and Use of Outer Space*, which provided that the provisions of the UN Charter, including limitations on the use of force, apply to outer space; outer space and celestial bodies are not subject to national appropriation by claim of sovereignty; states bear responsibility for parts of space vehicles that land on the territory of other states; the state of registry of a spacecraft has exclusive jurisdiction over it and any personnel it carries; and states shall regard astronauts as envoys and shall accord them assistance and promptly return them to the state of registry.[55] Although state practice was scant in the early years of space exploration, ICJ Judge Manfred Lachs concluded that "it is difficult to regard the 1963 Declaration as a

[52] Stephen Schwebel, "The Effect of Resolutions of the U.N. General Assembly on Customary International Law," 301, 302.

[53] *Military and Paramilitary Activities* (*Nicar. v. U.S.*), 1986 I.C.J. 106–07 (June 27).

[54] John O'Brien, *International Law* (London: Cavendish, 2001): 463–64; Bin Cheng, "United Nations Resolutions on Outer Space," 23.

[55] G.A. Res. 1962 (XVIII), Declaration of Legal Principles Governing the Activities of States in the Exploration and Use of Outer Space, December 13, 1963.

mere recommendation: it was an instrument which has been accepted as law."[56]

A second situation involved the NATO intervention into Serbia in an effort to prevent a potential genocide of ethnic Kosovar Albanians in 1999. It was significant that the situation was unfolding just five years after the UN failed to take action to halt genocide in Rwanda. When Russia and China prevented the Security Council from authorizing the use of force against Serbia, NATO proceeded to commence a seventy-eight-day bombing campaign without UN approval.[57] The near universal consensus, however, was that the intervention was justified under the circumstances, leading commentators to label the situation "unlawful but legitimate."[58] The international reaction to the 1999 NATO intervention prompted the General Assembly and Security Council to endorse a new doctrine known as "Responsibility to Protect," which would authorize humanitarian intervention in certain limited circumstances in the future.[59]

Finally, the systematic terrorist attacks against the World Trade Center and Pentagon on September 11, 2001, and the international community's reactions to those attacks, have had a profound impact on the global order[60] and "shattering consequences for international law."[61] Whereas the ICJ had previously opined in the 1986 *Nicaragua* case that states

[56] Manfred Lachs, *The Law of Outer Space: An Experience in Contemporary Law-Making* 138 (Leiden: Sijthoff, 1972).
[57] Richard A. Falk, "Kosovo, World Order, and the Future of International Law," *American Journal of International Law* 93 (1999): 850 ("In the months before the war, China and Russia appeared ready to veto any call for UN intervention, as well as any mandate that conferred upon NATO or any other entity such a right.").
[58] See, for example, The Independent International Commission on Kosovo, *The Kosovo Report* (New York: Oxford University Press, 2000): 4.
[59] Report of the International Commission on Intervention and State Sovereignty, The Responsibility to Protect (2001). Available at http://www.iciss-ciise.gc.ca/report2-en .asp; General Assembly Resolution A/60/L.1, World Summit Outcome Document, September 15, 2005 (world's Heads of State unanimously affirmed the Responsibility to Protect Doctrine); Security Council Resolution 1674, 28 April 2006 (reaffirms the provisions of paragraphs 138 and 139 of the 2005 World Summit Outcome Document regarding the responsibility to protect populations from genocide, war crimes, ethnic cleansing, and crimes against humanity).
[60] In the words of then–British Foreign Secretary Jack Straw, "Few events in global history can have galvanized the international system to action so completely in so short a time." British Foreign Secretary Jack Straw, *Order out of Chaos: The Future of Afghanistan, Address at the International Institute of Strategic Studies* (October 22, 2001), quoted in Anne-Marie Slaughter and William Burke-White, "An International Constitutional Moment," *Harvard International Law Journal* 43 (2002): 1, 2.
[61] Antonio Cassese, "Terrorism Is Also Disrupting Some Crucial Legal Categories of International Law," *European Journal of International Law* 12 (2001): 993.

could not resort to force in response to attacks by nonstate actors operating in other states,[62] a few days after the September 11 attacks, the UN Security Council adopted Resolution 1368, which was widely viewed as confirming the right to use force in self-defense against al-Qaeda in Afghanistan,[63] and there was little international protest when the United States invaded Afghanistan shortly thereafter. Invoking the term "constitutional moment" to describe these developments, Professor Ian Johnstone concludes that "in contrast to where the law stood in 1986...it is a fair inference today that self-defense may be invoked against nonstate actors."[64]

Commentators and courts should exercise caution, however, in characterizing situations as Grotian Moments. As one scholar has warned, "[i]t is always easy, at times of great international turmoil, to spot a turning point that is not there."[65] In this vein, the example of outer space principles might be discounted because the international community concluded a binding treaty on principles governing the activities of states in outer space in 1967, which has largely supplanted the 1963 UN Declaration of Legal Principles Governing the Activities of States in

---

[62] Military and Paramilitary Activities in and against Nicaragua (*Nicaragua v. US*) (Merits) [1986] ICJ Rep 14. The ICJ ruled that U.S. support for the Contras infringed on Nicaragua's territorial sovereignty in contravention of international law but concluded that the evidence did not demonstrate that the United States "actually exercised such a degree of control in all fields as to justify treating the contras as acting on its behalf."

[63] UN SCOR, 56th session, 4370th meeting, UN Doc. S/RES/1368 (2001). The resolution unequivocally condemns the terrorist attacks of September 11, 2001, calls on all states to "work together urgently to bring to justice the perpetrators, organizers and sponsors" of the attacks, and reaffirms the inherent right of self-defense in accordance with Article 51 of the UN Charter in the context of the September 11 terrorist attacks. Resolution 1378, adopted by the Security Council after the U.S. invasion, "condemn[ed] the Taliban for allowing Afghanistan to be used as a base for the export of terrorism by the Al-Qaeda network and other terrorist groups and for providing safe haven to Osama bin Laden, Al-Qaeda and others associated with them, and in this context support[ed] the efforts of the Afghan people to replace the Taliban regime." The resolution further endorsed U.S. efforts to set up a post-Taliban government in Afghanistan. UN SCOR, 56th session, 4415th meeting, UN Doc. S/RES/1378 (2001).

[64] Ian Johnstone, "The Plea of 'Necessity' in International Legal Discourse," 337. ICJ Judge Bruno Simma similarly concluded in his separate opinion in the 2005 *Armed Activities on the Territory of the Congo* case that "Security Council resolutions 1368 (2001) and 1373 (2001) cannot but be read as affirmations of the view that large-scale attacks by non-State actors can qualify as 'armed attacks' within the meaning of Article 51." Armed Activities on the Territory of the Congo (*Dem. Rep. Congo v. Uganda*), 45 I.L.M. 271, 308–09, Dec. 19, 2005 (DRC v. Uganda), separate opinion of Judge Simma, at para. 11.

[65] Ibrahim J. Gassama, "International Law at a Grotian Moment: The Invasion of Iraq in Context," *Emory Law Review* 18 (2004): 1, 30.

the Exploration and Use of Outer Space in the regulation of outer space activities.[66] The meaning of the "responsibility to protect" doctrine, in turn, is still under debate, and the doctrine has not yet been employed by the international community in a situation in which UN approval for the use of force was absent.[67] Finally, with respect to the right to use force in self-defense against nonstate actors, the ICJ has put the brakes on recognition of such a rule through its 2004 Advisory Opinion in the *Legal Consequences of the Construction of a Wall*[68] and its 2005 judgment in the *Armed Activities on the Territory of the Congo* case.[69] As established in the next section, Nuremberg, in contrast, was a prototypical Grotian Moment.

NUREMBERG AS GROTIAN MOMENT

The events that prompted the formation of the Nuremberg Tribunal in 1945 are probably more familiar to most than those that led to the creation of the modern-day international tribunals (ICTY, ICTR, Special Court for Sierra Leone, ECCC, and International Criminal Court) a half century later. Between 1933 and 1940, the Nazi regime established concentration camps where Jews, Communists, opponents of the regime, and others were incarcerated without trial; it progressively prohibited Jews from engaging in employment and participating in various areas of public life, stripped them of citizenship, and made marriage or sexual intimacy between Jews and German citizens a criminal offense; it forcibly

---

[66] Treaty on Principles Governing the Activities of States in the Exploration and Use of Outer Space, including the Moon and Other Celestial Bodies. Available at http://cns. miis.edu/inventory/pdfs/ospace.pdf.

[67] Carlo Focarelli, "The Responsibility to Protect Doctrine and Humanitarian Intervention: Too Many Ambiguities for a Working Doctrine," *Journal of Conflict and Security Law* 13 (2008): 191–213.

[68] Legal Consequences of the Construction of a Wall in the Occupied Palestinian Territory, Advisory Opinion, 2004 I.C.J. 136 (July 9), at p. 194, opining in dicta that using force under the right of self-defense against nonstate actors in the territory of another state requires evidence that the attack was imputable to that state.

[69] Armed Activities on the Territory of the Congo (*Dem. Rep. Congo v. Uganda*), 45 I.L.M. 271, 308–9, December 19, 2005 (*DRC v. Uganda*), at paras. 143–47, holding that Uganda could not rely on self-defense to justify its military operation in the Congo because (1) Uganda did not immediately report to the Security Council following its use of force as required by Article 51, (2) Uganda's actions were disproportionate to the threat, and (3) there was no evidence from which to impute the attacks against Ugandan villages by rebel groups operating out of the Congo to the government of Congo.

annexed Austria and Czechoslovakia; it invaded and occupied Poland, Denmark, Norway, Luxembourg, Holland, Belgium, and France; and then it set in motion "the final solution to the Jewish problem" by establishing death camps such as Auschwitz and Treblinka, where six million Jews were exterminated.[70]

As Allied forces pressed into Germany and an end to the fighting in Europe came into sight, the Allied powers faced the challenge of deciding what to do with the surviving Nazi leaders who were responsible for these atrocities. Holding an international trial, however, was not their first preference. The British and Soviet governments initially advocated summary execution for the Nazi leaders, but the United States persuaded them to establish jointly the world's first international criminal tribunal for four reasons: first, judicial proceedings would avert future hostilities that would likely result from the execution, absent a trial, of German leaders. Second, legal proceedings would bring German atrocities to the attention of all parts of the world, thereby legitimizing Allied conduct during and after the war. Third, they would individualize guilt by identifying specific perpetrators instead of leaving Germany with a sense of collective guilt. Finally, such a trial would permit the Allied powers, and the world, to exact a penalty from the Nazi leadership rather than from Germany's civilian population.[71]

The charter establishing the Nuremberg Tribunal, its subject matter jurisdiction, and its procedures was negotiated by the United States, France, the United Kingdom, and the Soviet Union from June 26 to August 8, 1945.[72] Nineteen other states signed onto the charter, rendering the Nuremberg Tribunal a truly international judicial institution.[73] The trial of twenty-two high-ranking Nazi leaders commenced on November 20, 1945, and ten months later, on October 1, 1946, the tribunal issued its judgment, convicting nineteen of the defendants and sentencing eleven to death by hanging. The judgment of the Nuremberg Tribunal paved the way for the trial of more than a thousand other German political and

---

[70] Michael P. Scharf, *Balkan Justice: The Story behind the First International War Crimes Trial Since Nuremberg*, (Durham, NC: Carolina Academic Press, 1997): 3–4.

[71] Ibid., p. 5.

[72] London Agreement of August 8, 1945, the Charter of the International Military Tribunal, and the Nuremberg Tribunal's Rules of Procedure are reproduced in Virginia Morris and Michael Scharf, *An Insider's Guide to the International Criminal Tribunal for the Former Yugoslavia* (Boston: Hotei Publishing, 1995), 675–691.

[73] Greece, Denmark, Yugoslavia, the Netherlands, Czechoslovakia, Poland, Belgium, Ethiopia, Australia, Honduras, Norway, Panama, Luxembourg, Haiti, New Zealand, India, Venezuela, Uruguay, and Paraguay.

military officers, businessmen, doctors, and jurists under Control Council Law No. 10 by military tribunals in occupied zones in Germany and in the liberated or Allied Nations.[74]

The United Nations' International Law Commission (ILC) has recognized that the Nuremberg Charter, Control Council Law Number 10, and the post–World War II war crimes trials gave birth to the entire international paradigm of individual criminal responsibility. Before Nuremberg, the only subjects of international law were states, and what a state did to its own citizens within its own borders was its own business. Nuremberg fundamentally altered that conception. "International law now protects individual citizens against abuses of power by their governments [and] imposes individual liability on government officials who commit grave war crimes, genocide, and crimes against humanity."[75] The ILC has described the principle of individual responsibility and punishment for crimes under international law recognized at Nuremberg as the "cornerstone of international criminal law" and the "enduring legacy of the Charter and Judgment of the Nuremberg Tribunal."[76]

Importantly, on 11 December 1946, in one of the first actions of the newly formed United Nations, the U.N. General Assembly unanimously affirmed the principles from the Nuremberg Charter and judgments in Resolution 95(I).[77] This G.A. Resolution had all the attributes of a

---

[74] Michael P. Scharf, *Balkan Justice* (1997), 10.

[75] Anne-Marie Slaughter and William Burke-White, *An International Constitutional Moment*, 13.

[76] See *Report of the International Law Commission on the Work of Its Forty-Eighth Session,* May 6–July 16, 1996, Official Records of the General Assembly, 51st Session, Supplement No. 10, at p. 19. Available at http://www.un.org/law.ilc/index.htm.

[77] Affirmation of the Principles of International Law Recognized by the Charter of the Nuremberg Tribunal, G.A. Res. 95(I), UN GAOR, 1st Sess., UN Doc. A/236, 11 December 1946, pt. 2, at 1144. Available at http://untreaty.un.org/cod/avl/ha/ga_95-I/ga_95-I.html. The resolution states in whole:

> The General Assembly,
>
> Recognizes the obligation laid upon it by Article 13, paragraph 1, sub-paragraph a, of the Charter, to initiate studies and make recommendations for the purpose of encouraging the progressive development of international law and its codification;
>
> Takes note of the Agreement for the establishment of an International Military Tribunal for the prosecution and punishment of the major war criminals of the European Axis signed in London on 8 August 1945, and of the Charter annexed thereto, and of the fact that similar principles have been adopted in the Charter of the International Military Tribunal for the trial of the major war criminals in the Far East, proclaimed at Tokyo on 19 January 1946;

resolution entitled to great weight as a declaration of customary international law: it was labelled an "affirmation" of legal principles; it dealt with inherently legal questions; it was passed by a unanimous vote; and none of the members expressed the position that it was merely a political statement.[78]

The ICJ,[79] the ICTY,[80] the European Court of Human Rights,[81] and several domestic courts[82] have cited the General Assembly Resolution affirming the principles of the Nuremberg Charter and judgments as an authoritative declaration of customary international law. Referring to General Assembly Resolution 95 (I), the Israeli Supreme Court stated in the 1962 *Eichmann* case that "if fifty-eight nations unanimously agree on a statement of existing law, it would seem that such a declaration would be all but conclusive evidence of such a rule, and agreement by a large majority would have great value in determining what is existing law."[83]

> Therefore,
>
> Affirms the principles of international law recognized by the Charter of the Nuremberg Tribunal and the judgment of the Tribunal;
>
> Directs the Committee on the codification of international law established by the resolution of the General Assembly of 11 December 1946, to treat as a matter of primary importance plans for the formulation, in the context of a general codification of offenses against the peace and security of mankind, or of an International Criminal Code, of the principles recognized in the Charter of the Nuremberg Tribunal and in the judgment of the Tribunal.

[78] See supra nn. 48–54 and accompanying text.

[79] *Legal Consequences of the Construction of a Wall in Occupied Palestinian Territory*, Advisory Opinion, 2004 I.C.J. 136, 172 (July 9).

[80] ICTY (*Tadić*, Opinion and Judgment, Trial Chamber, May 7, 1997, para. 623; and *Tadić*, Decision on the Defence Motion for Interlocutory Appeal on Jurisdiction, Appeals Chamber, October 2, 1995, para. 141).

[81] The European Court of Human Rights recognized the "universal validity" of the Nuremberg principles in *Kolk and Kislyiy v. Estonia*, in which it stated: "Although the Nuremberg Tribunal was established for trying the major war criminals of the European Axis countries for the offences they had committed before or during the Second World War, the Court notes that the universal validity of the principles concerning crimes against humanity was subsequently confirmed by, *inter alia*, resolution 95 of the United Nations General Assembly (11 December 1946) and later by the International Law Commission." *Kolk and Kislyiy v. Estonia*, Decision on Admissibility, 17 January 2006.

[82] The General Assembly resolution Affirming the Nuremberg Principles has been cited as evidence of customary international law in cases in Canada, Bosnia, France, and Israel. See *R. v. Finta*, Supreme Court of Canada (1994), 1 S.C.R. 701; *Prosecutor v. Ivica Vrdoljak*, Court of Bosnia and Herzegovina, July 10, 2008; Leila Sadat Wexler, "The Interpretation of the Nuremberg Principles by the French Court of Cassation: From Touvier to Barbie and Back Again," *Columbia Journal of Transnational Law* (1994): 289, summarizing *Touvier* and *Barbie* cases in French courts.

[83] *Attorney-General of Israel v Eichmann*, 36 I.L.R. 277 (29 May 1962) (*hereinafter* Eichmann II), para. 11. The fifty-eight states that signed the General Assembly

Finally, in submitting the draft statute for the ICTY to the Security Council in 1993, the UN Secretary-General emphasized the customary international law status of the principles and rules emanating from the Nuremberg Trial and other post–World War II jurisprudence. Specifically, he stated that the statute had been drafted to apply only the "rules of international humanitarian law which are beyond any doubt part of customary international law," which included the substantive law and modes of liability embodied in "the Charter of the International Military Tribunal of 8 August 1945."[84] Logic dictates that this 1993 statement about the content of customary international law also holds true for the time of the crimes in question before the ECCC (1975–79), as there were no relevant major developments in international humanitarian law between 1975 and the establishment of the ICTY in 1993. As Ciara Damgaard documents, "the origins of the JCE Doctrine can be found in the events surrounding the end of World War II."[85]

Although the Nuremberg Charter and Judgment never specifically mention the term joint criminal enterprise, a close analysis of the Nuremberg Judgment and the holdings of several Control Council Law Number 10[86] cases reveal that the Nuremberg tribunal and its progeny applied a concept analogous to JCE, which they called the "common plan" or "common design" mode of liability. In reaching its conclusion that JCE has existed in customary international law since the Nuremberg judgments, the Appeals Chamber of the Yugoslavia Tribunal in *Tadić* relied in part on ten post–World War II cases – six regarding JCE I,[87] two

Resolution Affirming the Nuremberg Principles constituted all of the members of the United Nations at that time. In the years since then, the United Nations has expanded to include numerous former colonies and other new states and now numbers 192 members.

[84] Report of the Secretary-General Pursuant to Paragraph 2 of Security Council Resolution 808, S/25704, May 3, 1993, paras. 34–35.

[85] Ciara Damgaard, *Individual Criminal Responsibility for Core International Crimes*, (New York: Springer, 2008): 132, 235.

[86] This law was based on the Nuremberg Charter and governed subsequent war crimes trials. Control Council Law Number 10, in *Official Gazette of the Control Council for Germany* (1946), vol. 3, at 50. Because Control Council Law Number 10 sought to "establish a uniform legal basis in Germany for the prosecution of war criminals," Article I of the law explicitly incorporated the Nuremberg Tribunal Charter as an "integral part" of the law. Pursuant to Article I, all the military commissions (U.S., British, Canadian, and Australian) adopted implementing regulations, rendering a defendant responsible under the principle of "concerted criminal action" for the crimes of any other member of that "unit or group." UN War Crimes Commission, *XV Law Reports of Trials of War Criminals* 92 (1949).

[87] *Trial of Otto Sandrock and three others; Hoelzer and others; Gustav Alfred Jepsen and others; Franz Schonfeld and others; Feurstein and others; Otto Ohlenforf and others.* (JCE I requires proof that the perpetrators share a common criminal purpose.)

regarding JCE II,[88] and two regarding JCE III.[89] Most of these cases were published in summary form in the 1949 Report of the UN War Crimes Commission.[90] According to the 1949 UN War Crimes Commission Report's Foreword, the "main object of these Reports [was] to help to elucidate the law, i.e., that part of International Law which has been called the law of war."[91] This authoritative and widely disseminated multivolume account of the trials, in which the war crimes tribunals recognized and applied JCE liability, supports the argument that the Khmer Rouge leaders had sufficient constructive notice in 1975–79 that their mass atrocity crimes would attract criminal responsibility under the JCE doctrine.

CONCLUSION

It was thus the paradigm-shifting nature of the Nuremberg precedent, and the universal and unqualified endorsement of the Nuremberg principles by the nations of the world in 1946, rather than the number of cases applying JCE liability at the time, that crystallized this doctrine into a mode of individual criminal liability under customary international law.[92]

---

[88] *Dachau Concentration Camp Case* (Trial of Martin Gottfied Weiss and thirty-nine others); the *Belsen Case* (Trial of Josef Kramer and forty-four others). (JCE II applies in the setting of concentration camps where all members of the camp's staff are presumed to share a common criminal purpose.)

[89] *Essen Lynching Case*; *Borkum Island Case*. For JCE III, the Appeals Chamber also cited several unpublished Italian decisions.

[90] Notably, the JCE III *Borkum Island Case* was not included in the report of the UN War Crimes Commission, but the charging instrument, transcript, and other documents of the case have been publicly available from the United States Archives. See Publication No. M1103, "Records of United States Army War Crimes Trials," *United States of America v. Goebel*, et al., February 6–March 21, 1946. In addition, a detailed account and analysis of the *Borkum Island Case* was published in 1956 in Maximilian Koessler, *Borkum Island Tragedy and Trial*, 47 *Journal of Criminal Law* 183–96 (1956).

[91] Foreword, *Law Reports of Trials of War Criminals*, XV UNWCC, p. vii (1949). Although the UN War Crimes Commission recognizes that where "there is no reasoned judgment . . . it is difficult in some cases to specify precisely the grounds on which the courts gave their decision," the Commission goes on to state that "[t]he difficulty is, however, to a large extent surmounted in [such cases] by examining carefully the indictment, the speeches of the counsel on both sides and the judgment."

[92] See Frank Lawrence, "The Nuremberg Principles: A Defense for Political Protesters," *Hastings Law Journal* 40 (1989), 397, 408–410, disputing the argument that "more than a single event is necessary for a proposed principle to be considered part of customary international law." In 2006, the European Court of Human Rights recognized the "universal validity" of the Nuremberg principles in *Kolk and Kislyiy v. Estonia*, Decision on Admissibility, January 17, 2006.

The example of the Cambodia Tribunal's use of the Grotian Moment concept in recognizing the validity of JCE demonstrates the value of the concept to explain an acceleration of the custom-formation process and the heightened significance of General Assembly resolutions in response to paradigm-changing events in international law. Although this chapter uses the lens of the Cambodia genocide trial to frame the analysis, it has implications with respect to some of today's most important international legal issues, such as whether there is a right to use force against terrorist groups acting in third States and whether there is a right to resort to humanitarian intervention to halt genocide.

5

Collective Responsibility and Transnational Corporate Conduct

Sara L. Seck

Corporations and other business enterprises are sometimes implicated in conduct that is considered criminally wrongful. At the domestic level, debates over corporate criminal liability often focus on the merits of holding corporations responsible for criminally wrongful conduct, as opposed to, or in addition to, convicting individuals for their role in the commission of corporate crimes. A second debate in the domestic context is over the significance of the distinction, if any, between a criminal and a regulatory offense when it comes to prosecuting and penalizing a legal person such as a business entity. In the international human rights context, however, the debates have focused on a different issue: whether corporations bear direct obligations under international human rights law for wrongful conduct that falls short of violating the egregious norms of international criminal law. This somewhat heated debate was recently settled at the United Nations Human Rights Council with the acceptance by states in June 2008 of the *Framework for Business and Human Rights*[1] developed by the Special Representative to the UN Secretary-General on Business and Human Rights, Professor John Ruggie. Curiously, it is international criminal law's preference for individual responsibility for mass crimes such as genocide that has opened the door to recognition of the legal responsibility of the corporation – a collective – for egregious human

I thank Jennifer Buttkus, Michael Misener, and David Vaughan for their excellent research assistance and the Social Sciences and Humanities Research Council of Canada for financial support.

[1] John G. Ruggie, United Nations Human Rights Council, 8th Session, *Promotion and Protection of All Human Rights, Civil, Political, Economic, Social and Cultural Rights, Including the Right to Development: Protect, Respect and Remedy: A Framework for Business and Human Rights*, UN Doc. A/HRC/8/5 (April 7, 2008).

rights violations, while keeping the legal door closed where less serious human rights violations are concerned.

The *Framework* speaks of the corporate responsibility to respect all human rights as part of a corporation's social license to operate even when not mandated by law. Yet the *Framework* also highlights the state duty to protect rights from harmful conduct by nonstate actors, including business. This suggests that a study of collective responsibility in the business and international human rights law context should consider both the collective responsibility of corporations and the collective responsibility of states. This chapter takes up the challenge. Although I follow Mark Drumbl's definition of collective responsibility as implying "noncriminal sanctions that attach to groups whose misfeasance or nonfeasance is supportive of, acquiescent in, causally connected to, or necessary"[2] for violations to occur, I do not limit the analysis to egregious violations of international human rights law with the status of international criminal law norms.

Although the *Framework* recognizes the fundamental nature of the state duty to protect rights, an unresolved issue is the extent of the jurisdictional scope of the duty for home states of transnational corporations.[3] The *Framework* and subsequent reports of the Special Representative have identified uncertainty surrounding the permissible scope of extraterritorial jurisdiction in the business and human rights context.[4] Indeed, the Special Representative has described extraterritorial jurisdiction as the "elephant in the room" about which "polite people" prefer not talk.[5] Yet, this chapter argues that the real elephant in the room about which

---

[2] Mark Drumbl, "Collective Responsibility and Postconflict Justice," Chapter 1, this volume.

[3] A home state may be defined as a capital-exporting country, whereas a host state may be defined as a capital-importing country. All developed and many developing states are both capital-exporting and capital-importing states. The transnational corporation or multinational enterprise is the usual vehicle through which foreign direct investment flows occur. See Cynthia Day Wallace, *The Multinational Enterprise and Legal Control: Host State Sovereignty in an Era of Economic Globalization*, 2nd ed. (The Hague: Martinus Nijhoff, 2002), 102, 139.

[4] Ruggie, *Framework*, para. 19; John G. Ruggie, United Nations Human Rights Council, 11th Session, *Business and Human Rights: Towards Operationalizing the "Protect, Respect and Remedy" Framework*, UN Doc. A/HRC/11/13 (April 22, 2009): para. 15; John G. Ruggie, United Nations Human Rights Council, 14th Session, *Business and Human Rights: Further Steps Toward the Operationalizing of the "Protect, Respect and Remedy" Framework*, UN Doc. A/HRC/14/27 (April 9, 2010): paras. 46–49.

[5] John G. Ruggie, "Keynote Presentation at EU Presidency Conference on the 'Protect, Respect and Remedy' Framework" (Stockholm, November 10–11, 2009). Available at http://www.reports-and-materials.org/Ruggie-presentation-Stockholm-10-Nov-2009.pdf.

even the Special Representative is unwilling to talk is the imperative to recognize the existence of home-state obligations to exercise jurisdiction to prevent and remedy harm by transnational corporate actors. The significance of this issue is evident in recent debates in Canada over proposed regulation of Canadian extractive industries operating internationally.[6]

Part I outlines the debates in the domestic context over individual and corporate criminal liability and between corporate criminal and civil or regulatory liability. The purpose of this part is both to lay out the conceptual framework for an analysis of collective responsibility and to provide a domestic law comparator for the international human rights law discussion to follow. Part II examines the three interdependent principles of the *Framework*. This part will highlight the intertwined nature of the legal and moral responsibilities in the *Framework*, as well as the uncertainty surrounding the jurisdictional scope of the home-state duty to protect rights. Part III critiques the conceptualization of collective responsibility for home states of transnational corporations under international law. This part proposes that a better understanding of international law would recognize that the state duty to protect human rights must include the responsibility of all states that, as institutional agents,[7] are in a position to exercise agency to prevent and remedy human rights violations by transnational corporations.

COLLECTIVE RESPONSIBILITY OF CORPORATE ENTITIES

Although common law states have embraced differing versions of corporate criminal liability for more than 150 years, most civil law jurisdictions

---

[6] Sara L. Seck, "Home State Responsibility and Local Communities: The Case of Global Mining," *Yale Human Rights and Development Law Journal* 11 (2008): 179–85, describing the history of this issue from 2005 to 2007. For more recent developments, see Canada, Bill C-300, *An Act Respecting Corporate Accountability for the Activities of Mining, Oil or Gas in Developing Countries*, 2nd Sess., 40th Parliament, 2009. Available at http://www2.parl.gc.ca/HousePublications/Publication.aspx?Docid=4330045&file=4. Department of Foreign Affairs and International Trade Canada, *Building the Canadian Advantage: A Corporate Social Responsibility (CSR) Strategy for the Canadian International Extractive Sector*, March, 2009. Available at http://www.international.gc.ca/trade-agreements-accords-commerciaux/ds/csr-strategy-rse-stategie.aspx#8.

[7] The phrase "institutional agents" is drawn from the work of Toni Erskine. See Toni Erskine, "Assigning Responsibilities to Institutional Moral Agents: The Case of States and Quasi-States," *Ethics & International Affairs* 15 (2001): 67–87. See also Michael Green, "Institutional Responsibility for Moral Problems," in *Global Responsibilities: Who Must Deliver on Human Rights?*, ed. Andrew Kuper (New York and London: Routledge, 2005).

have until recently been averse to it.[8] Several civil law jurisdictions in continental Europe still make no provision for criminal liability of corporations (legal persons) in their penal codes,[9] although they do provide for administrative fines when a representative of the corporation committed a criminal offence.[10] Despite increasing convergence of legal systems due to the increased transnational interactions of the global economic order, there is no clear move toward standardization of corporate criminal liability.[11] In fact, some international agreements specifically provide that countries that do not provide for criminal responsibility of legal persons are obligated to ensure that legal persons are subject to "effective, proportionate and dissuasive noncriminal sanctions, including monetary sanctions."[12]

The discomfort with corporate criminal liability is reflected in debates over individual versus corporate criminal liability. Some legal scholars prefer individual over corporate criminal liability on the basis of principle: the theoretical foundations of criminal law presuppose that crimes involve an act and a culpable mental state, yet neither culpable acts nor culpable mental states can be attributed to a corporation because it is a mere legal fiction.[13] A related principled argument against corporate criminal liability is that only individuals can possess the moral blameworthiness necessary to commit crimes of intent.[14] Finally, it is argued that crime is

---

[8] Celia Wells, *Corporations and Criminal Responsibility*, 2nd ed. (Oxford: Oxford University Press, 2001), 127, 138. See generally Celia Wells, "Comparative and International Solutions," Chapter 7 in *Corporations and Criminal Responsibility* (see n. 4).

[9] Thomas Weigend, "*Societas delinquere non potest?* A German Perspective," *Journal of International Criminal Justice* 6 (2008): 928.

[10] Ibid., 930–31; Wells, *Corporations and Criminal Responsibility*, 138–40; V. S. Khanna, "Corporate Criminal Liability: What Purpose Does It Serve?," *Harvard Law Review* 109 (1996): 1490–91.

[11] Wells, *Corporations and Criminal Responsibility*, 140–41.

[12] Ibid., 143, citing as an example Article 3(2) of the *OECD Convention on Combating Bribery of Foreign Public Officials in International Transactions* (1997, in force 1999).

[13] Vincent Todarello, "Corporations Don't Kill People – People Do: Exploring the Goals of the United Kingdom's Corporate Homicide Bill," *New York Law School Journal of Human Rights* 19 (2003): 486; Weigend, "*Societas delinquere non potest?*," 937; Khanna, "Corporate Criminal Liability," 1479. This position is rooted in the philosophical position known as methodological individualism. See Brent Fisse and John Braithwaite, *Corporations, Crime and Accountability* (New York: Cambridge University Press, 1993), 19–31; Brent Fisse and John Braithwaite, "The Allocation of Responsibility for Corporate Crime: Individualism, Collectivism and Accountability," *Sydney Law Review* 11 (1988): 475–88. See also Larry May, "Vicarious Agency and Corporate Responsibility," *Philosophical Studies* 43 (1983): 69–82.

[14] Khanna, "Corporate Criminal Liability," 1479–80; Weigend, "*Societas delinquere non potest?*," 938. See especially Susan Wolf, "The Legal and Moral Responsibility of

necessarily an *ultra vires* act of a corporation; liability cannot be imputed to a corporation because a corporation cannot be legally formed for the purposes of committing a crime.[15]

Practical reasons relating to effectiveness are also put forward by legal scholars who prefer individual criminal liability. Deterrence, retribution, and rehabilitation are frequent justifications for criminal punishment, yet because corporate punishment most often involves the imposition of a fine, none of these justifications may be met.[16] In theory, fines should confiscate any and all illegal profits generated by the offense; include compensation for victims and the costs to repair damage attributable to the offense; and punish and deter future violations by the offender and other similarly situated companies.[17] In practice, fines are often too low to have any deterrent effect,[18] whether general (deterring other corporations from committing the same crime) or specific (deterring the corporation in question from reoffending).[19] Deterrence also presumes that a diligent principal can control the behavior of corporate agents, yet fear of individual criminal liability may do a better job.[20] Retribution, historically downplayed in the corporate context, is also difficult to reconcile with differential fines imposed for identical offences, otherwise justified on the grounds of special deterrence when corporations are of different sizes.[21] Retributive effect is reduced as the impact of corporate punishment is dispersed across a broad section of society, including employees, shareholders, and consumers.[22]

Organisations," in *Criminal Justice: Nomos XXVII*, ed. Roland Pennock and John Chapman (New York: New York University Press, 1985).

[15] Todarello, "Corporations Don't Kill People," 486; Khanna, "Corporate Criminal Liability," 1480.

[16] Todarello, "Corporations Don't Kill People," 484; Weigend, "*Societas delinquere non potest?*," 941; Bruce Welling, *Corporate Law in Canada: The Governing Principles*, 3rd ed. (Mudgeeraba, Australia: Scribblers Publishing, 2006), 172.

[17] James Gobert and Maurice Punch, *Rethinking Corporate Crime* (London: Butterworths LexisNexis, 2003), 232.

[18] Ibid., 215. See John Coffee, "No Soul to Damn: No Body to Kick: An Unscandalized Inquiry into the Problem of Corporate Punishment," *Michigan Law Review* 79 (1981): 390–91, discussing the "deterrence trap."

[19] Gobert and Punch, *Rethinking Corporate Crime*, 217–20.

[20] Howard E. O'Leary, Jr., "Corporate Criminal Liability: Sensible Jurisprudence or Kafkaesque Absurdity?," *Criminal Justice* 22 (2008): 27–28; Khanna, "Corporate Criminal Liability," 1494–95.

[21] Gobert & Punch, *Rethinking Corporate Crime*, 219, 229.

[22] O'Leary, "Corporate Criminal Liability," 28; Todarello, "Corporations Don't Kill People," 493. Todarello makes this argument with respect to a reduction in deterrent effect. On punishment and externalities, see Coffee, "No Soul to Damn," 401.

Another problem with fines as punishment is evident if attention is given to theories of rehabilitation that suggest that education and denunciation are important in the corporate context because of the importance of both corporate culture and corporate reputation in the public eye.[23] Fines do not promote the structural reforms and systemic change necessary for rehabilitation.[24] Moreover, they fail to convey the message that serious corporate offenses are socially intolerable, instead converting corporate criminality from a wrong against society into a cost of doing business.[25] To overcome the practical problems with fines, some scholars suggest that other types of punishments should be used more frequently or in conjunction with fines, including community service orders, remedial orders, reputation-oriented sanctions such as adverse publicity orders or advertising bans, and restraint-oriented sanctions including the ultimate sanction of forced liquidation or corporate capital punishment.[26]

Principled and practical arguments are also put forward in support of corporate criminal liability. Practically, because of the difficulties that arise in punishing responsible individuals, the law may impose corporate criminal liability to spur companies to undertake internal disciplinary action and impose individual accountability (private policing).[27] Some scholars note that civil liability (as opposed to criminal liability) is insufficient and particularly unlikely to deter corporate criminality where the cost of harm exceeds the damages that are likely to be imposed on the corporation. The stigma and censure that accompany a criminal conviction are more effective as deterrents than the costs of civil liability or reaching a settlement.[28] In principled terms, scholars point to the collective nature of the corporation as supporting its capacity for moral action. Following an organic model, the corporation is more than a collection of individuals, creating an entity that is different from the sum

---

[23] Gobert and Punch, *Rethinking Corporate Crime*, 220; but see Khanna, "Corporate Criminal Liability," 1497–99, suggesting that cash fines are normally optimal.

[24] Gobert and Punch, *Rethinking Corporate Crime*, 215.

[25] Ibid., 233; Wells, *Corporations and Criminal Responsibility*, 36–37.

[26] Gobert and Punch, *Rethinking Corporate Crime*, 233–45. See also equity fine proposal and adverse publicity discussion in Coffee, "No Soul to Damn," 413–34.

[27] Fisse and Braithwaite, "Responsibility for Corporate Crime," 511. This "enforced accountability" paradigm has a deterrence aim. Coffee, "No Soul to Damn," 387, suggesting that law enforcement officials can achieve economies of scale by targeting both individuals and the firm.

[28] Gobert and Punch, *Rethinking Corporate Crime*, 51–52; see also Khanna, "Corporate Criminal Liability," 1497–1512, on sanctioning characteristics; Fisse and Braithwaite, "Responsibility for Corporate Crime," 512. Shaming of individuals by corporations is more effective than sentences imposed by the state.

of its parts.[29] A corporation is a conglomerate with internal decision-making procedures, unlike an aggregate, which is merely a collection of people.[30] Conglomerates can be described by flowcharts of responsibility and possess policies, operating procedures, and practices that evidence corporate aims, intentions, and knowledge and that are not reducible to individuals within the conglomerate.[31] The organizational flowchart is not itself responsible for corporate actions, but it represents the corporate "mind" and thus a "special kind of intentionality, namely corporate policy."[32]

In practice, the organizational flowchart of the corporate mind is highly significant in the application of corporate criminal liability. This is evident if consideration is given to the exercise of prosecutorial discretion and sentencing considerations. Whether the attribution of conduct to a corporation is based on the principle of *respondeat superior* as in the United States[33] or a variation of the identification doctrine as in the United Kingdom[34] and Canada,[35] for example, the existence of an effective compliance program may be used as a counter-indication to prosecution or as a mitigating factor in sentencing.[36] The organizational flowchart is

---

[29] Wells, *Corporations and Criminal Responsibility*, 75–80; Gobert and Punch, *Rethinking Corporate Crime*, 49.

[30] Wells, *Corporations and Criminal Responsibility*, 78–80. See especially Peter French, *Collective and Corporate Responsibility* (New York: Columbia University Press, 1984); and Fisse and Braithwaite, "Responsibility for Corporate Crime," 483–90. See also discussion in Erskine, "States and Quasi-States," 70–72; and Steven Ratner, "Corporations and Human Rights: A Theory of Legal Responsibility," *Yale Law Journal* 111 (2001): 473–75.

[31] Wells, *Corporations and Criminal Responsibility*, 79–80.

[32] Fisse and Braithwaite, "Responsibility for Corporate Crime," 483.

[33] Khanna, "Corporate Criminal Liability," 1490–94; Wells, *Corporations and Criminal Responsibility*, 131–36.

[34] Celia Wells, "Corporate Liability in England and Wales," chapter 5 in *Corporations and Criminal Responsibility* (see n. 4).

[35] Todd L. Archibald, Kenneth E. Jull, and Kent W. Roach, "The Changing Face of Corporate and Organizational Criminal Liability," chapter 5 in *Regulatory and Corporate Liability: From Due Diligence to Risk Management* (Aurora, Canada: Canada Law Book, 2005).

[36] Wells, *Corporations and Criminal Responsibility*, 136; Archibald, Jull, and Roach, *Regulatory and Corporate Liability*, 12–20. This observation is based in part on research conducted by the author in the late 1990s comparing the exercise of prosecutorial discretion and sentencing considerations in corporate criminal liability prosecutions in Canada, the United States, Australia, and the United Kingdom. This suggests that even when legal responsibility is ostensibly based on a form of vicarious responsibility, the notion that the collectivity is itself the agent remains important. See also Erskine, "States and Quasi-States," 70; Toni Erskine, "Kicking Bodies and Damning Souls: The Danger

also sometimes explicitly acknowledged in offense provisions. For example, the Australian Criminal Code Act 1995 recognizes that the fault element may be attributed to the corporation on the basis of "corporate culture."[37] Moreover, if civil or "regulatory" offenses are considered as well as "true crimes," recognition of the organizational mind is evident in "due diligence" defenses that often accompany strict liability or hybrid offences.[38] What all these examples have in common is the emphasis on encouraging corporations to adopt and implement policies and programs that will prevent future problems, rather than punishing business enterprises for wrongful past conduct. To be sure, if the corporate entity has not introduced an effective compliance policy or if senior management has participated in or condoned criminal conduct, no defense or mitigation will be available. This may be the exceptional case, however, rather than the rule.

Despite the potential significance of the stigma associated with a criminal conviction, the distinction between corporate criminal offenses and corporate civil or regulatory offences is not self-evident, and the two have more in common than is sometimes supposed.[39] According to some scholars, what the distinction reflects most clearly is the social construction of crime and the relative valuing of behavior by society: "more serious" behavior attracts the criminal sanction.[40] Yet, different jurisdictions may decide that certain corporate conduct should be subject to criminal

of Harming 'Innocent' Individuals while Punishing 'Delinquent' States," Chapter 10, this volume; David Luban, "State Criminality and the Ambition of International Criminal Law," Chapter 2, this volume.

[37] *Criminal Code Act 1995*, (Cth.), s.12.3(c) and (d); Wells, *Corporations and Criminal Responsibility*, 137; see John C. Coffee, "Corporate Criminal Liability: An Introduction and Comparative Survey," in *Criminal Responsibility of Legal and Collective Entities*, eds. Albin Eser, Günter Heine, and Barbara Huber (Freiburg: Ius crim, 1999).

[38] By strict liability, I am referring to the Canadian terminology, which includes a due diligence defense, unlike strict liability in the United Kingdom for which there is no defense, and is known in Canada as absolute liability. See generally Archibald, Jull, and Roach, "Evolution and Classification of Offences," chapter 2 in *Regulatory and Corporate Liability* (see n. 31): 5:40:40 – 5:40:50 and 6:20:10 – 6:20:20; Wells, *Corporations and Criminal Responsibility*, 101–3. Discussing hybrid offenses that incorporate a due diligence defense.

[39] Wells, *Corporations and Criminal Responsibility*, 21–22; Coffee, "No Soul to Damn," 424, 447–48. See also Khanna, "Corporate Criminal Liability," arguing that corporate criminal liability no longer serves a useful purpose. However, see Archibald, Jull, and Roach, *Regulatory and Corporate Liabiliy*, 14:20, indicating support for the distinction between regulatory and criminal liability.

[40] Wells, *Corporations and Criminal Responsibility*, 23.

sanction, although the same conduct is subject to regulatory prosecution in another very similar jurisdiction.[41] Indeed, domestic legislation increasingly provides for both: thus, a corporation may be charged for committing a true crime and committing a regulatory offense in relation to the same event.[42] This may be attributed to the persuasiveness of the idea of a regulatory enforcement pyramid developed by John Braithwaite and Ian Ayres, with the base of the pyramid representing action designed to coax compliance by persuasion, gradually moving up the pyramid to civil monetary penalties, criminal prosecution, and, ultimately, at the tip, permanent revocation of the licence to operate.[43]

As Steven Ratner points out, many scholars whose work has focused on determining "what societies might legitimately expect from corporations as a basis for holding them responsible" have built on the philosophical work of Robert Goodin, who "rejects a concept of responsibility that is centered on blame," instead emphasizing "the actors' responsibility for different tasks and their ex ante duties to ensure that certain harms do not happen."[44] Consequently, the distinction between civil responsibility and criminal responsibility is less significant.[45] Interestingly, the difference between an international crime and an international delict under the international law of state responsibility has also been somewhat controversial.[46] If lessons from domestic law were to inform international human rights law in relation to business conduct, it is arguable

---

[41] For example, in research conducted by the author in the late 1990s, price fixing was considered a criminal offense in Canada, a regulatory offense in Australia, and was subject to prosecution in the United States as either a crime or a regulatory offence (or both). See also Weigend, "*Societas delinquere non potest?*," 942, noting that whether a sanction is regarded as criminal differs from jurisdiction to jurisdiction.

[42] See Coffee, "No Soul to Damn," 434–35; Wells, *Corporations and Criminal Responsibility*, 5; Archibald, Jull, and Roach, *Regulatory and Corporate Liability*, 6:20. It is generally easier to convict of a regulatory offense than a true crime. Archibald, Jull, and Roach, *Regulatory and Corporate Liability*, 6:20; Khanna, *Corporate Criminal Liability*, 1492, 1512–20.

[43] Ian Ayres and John Braithwaite, *Responsive Regulation: Transcending the Deregulation Debate* (New York: Oxford University Press, 1992), 35–36, 39. See also Archibald, Jull, and Roach, "Responsive Regulation, Restorative Justice and Regulatory Pyramids," chapter 14 in *Regulatory and Corporate Liability* (see n. 31); John Braithwaite, *Restorative Justice and Responsive Regulation* (New York: Oxford University Press, 2002).

[44] Ratner, "Corporations and Human Rights," 474–75. See Robert E. Goodin, "Apportioning Responsibilities," *Law & Philosophy* 6 (1987): 181–83.

[45] Ratner, "Corporations and Human Rights," 474–75.

[46] Anthony Lang, "Punishing Genocide: A Critical Reading of the International Court of Justice," Chapter 3, this volume.

that the types of global governance tools engaged in the international realm should include both corporate criminal punishment and regulatory tools designed to focus on the prevention of harm. Moreover, if the conglomerate collectivity model of the corporation is applied to states as suggested by Erskine,[47] then international law should support notions of collective responsibility not only of corporate actors but also of state institutional agents.

THE 2008 FRAMEWORK FOR BUSINESS AND HUMAN RIGHTS

In 2005, the United Nations Human Rights Commission (now Council) appointed Harvard Professor John Gerard Ruggie as the Special Representative to the UN Secretary-General on the issue of human rights and transnational corporations and other business enterprises (SRSG).[48] His appointment followed the divisive controversy surrounding the draft *Norms on the Responsibilities of Transnational Corporations and Other Business Enterprises with regard to Human Rights*,[49] which were produced by the Sub-Commission on the Promotion and Protection of Human Rights in 2003.[50] In 2004, the UN Human Rights Commission rejected the *Norms*, describing them as a draft proposal of no legal standing that contained useful elements and ideas. According to the SRSG, his appointment was designed to move beyond the stalemate produced by the *Norms*.[51]

The SRSG's 2005 mandate included the need to "identify and clarify standards of corporate responsibility and accountability with regard to human rights," and to "elaborate on the role of states in effectively regulating and adjudicating business conduct with regard to human rights,

---

[47] Erskine, "States and Quasi-States," 70–72.

[48] John Gerard Ruggie, "Current Developments: Business and Human Rights: The Evolving International Agenda," *American Journal of International Law* 101 (2007): 821.

[49] The United Nations Sub-Commission on the Promotion and Protection of Human Rights, Doc. E/CN.4/Sub.2/2003/12/Rev.2 (August 26, 2003).

[50] David Weissbrodt and Muria Kruger, "Norms on the Responsibilities of Transnational Corporations and Other Business Enterprises with Regard to Human Rights," *American Journal of International Law* 97 (2003); David Kinley and Junko Tadaki, "From Talk to Walk: The Emergence of Human Rights Responsibilities for Corporations at International Law," *Virginia Journal of International Law* 44 (2004).

[51] John G. Ruggie, United Nations Commission on Human Rights, 62nd Session, *Promotion and Protection of Human Rights: Interim Report of the Special Representative of the Secretary-General on the Issue of Human Rights and Transnational Corporations and Other Business Enterprises*, UN Doc. E/CN.4/2006/97 (February 22, 2006): para. 55.

including through international cooperation."[52] The SRSG responded
with reports to the UN Human Rights Council in 2006 and 2007.[53]
Of note in the Ruggie 2007 report, *Mapping International Standards*,
is the SRSG's explicit recognition of the existence of direct legal obligations for business under international criminal law, despite the lack of an
international forum to hear these claims.[54] Corporate responsibility for
international crimes is the direct result of the "expansion and refinement
of individual responsibility by the international ad hoc criminal tribunals
and the ICC statute," combined with developments in domestic law.[55]
Because international criminal law can be enforced by domestic courts
where implementing legislation exists, it can be enforced against corporations in domestic jurisdictions that incorporate corporate criminal
liability.[56] Corporate entities may also be held liable civilly for violations
of international criminal law norms, as evident in the cases brought in U.S.
courts under the *Alien Tort Claims Act*.[57] However, enforcement of international criminal law in domestic courts may require a state to exercise
extraterritorial jurisdiction, particularly if enforcement is directed against
corporations that are not nationals of the enforcing state.[58] This type of
enforcement is usually justified in the context of international crimes as
an exercise of universal jurisdiction.[59] However, *Mapping International*

[52] Ibid., para. 1.

[53] Ibid.; and John G. Ruggie, United Nations Human Rights Council, 4th Session, *Business and Human Rights: Mapping International Standards of Responsibility and Account-ability for Corporate Acts*, UN Doc. A/HRC/4/35 (February 19, 2007).

[54] Ruggie, *Mapping International Standards*, paras. 21, 19–32. Notably, whereas the preparatory committee and the Rome conference on the establishment of the Inter-national Criminal Court debated a proposal that would have given the ICC jurisdiction over legal persons including corporations, no such provision was adopted because of differences in national approaches. Ibid., para. 21.

[55] Ibid., para. 22.

[56] Ibid., para. 24. Citing a survey of sixteen countries from a cross-section of regions and legal systems. See Anita Ramasastry and Robert C. Thompson, *Commerce, Crime and Conflict: Legal Remedies for Private Sector Liability for Grave Breaches of International Law – Executive Summary* (2006). Available at http://www.fafo.no/liabilities [hereafter *FAFO Survey*]. Of the 16, 11 were parties to the ICC and 9 had fully incorporated the three crimes of the Rome Statute; of these, 6 already provided for corporate criminal liability.

[57] Ruggie, *Mapping International Standards*, para. 27. Many of these concern allegations of complicity in the commission of a mass atrocity by "public or private security forces, other government agents, or armed factions in civil conflicts." Ibid., para. 30.

[58] Ibid., paras. 25, 29.

[59] Ibid., para. 25. See also *FAFO Survey*, which calculated that 11 jurisdictions adopted nationality jurisdiction, 5 universal jurisdiction, several both, and 9 also provided for some form of corporate criminal liability.

Standards also explicitly acknowledges that international law does not (yet) recognize direct legal obligations for business for violations of less egregious international human rights law norms. This is because there is no similar "observable evidence" of "national acceptance of international standards for individual responsibility" for other human rights violations.[60]

In June 2008, the SRSG presented the *Framework for Business and Human Rights*[61] to the UN Human Rights Council consisting of "differentiated but complementary responsibilities."[62] The *Framework* received unanimous approval from member states of the UN Human Rights Council, and the SRSG was given a renewed three-year mandate to build on and promote the *Framework* and to provide guidance for states, businesses, and other social actors on each of its three principles.[63] Despite the clear distinction in the Ruggie *2007* report between corporate obligations under international criminal law and in relation to other less egregious human rights norms, the *Framework* is aimed at all human rights. This is evident from its title, which speaks of "Promotion and Protection of All Human Rights, Civil, Political, Economic, Social and Cultural Rights, Including the Right to Development," and from specific discussion of the scope of the corporate responsibility to respect rights.[64] The *Framework* is also explicitly designed to "assist all social actors – governments, companies, and civil society – to reduce the adverse human rights consequences of "institutional misalignments."[65] The SRSG emphasizes that "there is no silver bullet," and everyone must learn to do many things differently.[66] The "root cause" of the business and human rights predicament today, according to the SRSG, lies in "governance gaps created by globalization – between the scope and impact of economic forces and actors, and the capacity of societies to manage their adverse consequences."[67]

The *Framework* consists of three core principles. The first and most fundamental is the state duty to protect against human rights abuses by nonstate actors, including business.[68] The second is the corporate responsibility to respect human rights,[69] and the third, the need for more effective access to remedy.[70] At first glance, the *Framework* appears to

---

[60] Ibid., para. 33 and generally paras. 33–44.
[61] Ruggie, *Framework*.
[62] Ibid., para. 9.
[63] Ruggie, *Towards Operationalizing*, para. 1.
[64] Ruggie, *Framework*, paras. 24, 52.
[65] Ibid., para. 17.
[66] Ibid., para. 7.
[67] Ibid., para. 3.
[68] Ibid., paras. 9, 27–50.
[69] Ibid., paras. 9, 51–81.
[70] Ibid., paras. 9, 82–103.

distinguish between the legal obligations of states under international human rights law (duty to protect) and the moral obligations of corporations (responsibility to respect) which legal pluralists might view as law, and business scholars might describe as corporate social responsibility. In fact, a legal/moral/pluralist mix of collective responsibilities appears throughout the *Framework*.[71]

The *Framework* describes the state duty to protect as having both legal and policy dimensions. From a legal perspective, "international law provides that states have a duty to protect against human rights abuses by non-state actors, including by business, affecting persons within their territory or jurisdiction."[72] International human rights treaty monitoring bodies "generally recommend that states take all necessary steps to protect against such abuse, including to prevent, investigate, and punish the abuse, and to provide access to redress."[73] Regulation and adjudication of nonstate actors are considered "appropriate" for the implementation of the state duty to protect, although states retain discretion as to exactly what measures to implement.[74]

Significantly, the precise jurisdictional scope of the state duty to protect is disputed, in particular as it concerns home states. According to the SRSG:

> Experts disagree on whether international law requires home States to help prevent human rights abuses abroad by corporations based within their territory. There is greater consensus that those States are not prohibited from doing so where a recognized basis of jurisdiction exists, and the actions of the home State meet an overall reasonableness test, which includes non-intervention in the internal affairs of other States. Indeed, there is increasing encouragement at the international level, including from the treaty bodies, for home States to take regulatory action to prevent abuse by their companies overseas.[75]

Although further refinements of the legal understanding of the state duty to protect by authoritative bodies at national and international levels are

---

[71] Notably, although Ruggie carefully distinguishes the corporate responsibility to respect from what is required by law, it is not clear that he considers it to be synonymous with a moral duty. Ruggie, *Towards Operationalizing*, para. 65.

[72] Ruggie, *Framework*, para. 18.

[73] Ibid. See further Ruggie, *Towards Operationalizing*, para. 14, noting that the state duty to protect is a standard of conduct, not a standard of result.

[74] Ibid.

[75] Ibid., para. 19. See further Ruggie, *Further Steps*, paras. 46–50, highlighting the importance of better understanding the acceptable scope of extraterritorial jurisdiction in the business and human rights context.

highly desirable, the *Framework* notes that at the same time, the policy dimensions of the state duty to protect "even within existing legal principles," require "increased attention and more imaginative approaches."[76] Accordingly, the *Framework* proposes that the question of how to foster a corporate culture respectful of human rights both at home and abroad should be an urgent policy priority of governments.[77] The *Framework* proposes four preliminary avenues to explore.

First, state governments can foster a corporate culture respectful of human rights by supporting and strengthening market pressures on companies to respect rights.[78] This might involve mandating sustainability reporting as part of stock-exchange listing requirements, redefining fiduciary duties in corporate law statutes so that companies owe duties to a broader range of stakeholders, and facilitating the consideration of shareholder proposals regarding human rights issues.[79] Governments could also redefine criminal accountability to reflect corporate culture in liability, sentencing, or prosecutorial discretion.[80] However, the SRSG implicitly suggests that fostering a corporate culture respectful of human rights is not part of current state obligations under international law, at least unless the business entity is a state-owned enterprise (SOE).[81] In this case, the SRSG notes that the state may be responsible for internationally wrongful conduct of the SOE if the SOE is an organ or agent of the state. Yet, even in the absence of legal obligation, states may experience reputational harm caused by SOEs, including the human rights impacts of investments by sovereign wealth funds.[82]

Second, the *Framework* suggests that changes need to be made to government policy alignment. At present, governments take on human rights commitments without regard to implementation (vertical incoherence), and government departments such as trade, investment promotion, development and foreign affairs work at cross-purposes with state agencies charged with implementing the state's human rights obligations (horizontal incoherence).[83] For example, bilateral investment treaties and

---

[76] Ibid., para. 21.   [77] Ibid., para. 27.
[78] Ibid., para. 30. See also Ruggie, *Further Steps*, paras. 33–43, identifying four policy tools that could address the systemic challenge of fostering rights-respecting corporate cultures and practices: "CSR policies, report requirements, directors' duties, and legal provisions specifically recognizing the concept of 'corporate culture.'"
[79] Ibid.   [80] Ibid., para. 31.
[81] Ibid., para. 32.
[82] Ibid. See also Ruggie, *Further Steps*, paras. 26–27, for similar comments but in the context of discussion of the state duty to protect when doing business with business.
[83] Ibid., para. 33.

host government agreements do not take into account the host government's duty to protect human rights because regulatory "freeze" provisions are routinely implemented in developing countries that are most in need of regulatory development.[84] Home-state export credit agencies (ECAs) finance or guarantee exports and investments in regions that are too risky for the private sector alone, yet few explicitly consider human rights.[85] This is despite the existence of a "strong nexus" between ECAs and the home state, which perform a public function mandated by the state.[86] Yet, again, the SRSG falls short of suggesting that ECAs are obligated under international law to "perform adequate due diligence on their potential human rights impacts," suggesting only that a "strong case" can be made for this on "policy grounds alone."[87]

Third, the SRSG highlights the need for more effective guidance and support for state policy coherence at the international level.[88] This includes recommendations and contributions to capacity building by international human rights mechanisms, as well as information sharing and capacity building between states.[89] Yet again, although the SRSG recommends partnerships between states with the "relevant knowledge and experience" and those who "lack the technical or financial resources to effectively regulate companies," particularly between home and host states, the SRSG does not suggest that international law obligates states to engage in this type of cooperation.[90]

Finally, the SRSG makes policy recommendations in relation to corporate conduct in conflict zones, where the "most egregious of human rights abuses" occur.[91] For example, the home state "could identify indicators to trigger alerts with respect to companies in conflict zones" and "could" then "facilitate access to information and advice" to help businesses address the "heightened human rights risks."[92] There may also be "a point at which the home state would withdraw its support altogether"

---

[84] Ibid., paras. 34–36. See further Ruggie, *Towards Operationalizing*, paras. 32–33; Ruggie, *Further Steps*, paras. 20–25. Notably, the discussion on this issue in Ruggie, *Further Steps*, is framed to focus on the host state's duty to safeguard its own ability to protect human rights, with no reference to the obligations of the other state party to the bilateral investment treaty.

[85] Ibid., para. 39.   [86] Ibid., para. 39.

[87] Ibid., para. 40. See also Ruggie, *Further Steps*, paras. 29–30, for similar commentary, but noting recent practice by the United States Overseas Private Investment Corporation as a sign of change.

[88] Ibid., para. 43.   [89] Ibid., paras. 43–44.

[90] Ibid., paras. 44–45.   [91] Ibid., para. 47.

[92] Ibid., para. 49.

from a company operating in a conflict zone.[93] However, the suggestions for home states are again not described as legal obligations. Moreover, the SRSG is careful to state that these suggestions would not detract from the host state's (legal) duty to protect against corporate violations of human rights.[94]

Although the state duty to protect is the core responsibility of the *Framework*, the SRSG stresses that active participation of business directly is also essential, and thus the second prong of the *Framework* is the corporate responsibility to respect rights. Because there are "few if any internationally recognized rights business cannot impact – or be perceived to impact – in some manner," companies should consider all rights.[95] The focus of the SRSG is on "identifying the distinctive responsibilities of companies in relation to human rights": "While corporations may be considered 'organs of society,' they are specialized economic organs, not democratic public interest institutions. As such, their responsibilities cannot and should not simply mirror the duties of States."[96]

The *Framework* describes the responsibility to respect rights as follows:

> In addition to compliance with national laws, the baseline responsibility of companies is to respect human rights. Failure to meet this responsibility can subject companies to the courts of public opinion – comprising employees, communities, consumers, civil society, as well as investors – and occasionally to charges in actual courts. Whereas governments define the scope of legal compliance, the broader scope of the responsibility to respect is defined by social expectations – as part of what is sometimes called a company's social licence to operate.[97]

The corporate responsibility to respect exists independently of the state duties, so one is not primary and the other secondary. As a baseline expectation, a company cannot compensate for human rights harms by performing good deeds elsewhere. Moreover, "'doing no harm' is not merely a passive responsibility" but "may entail positive steps," including the adoption of specific policies or programs.[98]

---

[93] Ibid.

[94] Ibid. See also Ruggie, *Further Steps*, paras. 44–45. Noting that Ruggie has convened a group of states to participate in informal discussions on how to address problems in conflict-affected areas, including potential roles for home-country embassies, and closer cooperation between home-state agencies and with host-state agencies.

[95] Ibid., para. 52.   [96] Ibid., para. 53.

[97] Ibid., para. 54. See further Ruggie, *Towards Operationalizing*, paras. 45–85, and Ruggie, *Further Steps*, paras. 54–87, elaborating the corporate responsibility to respect.

[98] Ibid., para. 55.

To discharge the responsibility respect, companies must exercise "due diligence."[99] Due diligence requires a company to take steps to "become aware of, prevent and address adverse human rights impacts."[100] The scope of due diligence will depend on the country context, the type of human rights impacts associated with company activity, and whether the corporation might contribute to human rights abuse through "relationships connected to their activities, such as with business partners, suppliers, State agencies, and other non-State actors."[101] The substance is to be found in international human rights law instruments that embody the "benchmarks against which other social actors judge the human rights impacts of companies."[102] The corporate responsibility to respect rights "includes avoiding complicity" under both international criminal law standards and in nonlegal contexts.[103]

The third and final principle of the *Framework* is effective access to remedy. Effective grievance mechanisms play an important role in both the legal and policy dimensions of the state duty to protect and in the corporate responsibility to respect. State regulation has little impact without the ability to "investigate, punish, and redress abuses," and the corporate responsibility to respect "requires a means for those who believe they have been harmed to bring this to the attention of the company and seek remediation, without prejudice to legal channels available."[104] The solution proposed is a mix of legal and nonlegal grievance mechanisms that together could remedy the current "patchwork of mechanisms" with "different constituencies and processes" that reflect "intended and unintended limitations in competence and coverage."[105] Accordingly, the *Framework* discusses the implementation of grievance remedies in six sections:[106] (1) judicial remedies, including through home-state courts;[107]

---

[99] Ibid., para. 56.

[100] Ibid., para. 56.

[101] Ibid., para. 57.

[102] Ibid., para. 58.

[103] Ibid., paras. 73–81.

[104] Ibid., para. 82. See further Ruggie, *Further Steps*, paras. 96, 103, noting that states have the responsibility within their territory and/or jurisdiction under the state duty to protect to ensure access to remedy through "judicial, administrative, legislative or other appropriate means," including ensuring the "functionality and facilitating access" to judicial mechanisms.

[105] Ibid., paras. 87, 102–3.

[106] Ibid., paras. 88–101.

[107] See further Ruggie, *Towards Operationalizing*, paras. 93–98; Ruggie, *Further Steps*, paras. 103–13. However, the SRSG is clear that international law does not require states to adjudicate the extraterritorial activities of businesses incorporated in their jurisdiction. See John G. Ruggie, United Nations Human Rights Council, 11th Session, *Addendum: State Obligations to Provide Access to Remedy for Human Rights Abuses*

(2) nonjudicial grievance mechanisms, which must be legitimate, accessible, predictable, equitable, rights-compatible, and transparent;[108] (3) company-level grievance mechanisms, part of the corporate responsibility to respect;[109] (4) state-based nonjudicial mechanisms, including national human rights institutions and the Organization for Economic Cooperation and Development (OECD) National Contact Points (NCPS) for the OECD Guidelines on Multinational Enterprises;[110] (5) multi-stakeholder or industry initiatives and mechanisms of corporate financiers; and (6) possibly a global ombudsperson. The SRSG is careful to note that "non-judicial mechanisms play an important role alongside judicial processes" both in societies with "well-functioning rule of law institutions" and in those without.[111] Moreover, although "Non-state mechanisms must not undermine the strengthening of State institutions, particularly judicial mechanisms," what they can do is "offer additional opportunities for recourse and redress."[112]

ANALYSIS: COLLECTIVE RESPONSIBILITY OF HOME STATES

The *Framework* recognizes the collective moral responsibility of states and corporations and at times recognizes that these responsibilities are also legally binding obligations under international law. Although the corporate responsibility to respect rights may include a legal obligation for violations of international criminal law, the obligation is not a legal one (beyond compliance with domestic law) for other international human rights norms. The *Framework* recognizes that the state duty to protect rights from violations by nonstate actors is a foundational obligation

---

    by Third Parties, Including Business: An Overview of International and Regional Provisions, Commentary and Decisions, UN Doc. A/HRC/11/13/Add.1, (15 May 2009): 4.

[108] See further BASESwiki, "Business and Society Exploring Solutions: A Dispute Resolution Community," http://www.baseswiki.org, an interactive online forum set up by the SRSG for sharing, accessing, and discussing information about nonjudicial mechanisms that address disputes between companies and their external stakeholders.

[109] See further Ruggie, *Further Steps*, paras. 91–95, noting that a "seventh principle specifically for company-level grievance mechanisms is that they should operate through dialogue and engagement rather than the company itself acting as adjudicator." Ibid., para. 94.

[110] See further Ruggie, *Towards Operationalizing*, paras. 102–4; Ruggie, *Further Steps*, paras. 96–102. "The universe of State-based non-judicial grievance mechanisms remains both under-populated and under-resourced." Ruggie, *Further Steps*, para. 101.

[111] Ruggie, *Framework*, para. 84.

[112] Ibid., para. 86. See further Ruggie, *Towards Operationalizing*, paras. 91–92; Ruggie, *Further Steps*, paras. 114–16.

under international human rights law. Yet the *Framework*'s focus is on policy recommendations for state implementation that are framed so as to resemble more closely state moral responsibilities than legal obligations, except perhaps where a state-owned enterprise is involved. Moreover, even the policy recommendations are couched in uncertainty because of disagreement over the jurisdictional scope of home state legal obligations. The *Framework*'s discussion of access to remedy suggests that although the possibility of legal remedy for breach of corporate legal obligations is clearly important (and currently lacking), legal remedy is only part of the puzzle. It would appear, then, that much of the *Framework* is structured in accordance with Mark Drumbl's plea for collective responsibility frameworks that "embrace multiple regulatory sites (international, national and local)" and integrate broad approaches to legal accountability as well as "quasi-legal or even fully extra-legal accountability mechanisms."[113] Curiously, from the perspective of this volume, critiques of the SRSG's approach to the problem of business and human rights sometimes call for what could be seen as the corporate equivalent of the individual "atrocity trial": an international court charged specifically with hearing cases addressing corporate abuse.[114]

For the purpose of this chapter, however, what is notably missing from the *Framework* is any discussion of how to ensure the collective responsibility of *states* that are in breach of obligations under the state duty to protect. Although one prong of the *Framework* is devoted to access to remedy, the remedies proposed all concern grievances brought against companies, not states. This is likely due at least in part to the uncertainty surrounding the scope of home-state obligations under international law, combined with the seeming futility of sanctioning those host states that, rather than being merely unwilling to regulate corporate conduct, in fact lack the capacity to do so effectively.[115] This omission is, however, also arguably due in part to the preoccupation in the business

---

[113] Drumbl, "Collective Responsibility," this volume.

[114] David Kinley, Justice Nolan, and Natalie Zerial, "'The Norms Are Dead! Long Live the Norms!' The Politics behind the UN Human Rights Norms for Corporations," in *The New Corporate Accountability: Corporate Social Responsibility and the Law*, eds. Doreen McBarnet, Aurora Voiculescu, and Tom Campbell (New York: Cambridge University Press, 2007), 467–68, 473–75. This is not to say that such a development should be discouraged. Moreover, Mark Drumbl specifically endorses Anthony Lang's call for a new international criminal court for groups that could adjudicate TNCs. See Drumbl, "Collective Responsibility," this volume; Anthony Lang, Jr., *Punishment, Justice and International Relations: Ethics and Order after the Cold War* (New York: Routledge, 2008).

[115] It may also be linked to a lack of clear guidance from the international human rights treaty bodies on state obligations in this context. See Ruggie, *Framework*, para. 43.

and human rights context with the need to sanction *business* for these failures, rather than even admitting to the possibility that *states* not only bear responsibility to regulate and adjudicate business but could – or even should – be sanctioned for failing to do so.[116] In this way, the contribution that the analysis in this section hopes to make is in keeping with David Luban's observation that the very nature of international law includes within it a "fetishism" of the state that international criminal law seeks to deflate.[117] Of course, the complexity of "enforcing" state obligations in the international human rights context must be recognized,[118] and with it the concerns raised by Toni Erskine over how to "effectively punish an institution while remaining faithful to the understanding of responsibility as nondistributive, which the model of institutional moral agency supports."[119] Because home-state institutional structures are designed to benefit citizens of the home state, it could be argued that citizens of the home state should be prepared to bear the burdens (or some types of burdens) that might accompany these benefits. Another approach would be to follow Erin Kelly's proposal to give up retributive notions of justice and seek reparative justice instead: "reparative justice articulates a conception of what wrongdoers could and should do: to repair the damage they have done, to address the needs of victims, or to prevent similar harms from occurring."[120]

Many would agree that the *Framework* is an accurate representation of current international law in the business and human rights context, and indeed the SRSG went to great pains to "map" the current state of international human rights law early on in his work.[121] The uncertainty over

---

[116] But see Ruggie, *Towards Operationalizing*, para. 87, noting in the context of a discussion of state obligations and access to remedy that states "may also be required to provide adequate reparation, including compensation, to victims."

[117] See generally David Luban, "State Criminality," this volume. According to Luban: "A full-fledged theory of state criminality would... blaspheme the sacred order of public international law, in which states are like gods."

[118] See, for example, Bruno Simma, "Human Rights and State Responsibility," in *The Law of International Relations: Liber Amicorum HansPeter Neuhold*, eds. August Reinisch and Ursula Kriebaum (Utrecht, The Netherlands: Eleven International Publishing, 2007), 359; and Jutta Brunnée, "International Legal Accountability through the Lens of the Law of State Responsibility," *Netherlands Yearbook of International Law* 36 (2005): 21, 31–34.

[119] Erskine, "Kicking Bodies," Chapter 10 this volume. However, note that Erskine raises her concerns while discussing the possibility of war as punishment, which is not under consideration here.

[120] Erin Kelly, "Reparative Justice," this volume.

[121] See Ruggie, *Mapping International Standards*, and four addenda submitted with the report (A/HRC/4/35/Add.1–4), including especially *State Responsibilities to Regulate and Adjudicate Corporate Activities under the United Nations' Core Human Rights*

the jurisdictional scope of home-state obligations is sometimes said to be due to the inherent limitations of the jurisdictional clauses of some international human rights treaties,[122] as well as misunderstandings regarding the scope of the permissive exercise of home-state jurisdiction under jurisdictional principles of public international law.[123] Yet, if international law is viewed as an exclusively state-based process, then all this means is that states, the primary subjects and objects of international law, have not consented to bind themselves with obligations to citizens in other states, nor do all states believe that they have given each other permission to protect the rights of citizens in other states. From a moral philosophy perspective that recognizes the collective responsibility of institutional moral agents like corporations and states, the justification for this limitation in law is not self-evident. Nor is it self-evident if the work of scholars who adopt Third World approaches to international law (TWAIL) is used to guide the interpretation of the international law principles of sovereign equality and noninterference in the territorial affairs of other states.[124]

There are other reasons to doubt the need for these limitations even from within traditional international law. For example, some

---

Treaties, UN Doc. A/HRC/4/35/Add.1. Whether the SRSG accurately mapped the corporate obligations under international human rights law is the subject of disagreement, as is the usefulness of such direct obligations for the protection of rights. On the accuracy of the mapping, see, for example, Kinley, Nolan, and Zerial, "The Norms are dead"; and David Bilchitz, "The Ruggie Framework: An Adequate Rubric for Corporate Human Rights Obligations?" (April 24, 2009). Available at Social Science Research Network: http://ssrn.com/abstract=1394367. On the usefulness of direct obligations, see, for example, Ratner, "Corporations and Human Rights," 465–71. There cannot be a state duty to protect human rights from violations by nonstate actors without nonstate actors having duties themselves; and see generally Andrew Clapham, "Corporations and Human Rights," chapter 6 in *Human Rights Obligations of Non-State Actors* (New York: Oxford University Press, 2006). However, see John H. Knox, "Horizontal Human Rights Law," *American Journal of International Law* 102 (2008): 47, suggesting that the current system of international law that places obligations indirectly on corporations to be enforced by states should be preserved and strengthened. This should be done by elaborating duties of governments with respect to corporations subject to their jurisdiction when these corporations violate human rights within the territory of governments unable or unwilling to regulate them adequately.

[122] F. Coomans and M. T. Kamminga, eds., *Extraterritorial Application of Human Rights Treaties* (Antwerp: Intersentia, 2004).

[123] Sara L. Seck, "Conceptualizing the Home State Duty to Protect Human Rights," in *Corporate Social and Human Rights Responsibilities: Global Legal and Management Perspectives*, eds. Karin Bhuman, Mette Morsing, and Lynn Roseberry (Palgrave Macmillan, forthcoming). See also Ruggie, *Further Steps*, paras. 46–50, highlighting the uncertainties associated with the permissive exercise of extraterritorial jurisdiction.

[124] See generally Sara L. Seck, "Unilateral Home State Regulation: Imperialism or Tool for Subaltern Resistance?," *Osgoode Hall Law Journal* 46 (2008), 598–603.

international law scholars contest the jurisdictional limitations said to exist within international human rights treaties,[125] whereas others note that the primary rules of international law in other contexts do not limit state obligations in the same way, particularly with regard to obligations to regulate and adjudicate nonstate actor conduct.[126] Two often-cited examples are international environmental law as applied to polluter responsibility[127] and antibribery law.[128] The limited nature of home-state obligations is also not clearly supported under the secondary rules of state responsibility under international law.[129] Moreover, if obligations extend to executive, legislative, and judicial organs of the state, as understood under the International Law Commission's *Draft Articles on Responsibility of States for Internationally Wrongful Acts (Draft Articles)*,[130] it becomes unclear why any jurisdictional limitation makes sense in the business and human rights context. Clearly, the traditional approach of attempting to directly attribute the conduct of the TNC to the home-state

[125] See especially Sigrun I. Skogly, *Beyond National Borders: States' Human Rights Obligations in International Cooperation* (Antwerp: Intersentia, 2006); Sigrun I. Skogly and Mark Gibney, "Transnational Human Rights Obligations," *Human Rights Quarterly* 24 (2002): 781; Mark Gibney, Katarina Tomaševski, and Jens Vedsted-Hansen, "Transnational State Responsibility for Violations of Human Rights," *Harvard Human Rights Journal* 12 (1999); and Mark Gibney and Sigrun Skogly, eds., *Universal Human Rights and Extraterritorial Obligations* (Philadelphia: University of Pennsylvania Press, 2010).

[126] The SRSG has recently noted that in policy domains other than business and human rights, states "have agreed to certain uses of extraterritorial jurisdiction." However, this comment speaks to the permissive exercise of extraterritorial jurisdiction, not the mandatory obligation to regulate and adjudicate discussed here. See Ruggie, *Further Steps*, para. 46.

[127] See citations in Ratner, "Corporations and Human Rights," 479–81. See also John Knox, "Diagonal Environmental Rights," in Mark Gibney and Sigrun Skogly, eds., *Universal Human Rights and Extraterritorial Obligations*, 86: "It is difficult to see why a state which has caused environmental harm that rises to the level of a violation of human rights should avoid responsibility for its actions merely because the harm was felt beyond its borders."

[128] See Ratner, "Corporations and Human Rights," 482–83; Seck, "Unilateral Home State Regulation," 571–72.

[129] See Rick Lawson, "Life after Bankovic: On the Extraterritorial Application of the European Convention on Human Rights," in *Extraterritorial Application of Human Rights Treaties* (see n. 111), 85–86; Nicola Jägers, *Corporate Human Rights Obligations: In Search of Accountability* (Antwerp: Intersentia, 2002), 168–69; and Robert McCorquodale, "Spreading Weeds beyond Their Garden: Extraterritorial Responsibility of States for Violations of Human Rights by Corporate Nationals," *American Society of International Law Proceedings* 100 (2006): 99, n. 30.

[130] International Law Commission, United Nations GAOR, 56th Session, Supp. No. 10, *Draft Articles on Responsibility of States for internationally wrongful acts*, UN. Doc. A/56/10 (2001), 29–365.

under the *Nicaragua* test of direction or effective control,[131] reproduced in Article 8 of the *Draft Articles* and endorsed in the *Bosnia* case, is only possible in exceptional cases.[132] However, if instead of trying to directly attribute TNC conduct to the state, the home state responsibility analysis were to focus on the conduct of state organs themselves, a more accurate picture of the relationship between TNCs and home states would emerge.[133] Moreover, this picture would more accurately reflect the agency of the state itself, as a collective.[134]

Under the principle of independent responsibility,[135] a home state is directly responsible for its own wrongful conduct in failing to regulate or adjudicate a TNC so as to prevent and remedy human rights violations when required to do so under international law – that is, failing to exercise due diligence. However, this does not mean that the state is necessarily directly responsible for the conduct of the TNC. This understanding of responsibility is described by Tal Becker as responsibility under the nonattribution and separate delict theory[136] and parallels the

---

[131] International Court of Justice, *Military and Paramilitary Activities in and against Nicaragua (Nicaragua v. United States)*, Merits, Judgment [1986] I.C.J. Reports, para. 115, cited with approval in International Court of Justice, *Application of the Convention on the Prevention and Punishment of the Crime of Genocide (Bosnia & Herzegovina v. Serbia & Montenegro)*, Merits, Judgment [2007] I.C.J. Reports, para. 399.

[132] Indeed, the Commentaries to Article 8 explicitly exclude a state's initial establishment of a corporation by special law or otherwise as a sufficient basis for attribution to the state of the entity's subsequent conduct. See International Law Commission, *Draft Articles*, Commentaries to Article 8, para. 6. See Jägers, *Corporate Human Rights Obligations*, 169–72; Clapham, *Human Rights Obligations*, 243–44; Olivier De Schutter, "The Accountability of Multinationals for Human Rights Violations in European Law," in *Non-State Actors and Human Rights*, ed. Philip Alston (New York: Oxford University Press, 2005), 235–37; Robert McCorquodale and Penelope Simons, "Responsibility beyond Borders: State Responsibility for Extraterritorial Violations by Corporations of International Human Rights Law," *Modern Law Review* 70 (2007): 609–10; Rüdiger Wolfrum, "State Responsibility for Private Actors: An Old Problem of Renewed Relevance," in *International Responsibility Today: Essays in Memory of Oscar Schachter*, ed. Maurizio Ragazzi (Leiden: Brill, 2005), 427–28; and Gibney, Tomaševski, and Vedsted-Hansen, "Transnational State Responsibility," 286. However, see Jägers, *Corporate Human Rights Obligations*, 171, arguing that the effective control test may be met due to the "economic, legal and political connection between the corporation and the home State."

[133] Indeed, this understanding may be evident in Ruggie, *Towards Operationalizing*, para. 14, where the SRSG indicates that the state duty to protect is a standard of conduct, not a standard of result.

[134] See distinction in Erskine, "States and Quasi-States," 70.

[135] International Law Commission, *Draft Articles*, Commentary to chapter 4, Commentary to Article 47, para. 3.

[136] Tal Becker, *Terrorism and the State: Rethinking the Rules of State Responsibility* (Oxford: Hart Publishing, 2006), 14–24, 19–41, and generally "State Responsibility

state responsibility accorded in the *Bosnia* case.[137] According to Becker, as the difference between a finding of direct responsibility and responsibility under the separate delict theory makes no difference in terms of the remedy available under international human rights law, the different theories of responsibility are often not clearly distinguished.[138] Although under certain circumstances, direct state responsibility for TNC conduct is possible,[139] the current "prevailing perception" is that the state "will be responsible for the conduct of its own organs or officials, but not for the conduct of non-State actors that is wholly private in nature. The State can, however, be held responsible for its own violations of a separate duty to regulate the private conduct."[140]

Accordingly, if home states are under a duty to regulate and adjudicate nonstate actor TNCs to prevent and remedy human rights violations, then the conduct of home state executive organs, legislative organs, and judicial organs must be subject to scrutiny.[141] The implications of this are broad, suggesting a rethinking of the role of not only government departments and agencies that provide support services to TNCs[142]

---

for Private Acts: the Evolution of a Doctrine," chapter 2. This type of responsibility is described by Scott as "indirect responsibility"; See Craig Scott, "Translating Torture into Transnational Tort: Conceptual Divides in the Debate on Corporate Accountability for Human Rights Harms," in *Torture as Tort: Comparative Perspectives on the Development of Transnational Human Rights Litigation*, ed. Craig Scott (Oxford: Hart Publishing, 2001), 47.

[137] See discussion in Drumbl, "Collective Responsibility," this volume; Lang, "Punishing Genocide," this volume.

[138] Becker, *Terrorism and the State*, 57, 62.

[139] Two possibilities are under Article 16 of the *Draft Articles* for complicity; see McCorquodale and Simons, "Responsibility beyond Borders," 611–15; Gibney, Tomaševski, and Vedsted-Hansen, "Transnational State Responsibility," 293–94; and Becker's analysis of causal responsibility, see Becker, *Terrorism and the State*, 289–94.

[140] Becker, *Terrorism and the State*, 66. The distinction between separate delict and direct responsibility is not specifically endorsed in the *Draft Articles*, which provide that a State is responsible for "all the consequences, not being too remote, of its wrongful conduct." International Law Commission, *Draft Articles*, Commentary to Article 31, paras. 10, 13.

[141] International Law Commission, *Draft Articles*, Article 4.

[142] These services include executive branch negotiations of bilateral investment treaties; trade commissioner services, overseas development agencies, export credit agencies, and sovereign wealth funds. See McCorquodale, "Extraterritorial Responsibility of States," 100–1; and Ryan Suda, "The Effect of Bilateral Investment Treaties on Human Rights Enforcement and Realization," in *Transnational Corporations and Human Rights*, ed. Olivier De Schutter (Oxford: Hart Publishing, 2006), 143. On the legal obligations of export credit agencies see Özgür Can and Sara L. Seck, *The Legal Obligations with Respect to Human Rights and Export Credit Agencies* (ECA Watch, Halifax Initiative

but also the legislation governing these departments and agencies and legislation creating "private" entities such as stock exchanges, financial institutions, and TNCs themselves. This observation highlights the complementary relationship between the state duty to protect and the corporate responsibility to respect, as within the state duty to protect is an obligation to enable or facilitate implementation of the corporate responsibility to respect.[143] Although the SRSG appears to be taking some steps in the right direction,[144] his policy prescriptions for states remain couched as optional recommendations – wise choices but not mandatory steps without which states would (or at least should) face consequences.[145]

Because judicial organs are also implicated and states are under a duty to provide access to remedy, then home-state courts must also be under an obligation to facilitate this access.[146] This highlights the complementary relationship in the *Framework* between the state duty to protect and the need for effective access to remedy. Again, the SRSG appears to be taking steps in the rights direction, indicating clearly in the Ruggie 2010 report that: "Under their duty to protect, States must take appropriate steps within their territory and/or jurisdiction to ensure access to effective remedy through judicial, administrative, legislative or other appropriate means."[147] Yet other language is more equivocal,[148] and nowhere does the SRSG suggest that the failure of a state to ensure access to remedy should or even must lead to the sanctioning of that state. This is even more so for home-state courts and access to judicial remedy.[149]

Coalition, and ESCR-Net, 2006); McCorquodale and Simons, "Responsibility beyond Borders," 607–8.

[143] This is hinted at in the discussion of corporate cultures. Ruggie, *Framework*, para. 30.

[144] See generally Ruggie, *Further Steps*, paras. 20–43.

[145] See, for example, Ruggie, *Further Steps*, paras. 39, 41, 43.

[146] See generally Jan Paulsson, *Denial of Justice in International Law* (New York: Cambridge University Press, 2005); Christopher Greenwood, "State Responsibility for the Decisions on National Courts," in *Issues of States Responsibility before International Judicial Institutions*, eds. Malgosia Fitzmaurice and Dan Sarooshi (Oxford: Hart Publishing, 2004). State responsibility would only arise once all means of challenging a lower court decision within the national legal system were exhausted. Greenwood, "State Responsibility," 72–73. See also Ruggie, *Addendum: State Obligations*.

[147] Ruggie, *Further Steps*, para. 96. See also ibid., para. 103. "It is essential that both States and companies act in a manner supportive of the independence and integrity of judicial systems."

[148] See, for example, Ruggie, *Further Steps*, paras. 102, 113.

[149] Ruggie, *Addendum: State Obligations*, 4.

The *Draft Articles* also provide various justifications for states that are unable to meet their legal obligations,[150] yet it is not clear that any would provide an excuse for a host state that lacked the capacity to implement such obligations effectively. From a moral philosophy perspective, the fact that a state has the capacity to deliberate and act is not sufficient to allow moral agency to be exercised, because the state must also have the "freedom to act and some degree of independence from other actors."[151] Despite the fundamental nature of the principle of sovereign equality to both international law and international relations, the limited nature of the sovereignty of many postcolonial or Third World states has been recognized by both international relations theorists[152] and TWAIL scholars.[153] Recognition of this limited sovereignty is not clearly evident in the *Framework*, however. This is most notable in the discussion of a role for home states in conflict zones, which indicates that the tentative policy recommendations put forward for home states do not detract from host-state obligations.[154] Yet, in the conflict zone situation, the host state is likely to be severely incapacitated and might be considered a "failed" or "collapsed" state.[155] Although caution should be exercised when considering restricting the recognition of institutional moral agency (and similarly legal responsibility) of what Erskine refers to as weak or "quasi-states," this caution may not apply to TNC conduct in "failed" or "collapsed" states, although in practice defining which states qualify

[150] However, the six "circumstances precluding wrongfulness" may not preclude the wrongfulness of any act of state that is not in conformity with an obligation arising under a peremptory norm of international law. See International Law Commission, *Draft Articles*, Articles 20–25: consent; self-defense; countermeasures; *force majeure*; distress; and necessity.

[151] Erskine, "States and Quasi-States," 74.

[152] See, for example, Robert H. Jackson, *Quasi-States: Sovereignty, International Relations and the Third World* (New York: Cambridge University Press, 1990); see discussion in Erskine, "States and Quasi-States," 74–83, of quasi-states as institutional moral agents and Jackson's distinction between positive sovereignty (the freedom to act and deter); and negative sovereignty (freedom from outside interference), 76.

[153] See generally Antony Anghie, *Imperialism, Sovereignty and the Making of International Law* (New York: Cambridge University Press, 2005); Balakrishnan Rajagopal, *International Law from Below: Development, Social Movements and Third World Resistance* (New York: Cambridge University Press, 2003); and discussion in Seck, "Unilateral Home State Regulation," 582.

[154] Ruggie, *Framework*, paras. 47–49.

[155] See Erskine, "States and Quasi-States," 79, discussing different terminology in relation to states that have "self-destructed by armed anarchy within."

as such may be not only complex but political.[156] This suggests that the
recognition of home-state duties in all conflict-affected areas should be
much stronger.[157]

On the other hand, as Erskine cautions, the role of the home state
in relation to TNC conduct in "quasi-states," or states that lack the
freedom to act because they are "deprived of the conditions necessary
to realize [their] capacity to act," raises several concerns. Recognition
of the disparate categories of "institutions similarly classified but differently situated" suggests that different states may have different capacities
for exercising their moral agency and therefore for bearing duties.[158]
Transnational corporations and First World home states are institutions
generally considered to have a greater ability to exercise their institutional
agency than Third World states.[159] Yet the *Framework* does not impose
stronger duties on these actors, in relation either to egregious human
rights violations or those of a lesser degree. Indeed, the obligations of
both TNCs and home states appear weaker under the *Framework* than
the obligations of host states, aside from the obligation of international
cooperation and capacity building imposed on all states.[160] Indeed, the
SRSG has explicitly stated that because corporations are "specialized economic organs, not democratic public interest institutions," their "responsibilities cannot and should not simply mirror the duties of States."[161]
Yet, although home states are democratic public interest institutions, the
public to whom they are generally held to account is a different public
from the public subject to transnational corporate human rights violations in host states. The weakness in the *Framework* could be overcome,
however, if uncertainties over the jurisdictional scope of state obligations
were surmounted. Moreover, if the constraints felt by First World states in
the global marketplace were also acknowledged, the solution would not

---

[156] For the problematic nature of the concept of "failed and collapsed" states from a TWAIL
perspective, see James Thuo Gathii, "Review: Neoliberalism, Colonialism and International Governance: Decentering the International Law of Governmental Legitimacy,"
Michigan Law Review 98 (2000): 2021.

[157] Notably, although the SRSG discusses this issue as a problem in "conflict zones" in the
Ruggie, *Framework*, the discussion in Ruggie, *Further Steps*, is focused on "conflict-
affected areas," suggesting a more nuanced understanding of the problem.

[158] Erskine, "States and Quasi-States," 80–81.

[159] This is not to say that First World states might not feel circumscribed by the power of
market forces, but as Erskine notes, "capacities for action and deliberation themselves,
can exist in degrees." Ibid., 82.

[160] Ruggie, *Framework*, paras. 43–45.   [161] Ruggie, *Framework*, para. 53.

be to limit home-state obligations but rather to recognize that these obligations to protect human rights should extend to wherever home-state TNCs operate, not just to locations in developing countries or Third World states. This would be in keeping with the understandings of many TWAIL scholars that we need to move away from a geographic understanding of the Third World, and instead understand it as a "historical and continuing experience of subordination at the global level" that is shared by "groups of states and populations which self-identify as Third World."[162] It would also acknowledge the reality that home states are increasingly Third World states.

CONCLUSIONS

This chapter began by canvassing the legal debates over the merits of corporate criminal liability. The three responsibilities under the UN Human Rights Council's 2008 *Framework for Business and Human Rights* were then explored, revealing a complex mix of law and policy addressed to both states and corporations. Part III then turned to the limitations imposed by international law on the jurisdictional scope of the home-state duty to protect rights and argued that these limitations make no sense in the business and human rights context. As concluded earlier, this chapter highlights the collective responsibility of home states as institutional actors in a position to prevent harm and takes the position that the existence of limitations on the enforcement of this responsibility should not detract from the importance of articulating its existence. In the words of Toni Erskine:

> Oddly and often tragically, our attention is focused on issues of imputation *following* international crises. Yet, addressing how responsibilities can be distributed is necessarily a prior step to understanding what it means to blame institutions for actions or failures to act. It is imperative to have some sense of who, or what, can bear duties before we deal with questions of imputation, blame and even punishment when these duties are abrogated. It is when an analysis of prospective responsibility is neglected that charges or retrospective responsibility are misdirected – as when the "international

---

[162] Obiora Chinedu Okafor, "Newness, Imperialism, and International Legal Reform in Our Time: A TWAIL Perspective," *Osgoode Hall Law Journal* 43 (2005): 174. See also Balakrishnan Rajagopal, "Locating the Third World in Cultural Geography," *Third World Legal Studies* 1 (1998–99).

community" is mysteriously imbued with agency and blamed for failing to respond to genocide, environmental crisis, or famine.[163]

Violations of human rights by transnational corporations are clearly linked to global crises, including not only genocide but also the most serious global crisis of our time, climate change.[164] As briefly alluded to in the introduction to this chapter, the question of whether home states such as Canada should enact legislation to regulate and adjudicate transnational corporate conduct in the extractive sector for compliance with international human rights and environmental standards is a highly controversial topic at present.[165] On the basis of this analysis, the answer is that Canada not only could but is mandated to do so under international law. The purpose of the chapter is to shed light on the blind spots of international law that shield the collective responsibility of home states as institutional agents of the global economic order, agents that are in the position to take prospective responsibility so that we might, in the future, "avoid . . . the need to speak retrospectively of responsibility in terms of guilt and culpability."[166]

[163] Erskine, "States and Quasi-States," 85.
[164] John H. Knox, "Climate Change and Human Rights Law," *Virginia Journal of International Law* 50 (2009), 9–11.
[165] See text at footnote 6.   [166] Erskine, "States and Quasi-States," 85.

6

Collective Punishment and Mass Confinement

Larry May

Due process rights are normally discussed in the context of particular prisoners who are in detention while awaiting trial or who have been sentenced. However some refugee camps should also be treated as forms of detention, even incarceration. Furthermore, the detention or confinement is itself especially problematic given its link to collective punishment. In such cases, what I will call Magna Carta legacy rights, those procedural rights that have been recognized as fundamental since the time of Magna Carta are in need of special protection not commonly recognized. In this chapter, I want to consider the relationship between collective responsibility and collective punishment by considering mass confinements of such people as those in detention while waiting extradition and those people who are forced into refugee camps.

Collective responsibility plays a prominent role in the supposed justification of detention imposed on a group when some of its members pose security threats and it is difficult to sort out who poses serious threats versus those who merely might. The United States used this rationale for incarcerating large numbers of people found on the "battlefield" in Afghanistan and sending them to prison in Guantanamo. Likewise, when the civil war in the Sudan reached a certain tipping point, large numbers of people were punished by being forced into refugee camps. I examine both sorts of arguments, finding them to be seriously flawed. I look to the debates in the Just War tradition and to contemporary international law for guidance.

In the first section, I consider the idea of collective responsibility and its relation to collective punishment. In the second section, I look at the Just War tradition, in which collective punishment was initially accepted but later rejected, especially by Grotius and his followers in international law, and in which most but not all forms of collective punishment are now condemned. In the third section, I discuss the conflict between security issues and the protection of rights of those who are confined or incarcerated, offering a compromise proposal. In the fourth section, I argue against collective punishment involving confinement in light of considerations of equity. Finally, in the fifth section, I respond to several objections to my view, most significantly the challenge that if one is critical of collective punishment, one must also be critical of collective responsibility.

COLLECTIVE RESPONSIBILITY AND PUNISHMENT

Over the past sixty years, collective responsibility has gained limited, if grudging, acceptance in theoretical circles.[1] At least in part, this is because of the recognition that in some ways, collective responsibility has become a fixture of our normal moral discourse to such an extent that when we speak of corporations or armies as responsible for various consequences, this is so common that we do not even think we are employing moral terms in any way that is especially problematic. Conceptions such as those of corporate responsibility even assume that some members will be held responsible for what other members have done – perhaps the hallmark of what was considered so objectionable about collective responsibility in the past. Of course, there have always been acceptable cases of vicarious responsibility, such as parents being held responsible for the actions of their children. Only recently, however, did theorists begin to see the large range of cases involving institutions and other large groups for which collective responsibility did not look that objectionable after all.

One of the main insights in recent years is that many of the most important social consequences are a product of the acts of multiple agents acting in concert. When we try to stick to the task of assigning responsibility only to what each person has done on his or her own, we fail to understand and account for the source of these social consequences. At the very least, we need to take account of how each person influences others, perhaps only in subtle ways. In addition, we need to realize that social consequences often result from the combination of efforts that could not have succeeded except for the organization as well as the direction that some of the members have provided to the joint effort.[2] Once all of this is recognized, certain forms of collective responsibility can be seen as

---

[1] Larry May and Stacey Hoffman, eds., *Collective Responsibility: Five Decades of Debate in Theoretical and Applied Ethics* (Savage, MD: Rowman & Littlefield, 1991).

[2] See the excellent treatment of this subject in Mark Osiel, *Making Sense of Mass Atrocity* (New York: Cambridge University Press, 2009).

plausible in ways that make the vast majority of the historical literature's harsh condemnation of collective responsibility nearly incomprehensible. Thus, the following question arises: if collective responsibility has been accepted, why is collective punishment still roundly condemned?

There are several forms of what might be called collective punishment in which individuals are punished for what others did:

1. punishing all members of a group for what has involved every member;
2. punishing all members of a group for what only some members have done, where it is difficult to figure out who did what;
3. punishing all members of a group for what only some members have done, even though it is known which members did what;
4. punishing one member, or some members, of a group for what some other members have done; and
5. punishing the institution or organization that contains the group without punishing any individual member.

Only some of these forms of collective punishment involve punishing some for what others have done.

In the first category, when all members of a group have together engaged in a wrongful act, punishing all members seems the most plausible of all the forms of collective punishment. What is unclear is whether this is best understood as full-blown collective punishment. It is possible still to assign punishment on the basis of what each has contributed, even as all members are punished. However, if all are assigned exactly the same punishment or penalty, even as it is known that their contributions were different, this is more problematic, although if there is an agreement to do the collective act on the part of all, it may not be implausible to punish all in the same way.

In the second category, punishing all for what some have done but it is unknown who did what, there is a kind of practical plausibility here, but not one on which to generalize. The plausibility here is merely due to the contingent fact that it is unknown who did what and that some should be punished for deterrent or retributive reasons. If, and when, it could be known what each contributed, it would be fairer to punish only those members of a group who contributed to a harm, and to do so based on their contributions. Thus, it is only fair to punish all members due to the contingent fact of lack of knowledge about who did what. The contingent plausibility of this form of collective punishment will not affect other forms.

In the third category, a classic case of collective punishment, I argue in subsequent sections that fairness is so offended by such punishment as to make it prima facie unjustifiable in all circumstances; the prima facie unjustifiability is only overridden, perhaps, if the group is so cohesive that what one member did was agreed to by all of the other members. Although this category is prima facie unjustifiable, there may be some circumstances in which other values are at stake that outweigh the prima facie unjustifiability of engaging in this form of collective punishment. We must nonetheless be careful here because it is so easy to abuse this category. In later sections of this chapter, I take up the problem of security as it butts up against fairness and rights issues in such cases.

I can see no plausibility for the fourth category of punishment, punishing some for what was known to be done by others, unless there are special ties between the members, causing one member to take on responsibility for what other members of a group are doing, such as in parent–child or employer–employee relations. However, if the only ties are those that form the group into a group in the first place, fairness seems to dictate that we should punish based on contribution. Nonetheless, perhaps punishment can exceed exact contribution in cases in which all conspired to act together, although only some members actually acted.

Finally, I suppose there might be forms of collective punishment, at least in theory, that involve punishing a group without punishing any of the members. The case that is often cited is that of punishing a state or corporation, perhaps with heavy fines. Although possible, it is nearly always likely that what appear to be nondistributive forms of punishment will turn out to be distributive forms because the members will suffer whenever their group is made to suffer, thereby raising fairness issues again, for only some members contributed to the wrong.

In thinking about the justifiability of collective punishment, one also needs to think about the wide range of sanctions that can be meted out under the label of collective punishment, including the following:

1. putting individuals in jail or prison after judicial proceedings,
2. putting individuals in jail or prison without judicial proceedings,
3. confining individuals in prisons for the protection of society,
4. confining individuals in refugee camps for entering illegally,
5. issuing monetary fines to individuals, and
6. barring individuals from the exercise of some of their minor freedoms.

Historically, and in contemporary discussion, when significant abridgments of liberty (1–4) are the type of sanction, it is more difficult to justify the collective punishment than if monetary fines or types of minor infringement of liberty (5–6) are the sanctions.

Although some of the types of collective sanction seem reasonable, the same difficulties faced by justifying collective responsibility afflict collective punishment. If it is minor infringement of liberty that follows on the attribution of collective responsibility, then perhaps the idea of collective sanctioning can still seem acceptable. However, when we turn to meting out criminal punishment to some for what others have done, the old worries seem to return in intensified form. There is an increased concern, for instance, for the fairness of putting some people in jail for what other people have done. Criminal punishment is almost always the kind of test case that causes one to pause in sanctioning some for what others have done. The one exception seems to be those individuals who were the ringmasters of great atrocities such as genocide, for which there is nearly universal condemnation for how they influenced others and it seems acceptable to employ criminal punishment, even though what the leaders are punished for is what those they should have restrained did.

Collective punishment is not necessarily exhausted by the idea that some can be punished for what others have done. There is an even more difficult type of collective punishment that follows on the heels of a type of collective responsibility that is itself not nearly so reviled. The general idea is that if it is true that a group of people is causally responsible for a wrongful consequence, then the entire group should be held responsible. To many people, this makes more sense than trying to figure out who played what role because it was the combination of acts, not the singular roles, that caused the harm. In addition, as we will see, it seems to matter if all somehow agreed with the harm that was being done by the group. Indeed, the recent debate about Israel's attack on Gaza raises this issue because, arguably, the people of Gaza voted Hamas into power knowing that Hamas would act violently toward Israel. Recently, in both philosophical and legal debates, the idea of collective punishment as a way to deal with groups in which the members entered voluntarily, knowing what the group was likely to do, was defended and even applauded.

Another wrinkle to the debates about collective punishment concerns cases in which it is clear that a single person was causally responsible for a given harm, but it is thought that deterrence, or some other social goal such as retaliation, demands punishing the entire group to which that person belongs, rather than merely the individual who is causally responsible. Views have changed over the centuries. There was quite a bit of support for this idea in earlier centuries, then a strong reaction against such practices in the late nineteenth and early twentieth centuries, followed by a recent return to acceptability of this type of collective punishment in recent years. In what follows, I am largely interested in this last case of collective punishment, although I occasionally discuss other cases as well.

My thesis is that the recent turn to collective punishment as a means of deterrence or retaliation is unsupportable, although there are cases in which it looks more plausible than others, especially when the cases are combined with other considerations, such as the inability to tell who was causally responsible – or at least who was the most causally responsible for a harm – or when people agreed to a given wrong even if they didn't contribute to it. In the next section, I look for guidance in addressing our issues from those who have historically considered them over the years and those who struggle with them practically as a matter of international law.

THE JUST WAR TRADITION AND INTERNATIONAL LAW

For those of us who have defended collective responsibility, one of the most difficult cases concerns collective punishment as a justification for war or the tactics of war.[3] Most contemporary theorists who have considered this issue are opposed to any form of collective punishment as a just cause for war.[4] In the Just War tradition, however, if a state committed a wrong, as a collectivity it was thought to deserve to experience retaliatory punishment, and hence there is a sense that this would be a justified form of collective punishment. War can be justified as a means of punishment because just cause focuses on wrongs, and punishment is about the proper response to wrongs committed, whether by individuals or by states. Indeed, if there is no likelihood that a state that commits a wrong will be punished as it deserves through any other means, war has seemed justified as a means to mete out such just deserts to an aggressive state and its people.

Writing in the early sixteenth century, Francisco Vitoria expressed this doctrine well when he quoted Thomas Aquinas as having said, "for a just war 'there must be a just cause, namely, they who are attacked for some fault must deserve the attack.'" Vitoria then quoted Augustine as having

---

[3] See my books, *The Morality of Groups* (Notre Dame, IN: University of Notre Dame Press, 1987), and *Sharing Responsibility* (Chicago: University of Chicago Press, 1992).

[4] See Kenneth W. Kemp, "Punishment as Just Cause for War," *Public Affairs Quarterly* 10 (October 1996): 335–53.

said, "It is involved in the definition of a just war that some wrong is being avenged, as where a people or state is to be punished for neglect to exact amends from its citizens for their wrongdoing or to restore what has been wrongfully taken." Here it is clear that Vitoria advocated war as a means to punish a people or state collectively. Vitoria summarizes the 300-year tradition since Aquinas as follows:

> Where, then, no wrong has previously been committed . . . there is no cause for just war. This is the received opinion of all the doctors, not only of the theologians, but also of the jurists . . . and I know of no doctor whose opinion is to the contrary.[5]

Up to Vitoria's time, in the early part of the sixteenth century, war was largely thought to be justified as retribution or retaliation for wrongs done.

In the seventeenth century, things changed. Hugo Grotius, for instance, said that "guilt attaches to the individuals who have agreed to the crime, not to those who have been overmastered by the votes of others."[6] In discussing the sharing of punishment, Grotius said that individuals who have not consented to the "wrong done by the community" cannot be punished.[7] On the Grotian account, for war to be just, it must be for the common good, not merely to avenge a wrong done to a specific state or individual.[8] Although Grotius was seemingly unsure how best to characterize the issue, he was sure that war is just when it is waged to deter or repair wrongdoing. Retaliation that achieves neither of these goals is much more problematic, however.[9]

If a war is fought to punish a state for wrongdoing, there is support for the justifiability of this war in the Just War tradition, especially if aimed at deterrence. If war is fought to punish a people that constitutes part of the population of a state, problems are soon recognized, however, even though it is unclear how a war could be waged to punish a state without also, to a certain extent, punishing various parts of the population of that state. Here is the crux of the problem concerning collective punishment: it can be understood on the model of collective responsibility as involving

---

[5] Francisco Vitoria, *On the Indians (De Indis et de Ivre Belli Relectiones)*, trans. John Pawley Bate, ed. Ernest Nys, Section II, para. 11 (Washington DC: The Carnegie Institution of Washington, 1917), pp. 143–44.

[6] Hugo Grotius, *De Jure Belli Ac Pacis* (On the Law of War and Peace), trans. Francis W. Kelsey (Oxford: Clarendon Press, 1625/1925), 535.

[7] Ibid., p. 544.   [8] Ibid., pp. 482, 502–3, and elsewhere.

[9] See ibid., p. 462.

either distributed or nondistributed liability. If one thinks of punishing the state for its wrongdoing, one tends to think of nondistributive responsibility, and this may indeed be accomplished in some cases if there are assets of the state that, when lost, do not harm the populace of the state. However, in most cases of collective punishment of a state, what in fact happens is that punishing the state is a form of distributive collective liability in that the populace will bear the weight of the punishment, not the state itself. Then we run afoul of the Grotian dictum that punishment needs to be assigned only to those individuals who have done wrong, or at least agreed to its having been done.

Let us now turn to considerations of international law for more guidance on our topic. In the various formulations of the laws of war, it appears that before the first Hague Peace Conference in 1899, collective punishment as a rationale for waging war and for various tactics during war was considered legal. Even the famous rules set out to govern the conduct of Union soldiers during the U.S. Civil War seem to allow collective punishment on the battlefield. The Lieber Code stipulated that "The citizen or native of a hostile country is thus an enemy, as one of the constituents of the hostile state or nation, and as such is subjected to the hardships of war."[10] And while other provisions of the Lieber Code placed restrictions on acts of retaliation and revenge, the general idea that the members of a population could be subject to the hardships of war merely because they were part of a State that had done wrong was not disputed.

At the end of the nineteenth century, however, the consensus in international law seemed to have shifted dramatically. Article 50 of the Hague Regulations, adopted at the Hague Peace Conference of 1899, provides that "No general penalty, pecuniary or otherwise, can be inflicted upon a population on account of the acts of individuals for which they can not be regarded as jointly and severally responsible."[11]

Yet, despite the fact that many significant statements of a similar sort were incorporated into sources of international law, collective punishment continued as a practice through both World Wars, especially on the part of Germany. In 1939, during the Second World War, Reich Protector for Bohemia and Moravia, Konstantin Von Neurath, declared that "the responsibility for all acts of sabotage is attributed not only to

---

[10] Instructions for the Government of the Armies of the United States in the Field, General Orders No. 100 (1863), the Lieber Code, Article 21.

[11] See Shane Darcy, *Collective Responsibility and Accountability under International Law* (Leiden: Transnational Publishers, 2007), 17.

individual perpetrators but to the entire Czech population."[12] As late as 1948, an Italian military tribunal declared that the expression "collectively responsible" refers to an exceptional rule in occupied territory when "the normal proceedings have not led to positive results. In substance, collective responsibility may arise where it has appeared impossible to establish who was or who were the culprits."[13]

There is also quite a difference in the recent international law debates if the subject is whether fines can be extracted as a collective punishment as opposed to the more common forms of physical assault and abuse that is inflicted on the battlefield or the restrictions to basic liberties when prisoners are being held in captivity. The Hague Conventions seem to rule out even monetary fines, but the actual practice appears to be that monetary fines were treated quite differently from physical force as a form of collective punishment. Collective punishment during war meted out as a kind of tax is seen as not nearly as noxious as collective punishment meted out in terms of killing or jailing.[14]

There is one controversial kind of collective punishment that seems to be accepted in international law in some form – namely, what is sometimes called "protective retribution." This appears to be the only form of collective punishment not tied to deterrence that is recognized in international law, but this is also somewhat misleading. Although the punishment must be proportional to what was inflicted, the salient consideration is that the purpose is to coerce "the law-breaking party to cease its violative conduct."[15] Thus, this form of collective punishment is actually closer to deterrence than retribution, despite its name, and when retaliation seems to have limited deterrent objectives, even if there is a deterrent objective, proportionality considerations come to the fore and make it much harder for the practice to be justified in international law. Yet many of the practices that seem to be based on self-protection are only loosely so based, with retaliation instead being the main objective. Pure collective retaliation, even when somewhat "protective," is simply and properly condemned in international law.

Indeed, the very idea of collective punishment either as a retributive rationale for initiating war or as a rationale for using certain tactics during war has been roundly condemned by most international agreements since

---

[12] International Military Tribunal (Nuremberg) Judgment and Sentences, October 1, 1946.

[13] *In re:Kappler*, Italy, Military Tribunal of Rome, July 20, 1948, Case No. 151.

[14] See James Gardner, "Community Fines and Collective Responsibility," *American Journal of International Law* 11 (1917): 511–37.

[15] *Oxford Manual on the Laws of War*, 1880.

1899. One of the strongest such statements comes from the International Law Association, which declared in 1921 that "Collective punishments shall not be imposed on account of the misconduct of individuals."[16] War is simply too serious a matter to be justified by such questionable rationales as collective punishment. Contemporary international law adopts the Grotian maxim that punishment should only be inflicted for what the individual person has done or agreed to.

COLLECTIVE LIABILITY, SECURITY, AND DETAINEES

Detention is much less severe than war, and so one might think that collective punishment directed at confinement or detention rather than war would be easier to justify. This is indeed the case, but not as helpful as one might think in cases such as the mass confinement at Guantanamo. There are two reasons that collective detention as a form of collective punishment has been much easier to justify than full-scale wars on the basis of the rationale of collective punishment. First, loss of liberty in detention is not as serious as loss of life in war. Second, security considerations are much less problematic in the justification of collective detention than war. There are, however, other problems with collective detention that make it difficult to justify, as we have seen to be generally true of collective punishment.

The two kinds of collective detention cases I am most interested in are, first, those detainees in detention centers such as Guantanamo Bay who were picked up on the battlefield, for which little evidence exists to link them individually to crimes but who are claimed to be a threat to the United States. Second, I am interested in people who are stateless and currently occupying refugee and displaced-person camps who were forced to flee from their home countries, and yet have not been accepted into the host countries where the camps are established. Considering such cases helps us see why it is somewhat easier to justify collective detention than collective punishment in war, but also why such cases are nonetheless problematic.

These two groups of detention cases are similar in that the people detained are not treated in terms of what these individuals have done or even as deserving of rights protection – indeed, the point of the punishment is to deprive these individuals of the protection of their rights. Noncollective detention may deprive people of their rights as well, but

---

[16] International Law Association, declaration of 1921.

collective detention almost always does so, for when whole groups are detained, there will inevitably be different degrees of culpability among the group members, and often some members will have no culpability at all, except perhaps for the loosest of complicity. Indeed, there is good reason to believe that most of the people held at Guantanamo did nothing to warrant their detention.[17] Likewise, those held in refugee camps generally did not individually do sufficient wrong to warrant their detention.

There is a sense that collective detainees have become "outlaws," people who exist outside the protection of domestic or even international law. At about the time of Magna Carta, it was apparently a practice in England to exile within England itself those who were members of disfavored groups or groups thought to be dangerous or who were in some other way suspicious. For this to be accomplished, the group members were removed from the populous regions of England where the king's law was enforced into a region where no laws were enforced, or they were placed into prisons that were similarly beyond the reach of normal procedural restraints of the law. The term "outlaw" merely refers to those who exist outside the jurisdiction and protection of the law.

Being an outlaw was recognized at the time of Magna Carta as something against which a person needed specific procedural protections. Indeed, there is a sense that the entire of Magna Carta's famous Chapter 29 can be understood as an attempt by the barons to extract from the king a set of guarantees that people in England would not be rendered as outlaws. Here is Chapter 29 in one of its versions:

> No freeman shall be taken or imprisoned or desseised or exiled or outlawed or in any way destroyed, nor will we go upon him nor send upon him, except by the lawful judgment of his peers or by the law of the land.

These rule-of-law constraints were aimed at various problems, not the least of which was collective confinement and detention.

Refugee detention centers are good examples of detention that is seemingly justified, if at all, by collective liability. The people who are so detained, because they have not been detained because of what they have personally done, are in a no-man's-land concerning the protection of their individual rights. Collective punishment schemes that diminish the importance of determining whether a given person is indeed guilty have been at

---

[17] In a recent article, it was claimed that more than 90 percent of the 779 men held at Guantanamo were originally captured under suspicious circumstances. See Jacob Sulum, *Reason Magazine* (January 21, 2009): pp. 1–2.

the center of the problem of collective detentions. Thus, even though collective detention may be easier to justify than collective liability rationales for war, collective detention should also be roundly condemned.

There is a rationale for detention, even for collective detention, that is similar to that for anticipatory self-defense in cases of justified war. Here a concern for security could propel one to round up all those who are judged to be dangerous to the state and to detain them until the threat to the state has abated. Indeed, even the right of habeas corpus – the right to be removed from prison and told of the charges against one, which is sometimes seen as the most significant of all rights in the Anglo-American legal system – can be suspended when security considerations warrant it, as is also true for another Magna Carta legacy right, nonrefoulement.

Habeas corpus, since before the time of Magna Carta, was identified with protecting rights of those most vulnerable. In the U.S. Constitution, only one right is listed in the main body, not in the first ten amendments, of this document. Article 5, section 2 states:

> The Privilege of the Writ of Habeas Corpus shall not be suspended, unless when in Cases of Rebellion or Invasion the public Safety may require it.

This clause of the U.S. Constitution is most commonly referred to as "the suspension clause" rather than the "habeas corpus rights clause," referring to its justifiable abridgement in emergency situations rather than to its protected status in normal times.

One of the first expressions of the idea of nonrefoulement, that individuals cannot be sent to countries that are likely to torture or kill them, is in Article 33 of the 1951 Refugee Convention:

1. No Contracting State shall expel or return (*"refouler"*) a refugee in any manner whatsoever to the frontiers of territories where his life or freedom would be threatened on account of his race, religion, nationality, membership of a particular social group or political opinion.

The Convention goes on to specify security exceptions, however:

2. The benefit of the present provision may not, however, be claimed by a refugee whom there are reasonable grounds for regarding as a danger to the security of the country in which he is, or who, having been convicted by a final judgment of a particularly serious crime, constitutes a danger to that community.

Thus, like habeas corpus, nonrefoulement can be abridged when security concerns warrant it. Yet, neither the U.S. Constitution nor the Refugee

Convention gives clear criteria for when such abridgement can legitimately occur. As we will see, it is this gap that has allowed for abuse to occur that further underlies the need for truly global protection of these rights.

Perhaps the best example of where there is a disparity between the protection of rights, especially between procedural rights such as habeas corpus and nonrefoulement on one hand and threats to security on the other, is in the fight against terrorism in the United States. The United States has consistently claimed that it is not possible to protect the rights of detainees and at the same time protect the security of the United States, whether habeas corpus rights at Guantanamo or rights of nonrefoulement of those who are illegal or undocumented immigrants. I do not agree with the U.S. government position on this issue, but I agree that there is a serious problem about how to afford maximal rights protection to those who are accused of actually or possibly being a security threat to a country.

In my view, when the few cases of straightforward conflict between rights protection and security do arise, the benefit of the doubt should go to the right holder, although exceptions should be allowed. When the individual is made less secure, there is a diminishment of the aggregate security of the larger society. If rights are claimed to be offset by a mere *risk* of loss of security to the larger society, it seems that we must discover what the extent and likelihood of that risk to society is. If it is determined that the risk to society should outweigh the risk to the individual, then it must be clear that this is an exceptional case and not one on which a precedent can be established. Most of all, it must not be allowed that a state like the United States can use the threat to national security as a pretext to detain individuals collectively for lengthy periods of time long after the strong likelihood of the threat being realized has passed.

It may be difficult indeed to find a state to take detainees who the home state believes constitute a continuing threat merely by their presence in that state. Here there seem to be only two choices: deport them to a state that is highly likely to mistreat the detainees or submit the detainees to open-ended detention, even though there has been no judicial decision that the person indeed deserves punishment through incarceration. It seems that no matter what is done to protect security, some rights of the detainee will be abrogated, and these rights will be of the most fundamental sort, including jeopardizing the security interests of the persons to be deported. Collective detention is here worse than individual incarceration or detention, especially if the detention facility is horrible, as is true of nearly all refugee camps and most mass detention centers, and thus solving the problem is of considerable urgency.

One way to respond to these problems is to articulate an emergency exception to even fundamental human rights.[18] If we are to pursue this strategy, however, I would propose that we also consider exceptions to the assumed priority of security as well, so that we have a kind of compromise achieved in which neither rights nor security should be unduly sacrificed for the other. Such an arrangement – let's call it the security–rights compromise – is premised on the idea that rights can really only be protected when there is a modicum of security and that security only has value when it is in the service of rights protection. The idea behind the security–rights compromise is, however, that it is security of rights that is the underlying rationale and so individual denial of rights can only be justified if it is clear that more security of rights are advanced by denial of individual rights.

The security–rights compromise can also be characterized in terms other than compromise if we take seriously the interdependent relationship between security and rights that I have defended elsewhere.[19] Indeed, there is a sense that the most important considerations for when security and rights can be abridged has to do with method and procedure. Fairness is the key consideration, and visibility or transparency is also extremely important. This underlines the importance of having some kind of global court or other institution in place where people can appeal when fairness seems to them to be denied. Thus, as we search for an appropriate adjusted relationship between rights and security in emergency situations, we should focus on the correct methods and procedures for dealing with people and problems. Here the common denominator is that the emergency regime should be one that is fair in that the methods and procedures are ones that people from all perspectives will find acceptable.

Emergency situations, like most other hard cases, make for bad rules. This is not to say that we should avoid discussing them, just that we should not radically alter our original conceptualizations to accommodate them. This is an aspect of fairness that seems to elude government officials in times of crisis. Government officials often use emergency situations

---

[18] See Michael Walzer, "Emergency Ethics," in his book, *Arguing about War* (New Haven, CT: Yale University Press, 2004), 33–50.

[19] See Larry May, "Global Procedural Rights and Security," in *Security: A Multi-Disciplinary Approach*, ed. Cecilia Bailliet (Leiden: Brill and Martinus Nijhoff Publishers, 2009), 249–60.

to reframe the relationship between security and rights in their desired direction long after the crisis is over.[20] Such maneuvers are unfair in that they exploit the crisis in ways that readjust the security–rights divide initially portrayed as a one-time response to an emergency crisis in ways that the overall population would not find acceptable after the crisis was over. Indeed, as the next section shows, such rights violations are violations of equity.

REFUGEE DETENTION AND EQUITY

Collective confinement and detention is problematic in nearly every case because it violates the Grotian maxim that people should only be punished for what they have done or agreed to. Some forms of collective punishment may be justifiable on the Grotian maxim if all of the members of the group supported each other in performing a wrongful collective action. And it may even be possible to justify collective punishment if there was a democratic process that led to a wrongful collective action. However, these possible rationales will not succeed in justifying mass confinement of those who did not engage in collective action but who were treated as a group simply because of similarities of behavior, such as all being found in the same place where wrongful behavior was occurring. Here there is a lack of either action or agreement in a wrongful collective action. If these situations can be justified at all, it will be only on grounds of security considerations.

Yet, as I argued earlier, it will be difficult to justify mass confinement on security grounds. In any event, the possibility of abuse of the security rationale makes it especially important that strong procedural constraints be in place. In my other work on this topic, I have continually stressed the special importance of Magna Carta legacy procedural rights in providing these constraints and protections from abuse by states. Procedural rights have not received the attention they deserve in the debates about human rights in global justice contexts.[21] In my view, cases like that of the

---

[20] See Oren Gross and Fionnuala Ni Aolain, *Law in Times of Crisis: Emergency Powers in Theory and Practice* (New York: Cambridge University Press, 2006). Also see Michael Gross, *Moral Dilemmas of Modern War: Torture, Assassination, and Blackmail in an Age of Asymmetric Conflict* (New York: Cambridge University Press, 2010).

[21] My own previous work on global justice has concerned substantive rather than procedural issues. See *Crimes against Humanity: A Normative Account* (New York: Cambridge University Press, 2005); *War Crimes and Just War* (New York: Cambridge University

Guantanamo detainees highlight the problem faced when states seemingly abuse their power to arrest en masse and detain people who do not satisfy the Grotian maxim.[22]

One category of people most in need of protection from the abuses of collective punishment are those refugees who have been forced to flee their home states because of war or the bad behavior of the home states and who have not been accepted as subjects or citizens of the state in which they find themselves. The refugee camps of the world are largely centers of "detention" if that term is used a bit more broadly than normal, where the inhabitants are also practically rightless in that no state is willing to protect them from the most severe of human rights threats, including the threat of death, rape, torture, and other serious harm. Although these people are recognized as stateless and there are international treaties that afford them rights protection, there are so many gaps here that being in a refugee camp most closely resembles being in a Hobbesian state of nature rather than in a state of civil society.

One of the reasons for the problem of rights enforcement in refugee camps is that some of the people in these camps are people who are considered a current threat or who have a criminal past, even though the overwhelming majority of these people are innocent men, women, and children. But the fact that there are some miscreants in these camps has given some host states the ability to claim that it does not have to protect any of the rights of these refugees who are detained because collectively they pose a threat to the safety or security of that State. Worse yet, it has sometimes given the host state what it believes is a right to attack the people in the refugee camps on grounds of collective punishment. Thus, there is a clear issue here that needs to be addressed by something like a court of equity or a similar international institution that can redress these rights abridgements.[23]

In the discussion of the application of the Geneva Conventions, the International Committee of the Red Cross Commentary authors state that the clear intention of the Geneva Convention drafters was that the

---

Press, 2007); *Aggression and Crimes against Peace* (New York: Cambridge University Press, 2008); and *Genocide: A Normative Account* (New York: Cambridge University Press, 2010).

[22] See my forthcoming book, *Global Justice and Due Process*, forthcoming with Cambridge University Press, 2011.

[23] Amnesty International, in a 2009 report, cites a "dramatic increase" in detention of immigrants with such detentions increasing threefold in just over a dozen years. *Amnesty International Report on United States Immigration Detentions (2009)*, reported in *International Law in Brief*, American Society of International Law (April 17, 2009): 2–3.

Geneva Conventions would not have gaps such that some people would not be protected during war.[24] I will here make a similar argument for the gapless reach of international law concerning those who are forced to suffer in the aftermath of war or atrocity. It should not matter whether one is in a refugee camp or on the soil of one's home state in terms of whether human rights protection can be claimed, assuming that the basis of the claim is a good one. In general, there should not be some people whose State protects their rights and other people who are practically rendered rightless because no State will protect them.

Since the time of Aristotle, equity has been the category in which gap filling is discussed. In the current condition of world affairs, in which states dominate, most human rights protection occurs at the state level. There are various gaps in human rights protection, however, because states mainly care about protecting the rights of their own citizens but rarely care about noncitizens. Equity is especially offended when there are gaps in human rights protection, but many have thought that such gaps in human rights protection can be justified if security is threatened, particularly in situations in which it is unclear who is truly dangerous and who is not within a group of people who are being considered for detention.

Detention for security reasons does not only occur collectively, for there is an increasing use of protective detention for those convicted of sex offenses and who have served their sentences, but who are thought likely to commit sex offenses again if released back into the general population. Here, as in cases of collective detention that are not based on the conviction of each person for what he or she has done, there is a serious failure in terms of equity. It is true that collective detention treats the members of a certain group equally, in that all are detained who seem to constitute a similar threat or risk. Equity is not the same as equality, however. The appropriate question to ask is whether the treatment is just as a matter of fairness.

The problems with the case of refugee detention arise because of the patently unfair way that the "punishments" of detention are inflicted. Once in detention or confinement, people are punished for being associated with others who are either high risk or who have actually committed serious wrongs. Some of the people in detention may deserve severe punishment, but many of the detainees do not, and thus it is patently unfair to

---

[24] See *Commentary on Geneva Convention IV*, ed. Jean S. Pictet (Geneva: International Committee for the Red Cross, 1958): 51.

treat them all "equally," in the sense of disregarding relevant differences. As Aristotle first recognized, equity is a correction of normally functioning justice. Equity clearly calls for the application of the Grotian maxim that people only be punished if they have done wrong or agreed in some way to the wrong being done.

My point is that if human rights have meaning, it is that people have significant rights merely by being members of the human or world community. This is the only fully justifiable collective membership that should matter morally. When a person is deprived of human rights protection by falling through the cracks of the regime of international rights protection, that person is practically rendered not fully human. Collective detention, in most cases, treats a human person not as a responsible agent but merely as a means to someone else's end. When this is done to deter the person being detained, it can be justifiable in some cases, but in most cases, in which the intent is not deterrence of this individual but of others, collective detention violates the underlying principle behind human rights. Even when detention is for emergency situations, the burden must remain on the detainer to prove that the detention is necessary and is not a mere pretext for long-term retaliation for unproven offenses or security threats, in a similar way to the justifications for supposedly protective retribution as a just cause for war.

Eight hundred years have elapsed between Magna Carta and Guantanamo, but the principles enunciated in Magna Carta, especially concerning arbitrary imprisonment, outlawry, or exile, are still relevant, especially as a stop to practices of collective confinement and detention, as a form of collective punishment. In a similar vein, war cannot be justified by reference to collective responsibility and punishment either – except in the cases of deterrent or self-defensive war. In those cases, however, it is misleading to talk of collective punishment, especially of "protective retribution" when what is really at stake is simple deterrence of those who have already caused harm and are likely to do so in the future. It can be similarly problematic to talk of "protective detention" because it is often merely a euphemism for what is really collective detention in violation of deep-rooted principles of equity.

OBJECTIONS

The first objection to consider is that I have set myself up for a serious challenge by suggesting that states have duties to refugees who are no longer on their soil, thereby suggesting a set of cosmopolitan duties that could sweep so far as to swamp the resources of most states. Once refugees are indeed in refuges outside a state's borders, it is a mistake to think that the state continues to have significant obligations to them. In any event, it will be difficult to make sure that some states are not unduly penalized for having lots of their citizens become refugees, especially those states that already have trouble supplying needed resources to those who remain within their borders.

My response is to acknowledge this as a serious problem to be addressed. One strategy of response is to argue that only those states that have caused their citizens to become displaced refugees by acting wrongly toward them are those that have strong duties to protect the rights of these refugees, even though they are no longer on the soil of the state in question. Merely because a state's citizens have left or even fled due to no fault of the state in question does not bring forth obligations on the State to protect these refugees. In many refugee camps, however, the refugees have been forced to leave their home states either by being subject to rendition or by being persecuted to the point where they see no other option but to flee. In these cases, it makes sense to see the home state as having a continuing obligation, under international law, to protect the rights of these refugees.

A second objection to consider is that I have overstated what happens when rights protections are not granted to a person. Surely, it is too strong to say that individuals lose their rights, become rightless, when their home state does not protect their rights. Indeed, it is difficult even to make the point that one has been treated badly if one makes the having of rights conditional on them being protected. It seems conceptually and normatively better to separate completely the having of rights from the protecting of those rights. Even the claim that one has *practically* lost one's rights risks the misleading impression that human rights can indeed be lost when protection of rights is not efficacious.

I certainly do not want to suggest that a person literally ceases to be a human if his or her human rights are not protected, but there is nonetheless such a significant loss here that it makes sense to speak of a person being not treated as fully human in terms of the respect that should be afforded when rights are not protected. Having rights is both a normative and an empirical matter. As an empirical matter, having rights entails that one is in a position to make claims and those claims are recognized as ones that need to be responded to. It is true that rights are also normative in the sense that they are hortatory – setting out a status that should be respected and for which this normative status is independent of whether one is so respected. However, it is a mistake to think that having rights in general can be practically divorced from being in a position to make claims that are recognized.

A third objection is that my security rights compromise does not give states enough leeway to protect their citizens from attacks, especially in our age of asymmetrical warfare and terrorism. In asymmetrical warfare, in which one side is either not a state or does not recognize the normal rules of war, nonrogue states must be able to protect themselves in ways that would otherwise be regarded as violating the rules of war. If these rules are not abridged in such conflicts, nonrogue states will be rendered hostage to the rules that only they are following and not sufficiently able to protect their populations from those rogue states that are not following the rules.

I have tried hard to give states some leeway in the way that I sketched a security–rights compromise, but I am not willing to grant to states more ground than I have because I would risk undercutting the rights of those who are deemed to be security threats. It is too easy for states to claim that a person represents such a threat as a way to remove those whose only threat is to the political leadership's attempt to curtail dissent. It is important not to sacrifice the very ideals on which support for nonrogue states has been built by allowing states to get a pass when they violate their own highest ideals. In any event, I have not advocated an absolutist approach in these regards because I have allowed for some forms of compromise, thereby giving states the ability to protect themselves as long as doing so does not undermine the ideals the state should hold dear.

A fourth objection is that I have stretched too far the idea of confinement and detention in including cases of refugee camps. We should restrict the idea of detention to those who are forcibly under the guard of the state rather than those who are living in a camp that they can leave, even if it might cause hardship to do so. It is important, so the objection would run, to keep our strong condemnation of arbitrary detention and confinement only for those who have been subject to imprisonment at the hands of the state, rather than to dilute the idea by including marginally similar cases of those in refugee camps. Refugee rights should be protected, but they shouldn't be assimilated to rights of those who are citizens or residents of a state.

Detention and confinement are terms that admit of several meanings. Detention normally implies that one is being restrained, and confinement similarly has the normal implication that one is forcibly prohibited from leaving. Yet, in both cases, there are also meanings of the term that imply restrictions that are moral rather than physical, as when one is restrained by rules. In urging that we think of some refugee camps as centers of detention or confinement, I am thinking of those camps where fear or economic circumstance confines the refugees and where these factors act to confine just as effectively as if there were bars and guards at the door. What becomes crucial is how these circumstances were created. If a state is responsible for creating these conditions, just as a state is responsible for creating the conditions of imprisonment, then it may be appropriate to talk of the cases in similar terms.

A final objection is to wonder how someone, such as me, who has strongly supported notions of collective responsibility can nonetheless strongly condemn collective punishment. How can one support collective responsibility without supporting what seems naturally to follow from such support – namely, support for collective punishment? Is it even conceptually possible, or normatively plausible, for there to be responsibility without punishment? It is hard not to draw the inference that if I condemn collective punishment I would have to abandon my previous support for collective responsibility.

In this chapter, I have not condemned all forms of collective punishment; indeed, the issuing of fines or barring of individuals in the exercise of some of their nonbasic freedoms seem to me, in some cases, to be appropriately directed at members of a group, especially when it is hard to tell who is a threat and who is not. What I have objected to is the deprivation of basic freedoms that comes from incarceration as well as other forms of detention and confinement directed at the members of a group. I can support collective responsibility that has as its consequence moral blame or various forms of legal sanction, including penalties and nonbasic liberty deprivation. Thus, although my earlier strong support for collective responsibility will surely be somewhat weakened by the considerations about collective punishment in this chapter, I can still support collective responsibility.

Throughout this chapter, I have been motivated by the Grotian maxim that no one should be deprived of basic liberties unless that person has done something that is wrongful or agreed to that wrong. Collective responsibility can still make sense practically even when it is associated with restricted kinds of collective penalization. As Mark Drumbl has argued, members of groups so penalized "could be permitted to avoid footing the bill, or foot less of the bill than others, by affirmatively demonstrating what they did to prevent genocide or oppose the State,"[25] for instance. However, subjecting people to mass confinement based on what others have done is simply not morally acceptable except in the most extreme emergency. The mass detention centers and refugee camps of the world are insupportable unless they conform to the Grotian maxim. Thus, what has been recognized as true about the use of war as a vehicle for collective punishment should also be true of the use of mass confinement.[26]

[25] Mark Drumbl, *Atrocity, Punishment, and International Law* (New York: Cambridge University Press, 2007), 204.
[26] I thank Gabby Blum, Michael Zimmerman, Antony Duff, Toni Erskine, David Luban, Erin Kelly, and Nancy Sherman for valuable feedback on this chapter.

PART II

Distributing Accountability

7

Reparative Justice

Erin I. Kelly

This chapter argues for a notion of reparative justice: when persons participate in an injustice, they may incur reparative obligations. Reparative obligations will take different forms depending on the nature of the injustice and a person's relation to it. When the injustice in question is a crime, reparative obligations could be a basis for criminal punishment. Under this rationale, it would be important that the punishment serve a productive social purpose, such as deterrence or the codification of relevant social norms, or the reparative aim is not accomplished. Other reparative aims could include truth telling, repudiation of wrongs done, restitution or aid to victims, community service, and institutional reform. Obligations to promote reparative aims need not presuppose criminal liability. When the burdens of reparative justice are less onerous than criminal punishment, they may be underwritten by weaker notions of fault than what is required by criminal law. An aim of this chapter is to develop a notion of reparative justice that could include, but is broader than, criminal justice. This renders a reparative approach a fitting response to the various forms collective wrongdoing might take.

I am led to the topic of reparative justice from skeptical worries about the nature of individual responsibility. Our understanding of human psychology should lead us to be skeptical about notions of freedom that individual culpability requires. We are shaped by environment, genetics, and experience in a way that affects what we perceive as reasons and narrows the horizon of possibilities for action. Environmental, genetic, and psychological factors all shape what count as reasons for a person.

I am grateful for comments I received from participants at the Collective Punishment conference, The University of Western Ontario (UWO), April 2009. I would also like to thank Richard Vernon, Tracy Isaacs, and the Nationalism and Ethnic Conflict Research Group at UWO for sponsoring the conference.

Recognizing this should challenge our confidence that a given wrong-doer was morally capable of doing better. Without this confidence, I argue, we should give up retributive notions of justice and become more modest about blaming. We should revise judgments and attitudes that commonly underlie our practices of punishment. Judgments of culpability and desert are modes of evaluation that should consult the agent's perspective. If reasons to act as morality requires are unavailable to an agent, this undermines judgments of culpability and desert, or at least significantly weakens their force. As a consequence, punitive responses become hard to justify, particularly when they are retributive in character.[1]

Reparative justice is an alternative to retributive justice. Instead of focusing on the condemnation and suffering that blameworthy wrongdoers deserve, where what is deserved is determined apart from any beneficial consequences of dealing it out, reparative justice articulates a conception of what wrongdoers could and should do: to repair the damage they have done, to address the needs of victims, and to prevent similar harms from occurring. I submit that a notion of reparative justice puts less pressure on notions of individual culpability than does retributive justice. This is because its rationale depends heavily on the value of producing outcomes that are beneficial to persons who have unjustly suffered, rather than on punishment itself as the aim of justice. Reparative justice represents a way to shift the burdens of wrongful harms from victims to those who caused or were complicitous in the unjust harm. Although this burden shifting must be justified, the conditions of its justification are weaker than what would be required for any reasonable defense of retributive justice.

To justify obligations of reparative justice, an agent's behavior must be faulty enough to support the conclusion that it would be morally better for her or him to absorb reparative costs rather than (1) to allow persons whom the person has harmed to absorb the costs of those harms or (2) to distribute the reparative costs more broadly to persons who have done nothing wrong. I submit that the threshold of fault may be met without establishing deep responsibility – full moral culpability or deservingness on the part of the agent who caused or contributed to unjust harms.[2] For the purposes of this chapter, I understand full moral culpability as a condition of agency that would be required to render retributive sentiments appropriate. Morally culpable agency, in this sense, requires more than wrongdoing. It requires the agent's capacity to understand and to

---

[1] For further discussion, see Erin I. Kelly, "Criminal Justice without Retribution," *The Journal of Philosophy* 106 (2009): 419–39.

[2] Thus we may have something like a notion of shared liability without guilt. See Avia Pasternak, "The Distributive Effect of Collective Punishment," Chapter 8, this volume.

feel moved by moral reasons. I submit that some wrongdoers lack the capacity to understand and to be motivated by morality. It might be true of a person that a harmful action is attributable to her and that what she has done is morally objectionable even though her capacity for morality is diminished or even nonexistent. Perhaps she is morally unperceptive, and her heart is cold. Still, because she has acted with disregard for others and caused objectionable harm, it may be morally better for her to absorb reparative costs rather than to allow persons whom she has harmed to be burdened by the costs of those harms or to distribute the reparative costs more broadly to persons who have done nothing wrong. It may be morally unacceptable to impose burdens on fully innocent persons, some of whom have already suffered unjustly. Thus, it seems that wrongfully causing harms makes a moral difference that can render wrongdoers, but not uninvolved third parties, liable to reparative obligations. Even blameless wrongdoers are not like bystanders, although there is considerable room for moral bad luck in the reparative obligations that befall us. We may not be able fully to establish the moral blameworthiness of those who incur reparative obligations, even when the wrongs are criminal.

I am especially interested in reparative duties that are incurred by the way a person's actions interact with the objectionable actions of other people. When persons are complicitous in a collectively generated outcome, reparative duties would be jointly incurred. This might be the case in a strong sense, even when collective aims are not jointly intended.[3] Participants may not all share the same aims. The intentions of participating members might overlap without converging, and when the group is large enough or its structure complex, the coordination required for the group to act may not extend to all members. Some members may adjust their plans in response to the actions and intentions of other group members only quite locally and as needed. The sense in which each participant coordinates his actions with other members may be limited in these ways. A person might participate in a broader economic system primarily by working together with others in a particular firm. Citizens might help to fund their government's unjust foreign intervention through a desire to avoid penalties for tax evasion. Some may participate more directly in a larger war effort by seeking employment through the military. In

---

[3] Margaret Gilbert analyzes a strong notion of joint intention that involves joint commitment to pursuing the same aim together; see *Sociality and Responsibility* (Lanham, MD: Rowman and Littlefield, 2000), especially chap. 2. Christopher Kutz develops an account of complicity that depends on overlapping intentions; see Christopher Kutz, *Complicity: Ethics and Law for a Collective Age* (Cambridge: Cambridge University Press, 2000), especially chap. 2. Gilbert and Kutz's work has been helpful to me in understanding collective action and collective responsibility.

all these cases, the broader aims and implications of the group's actions might remain largely unexamined by many, and perhaps even all, of the group's members. The contributions of individual members may have been marginal and causally inefficacious and have come from seemingly innocuous motives. These factors may well be taken to mitigate the blame individual members deserve, but they do not necessarily undermine the case for reparative obligations that could burden all participants.

Reparative justice addresses collectively generated wrongs and harms while avoiding many of the difficulties involved in distributing blame among group members for what the group has done. Participation in collective action schemes is an important source of moral pressure to accept reparative obligations for harms participants may not intend or foresee and for which members may not individually be to blame. This is not the only source of moral pressure, which derives also from more general duties of humanitarian assistance, fair play, or political membership, but a principle generating reparative obligations may not be superseded by these other principles. Further, it may work in tandem with other principles to make a sense of obligation harder to evade.

Acknowledging that the influences of our social and natural world compromise the sense in which individual choices and actions are autonomous does not negate the possibility that people might take responsibility for their actions, whether acting on their own or as members of groups. What I am proposing, more narrowly, is that we replace the enterprise of dealing out desert with an acknowledgment of the ethical and political importance of taking responsibility for wrongs done and harms caused.[4] Taking responsibility involves acknowledging that a morally objectionable outcome was attributable to you and responding appropriately to this fact by, for example, taking steps to acknowledge, to rectify, or to compensate for wrongs done and harms caused. Reasons to take responsibility may stem from a person's causal responsibility for wrongdoing or from her participation in a group that acts unjustly. Individual or collective wrongdoing may be adequate to support the demands of reparative justice, even though it fails to justify retributive responses.

TAKING RESPONSIBILITY

In 1946, not long after the defeat of the Nazi regime, Karl Jaspers delivered a series of lectures titled "The Question of German Guilt." In these

---

[4] See the helpful discussion by Jeffrey Blustein, especially on the point that taking responsibility need not presuppose blameworthiness. *The Moral Demands of Memory* (Cambridge: Cambridge University Press, 2008), chap. 3.

lectures, he grappled with the question of the German people's responsibility for World War II and for the atrocities of the Nazi regime. He was addressing a defeated and demoralized population that had suffered greatly. The allies had bombed Germany heavily in the last phases of the war. Its cities lay in ruins. Poverty and the devastation of war marked the entire country, and Germany seemed to be left with little to build a future. The German people were also a population lacking sympathy from the rest of the world. Germany had come to represent evil on a heretofore unknown scale. The allies demanded reparations from the German people, and Nazi leaders accused of war crimes would be tried in Nuremberg.

Jaspers and other anti-Nazi professors were returning to their posts after having been banished from the universities under the Nazis. As Jaspers addressed students at the University of Heidelberg, he assumed the task of helping young people to face both the past and future of Germany. Naturally Jaspers would have to address the meaning of guilt, the point of guilt, and where an acknowledgment of guilt might leave Germany and its citizens. Although his audience was German, Jaspers must have felt the scrutiny of the rest of the world.

The lectures bear some striking themes. Despite the dangers of appearing to "excuse" German citizens for their complicity, Jaspers acknowledges the power of culture and politics to shape our individual experience and possibilities for action. He writes, for example, that "the conduct which made us liable rests on a sum of political conditions whose nature is moral, as it were, because they help to determine individual morality. The individual cannot wholly detach himself from these conditions, for – consciously or unconsciously – he lives as a link in a chain and cannot escape from their influence even if he was in opposition."[5] By describing individuals as links in a chain from which they cannot escape, Jaspers emphasizes the social context that shapes our moral possibilities. He argues that a people's way of life restricts the possibilities for individual choice and sets political events into motion. History attests to a cycle of influence between culture and politics. As Jaspers puts it, "The way of life effects political effects, and the resulting political conditions in turn place their imprint on the way of life."[6] This picture may seem to leave no room for personal guilt. Where and how in this chain of causes could personal guilt be located? How might individual responsibility enter the cycle?

---

[5] Karl Jaspers, *The Question of German Guilt,* trans. E. B. Ashton with intro. by Joseph W. Koterski, S. J. (New York: Fordham University Press, 2000), 70.
[6] Jaspers, *The Question of German Guilt,* 71.

One might insist on the "compatibilist" position that natural causes pose no threat to moral responsibility. Persons are accountable for the role they have actually played unless the causes or consequences of their behavior were of an "abnormal" sort. Common causes do not exculpate. In fact, the idea that guilt is compatible with lack of control and even lack of agency pervades Jaspers's notion of "metaphysical guilt." Metaphysical guilt is survivors' guilt: the guilt a person might feel for living when others are killed. This notion of guilt can accompany complete powerlessness; one might feel guilty even when there is nothing one could have done that would have made any difference. Its basis is not individual freedom but human solidarity and sympathy. In that sense, it seems to go to the core of an impartial morality. Metaphysical guilt expresses the felt connectedness of persons who have transcended the limits of self-concern and group partiality and are sensitive to the value of human life. Yet, it also lacks moral edge. Guilt is set adrift from any recognizable sense of wrongdoing. For that, human agency is required.

Yet, something important is acknowledged through Jaspers's notion of metaphysical guilt. Specifically, through it we might acknowledge that others did not deserve their fate and that the moral standing of each of us is influenced by contingencies that we do not control. Others have recognized the moral relevance of contingency through the notion of "moral luck." Thomas Nagel defines moral luck as follows: "where a significant aspect of what someone does depends on factors beyond his control, yet we continue to treat him in that respect as an object of moral judgment."[7] Nagel believes we accept moral luck in how things turn out when a person acts, in the circumstance in which a person is faced with questions about how to act, in the facets of a person's character, and in the causal antecedents, in mental space, of a person's choices themselves. If you leave the baby in the bathtub while you answer the phone, you have done something far worse if the baby happens to drown. Of course, moral luck infects praiseworthy qualities as well. As Frog remarks to Toad after their all-too-desirable cookies are eaten by birds, "Now we have ... lots of will power."[8]

Nagel's point is that although our ordinary idea of moral assessment maintains that persons are not responsible for what is not their fault or due to factors beyond their control, in practice we find it acceptable

[7] Thomas Nagel, "Moral Luck," in *Mortal Questions* (Cambridge: Cambridge University Press, 1979), 26.
[8] Arnold Lobel, *Frog and Toad Together* (New York: Scholastic Books, 1971).

morally to judge persons even when a significant aspect of what they do depends on factors beyond their control. We do in fact hold people accountable for the way things turn out when they act badly. We judge people for character traits they have developed, almost whatever the cause. We blame people for failing to make good choices under difficult circumstances that most of us are fortunate not to have faced. However, the relevance of contingency to morality is difficult to reconcile with retributive notions of blame and punishment. In particular, I have emphasized the troublesome nature of moral luck in the horizon of a person's possible reasons to act. Retributive notions of blame and punishment presuppose that a blameworthy person could have acted as she morally ought to have acted. If she is not capable of taking moral reasons seriously, her culpability should be accordingly limited. Yet, as compatibilists would readily affirm, this possibility haunts any of our ascriptions of culpability. Moral reasons may or may not have been available to a person who has violated morality's requirements, and we might not be able to tell the difference. Retributive notions of blame and punishment are in trouble.

In response, we might reject the notion that responsibility is a wholly backward-looking notion. We could relinquish retributive notions of moral desert and look instead to the role ascriptions of responsibility play in an obligation-centered morality. Reparative obligations are responsive to what has happened. They are historically rooted in what we have done, yet they also involve a forward-looking directive. They can largely abstract from questions of blame. Their point is to guide us in understanding and responding to what we have done. Jaspers construes responsibility as a task that the citizens of Germany ought to take on for the sake of Germany's future, as well as their own. He thought the hope of dissociating from a horrifying and shameful past and committing to a better future depended on it.

How one has acted is a basis for reflection, reconsideration, and change in a context in which we can recognize, nevertheless, the many factors that impinge on our agency. An appreciation of our own agency that is grounded by a sensible grasp of our limitations can produce, ironically, a stronger sense of identity, purpose, and self-control. It can lead us to understand more clearly the importance of the choices available to us and prepare us to negotiate our way around difficulties and troublesome incentives we do not create. It can also strengthen and humanize relationships by opening possibilities for reconciliation.

What unifies a person as an agent over time is a person's self-conception – a self-conscious appreciation of and identification with principles of action.[9] We make sense of action-possibilities by reference to a reasons framework of practical deliberation. A deliberate course of action is identifiable as such in terms of reasons that justify or at least rationalize it; we cite an agent's motives or reasons for acting. We analyze what a person should and will do, as well as what she has done, in this way. Unless we situate his actions within a framework of normative considerations, we cannot discriminate deliberate bodily movements from those merely preceded by certain thoughts (such as that I ought to do something).

In making sense of our past behavior, we cite reasons we can understand, even if we are now critical of them. An action might be understandable, given an agent's priorities at the time of acting, although those priorities were misguided. Misguided priorities provide a basis for criticism, including self-criticism. Of course, self-criticism can produce a serious sense of alienation from self and, accordingly, a sense of disunity. This is avoided and a unified self-conception is preserved when self-understanding relies on principles that contain something with which the self-critical agent can identify – for instance, the notion that a person's personal goals and commitments present her with some reasons to act. Principles such as this function as a kind of bridge between a person's current values and the values she held at the time of acting.[10] She can rely on such a principle to take responsibility for what she has done and to orient her future behavior and obligations. Although she may now reject her former goals, she can understand how at the time she could have taken herself to have reasons to act as she did, reasons that were rooted in her commitment to the goals she had. She can identify with herself as a person who had commitments that she tried rationally to realize.

Without active identification, a person's behavior is indistinguishable from mere happenings, for instance, that she happened to be someone (or that there happened to be someone) with misguided priorities. Our tendency to dissemble and to rationalize actions we are ashamed of is evidence of the value we place on unified agency and its underlying principles. Persons seek a way to reconcile themselves with what they have

---

[9] See Christine M. Korsgaard, *Self-Constitution: Agency, Identity, and Integrity* (New York: Oxford University Press, 2009). See also Harry G. Frankfurt, *The Importance of What We Care About* (Cambridge: Cambridge University Press, 1988).

[10] Charles Griswold makes the point that a wrongdoer's repudiation of past wrongs depends on a recognizable continuity of self, something the offender offers through a narrative account of how she came to do wrong. See Charles L. Griswold, *Forgiveness: A Philosophical Exploration* (Cambridge: Cambridge University Press, 2007), especially 47–53.

done, even if this means lying to themselves. Self-deception preserves agency, but a self-deceived agent is also fragile and vulnerable to fragmentation. By contrast, an agent who finds a way to identify with her mistakes can take responsibility for what she has done while affirming principles for better choices. By specifying some normative bridging principles, identification through self-criticism and change is possible. The self-critical agent can put acknowledging her past faulty conduct and the mistaken values that guided it in the context of some (if more abstract) continuity in her values. At the same time, her present commitment to better principles of action allows for the possibility of growth. A person can identify with something that contributed to her decision to act as she did while asserting that principles she now affirms would have led her to act differently. Her current values help her to understand and to claim her mistakes without repudiating her own agency.

In sum, an action is oriented toward a goal, aim, or purpose the agent commits herself to as worthwhile. This orientation calls attention to principles or norms guiding an agent's pursuits. These norms include a principle of instrumental rationality, but also substantive commitments and principles that characterize someone as a person of a certain sort. Adherence to norms unifies agency over time. Even with revision of some aims and their supporting norms, a subset of relevant principles may provide continuity over time sufficient for agency and identity. Action-guiding principles provide a basis for the agent to take responsibility for her mistakes, a stance from which a person could acknowledge reparative obligations.

COMPLICITY

Taking responsibility extends to acknowledging the role one has played as a member of a group. A person contributes to the action of a group of which she is a part through her complicity with what the group does. We can understand this by considering what it is for a group to act and what it means for an individual to be complicit with a group's wrongdoing. A group or collective action should be distinguished from the aggregated effects of separate individual actions. In the latter case, there is no collective agent.

Like individual agents, a collective agent commits itself to goals, aims, or purposes it takes to be worthwhile. There is something at which it aims in acting and it does so for reasons that it accepts as having normative force. A collective agent achieves a meaningful conception of itself as subject to normative directives through its representatives and participants. Collective self-understanding is attained through each member's conception of her aim in acting as shared with some other members of the group and as guided by rules or principles to which they are committed. Each participant understands herself to be doing something together with other members: electing a leader, doing business, fighting a common enemy, abiding by the law. In acting, each member intends to play a part in advancing a shared and mutually affirmed enterprise. Furthermore, the relevant aims and action-coordinating principles are public. They are not merely held privately by individuals but are affirmed by the group through, for example, legislation, delegation, or an agreement on plans. This is true even if the group's aims are multiple and not all endorsed by all members.

Thus, aims and action-guiding principles expressed in collective action are set together by a group of people or by individuals who represent the group and are authorized to act on its behalf. Those with representative authority advance aims in the name of collective interests, principles, and goals. The coordination of multiple aims and of the parts played by various participants to advance those aims is achieved through accepted structures of authority, decision-making procedures, public conventions that express norms and values characterizing a shared way of life, and the like. Multiple aims might be coordinated institutionally without the oversight of particular persons.

When people act according to a common scheme, each person enlarges the scope of his or her agency. Each person acts together with other people at the same time she does something herself. It follows from this that collective agency can have ethical ramifications for individual members. First of all, collective commitments and actions that serve them can be subjected to moral criticism. Members whose contribution to harms done by a group is marginal or causally inefficacious may nevertheless be at fault together with their comembers for harms the group causes, and, I submit, they may incur reparative obligations together with comembers for their participation in collective wrongdoing. While you are not generally responsible for acts that are committed by another person, harms committed by other people are a basis for your accountability when a person whom you have empowered to represent you, or with whom you coordinate actions that together bring about the objectionable result, commits the harmful act. Delegation and other forms of coordination establish an ethically relevant sense in which you are a collective agent and have generated the harmful result together. This means that each participant bears some responsibility for what other group members do.

When there is no collective agency, by contrast, individuals whose relation to a harmful outcome is marginal or causally inefficacious may bear no responsibility. They have not significantly participated in its creation. The last driver who crossed the I-35 W Bridge in Minneapolis before the bridge collapsed may have weakened it to the breaking point, but surely that person would not be thought to have caused the collapse nor to be at fault, even in a small way or together with other persons.

The picture I have just sketched posits the ethical significance of collective action for evaluating individual behavior. This picture might be challenged. It might be thought that collective responsibility is an illusion and that all reparative obligations must be traced to individual contributions and proportionally distributed. A robust conception of individual responsibility may be thought to be an adequate basis for distributing reparative obligations – for example, a conception of responsibility maintaining that marginal contributions can be morally significant and that causally inefficacious contributions are morally significant if they might foreseeably have made a difference. Thus, it might be argued, reparative duties can be rooted entirely in individual responsibility. We need only to acknowledge the reasonably foreseeable results of what individuals do, in a social context in which other people act or might act. Notions of collective action and complicity are not required to generate the full range of reparative obligations.

There is something to these claims. It does seem true that we tend to underappreciate the moral significance of marginal contributions and the counterfactual properties of our actions. Individual polluters are open to moral criticism, even if their overall contribution to the problem of pollution is small. Moral criticism could be proportioned in accordance with the commonly recognized moral intuition that we are each responsible for what we ourselves do, but not for what other people do. Indeed, this principle may seem to be fundamental to morality. Yet, it does not stand up to its intuitive appeal. In morally evaluating what a person has done, we should not underestimate the moral and political significance of coordination: what a person does together with other people. Many harmful results, for example, those generated in war or through corporate greed, would not have occurred but for socially coordinated schemes in which we most meaningfully analyze agency in collective terms. Persons act as they do because they share intentions and plans. They enable each other to act for shared reasons that can be evaluated ethically. Social cooperation implies that individual contributions should be understood, ethically speaking, not merely in terms of their causal interaction but also as a matter of their common design.

Because collective agency can be understood by plausibly expanding our understanding of what participants do to include what they do together, we should reject the common belief that we cannot be responsible for what other people do. Each participant may be responsible, albeit to varying degrees, for what the group does. In this way, moral criticism of participants is not confined only to the role a participant has played in the group's action. Each participant can also be criticized for what she did together with other group members, that is, for what the group has done.

In sum, complicity relates individual members of a group to what a group does and, accordingly, expands the domain of personal responsibility. Coordination, delegation, and strategic planning raise the moral stakes of seemingly inconsequential actions, linking these actions to what the group does, even though the group's action is also the product of other people's choices. When participation creates a group agent, responsibility for its actions extends in some measure to all individual members. Thus, a person's willingness to plan and coordinate with others can be morally significant, beyond merely marginal, if any, harms that person individually causes.

COLLECTIVE CRIMINALITY

The ethical significance of complicity has been recognized in the criminal law. Notions of collective criminality are developed in both domestic law and international law. These notions include doctrines of conspiracy as well as other modes of complicity, such as aiding and abetting, through which persons who are not the direct agents of a criminal act are nonetheless liable as coperpetrators. The crime of conspiracy enlarges the scope of individual accountability to include concrete criminal plans made with other persons. All conspirators are liable to criminal sanctions, whether or not the criminal plan is executed. In other words, conspiracy is a separate crime that can be added to charges for particular substantive criminal acts. In U.S. law, a person is guilty of conspiracy when it has been established that he was party to an agreement to achieve an unlawful objective and that he knowingly participated in the joint criminal enterprise with the intention of helping it to succeed. Thus conspiracy requires both intention and knowledge on the part of coperpetrators.

Modes of participation, such as aiding and abetting, derive coperpetrators' liability from the criminal acts of their associates. These modes of participation also require knowledge and intention on the part of coperpetrators. They clearly emphasize the agency of coperpetrators, even those who are not the direct agents of the crime.

More controversial are statutes that expand criminal liability to include "reasonably foreseeable consequences" of a criminal associate's behavior. The Pinkerton Rule in U.S. federal law maintains that coconspirators are liable for all reasonably foreseeable substantive crimes committed by their coconspirators in furtherance of the conspiracy.[11] Criminal liability requires neither direct participation nor knowledge. "In furtherance of the conspiracy" seems to be interpreted to mean, "in the course of carrying out the conspiracy," whether or not the substantive crime in question was instrumental or necessary for completing the conspiracy. This statute and others like it loosen requirements of intention and knowledge, permitting criminal liability to be ascribed to members of a criminal enterprise for crimes committed by their associates even though liable members may not have intended or known about the particular criminal acts in question. The notion here is that the crime in question was a reasonably foreseeable consequence of the joint criminal enterprise. This standard is "objective" rather than "subjective" – in other words, it does not entail that the offender actually foresaw the result. The standard appeals instead to the judgment of a "reasonable person."

My concern is with what is required to meet the agential requirements of criminal liability, and whether "reasonably foreseeable consequences" can plausibly be said to fit these requirements. We have seen that when a person is complicit with group wrongdoing, that individual may incur reparative obligations for harmful actions committed by other group members. The question with which we are now occupied concerns how tightly coordinated and planned the group's actions must be, if each member is to be held criminally liable for what comembers do.

I submit that less here in the way of individual fault is required than would be required for the retributivist to show that individual members deserve punishment, but something more than "reasonably foreseeable"

---

[11] *Pinkerton v. United States*, 328 U.S. 640 (1946). See discussion by David Luban, Julie R. O'Sullivan, and David P. Stewart, in *International and Transnational Criminal Law* (New York: Aspen Publishers, 2010), chap. 17. Chapter 17 also discusses a similar criterion, "joint criminal enterprise," found in international law as shaped by the Yugoslav Tribunal. See *Prosecutor v. Tadić*, Case No. IT-94-1-A, Judgment (July 15, 1999).

results of what the group does must be established. Forseeability is too weak a basis criminally to implicate each individual member of the offending group. Another person's act that was not assisted or intended by an alleged coconspirator typically breaks the causal chain, in the eyes of the law.[12] This is how boundaries of responsibility are typically drawn in the law so as to preserve *mens rea* considerations designed to ensure that the main focus of law is to guide people's choices and that only persons who had a fair opportunity to avoid committing a discrete crime are liable to criminal charges.[13] Only thus are individual rights respected. We need some compelling grounds to override this presumption. We need some ground for thinking not just that B's action P was predictable given what A did, but that B and A share criminal responsibility for P.

This can be seen as a question about how the boundaries of agency should be drawn for the purposes of criminal law. If we are to understand collective criminality such that culpable participation does not require conspiring, inducing, or assisting, some other relevant criterion must be established. Moreover, as I have suggested, this criterion must be compatible with the notion of agency that gives a system of law its point: to guide choices without encroaching on individual rights. The question is whether reasonably foreseeable results of one party delegating responsibility or empowering another party to act establish joint criminal liability. Because I will assume that there are good moral reasons not to eliminate the notion of responsibility that *mens rea* considerations aim to capture, we need an account of how weakening their requirements could be compatible with treating individuals fairly and with acknowledging the moral significance of choice.

We have seen that marginal causal contributions could be a basis for complicity when coordination produces collective action, but I also expressed skepticism about whether complicity entails blameworthiness. When it comes to criminal charges, it would seem that something akin to blameworthiness is required. There must be a relevant way directly to connect complicitous individuals with objectionable outcomes if those outcomes are to count as their crime. Unless a person has chosen to participate in a given crime, whether or not she is involved with the

---

[12] H. L. A. Hart and Tony Honoré, *Causation in the Law*, 2nd ed. (Oxford: Oxford University Press, 1985), chap. 12.

[13] See H. L. A. Hart, "Legal Responsibility and Excuses," and "Punishment and the Elimination of Responsibility," in *Punishment and Responsibility* (Oxford: Oxford University Press, 1968).

agents of that crime, she cannot meaningfully be said to have disregarded a fair opportunity to have avoided liability to criminal charges. Guilt by association is an inadequate notion of criminal responsibility.

A promising strategy is to argue that expressing approval of results that are directly connected to collective wrongdoing in which one has participated is evidence of the requisite *mens rea* and implies that one shares criminal responsibility for the group's wrong. The same might be said about accepting benefits that are so connected. Expressing approval or accepting benefits is evidence that coperpetrators were reconciled to the harmful results that in fact occurred, even if they did not conspire to commit the criminal act in question nor directly assist in its execution.[14] Evidence might include accepting stolen property, rewarding corrupt employees, consolidating political power after the illegal use of force by associates, affirming victory in a rigged election, claiming territory that was obtained illegally, and the like. The approval by or benefit to coperpetrators points to their culpable disregard for the laws directives. Without evidence that an alleged coperpetrator was reconciled to the result, there may be no relevant description of his participation in the crime that fits with principles on which he has acted. Thus, there would be no relevant sense in which she is criminally implicated by the group's action, even if other people's actions would count as reasonably foreseeable results of a scheme in which she is involved. On the other hand, when a coperpetrator is reconciled to the results of foreseeable collective wrongdoing, she can be said to endorse the group's action as her own.

I submit that if an individual was not herself the direct agent of a collectively produced wrong, her criminal liability must presuppose that she agreed to participate, enabled the harm, approved of the wrong, or accepted benefits from it. Otherwise, even if the event was reasonably foreseeable, it could not be said to express the coperpetrator's culpable agency.

Thus, criminal responsibility may be generated by complicity in group behavior, provided there is evidence that coperpetrators were reconciled to the criminal result, even if they did not all in fact intend or know

---

[14] I am indebted to David Luban for suggesting to me that an individual may demonstrate *mens rea* by being reconciled to an unjustifiable risk. Luban and his coauthors discuss this idea and its connection with the German notion of *dolus eventualis* in Luban, O'Sullivan, and Stewart, *International and Transnational Criminal Law*, chap. 17. See also *Prosecutor v. Lubanga*, Case No. ICC-01/04–01/06, Decision on the confirmation of charges (January 29, 2007).

about it in advance. The form their reparative obligations may take could include nonretributive forms of criminal punishment, provided that culpability, thus understood, can be established, or so I have argued.

CONCLUDING THOUGHTS

In noncriminal cases, the criterion for establishing a morally relevant sense of collective responsibility could be considerably weaker. Specifically, accepting benefits that are only indirectly connected to the wrong in question might suffice. Institutional sources of support for racial discrimination, for example, may cast the net of complicity quite broadly. Accepting indirect benefits such as financial advantage, status advantage, or political power may establish the complicity of individuals with a group's actions they do not intend or foresee, even when their participation in marginal. Reconciliation with the results of collective wrongdoing in this sense may not even be necessary to establish an individual's complicity with group wrongdoing that the individual participant did not intend or directly assist. It may be enough that a group member has embraced principles that rationalize aspects of the group's organization as he participates in facets of the group's activities and that the group's wrongdoing was a significant possibility. Complicity, so understood, may constitute moral grounds to shift the burdens of liability onto complicitous members, rather than burdening those who have not participated, even marginally, in wrongdoing. Complicity provides members of a group with reasons to take responsibility for the group's action, by acknowledging, compensating, repairing, and the like. It would not, however, justify collective or individual punishment.

Reparative obligations acknowledge the moral importance of an individual or a group's causal responsibility and allow wide scope for moral luck. It is often appropriate that an agent (individual or collective) who caused harm take responsibility for it, even when that agent is not fully to blame for the harm, or perhaps is not blameworthy at all. The alternative is that others who have done nothing wrong nor caused harm should absorb the cost of her harmful and morally objectionable acts. These costs provide compelling reasons for persons who are causally connected with the harms in question, either directly or via complicity, to take responsibility for them. We should protect persons who are not the agents of their own suffering from other people's harmful behavior. This is imperative within a rights-based conception of justice. I have been discussing factors that bear on how the costs of this "responsibility to protect" ought to be distributed.[15]

Socially responsible persons aim to counteract the possibility of injustice. Responsible membership in a collective agent is not best gauged by a shared sense of pride and celebrated values but by a cautious thinking ahead to how things might go wrong. This requires critical analysis that acknowledges past wrongs and grapples with the political and social dynamics that made them possible. The historical record of the social institutions in which we participate, willingly and even unwillingly, influences our responsibilities as members of groups. Our critical grasp of these influences may open action possibilities that would not otherwise have been available to us. This is especially true when critical appreciation of the dynamics of injustice is public and shared. Then critical scrutiny can be joined with a collective commitment to taking responsibility for social injustice.

I have contrasted reparative justice with retributive justice. Reparative justice enables us to recognize that how one has acted and been complicit is a basis for reparative duties in a context in which we can also recognize the many factors that impinge on our agency. It may be a person's bad moral luck that she morally ought to assume responsibility for what she has done. Taking responsibility involves aiming to acknowledge, self-examine, and rectify or compensate for wrongs done and harms caused. Central to this moral conception of responsibility is a recognition that participation in group wrongdoing has moral implications for the group's members, despite the influence of factors beyond an individual participant's control.

---

[15] For illuminating discussion of the notion of "responsibility to protect," see Report of the International Commission on Intervention and State Sovereignty, *The Responsibility to Protect* (Ottawa: The International Development Research Centre, 2001).

8

The Distributive Effect of
Collective Punishment

Avia Pasternak

Collective punishment has a notorious reputation among moral philosophers. If we take it to mean the imposition of punitive measures on groups
(I elaborate on this meaning later in the chapter), collective punishment
raises two normative issues that many philosophers find particularly troubling. The first concerns the extent to which *groups* are the appropriate
subjects of punishment. Here the question is, are groups moral agents
that are responsible for their actions and should be held to account when
they act wrongly? The second difficulty concerns the impact of collective punishment on group *members*. Here the question is, is it justified
to impose burdens on individuals by virtue of the fact that their group
caused a collective harm?

To see these problems more clearly, consider the proposed academic
boycott against Israeli universities (the subject of heated debates in recent
years in British academia). Briefly, the proponents of the boycott recommend the elimination of professional ties with Israeli academic institutions, in light of the latter's alleged support of the Israeli government
policies.[1] However, does it make sense to argue that academic *institutions*

I am grateful for comments and suggestions by the participants of the workshop on
collective punishment at The University of Western Ontario, April 2009; the participants
of the Center on Ethics workshop at Stanford University; and one anonymous reviewer
from Cambridge University Press.

[1] Proposals to impose a boycott on Israeli universities have been considered in recent
years by the University and College Union (UCU), the largest academic trade union in
the United Kingdom. Delegates to the UCU annual meeting voted on several occasions
for motions in support of a boycott. All motions were met with much criticism and
objections from within the union and were subsequently revoked on legal grounds. At
the UCU 2007 annual meeting, delegates voted for a circulation of the boycott call to all
its branches and local organizations. This vote raised a heated debate within the union.

act in a condemnable manner? Are *institutions* themselves the proper subject of moral reactions such as anger, resentment, or condemnation? Moreover, even if it can be shown that Israeli academic institutions acted in a way that merits condemnation, boycotting them will harm the individual academics who work in those institutions. Can this distributive effect be justified?

In recent years, much attention has been given to the first of these challenges: which groups should be classified as moral agents that are collectively responsible for their actions?[2] At the same time, the problem of the impact of collective punishment on such groups' members has not gained much attention. Here, to assess the legitimacy of such impact, two separate issues must be addressed. The first concerns the *character* of the impact of collective punishment on group members: is it a form of punishment, or perhaps another type of burden? The second concerns the *pattern* of the impact of the collective punishment on group members: how are the different group members affected by the punishment relative to each other, and what is the justification for that pattern of distribution? The answers to these questions would help us to understand under what circumstances the distributive effect of collective punishment is morally permissible and how this effect should be managed.

In this chapter, I begin to address these issues. The starting point of the discussion here is the (admittedly controversial) assumption that some groups have a collective moral agency that is independent of their members' agency and that, as such, they are collectively responsible for their actions. The first section distinguishes between two types of burdens that groups can be made to bear in the aftermath of an injustice or harm for which they are responsible. The first is collective (or, more precisely, corporate) punishment, a burden with the purpose of condemning the group for the harm it caused. The second is collective (or corporate) liability, a burden with the purpose of assigning the costs of the harm to the group

---

It was subsequently revoked after it had been pointed out that an academic boycott is likely to infringe on UK antidiscrimination legislation. At the 2008 annual meeting, delegates decided to call on the UCU members to "consider the moral and political implications of educational links with Israeli Institutions." This decision was also met with much internal criticism and threats for legal action and was not implemented. In 2009, delegates voted for a "boycott, disinvestment and sanctions campaign" against Israeli universities. The vote was immediately declared void by the union's leadership.

[2] See, for example, the collection of works in Peter A. French and Howard K. Wettstein, eds., *Shared Intentions and Collective Responsibility*, vol. XXX, Midwest Studies in Philosophy (Oxford: Blackwell Publishing, 2006).

but in a way that does not carry with it a condemning quality. When groups are being punished or held liable for their actions, their individual members are bound to be affected as a result. However, using the case of the academic boycott as a case study, I suggest that this effect does not necessarily amount to the personal condemnation and *punishment* of individual group members. Rather, group members may end up being merely *liable* for harms that their group has caused, without that burden implying that they personally have acted wrongly. Nevertheless, as I discuss later in the first section, even if collective sanctions do not punish group members, they affect them adversely, and sometimes heavily. This fact raises important questions about the proper model for the distribution of the collective burden that is created by the sanction, between the group's individual members.

The second section deals with this problem. I suggest that, once a group is being collectively sanctioned, there are three ways in which the impact of the sanctions can be further distributed between its members: on a proportional basis, on an equal basis, and on a random basis. A proportional distribution of the impact takes into account the group members' personal association with the collective harm; an equal distribution distributes its costs on an equal basis; and a random distribution lets the collective burden fall randomly. A group that is subjected to corporate sanctions must choose between these three models. The third section analyzes both the normative and practical considerations that should guide a group's choice in this matter. As the discussion shows, the three models of distribution fare differently from each of these perspectives: a proportional distribution is potentially the least practical distribution, but it has a solid normative justification that revolves around the principle of fairness. A random distribution is hard to justify on normative grounds, but is the easiest to implement. Finally, an equal distribution is located somewhere between the two other distributions on both scales: it is more practical than a proportional distribution and harder to implement than random distribution. On the normative scale, although it is not as clearly supported by a normative premise as proportional distribution, there are cases in which it can be justified on normative grounds. For example, as I suggest here, in cases in which the group in question is the state, it can be argued that citizens ought to accept an equal distribution of their governments' collective burden because doing so is constitutive of a certain ethical understanding of the meaning of citizenship. Finally, the fourth section draws on the discussion to provide some recommendations for the proper scope and limits of collective sanctions.

IMPOSING SANCTIONS ON COLLECTIVES

In this section, I examine the nature of the impact of collective punishment on group members. As a prelude to the discussion, it is important to draw two conceptual distinctions. The first distinction is between "punishment" and what I would refer to here as "liability." Following Joel Feinberg, I define punishment as a "device for the expression of attitudes of resentment and indignation, and of judgments of disapproval and reprobation, either on the part of the punishing authority himself or of those 'in whose name' the punishment is inflicted."[3] According to this definition the key function of punishment is the expression of condemnation through some form of hard treatment. Liability, in contrast, is a notion that refers to the burdens that are imposed on an agent in the aftermath of an undesired situation but that do not necessarily carry with them the implication that she acted wrongly. Examples are fines and penalties – costs that are imposed when agents have broken the law but that lack symbolic significance,[4] and compensatory duties to the victims of harm, which are sometimes assigned to agents who acted without fault or who have not even contributed to the harm in question (e.g., companies' liability for the quality of their products or for the conduct of their employees).[5]

---

[3] Joel Feinberg, "The Expressive Function of Punishment," *Monist* 49, no. 3 (1965): 400.

[4] See discussion in ibid. As Feinberg points out, fines, penalties, or the withdrawal of state benefits can become a form of punishment if they carry with them a symbolic significance.

[5] See discussion in Joel Feinberg, "Collective Responsibility (Another Defence)," in *Collective Responsibility: Five Decades of Debate in Theoretical and Applied Ethics*, ed. Larry May and Stacey Hoffman (Savage, MD: Rowman & Littlefield Publishers, 1991). Notice that the notion of liability as it is used here is different from the notion of "outcome responsibility" as developed by Tony Honoré and more recently by David Miller (Tony Honoré, "Responsibility and Luck: The Moral Basis of Strict Liability" in *Responsibility and Fault* (Oxford: Hart, 1999); and David Miller, *National Responsibility and Global Justice* (Oxford: Oxford University Press, 2007), 86–90). According to Honoré, outcome responsibility means "being responsible for the good and harm we bring about by what we do," and it justifies the assignment of costs (or benefits) to agents for outcomes they have brought about even when their conduct was without fault (Honoré, "Responsibility and Luck," 14). Although my notion of liability is also concerned with the distribution of the costs (and benefits) of certain outcomes, I wish to also include in it cases where the liable agent is not related to the outcome through her own conduct. My reason for preferring this notion of liability is that, as the discussion later on would reveal, it covers cases in which the responsibility of a group is distributed between group members, sometimes regardless of their own conduct. The notion of outcome responsibility seems inapplicable to those cases.

The second distinction is the familiar distinction between corporate and shared responsibility. Briefly, corporate responsibility refers to the responsibility of a group, as an agent independent of its individual members. Shared responsibility, in contrast, refers to the responsibility of group members, with relation to actions performed by the group or by other group members.[6] The idea that groups are corporately responsible for their actions, and as result can be held liable or punished when their actions lead to bad outcomes, is often grounded in the metaphysical claim that groups can have a collective moral agency independent of their members. Several familiar accounts in the literature support this claim, and what they all share in common is the assumption that at least highly institutional groups can form collective intentions and can act collectively.[7] The collective intentions and actions of groups have a derivative nature in the sense that they are exercised through the intentions and actions of individual group members. However, at least in highly institutional groups with formal decision-making mechanisms, the collective intention of the group would not necessarily be the intention of all group members, and even if all group members share the collective intention, they may be doing so to varying degrees. In the rest of the discussion, I assume that a group agent that acts in a condemnable manner is corporately responsible for its behavior, but it does not follow that all its members acted in a condemnable manner; even if they did, then not necessarily to an equal degree.

Do Corporate Sanctions Punish Group Members?

We can now turn to examine the distributive effects of collective punishment and of collective liability. On the basis of the aforementioned

---

[6] This distinction appears in many discussions of collective responsibility. See, for example, Virginia Held, "Can a Random Collection of Individuals Be Morally Responsible?," in *Collective Responsibility*, ed. Larry May and Stacey Hoffman. Larry May, *Sharing Responsibility* (Chicago: University of Chicago Press, 1992), 37–38. Gregory Mellema, *Collective Responsibility*, Value Inquiry Book Series, Vol. 50 (Amsterdam: Rodopi, 1997).

[7] See, for example, Peter French, *Collective and Corporate Responsibility* (New York: Columbia University Press, 1984). Larry May, *The Morality of Groups: Collective Responsibility, Group-Based Harm, and Corporate Rights* (Notre Dame, IN: University of Notre Dame Press, 1987); Philip Pettit, "Groups with Minds of Their Own," in *Socializing Metaphysics: The Nature of Social Reality*, ed. Frederick F. Schmitt (Oxford: Rowman & Littlefield Publishers, 2003); Christopher Kutz, *Complicity: Ethics and Law for a Collective Age* (Cambridge: New York: Cambridge University Press, 2000), 191–97. According to some of these accounts, noninstitutional groups can also be corporately morally responsible.

distinctions, I take "collective punishment" to mean the imposition of *corporate* punishment, or the punishment of a group. Accordingly, collective punishment amounts to a hard treatment of a *group* with the purpose of expressing resentment, indignation, disapproval, or reprobation of the group's behavior.[8] But is it possible to punish a group without also punishing its members? After all, groups are made of flesh and blood individuals, and it seems that, at least usually, whatever treatment the group itself is subjected to would pass on to them.[9] To see this problem more clearly, consider the aforementioned example of the proposed academic boycott against Israeli universities.[10] Supporters of the boycott call for the elimination of professional contacts with Israeli academic *institutions*. By eliminating those professional contacts, the boycotting academics express their condemnation of the alleged collaboration of Israeli academia with Israel's foreign policy.[11]

The calls for an academic boycott on Israeli universities have been met with much critique. Some opponents question the alleged collaboration of Israeli universities with the Israeli government's policies. Others doubt whether a boycott is the most appropriate means to express condemnation

---

[8] Notice that in common speech, the term "collective punishment" is often used to describe not just the punishment of a group but also the imposition of burdens on group members by virtue of their membership. According to my proposed terminology, the latter type of burden should be called "shared punishment" or "shared liability."

[9] For the various ways in which group members are affected by the punishment of their group, see the chapter by Toni Erskine in this volume. Notice that the punishment of the group would not always pass on to its members. For example, it is possible to characterize the revocation of a corporation's charter as a form of "capital punishment" of the corporation, but not of its members. These are more rare examples, however, and they raise a host of separate questions such as, for example, should we classify a revocation of a charter as punishment at all, if it does not inflict suffering on real flesh-and-blood agents? These problems are briefly discussed in French, *Collective and Corporate Responsibility*, chap. 14.

[10] Boycotting is, of course, different from punishment, *inter alia* because a boycott does not have a retributive function. Nevertheless, both boycotts and punishments have the function of expressing the condemnation of their subject's behavior, and for that reason, I think the example of the boycott is relevant for the discussion here.

[11] Such public expression of condemnation is meant to serve several goals, according to the supporters of the boycott: it would put pressure on the Israeli public and government; it would express solidarity with Palestinian academics and with Israelis who oppose their government's policies, and it would raise international consciousness to the Israeli–Palestinian conflict. Whether these goals justify the use of boycott as a means and whether these goals would realistically be achieved by a boycott are important questions, but they are not the subject of this chapter. For a related discussion on these issues with regard to international economic sanctions, see Avia Pasternak, "Sanctioning Liberal Democracies," *Political Studies* 57, no. 1 (2009), 54–74.

of academic institutions and to achieve the boycott's proclaimed goals. Finally, there is the worry that an academic boycott would seriously compromise academic freedom. These are heavy charges against the academic boycott, and its supporters do not necessarily have adequate replies to them. However, in what follows I wish to leave these debates behind and instead focus on the problem of the impact of the boycott on individual academics. This problem was raised, for example, by Martha Nussbaum, in her recent critique of academic boycotts. According to Nussbaum, the primary target of an academic boycott is the academic *institution*, but it inevitably bans *individual* academics from participation in the international academic community. By doing so, it signals that "all *members* of the institution deserve condemnation."[12] Using the distinctions I drew earlier, we can say that Nussbaum is concerned that the type of treatment that individual academics face when their institution is boycotted is a form of shared punishment, because it shames and condemns *them*, not just their institution. This is a heavy accusation, because it implies that the boycott violates the basic moral premise according to which expressive condemnations such as punishment or boycotting must condemn the specific agent that behaved wrongly.[13] When the group itself is the agent that behaves wrongly but its members are the ones who end up being condemned, then the necessary connection between responsibility and punishment (or boycotting) is broken.

If collective sanctions such as punishment or boycott do inevitably turn into a form of *shared* punishment, as Nussbaum seems to suggest, then we have an additional good reason to reject such practices. However, in what follows, I argue that this is not obviously the case. I take the lead here from Peter French's defense of the practice of punishing

---

[12] Martha Nussbaum, "Against Academic Boycotts," *Dissent* 54, no. 3 (2007): 33. Emphasis added. Nussbaum lists several other objections to academic boycotts in general and to the boycott against Israeli institutions in particular.

[13] Anthony Flew, "The Justification of Punishment," *Philosophy* 29, no. 111 (1954): 293. Mark Reiff explores an alternative view that does not share this basic moral premise about the necessary connection between responsibility and punishment. This view, as he suggests, is the most plausible basis for terrorist acts against civilian populations. It postulates that people can be *punished* for things which their group has done but for which they share no responsibility (e.g., wrongs committed in the distant past). Reiff demonstrates how this view suffers from internal inconsistencies and leads to conclusions which are unacceptable by its own lights. See Mark Reiff, "Terrorism, Retribution, and Collective Responsibility," *Social Theory and Practice* 34, no. 2 (2008), 209–42.

criminal corporations.[14] In reply to the objection that corporate punishment harms the individual members of corporations (such as shareholders), French makes the following observation: "when a natural person commits a felony and is convicted and punished, his or her associates, often family members and dependents, are frequently cast into dire financial circumstances." Yet, as he continues, "in many jurisdictions little or no official interest is paid to these innocent sufferers."[15] One way to interpret this statement is as a suggestion that the costs that are imposed on those who are related to the punished agent, whether an individual or a corporation, are mere side effects.[16] They have no expressive and condemning function and are therefore not a reason, in and of themselves, to reject the practice of punishment (although, as French himself later on notes, considerations of proportionality could play a role here).[17] A similar line of argument could be employed with regard to the academic boycott. According to this line, the costs that pass on to individual Israeli academics as result of the boycott are not intended to condemn *them*. Rather, although the social meaning of the boycott is a form of corporate condemnation of Israeli academic institutions, the social meaning of its distributive effect on individual academics is a form of shared *liability*. It is a burden that they end up carrying as a result of the fact that the institution they work in acted wrongly. This burden is part of the costs that come with being a member of an academic institution. In this respect, it is equivalent to a fine or to the attribution of strict liability – namely, costs that, although unpleasant, do not necessarily express indignation, resentment, or disapproval. As I mentioned earlier, there are other objections to the boycott (and to other forms of corporate punishment) that should be taken into account when we evaluate it. However, the specific objection that a boycott of an institution necessarily condemns all the members of the institution can be rejected, at least when a boycott is designed and

---

[14] In French's terminology, corporations are 'conglomerates,' or groups with a moral personality. On the definition of conglomerates see French, *Collective and Corporate Responsibility*, 13–18.

[15] Ibid., 189–90.

[16] The analogy between the corporation and the criminal is made also by Peter Cane, *Responsibility in Law and Morality* (Oxford: Hart, 2002), 146). See also David Runciman, "The Concept of the State: The Sovereignty of Fiction," in *States and Citizens: History, Theory, Prospects*, ed. Quentin Skinner and Bo Stråth (Cambridge: Cambridge University Press, 2003).

[17] I refer to the issue of proportionality in the conclusions to the chapter.

advertised in a way that separates the condemnation of the institution from the condemnation of its members.[18]

The Problem of Distributing Shared Liability

I suggested thus far that the distributive effects of corporate sanctions like punishment or boycott should not necessarily be rejected on the grounds that they amount to a form of shared punishment. If the sanction is designed in a way that does not condemn the group members, then the burdens they suffer as a result are a form of shared liability. However, in what follows, I point to a different normative difficulty that the effects of corporate sanctions raise. This difficulty concerns the way in which the effect of the corporate sanction is distributed between group members. To see this problem more clearly, consider again French's example of the family who is cast into financial difficulties as a result of the arrest of a family member. Imagine a criminal whose family consists of a sister and a mother. Both women were financially dependent on the criminal before he was sent to prison. The mother, who is old and ailing, was unaware of the fact that her son perpetrated a crime. The sister, however, was in a position to prevent the crime, but failed to do so and in that specific sense shares some moral responsibility for it. Under these circumstances, we are likely to think that *within* the family, there are better and worse ways to distribute the new financial burden that resulted from the arrest. For example, we may think that the sister should carry a greater portion of the burden, for after all, she shares greater responsibility for the crime than her mother. As this example demonstrates, even if the burdens that are imposed on those that surround the punished are not punitive in and of themselves, they raise an important normative question about the proper distribution of the burden among those who are affected by the punishment.

The question of the proper distribution of the effects of sanctions is especially pertinent when the sanctioned agent is a group. For after all, it is usually the case that when a group is sanctioned, these sanctions cannot

---

[18] Notice that many supporters of the academic boycott on Israeli institutions have failed in that respect. See, for example, Mona Baker and Lawrence David, "In Defence of the Boycott," *Counterpunch*, September 18, 2003. Available at http://www.counterpunch.org/baker09182003.html. The authors of this piece argue that the target of the boycott is Israeli institutions but also suggest that the boycott is justified because all Israeli academics share the blame for the wrongs of the Israeli occupation (thus pointing the finger at individuals rather than at the institution).

be contained to the level of the group and almost always are bound to have a distributive effect. We saw this effect in the case of condemning sanctions such as the academic boycott: its adoption cannot avoid imposing burdens on the institution members. This scenario repeats itself in the case of corporate *liability*. Consider, for example, the common practice of holding states liable for injustices they caused (e.g., war crimes).[19] When a state pays compensation to its victims, the material losses it suffers pass on to its citizens, either directly or indirectly. By direct transfers I mean that the government taxes citizens more, to cover for the assets it lost. By indirect transfers, I mean that the government covers for its losses using resources that would otherwise have been used for other public goods and services, thus lowering the overall welfare level of the population. Because the population will end up bearing the liability of the state, it is important to stipulate the rules for the distribution of this effect.[20]

To sum up, I distinguished between the notions of punishment and liability and between shared and corporate responsibility. I suggested that if we take collective punishment to mean corporate punishment, it can have two types of effect on group members: first, the punishment imposed on the group (e.g., boycotting) may carry a condemning quality

[19] On states' agency, see Toni Erskine, "Assigning Responsibilities to Institutional Moral Agents: The Case of States and Quasi States," *Ethics and International Affairs* 15, no. 1 (2001), 67–86.

[20] This example points to the relevance of the problem of the distributive effects of corporate sanctions to individualist as well as to corporatist theorists. Corporatists take collectives such as states to be independent moral agents that can be held responsible and liable for their actions. This position is not shared by individualists, who reject the metaphysical assertion that groups have a moral agency; see discussion in H. D. Lewis, "Collective Responsibility (a Critique)," in *Collective Responsibility: Five Decades of Debate in Theoretical and Applied Ethics*, ed. Larry May and Stacey Hoffman (Savage, MD: Rowman & Littlefield, 1991; Mellema, *Collective Responsibility*, chap. 4.) For that reason, individualists are likely to argue against the practice of punishing collective entities such as states. Nevertheless, even individualists can agree that, as a matter of practicality, states are the institutional units that should be held *liable* for the bad outcomes brought about by their governments and sometimes its citizens. Indeed, many authors assign liability to states but remain silent about their separate moral agency. See, for example, Christian Barry, "Applying the Contribution Principle," in *Global Institutions and Responsibilities: Achieving Global Justice*, ed. Christian Barry and Thomas Pogge (Malden, MA and Oxford: Blackwell, 2005); John Rawls, *The Law of Peoples* (Cambridge, MA: Harvard University Press, 1999), 105–6; Henry Shue, "Global Environment and International Inequality," *International Affairs* 75 (1999), 531–45. As I suggest, if the state is regarded as the liable agent, even if for practical reasons alone, there is room for thinking about the way in which this collective burden will be distributed among citizens.

for the group members as well. As we saw, the transfer of such punitive measures to group members is morally objectionable because it violates the necessary connection between punishment and responsibility. Next, the punishment imposed on a group may create further nonexpressive burdens for its members (e.g., damage to one's academic career in the case of the academic boycott); similarly, corporate liability is likely to be translated into shared liability (e.g., higher taxes for citizens). I suggested that even when the burden that group members bear is mere liability and not punishment, important questions arise about the way this burden should be distributed among them. In the next sections, I turn to address this issue by examining several rules for the distribution of the impact of corporate sanctions.

THREE WAYS TO DISTRIBUTE CORPORATE SANCTIONS

In the previous section, we saw that it is common practice to hold collective entities responsible for their actions and to impose corporate sanctions on them when they act wrongly. Furthermore, we saw that whenever a group is corporately sanctioned, its members will be liable for those costs, and this fact calls for thinking about the proper rules for the distribution of the burden. In this section, I stipulate what I take to be the three possible ways to distribute the impact of corporate sanctions within a group.[21]

The first rule for the distribution of the impact of corporate sanctions is what I call "proportional distribution." According to this rule, the group allocates the collective burden that was assigned to it in proportion to members' differing levels of personal association with the collective harm. There are different ways in which group members may be associated with a collective harm that their group caused: their contributions to the harm, their failure to prevent it, and even the personal benefit they derived from the harm. Putting aside the differences between these various considerations, for the purposes of the discussion here, I'll define proportional distribution (PD) as any form of distribution that identifies some way in which individual group members are personally associated with the collective harm and apportions their share of personal liability in proportion to their association. It is not difficult to find supporters for some version of

---

[21] For the time being, I am treating the question of the distribution of corporate sanctions as an internal question that is directed to the sanctioned group itself. Later on, I reflect on the implications of this question also for the external agents who impose the sanctions on the group (I thank David Luban for pointing out this distinction).

a PD in the literature. For example, Larry May expresses support for a PD when he suggests that the punishment of criminal organizations should be distributed "among those key members of the corporation who can be linked to the harm by their positions of authority and then also by the specific guilty state of mind they each had."[22]

The second rule for the distribution of the impact of corporate sanctions is what I call "equal distribution" (ED). In contrast with a PD, an ED ignores members' personal association with the harm, and instead apportions to each liable member an equal share of the burden. The precise definition of an equal share of the burden will be informed by further distinctions about the nature of equality. For example, an ED may take into account members' relative capacity to pay, so that the burden has an equal impact on each. However, these further distinctions are not important for the discussion here, so long as the distribution is not guided by considerations which relate to members' association with the harm. An ED of one specific type of collective burden is advocated by Iris Young, in her work on responsibility for global labor injustice. According to Young, citizens of developed and underdeveloped countries have a duty to work toward a more just global supply chain system, regardless of their personal involvement with this injustice.[23]

---

[22] May, *The Morality of Groups*, 100. The crude–careful approach to collective responsibility that Mark Drumbl stipulates in his contribution to this collection is another example of proportional distribution. Other supporters are Cass Sunstein and Eric Posner in their work on the costs of climate change injustice. They note with regard to the distribution of these costs that "many Americans today do not support the current American energy policy, appear not to benefit from it, and already make some sacrifices to reduce the greenhouse gas emissions that result from their behaviour.... [A]n approach that emphasized corrective justice would attempt to be more finely tuned, focusing on particular actors, rather than on Americans as a class." Cass Sunstein and Eric Posner, "Climate Change Justice," (John M. Olin Program in Law and Economics Working Paper Series, University of Chicago Law School, 2007), 22. Thomas Pogge expresses a similar position in *World Poverty and Human Rights*, where he argues that the scope of individuals' duty to reform unjust institutions is determined in light of their level of participation in these institutions and contribution to the injustices they commit. See Thomas Pogge, *World Poverty and Human Rights: Cosmopolitan Responsibilities and Reforms* (Cambridge: Polity Press, 2002), 50.

[23] Iris Marion Young, "Responsibility and Global Labor Justice," *The Journal of Political Philosophy* 12, no. 4 (2004): 385. For a similar line of argument that is grounded in consequentialist premises, see Robert Goodin, "Apportioning Responsibility," *Law and Philosophy* 6, no. 2 (1987). Young develops a further principle (which includes the capacity to engage in political activity) that specifies what an equal share of the task of opposing global labor injustice precisely entails for each individual. Notice that the burdens associated with the task of opposing global labor injustice do not clearly fall into the category of "liability costs." Like liability costs, however, they are burdens that

Finally, the third possible way to distribute the costs of corporate sanctions is what I call random distribution (RD). RD is distinct from PD and ED by the fact that it allows the distribution to be guided by pure luck or chance, rather than by a systematic principle. Consider, for example, the case of the academic boycott. If Israeli universities will be boycotted, their individual members are likely to suffer as a result, and we can imagine the distribution of this burden to be neither proportional nor equal: it will impose different burdens on different academics, and this burden will not necessarily fall in proportion to members' association with the collective harm (e.g., academics with a higher international profile will suffer more than academics who publish only in Israeli journals). Furthermore, the burden in question (damage to one's international career, etc.) can hardly be transferred between members within the group, and for that reason, the group cannot shift to a proportional or equal distribution. In this case, the distribution then remains random: some members simply have the bad luck of being more vulnerable to the collective harm than others.

EVALUATING THE THREE FORMS OF DISTRIBUTION

We saw that there are three ways in which a group that is liable or punished for its actions can pass the burden on to its members. The question I now turn to address is under what circumstances would each of the models be recommended?[24] When answering this question, we should distinguish between practical and normative considerations. As we will see, at least as a general rule, the three models fare differently from each of these perspectives. Let us first look at practical considerations such as the feasibility and the financial cost of the chosen distribution. On this scale, a PD is likely to fare worse than the other two models. After all, according to the PD model the group has to engage in calculations of members' personal association with the collective harm (their personal contributions, omissions, benefit, and so on) to determine their share of liability. Such calculations are potentially costly and time-consuming (if not impossible), at least in very large groups such as states or big

---

are imposed on agents as a result of harm or injustice, and they do not have a symbolic significance. For these reasons, I think the example is relevant for the current discussion.

[24] I am assuming here that the group can make a viable choice between the three models. This implies, for example, that the costs are at least partly transferrable and that the group is not forced to remain with a random distribution.

corporations.[25] An ED and an RD, in contrast, do not require similarly complex calculations, because they are not based on information about individual members' personal behavior with relation to the collective harm. Furthermore, at least as a general rule we can assume that an ED, although potentially less costly than a PD, would be more costly than a RD. After all, an ED requires some transfer of resources between the members of the group – from those who were encumbered with a greater share of the burden to those who paid less or from everyone an equal share to the general pool. A RD would avoid the procedural costs that such transfers would entail, simply because it does not call for any redistribution within the group.[26]

Turning next to the normative set of considerations, it is hardly surprising that an RD fares badly in this respect, for as we saw, an RD provides little in terms of normative justification for why some group members rather than the others end up with the costs. That is not to say that an RD can never be justified on normative grounds. An RD may arguably be deemed normatively acceptable under some circumstances, usually if it is assumed to lead to an overall significant benefit. Consider for example the legal practice of "solidarity liability." This practice gives a claimant who was harmed by several parties the right to seek full compensation from any of those parties. As Peter Cane explains, "the sharing of the liability is a matter between the various responsible parties ... it is no answer to a claim for full compensation that the party sued was only one of several responsible parties."[27] At least in its initial stage, solidarity liability is a form of RD, because it does not provide a systematic principle according to which we are able to foretell on which of the guilty parties the collective expense will fall.[28] This legal practice, as Cane notes, is highly controversial, but its supporters justify it by pointing to the fact that, as a general rule, it serves to protect the interests of victims, who

[25] In his contribution to this collection, Mark Drumbl deals with some of the practical critiques of PD.

[26] An RD may incur additional negative costs for the group in the long run. For example, it may have negative side effects that will harm the group as a whole (e.g., it will create resentment among those individuals who end up paying more than others). Notice, however, that PD and ED may also have long-term side effects in terms of their influence on the behavior of group members. Because it is hard to determine what such side effects would be without a more detailed sociological account, I do not consider them here.

[27] Cane, *Responsibility*, 178.

[28] Notice, however, that in this example, RD is imposed on the members of the group from the outside, and only at an initial stage. After that initial stage, the group can decide to leave the distribution in its random form or to continue and redistribute the burden (where possible) on a proportional or an equal basis.

do not have to go through the cumbersome process of proceeding against several parties. Another example of cases in which RD may be justified is when the sanctions that are imposed on a group simply cannot, by their nature, be transferred between group members (whether on an equal or proportional basis). Here, if there are good reasons to think that sanctioning the group would stop it from perpetrating greater wrongs, then the fact that this measure would have an impact on group members on a random basis should perhaps be ignored.[29] Note, however, that in both these examples, RD is a moral compromise, permissible not because it is supported by some underlying normative principle but by virtue of the fact that it produces an overall desired outcome.

In contrast to RD, a PD has a solid normative basis to support it. After all, as we saw in the example of the family of the criminal, PD is compatible with our basic intuitions about fairness. Fairness requires that a distribution of gains and burdens will allocate them to the parties in question according to some relevant factors. A PD of a group's collective burden does precisely that, by identifying those individuals who are personally associated with the collective harm through their own actions and omissions. This conclusion is not unfamiliar in the literature. For example, it is the driving force behind May's aforementioned argument that the punishment of corporations should be directed at decision makers in the corporation rather than at powerless shareholders.[30]

The picture becomes more complex, however, when we examine the normative status of ED. As we saw, an ED gives each group member an equal share of the group's collective burden. In this respect, it can be argued, an ED fails to comply with basic standards of fairness: it treats alike those who are more and those who are less associated with the collective harm. Can an ED ever be justified on normative grounds? The

---

[29] Although as some authors argue, an RD is justified in such cases only if all the group members share some responsibility for the collective harm. Erin Kelly's work on the justification of collective sanctions against unjust states arguably takes this line: she argues for collective sanctions against unjust states, which include even bombing from the air. These measures are likely to impose nontransferrable burdens on the citizens of the sanctioned state. As such, they cannot be redistributed on an equal or proportional basis. Nevertheless, Kelly suggests that such impositions can be justified in cases in which all the citizens of the target state share some responsibility for their government's unjust policies. See Erin Kelly, "The Burdens of Collective Liability," in *Ethics and Foreign Intervention*, ed. Deen Chatterjee and Don Scheid (Cambridge: Cambridge University Press, 2003).

[30] May, *The Morality of Groups*, 104: Sunstein and Posner, "Climate Change Justice," 32.

answer to this question partly depends on the type of group in question. In the case of voluntary groups, such as corporations or partnerships, an ED would be legitimate if the rules of distribution of the group's collective burdens are publicly known, and members are generally aware of the fact that, were the group to be punished or held liable, they would be expected to share the costs on an equal basis.[31] An ED is much harder to defend in nonvoluntary groups, whose members do not choose to join nor can they easily exit them. The paradigmatic example of such groups is, of course, the state: in most states, the majority of citizens do not choose their country of nationality, nor can they leave it without incurring serious costs. Moreover, it is usually the case that policy makers prefer an ED over a PD of the costs of the state's collective liabilities. Consider, for example, a state that is demanded to pay compensation for a harmful or aggressive behavior toward another country. State officials are unlikely to attempt to design a tax scheme that would identify those citizens who have supported the harmful policies, failed to prevent them, or benefited from them. Instead, they will raise a general tax that would distribute the burden among *all* citizens, regardless of their personal association with the harm.

Of course, it could be argued that political decisions of this nature are guided primarily by considerations of practicality (such as the costs of a PD to the state as a whole). However, can such practices be defended on normative grounds as well? I would argue that they can, at least under certain circumstances. The starting point of my defense is the intuition that a PD of the collective burden that results from governments' policies seems somehow inappropriate. This intuition is voiced, for example, by Michael Walzer, in his discussion of reparations for unjust wars.[32] There Walzer briefly notes that

> Reparations are surely due to the victims of aggressive war, and they can hardly be collected only from those members of the defeated state who were active supporters of the aggression. Instead the costs are distributed through the tax system, and through the economic system generally, among

[31] As I noted earlier, members may have good reasons to prefer an ED to PD, in light of the latter's potentially considerable costs.
[32] See similar comments in Hannah Arendt, "Collective Responsibility," in *Amor Mundi: Explorations in the Faith and Thought of Hannah Arendt*, ed. James William Bernauer (Boston: Nijhoff, 1987); Karl Jaspers, *The Question of German Guilt* (New York: Fordham University Press, 2000), 55–57; Debra Satz, "What Do We Owe the Global Poor?," *Ethics and International Affairs* 19, no. 1 (2005): 50.

all the citizens . . . in this sense, citizenship is a common destiny, and no one, not even its opponents . . . can escape the effects of a bad regime.[33]

I would suggest that this quote points to a normative defense of the practice of ED in states. According to this defense, an ED is part and parcel of a certain ethical view of the meaning of citizenship. More specifically, on this view, citizens should see themselves as having equal shares in their joint political activities and as equal bearers of responsibility for them.[34] This view, I would venture, is not uncommon in the real world. It is reflected, for example, in the powerful sense that citizens often have that "this is *their* government," even when they did not personally authorize it and even if they protest against its policies; in the familiar sense of shame, or at least discomfort, we tend to feel when our governments act badly, even if we personally "off-set" our contributions to the objectionable policy. These common sentiments reflect a certain understanding of the bond of citizenship, according to which each citizen is tied to outcomes of the political community's shared political goals and institutions in a way that does not depend on his or her own personal contributions to it.

The perception that citizenship is a common destiny is not the only available interpretation of the meaning of citizenship. One could point to alternative accounts of citizenship that are more individualistic. However, the idea of citizenship as a common destiny has an intrinsic value that other perceptions arguably do not share. Its value is generated, first by the fact that it connects citizens to each other in a deep and important sense,[35] and second, by the fact that it enhances citizens' willingness to participate in and contribute to their political lives together. Consider, for example, the case of soldiers who are asked to fight a war for their

---

[33] Michael Walzer, *Just and Unjust Wars: A Moral Argument with Historical Illustrations*, 2nd ed. (New York: Basic Books, 1992), 297. In the sentence omitted from the quote, Walzer refers to the fact that current generations are often made to pay for injustices perpetrated in the past. The problem of transfer of collective burdens between generations raises a host of other questions, which I cannot refer to in the scope of this chapter.

[34] For a detailed account of this particular understanding in general and in political communities in particular, see Avia Pasternak, "Sharing the Costs of Political Injustice," *Politics, Philosophy, Economics* (forthcoming). An argument in similar spirit appears in Amy Sepinwall's contribution to this collection (Chapter 9).

[35] On the importance of this specific deeper connection see, for example, Alasdair MacIntyre, "Is Patriotism a Virtue?," in *Theorizing Citizenship*, ed. Ronald Beiner (Albany: State University of New York, 1995), 224; Robert Nozick, *The Examined Life: Philosophical Meditations* (New York: Simon & Schuster, 2006), 289.

country. The sacrifice these soldiers may have to make can be high, and they are more likely to be willing to make it if they are certain that the rest of the citizenry will share the burden of the actions that they are performing for the collective.

I suggested that according to one common and valuable understanding of citizenship, citizens who act together to execute their common political will through their representative institutions should see themselves as having equal shares in their joint political activities. Although an ED of the costs of government policies expresses precisely this idea, a PD or an RD undermines it: a PD highlights the individualized actions of citizens with regard to government's policies, thus treating some as participants and others as not. An RD lets the burden fall only on some citizens and thus undermines any sense of collective solidarity. Because an ED is constitutive of a valuable ethical understanding of the meaning of citizenship, citizens have ethical reasons to preserve and protect it.[36]

To sum up, a group that is held liable or punished for its actions must choose between the three models of distribution, and – at least as a general rule – normative and practical considerations are likely to pull in opposite directions. An RD may cost less to the group as a whole, but it can rarely be justified on normative grounds. A PD may be costly for the group, but from a normative point of view, it is compatible with the principle of fairness.[37] Finally, an ED is potentially less costly than a PD, but harder to justify on normative grounds. Still, as we saw, there are instances in which an ED is morally acceptable. For example, I suggested that an ED can be justified in voluntary groups, if it is a matter of public knowledge. I also suggested that even in nonvoluntary groups such as states, an ED could be justified because it is constitutive of a certain

---

[36] Notice that rejecting PD would be more difficult than rejecting RD, because PD, as we saw earlier, is compatible with the principle of fairness. Groups like the political community thus face a choice between two visions: the idea of citizenship as a common destiny, and an alternative view of citizenship that emphasizes fairness and personal responsibility. Both are legitimate views of citizenship, and my goal here is not to judge between them but rather merely to point out to a possible defense of ED that could outweigh fairness considerations.

[37] An important caveat to be mentioned here is that if the costs of PD are high, attempting to implement it might have residual normative costs; for example, it would take a long time until the victims of the injustice received their due compensation; or the group's ability to provide other goods would be diminished. Such problems do not necessarily call for a complete break with PD but perhaps, where possible, for a partial PD, which will be easier to implement.

understanding of the civic bond, according to which citizenship is a common destiny.[38]

CONCLUSIONS

I noted in the introduction that collective punishment has a notorious reputation among moral philosophers. My goal here was not to redeem the reputation of the practice of collective punishment but rather to distinguish between the various ways in which the punishment of groups can be managed and to show which of these are more morally acceptable than others. As I argued in the first section, even if we accept the claim that groups are independent agents that merit condemnation when they behave badly and should be held liable for their actions, we must acknowledge that corporate sanctions will usually affect group members adversely. This does not necessarily imply that corporate punishment translates into the unjustifiable shared punishment of group members. Rather, the costs that group members suffer as a result of the sanctioning of their groups may be merely a form of shared liability. Even so, there are good reasons to stipulate the rules for the further distribution of that type of burden between group members because the various possible patterns of distribution have different strengths and weaknesses.

The second and third sections pointed to what I take to be the three possible ways in which the costs of corporate sanctions may fall on group members: on a proportional basis, which takes into account their personal responsibility for the collective harm; on an equal basis, which allocates each an equal share; and on a random basis, which lets the burdens lie where they fall. An RD may be the most feasible and least costly to the group as a whole because it does not require transfer of resources between group members. However, it is bound to raise deep moral objections precisely because it does not provide any normative explanation for why some group members and not others end up carrying the burden. A PD may be hard to implement in large groups, but it sits well with our intuitions about fairness and personal responsibility: those group members who have a greater share of personal association with the collective harm end up bearing a greater share of the burden. Finally, I suggested that an ED can be defended from a normative point of view when it is

---

[38] This defense is developed more fully in Pasternak, "Sharing the Costs of Political Injustice." For an alternative defense see Anna Stilz, "Collective Responsibility and the State," *Journal of Political Philosophy* (forthcoming).

constitutive of a certain valuable perception of group membership as common destiny. This argument can perhaps serve to explain why, in many states, an ED of the costs of the states' corporate burden is a common practice that, I would venture, is largely supported by common sentiments.

The discussion thus far analyzed the impact of collective punishment on group members. As a final point, I turn to assess how this distributive nature of collective punishment should shape our general assessment of the practice of corporate sanctions. First, as was mentioned in the first section, corporate punishment should be designed in a way that does not translate into punitive measures on group members. This implies that to whatever condemning treatment the group is made subject, that treatment should not condemn its members simply because they belong to the group. This restriction will put limits on the type of treatment to which groups can be subject when they are punished for their actions. For example, going back to the case of the academic boycott, if it turns out that the sanctioning of individual academics (which results from the general boycott) is generally interpreted as a mark of their condemnation, this would be a good reason to avoid this practice.

The distributive effects of corporate sanctions should also be taken into account when they do not have a condemning implication for group members. Here I would agree with French that, as a general rule, the fact that the sanctioning of a group would have derivative effects on its members should not forbid the sanctioning of that group (in the same way, to recall French's example, that the fact that the punishment of a criminal affects his family members should not lead to his pardoning). In that spirit, I presented the question of the distribution of the effects of corporate sanctions as an internal question that the group itself needs to deal with in the aftermath of the bad outcome it had brought about. However, although as a general rule the problem of distribution is an internal question, it can nevertheless affect the choice of measures that are imposed on the group in question by external agents. First, if a result of the punishment of the group, group members will inevitably suffer extreme costs that are highly disproportional to either the harm caused or to their involvement in the collective harm, then this poses a good reason to reconsider the chosen mode of corporate sanction itself (as it may do in the case of sanctions imposed on individual actors). Second, we are led to the conclusion that at least where possible, corporate sanctions should be designed so that they give the sanctioned group the opportunity to redistribute their costs between group members on some normatively justified basis (namely, a

PD or in some circumstances an ED). This would imply, for example, that corporate sanctions that impose material and transferrable costs on group members are preferable to sanctions that impose nontransferrable costs. Moreover, it implies that sanctions should be imposed with much greater care and with more attention to their distributive effects, when the target group does not have the organizational capacity to redistribute the costs between its members. Consider again the academic boycott: even if we agree that Israeli universities should be boycotted for their allegedly condemnable behavior, the costs that an academic boycott would impose on Israeli academics are likely to be nontransferrable. Moreover, academic institutions are not the type of institutions that have the authority to redistribute the impact of the boycott among their members. These facts suggest, as we saw throughout the discussion, that boycotting or punishing academic institutions is by far more problematic from a normative point of view, because the distributive effects of these measures cannot be mitigated. As I noted earlier, this fact does not imply that an academic boycott is never permissible. There may be cases in which such a boycott could be justified on the grounds that it prevents greater evils. Nevertheless, if my arguments in this chapter are correct, then corporate sanctions in this particular type of case would likely to be a serious normative compromise. However, when the effect of the sanction can be transferred, and the group has the tools to do so, then the fact that group members suffer as a result of the corporate sanction is not, in and of itself, a detrimental objection to the practice of corporate punishment.

9

Citizen Responsibility and the Reactive Attitudes: Blaming Americans for War Crimes in Iraq

Amy Sepinwall

[I]f today I heard that some American had committed suicide rather than live in disgrace, I would fully understand.

– J. M. Coetzee, *Diary of a Bad Year*[1]

INTRODUCTION

It is now horrifyingly apparent that American prosecution of the war in Iraq, and its attendant detention policies, have been rife with abuses.

For very helpful comments and suggestions, the author wishes to thank Margaret Little, David Luban, and Andrew Siegel, as well as attendees of the April 7, 2010, Philosophers' Lunch, University of Pennsylvania Philosophy Department, and participants in the Collective Punishment Workshop, Windermere Manor, The University of Western Ontario, April 17–19, 2009.

[1] J. M. Coetzee, *Diary of a Bad Year* (New York: Penguin, 2007), 43 (reflecting on American shame in the face of human rights abuses committed in the course of the war in Iraq). In a probing critique of this passage, Jeff McMahan argues that "even if there are institutional connections between ordinary Americans and their government that make it rational for them to feel personal shame over its deeds, to suggest that it might be desirable, meritorious, noble, or even morally necessary for them to kill themselves is to attribute vastly disproportionate significance to the grounds for shame." Jeff McMahan, "Torture and Collective Shame," in Anton Leist and Peter Singer, eds., *J.M. Coetzee and Ethics: Philosophical Perspectives on Literature* (New York: Columbia University Press, 2010). Earlier in his essay, McMahan roundly rejects the notion that the generic American might bear any guilt for the torture of Iraqis. Operating with an unfailingly individualist conception of responsibility, McMahan contends that if he neither participated in torture nor failed to prevent torture that it was in his power to prevent, he cannot be said to bear individual guilt for torture perpetrated by his government. The most that can be ascribed to the generic American is, for McMahan, a kind of moral taint by association. It is for this reason that suicide seems to McMahan so grossly disproportionate – a product of megalomania or else an obsessive need for moral purity. In contrast to McMahan, this essay takes seriously the notion that Americans

American soldiers killed Iraqi civilians by throwing them into the Tigris,[2] shooting them in "massacres" at Haditha and Mahmoudiya,[3] or running them over in supply-carrying convoys intent on moving through traffic.[4] During raids, it became "very common" to shoot the family dog in front of the family who owned it and routine to "destroy" the family's property with no subsequent compensation.[5] Detainees died after having been exposed to extreme temperatures[6] or subjected to stress positions;[7] in one case, an Iraqi prisoner suffered a lethal heart attack after he was forced to do long sessions of jumping jacks with a sandbag over his head.[8]

Cries of ignorance, perhaps once possible, are now unavailable and unavailing. The pictorial evidence has been too graphic, the pleas for judicial relief too numerous, and the revelations by journalists and veterans too widespread and wrenching, for Americans to invoke the Bush administration's penchant for secrets and deceit (and sometimes that of the Obama administration as well) as sources of immunity.[9] The

---

are individually blameworthy for torture, and other human rights abuses, committed in the course of the war in Iraq. Nothing in this essay should be taken to endorse suicide as an appropriate response to America's transgressions, but the arguments advanced herein should nonetheless help to make sense of the sentiment underlying the epigraph.

[2] Dexter Filkins, "The Fall of the Warrior King," *New York Times* (October 23, 2005).

[3] Tim McGirk, "Collateral Damage or Civilian Massacre in Haditha?," *Time* (March 19, 2007); Richard Engel, *War Journal: My Five Years in Iraq* (New York: Simon & Schuster, 2008), 279.

[4] Chris Hedges and Laila Al-Arian, "The Other War: Iraq Vets Bear Witness," *The Nation* (July 30, 2007).

[5] Ibid.

[6] Glenn Greenwald, "Senate Report Links Bush to Detainee Homicides," *Salon* (December 15, 2008).

[7] Seth Hettena, *Iraqi Died while Hung from Wrists*, Associated Press (February 17, 2005).

[8] Greenwald, supra n. 6.

[9] For examples of statements issued by the Bush administration intended to deny its role in these abuses, see, for instance, Dan Froomkin, "Pack of Liars," *Washington Post* (December 12, 2008). Available at http://www.washingtonpost.com/wp-dyn/content/blog/2008/12/12/BL2008121201873.html. The Obama administration has at times upheld the Bush position. For example, the Obama administration followed the Bush strategy of invoking the state secrets defense to thwart an American Civil Liberties Union lawsuit challenging the U.S. program of rendition, under which alleged terrorists were abducted and sent to other countries to be tortured. See, for example, Glenn Greenwald, "Obama Fails His First Test on Civil Liberties and Accountability – Resoundingly and Disgracefully," *Salon* (February 9, 2009) http://www.salon.com/news/opinion/glenn_greenwald/2009/02/09/state_secrets; David Luban, "You Cover It Up, You Own It," *Balkinization*, February 10, 2009, http://balkin.blogspot.com/2009/02/you-cover-it-up-you-own-it.html.

question of responsibility therefore presses upon us: what responsibility do Americans bear for these war crimes?[10]

For most commentators and scholars, the answer is "none," at least if we are referring to the responsibility of Americans who did not directly participate in the crimes in question. Instead, the tendency is one of deflection (onto, for example, George W. Bush)[11] or submersion (by the administration of Barack Obama, which implores the American public to move forward).[12]

These responses find support in a conception of responsibility familiar to us from criminal law, in which individual causal responsibility is seen to be the sine qua non of culpability.[13] Yet, as a handful of scholars have recently argued, the collective nature of crimes of war escapes the bounds of the individualist paradigm of Western criminal law.[14] Thus, Mark

---

[10] My use of the term "war crimes" is not intended to be polemical. A Spanish prosecutor, for example, recently filed a complaint seeking an indictment against six high-level Bush officials for the torture of detainees as a war crime. A copy of the complaint can be found here: http://www.publico.es/resources/archivos/2009/3/27/1238184153397QUERELLA_VERSION_FINAL.pdf. See generally Jeremy Brecher, Jill Cutler, and Brendan Smith, eds., *In the Name of Democracy: American War Crimes in Iraq and Beyond* (New York: Metropolitan Books, 2005). Cf. Neta C. Crawford, "Individual and Collective Moral Responsibility for Systemic Military Atrocity," *Journal of Political Philosophy* 15 (2007): 187, arguing that the killing of Iraqi civilians by American soldiers at Haditha and Ramadi constitute "systemic atrocities" – that is, those that are unintended but foreseeable, resulting from the constraints of a larger social structure rather than any individual's intentional act.

[11] See, for example, Andrew Sullivan, "Dear President Bush," *The Atlantic* (October 2009), http://www.theatlantic.com/doc/200910/bush-torture/1.

[12] See, for example, Shailagh Murray, "A Commission on Enhanced Interrogation? Obama Rebuffs Idea," *Washington Post* (April 23, 2009), http://voices.washingtonpost.com/44/2009/04/23/a_commission_on_enhanced_inter.html.

[13] For a statement embracing the principle of individual culpability in international law, see the Appeals' decision in *Prosecutor v. Tadić*, before the International Criminal Tribunal for the Former Yugoslavia (ICTY): "The basic assumption must be that in international law as much as in national systems, the foundation of criminal responsibility is the principle of personal culpability: nobody may be held criminally responsible for acts or transactions in which he has not personally engaged or in some other way participated (nulla poena sine culpa)." *Prosecutor v. Tadić*, Case No. IT-94-1-A (Int'l Crim. Trib. for the Former Yugoslavia Appeal Judgment, July 15, 1999), at ¶ 186 (footnotes omitted). Resistance to accomplice liability in domestic law is a prominent place exhibiting reverence for the principle of individual culpability as, for example, in Joshua Dressler, "Reassessing the Theoretical Underpinnings of Accomplice Liability: New Solutions to an Old Problem," *Hastings Law Journal* 37 (1985): 91–140.

[14] See, for example, Mark A. Drumbl, "Collective Violence and Individual Punishment: The Criminality of Mass Atrocity," *Northwestern Law Review* 99 (2005): 542: "The dominant discourse determines accountability through third-party trial adjudication premised on liberalism's construction of the individual as the central unit of action.

Drumbl forcefully argues in this collection that "[t]he collective nature of [atrocity] sits uncomfortably with international criminal law's predicate of individual agency, action, and authorship."[15] Similarly, George Fletcher contends that "the liberal bias toward individual criminal responsibility obscures basic truths about the crimes that now constitute the core of international criminal law. The[se] crimes ... are deeds that by their very nature are committed by groups and typically against individuals as members of groups."[16]

One might have thought that dissatisfaction with the conception of responsibility underpinning the response to atrocity would have occasioned support for the notion of collective guilt, but the alternatives proposed by critics such as Fletcher and Drumbl are far more modest. Fletcher's interest in collective guilt is intended not to implicate those who acquiesced in atrocity but instead to mitigate the responsibility of those who committed it.[17] Drumbl is prepared to countenance group-based responsibility, but only if individual group members are permitted "the subsequent opportunity ... to affirmatively demonstrate why they should be excluded from the liable group."[18] Accordingly, on Drumbl's account, group members who resisted or spoke out against mass atrocity would be exempt from having to contribute to a collective sanction levied against other members of the group.[19] Similarly, others who have entertained the

---

This means that a number of selected guilty individuals squarely are to be blamed for systemic levels of violence" (footnote omitted); George P. Fletcher, "The Storrs Lectures: Liberals and Romantics at War: The Problem of Collective Guilt," *Yale Law Journal* 111 (2002): 1499–73. Cf. Larry May, *Crimes against Humanity: A Normative Account* (New York: Cambridge, 2005), 246–49, advocating collective responsibility as a supplement to individual responsibility in "situations of group-based harm, [where] many members of the society may have chosen to play a role in the climate that has been instrumental in nurturing the harmful conduct"; Larry May, *War Crimes and Just War* (New York: Cambridge, 2007), 247–56, offering a qualified defense of joint criminal enterprise as a kind of collective responsibility when the responsibility of each member turns on his having an intention to participate in the collective injury.

[15] Mark Drumbl, "Collective Responsibility and Post-Conflict Justice," at 1. See also Mark A. Drumbl, *Atrocity, Punishment and International Law* (New York: Cambridge, 2007), 37: "[i]nternational criminal culpability is too crude a device to assimilate and measure the small things many people do that make the larger things fewer people do truly pandemic."

[16] Fletcher, supra n. 14 at 1513.   [17] Fletcher, supra n. 14 at 1541–42.

[18] Mark Drumbl, "Collective Responsibility and Post-Conflict Justice," supra n. 15 at 25.

[19] Drumbl, *Atrocity, Punishment and International Law*, supra n. 15 at 208. Drumbl worries that an assessment that ignores individual culpability will entail not only that the debtor class will include "innocent" group members but also that the beneficiary class will include complicit group members. Such an assessment "would restitute some individuals while unjustly enriching others." Idem at 200. Although I go on to defend

notion of collective sanctions in this context contemplate internal rights of contribution, which would allow the group to apportion group-based sanctions according to members' relative amounts of wrongdoing.[20] In short, those who call for a more encompassing understanding of responsibility for atrocity have nonetheless remained faithful to the principle of individual culpability embodied in international criminal law.

By contrast, this chapter takes seriously the notion that individuals may bear responsibility for the transgressions of their group even where they do not bear the hallmarks of individual culpability. More specifically, I contend here that citizenship itself can ground responsibility for the crimes of one's nation-state. To be clear, my interest here lies not in uncovering when and why it is appropriate to hold *groups* responsible (whether conceived as nations or states), questions addressed in the chapters by Toni Erskine and Tony Lang in this volume; nor am I interested in determining the circumstances when, and the grounds on which, it is appropriate to transmit sanctions imposed on the group to its members, which is the question Richard Vernon and Avia Pasternak confront in their contributions. I am interested instead in locating and interrogating the grounds on which we may, *in the first instance*, hold group members responsible for a transgression of their group. The focus here is then on responsibility assigned directly to members and not derivative of the responsibility of the group.

Moreover, the kind of responsibility I have in mind is not simply the forward-looking variety, which is what many forms of civil liability and reparations programs contemplate; nor is it simply outcome responsibility, which arises where an individual deserves to incur the material consequences of his or her acts, but not moral sanction.[21] Instead, I argue

---

an assignment of responsibility that Drumbl deems "crude," I see no reason why this assignment could not function alongside a careful delineation of the individuals entitled to compensation.

[20] See, for example, Mark Osiel, "The Banality of Good: Aligning Incentives against Mass Atrocity," *Columbia Law Review* 105 (2005): 1842–59, advocating the imposition of collective *civil* sanctions on military units and arguing that these are just because they allow military officers to redistribute the sanction internally so that it is levied in accordance with individual guilt. Cf. Daryl Levinson, "Collective Sanctions," *Stanford Law Review* 56 (2003): 345–428, advocating collective sanctions within criminal law, but anticipating that the sanctions will work themselves out internally, to cohere with principles of individual culpability.

[21] See, for example, David Miller, "Holding Nations Responsible," *Ethics* 114 (January 2004): 244–46; Richard Vernon, "Punishing Collectives: States or Nations," Chapter 11, this volume.

that U.S. citizens are legitimate targets of *blame* for abuses committed in the course of the war in Iraq.[22]

The account of citizen responsibility that I advance differs from the individualist account insofar as it severs moral and causal responsibility: Again, I argue that citizens may bear moral responsibility even though they did not participate in, facilitate, or even tolerate the abuses committed in their midst. The account also severs the notions of guilt and blameworthiness: I argue that citizens may be appropriate objects of blame (and hence appropriately subject to resentment and indignation) even though they need not conceive of themselves as guilty. I suggest that this fracturing of the traditional troika of guilt, resentment, and indignation has implications for the way we think about moral responsibility more generally.

I begin by articulating an account of the relationship between citizens and their nation-state that grounds citizens' responsibility for a transgression of their nation-state independent of the extent of their participation in that transgression. I do not anticipate, however, that that account will induce guilt in every American who encounters it. The resistance to guilt is itself interesting, and in the second part of the chapter, I seek to investigate its source. To that end, I undertake an exploration of the moral psychology of guilt and resentment, especially as these emotions pertain to understandings of responsibility for war crimes among members of

---

[22] Most accounts that seek to assign responsibility to group members who did not participate in the group transgression contemplate forward-looking responsibility, not responsibility as an assignment of blame. For example, John Parrish has sought to argue that Americans bear responsibility for illegal killings and other injuries suffered by Iraqi civilians. Although Parrish assigns responsibility to Americans independent of individual blameworthiness, he understands responsibility to consist of an obligation of repair and not as liability to blame. John M. Parrish, "Collective Responsibility and the State," *International Theory* 1 (2009): 119–54. Similarly, in other contexts, theorists have argued that citizens may be held responsible to *redress* harms of their nation-state, although these citizens are innocent of wrongdoing. See, for example, Debra Satz, "What Do We Owe the Global Poor?," *Ethics and International Affairs* 19 (2005): 47–54.

Juha Raikka is one who has argued that even those who dissociate themselves from their group's wrongdoing may nonetheless deserve blame for that wrongdoing. Juha Raikka, "On Disassociating Oneself from Collective Responsibility," *Social Theory and Practice* 23 (1997): 93–108. In brief, Raikka argues that dissidents come to bear responsibility for group acts that they oppose where they must participate in, or otherwise support, an evil practice to oppose that same or another evil practice. Raikka's account is not as far-reaching as my own, and it is particularly unhelpful here, because it is far from clear that American opponents of the war in Iraq need participate in any evil practice to voice their opposition.

the perpetrator and victim populations. I end by gesturing to the ways in which the account challenges accepted truths about moral responsibility and its relationship to the reactive attitudes.

Some words about terminology first: by "morally responsible," I mean "appropriately subject to blame," which I take to mean the same thing as "blameworthy." Further, I conceive of the experience of guilt as being constituted, at least in part, by the judgment that one has breached an expectation whose authority one recognizes.[23] Whether that experience is also constituted by guilt feelings is a question I have occasion to consider in what follows. For now, it is sufficient to note that by "guilt feelings," I mean the phenomenological correlates of the judgment involved in experiencing guilt – typically, pain, sadness, and so forth.[24] Finally, I refer to the entity whose acts occasion responsibility as the "nation-state."[25]

CITIZEN RESPONSIBILITY

The notion that one may be held morally responsible for a group wrong not in virtue of one's participation in it but instead in virtue of group

---

[23] Cf. Gabriele Taylor, *Pride, Shame and Guilt: Emotions of Self-Assessment* (New York: Oxford University Press, 1985), 85 ("To feel guilty, [an individual] must accept not only that he has done something which is forbidden, he must accept also that it is forbidden, and thereby accept the authority of whoever or whatever forbids it."). Though Taylor here speaks of "feel[ing] guilt," she clearly has the cognitive component of guilt in mind and so her description fits what I have referred to as the judgment involved in the experience of guilt.

[24] See, for example, Margaret Gilbert, "Collective Guilt and Collective Guilt Feelings," *Journal of Ethics* 6 (2002): 118–19.

[25] In his contribution to this volume, Richard Vernon offers an incisive inquiry into whether the responsible collective ought to be understood as the state or the nation and settles on the former. Vernon persuasively argues that the transmission of liability from a sociopolitical entity to its members can be defended for states but not for nations, because it is the open-ended delegation of authority to the state that legitimates our imposing on citizens the consequences of that delegation (here, the sanctions arising in the aftermath of state crime), and this open-ended delegation of authority is an essential feature of the state but not the nation. All of this seems correct if one is concerned with citizens' derivative liability, as Vernon is, but I am concerned with citizens' individual moral responsibility. For my purposes, something more normatively robust than the mere state is required. More specifically, the collective entity in question must possess the political character of a state because, as Vernon rightly notes, it is in its political aspect that the collectivity commits crimes of war. However, mere states, we shall see, need not encompass the normative obligations of fidelity to fellow members and the group itself that ground responsibility here. For these reasons, I invoke the nation-state as the collective actor of interest.

membership alone has been termed "tribal,"[26] and even "barbarous."[27] Indeed, those who seek to blame Americans for abuses committed in the war in Iraq have been accused of succumbing to the same kind of spurious logic that allowed the 9/11 terrorists to kill American civilians in retaliation for (purported) grievances against the American government.[28] What these critics fail to see (and what the 9/11 terrorists, tragically, failed to see) is that assignments of responsibility need not be one size fits all. Instead, we may hold different people responsible *to different degrees* for the same event or state of affairs, which may lead to our imposing on them different kinds or amounts of sanction. It is worth beginning our inquiry into citizens' responsibility by considering two factors that govern the magnitude of a responsibility assignment.

First, and most obviously, responsibility turns on the nature of the injury in question, which we may call the *object* of responsibility. Thus, the murderer is more blameworthy, *ceteris paribus*, than is the assailant whose victim sustains only nonlethal injuries. Second, the magnitude of a responsibility assignment varies according to the nature of the individual's relationship to the injury for which we seek to assign responsibility. Thus, for example, Kitty Genovese's assailant bears more responsibility for her death than do the residents of Kew Gardens; the former intends her death, whereas the latter recklessly refuse her rescue and thereby contribute to her death.[29] We may refer to this second factor as the *ground* of responsibility.

Now, the claim to be defended in this section is that *all* Americans of majority age bear responsibility for American transgressions – that is, the *object* of responsibility is the same for all. It is worth noting up front, however, that the *ground* of responsibility differs in accordance with the nature of the relationship of each American to the transgression in question. In particular, perpetrators, bystanders, and opponents of the transgression each bear a different relationship to it, and these differences

---

[26] See, for example, Nick Smith, *I Was Wrong: The Meaning of Apologies* (New York: Cambridge, 2008): 188.

[27] See, for example, H. D. Lewis, "The Non-Moral Notion of Collective Responsibility," in *Individual and Collective Responsibility: The Massacre at My Lai*, ed. Peter A. French (Cambridge, MA: Schenkman, 1972): 121.

[28] See, for example, Crawford, supra n. 10 at 205.

[29] The standard account of the Kitty Genovese case has recently been disputed. See Rachel Manning, Mark Levine and Alan Collins, "The Kitty Genovese Murder and the Social Psychology of Helping: The Parable of the 38 Witnesses," *American Psychologist* 62 (2007): 555. I nonetheless employ the standard account here for illustrative purposes.

entail differences in the *magnitude* of responsibility to be assigned to members of each camp.

To take one example: The complacent bystander (but not the dissident) has done nothing to diminish the perpetrator's motivation to commit the atrocity in question. The complacent bystander thereby signals to the perpetrator (as well as his victim, perhaps) that the victim's treatment does not merit opposition. In this way, he helps to normalize this treatment. So the ground of the complacent bystander's responsibility, but not that of the dissident, includes the support through silence that complacency confers. The complacent bystander will thus come to bear more responsibility than will the dissident.[30]

More generally, it cannot be denied that the perpetrators and facilitators of atrocity are related to the atrocity in ways that the dissident, and other nonparticipants, are not. There is, however, one way in which *all* adult citizens are related to the atrocity, and it is this relationship on which I focus here.

Each citizen bears a *commitment* to the nation-state, and this commitment, as I argue at greater length elsewhere,[31] provides a ground for holding each citizen responsible for the nation-state's acts, no matter the extent of his or her participation or opposition. More specifically, the citizen's *commitment* to the nation-state contains a normative dimension that requires citizens to accept responsibility for their nation-state's transgressions.

To get a better handle on the normative dimension of commitment, it is useful first to contemplate other, more intimate contexts of commitment. Consider the marital union, for example. Individuals in a marriage must

---

[30] To be sure, there may be many complacent bystanders – so many that the causal role of any one of them may be insignificant. However, moral responsibility is not a zero-sum matter, with the portion of responsibility for each individual turning on the number of people sharing it. For one thing, that complacency is rampant is a matter of moral luck. The complacent bystander should not be treated more leniently, then, just because others join him or her in providing psychic support to the atrocity's perpetrators. Indeed, we might say something even stronger than this: each of these bystanders reinforces the complacency of the other and thereby comes to bear responsibility not only for the atrocity the complacency supports but also the complacency itself. Cf. Larry May, *Sharing Responsibility* (Chicago: University of Chicago Press, 1996), 47, arguing that those who hold racist attitudes "causally contribut[e] to a climate that influences others to cause harm."

[31] Amy Sepinwall, "Responsibility for Group Transgressions," Ph.D. diss., Georgetown University, 2010.

act with a certain regard for their union.[32] Although exit is a real option, each nonetheless bears an obligation to the other to put the possibility of exit out of his or her mind, at least while less disruptive options exist. Further, each is obligated to the other to present a united front to the world, for maligning one's spouse to others would degrade the union and violate marital trust.

Similarly, individuals in a joint business partnership must also operate with a certain regard for the joint venture and commit themselves to working out the kinks of the operation before contemplating dissolution. Where one partner is empowered to, say, manage the partnership's business, the other partner may not publicly disparage the result or disavow responsibility for it. To do so would be to make a fool of the producing partner and to exhibit a reproachable lack of loyalty.

Now we should note that the strength of the obligations each member of the joint venture bears to the other(s) will depend on the strength of the commitment the joint venture expects of its members. Thus, spouses typically have greater obligations of fidelity to each other than do business partners because a marriage typically demands more of the individuals comprising it than does a business venture. Nonetheless, some amount of fidelity follows from membership in the partnership just as it does in the marital union. *Mutatis mutandis*, I now argue, some amount of fidelity follows from membership in the joint project that is the United States. By way of establishing this point, I offer first some general remarks about the ways in which citizenship can entail a commitment of the kind that grounds responsibility. I then describe the ways in which the United States might be understood as a joint project.

Citizens harbor a commitment to the nation-state, and that commitment obligates them in special ways to their fellow citizens. Citizens have an obligation (although not an insuperable one) to operate with a certain regard for the ways in which their acts reflect on or contribute to the nation-state. They must demonstrate a loyalty that requires, among other things, that they seek to change their country's conduct or policies before jumping ship, as it were. Most relevant here, their commitment entails

---

[32] Cf. Herbert Morris, *On Guilt and Innocence: Essays in Legal Philosophy and Moral Psychology* (Berkeley: University of California Press, 1976), 124–25, arguing that a husband's intention to commit adultery, even if never acted upon, constitutes a betrayal of his spouse because marriage "is defined partly by each partner being prepared to exercise restraint out of love and respect for the other. The man's intention reveals that he is no longer prepared to abide by this condition."

that they may not step outside the nation-state to point a finger in righteous indignation at the state's transgressions; instead, the citizen must face judgment with fellow citizens, in recognition that the nation-state is his as well as theirs. To do otherwise is to denigrate the shared venture; it is to demonstrate an atomism incompatible with citizenship.[33]

Importantly, the commitment that grounds the citizen's responsibility is a normative component of citizenship. This commitment may well have attendant psychological effects – in particular, it may be accompanied by a feeling of loyalty toward one's fellow citizens and the nation-state itself, a feeling of pride at their or the nation-state's successes, or a feeling of shame in the face of their or its misdeeds. Indeed, the commitment entails a normative expectation that the citizen will experience just these feelings in the appropriate contexts. However, the psychological concomitants of the citizen's commitment are not themselves the ground of his responsibility.[34] If they were, a citizen could deny responsibility simply by disclaiming any psychological attachment to the nation-state. Instead, the disaffected citizen bears an amount of responsibility for the nation-state's transgressions that corresponds to the strength of the commitment citizenship entails, regardless of whether the citizen has fulfilled his or her commitment by harboring the feelings of loyalty that the commitment demands.

That citizenship has the normative cast invoked here is a contingent, and not a conceptual, matter; citizenship need not function in this way everywhere and at all times. For example, loose political associations in which citizenship is a shorthand for eligibility for a set of legal entitlements and obligations, with no attendant sense that citizens are joined in

---

[33] Because, on at least some accounts, responsibility presupposes freedom, I note here that the account of citizen responsibility I advance depends on a genuine right of exit and, as such, applies only when each citizen can emigrate and is not unduly deprived by the state of the resources necessary to do so. I take it that it is relatively uncontroversial to presuppose that Americans possess genuine rights of exit.

[34] See, however, Farid Abdel-Nour, "National Responsibility," *Political Theory* 31 (2003): 703, contending that citizens' national responsibility "*only extends to the actions that have historically brought about the objects of their national pride*" (italics in original); Meir Dan-Cohen, "Responsibility and the Boundaries of the Self," *Harvard Law Review* 105 (1992): 959–1003. Both Abdel-Nour and Dan-Cohen argue that citizens can share responsibility for the nation-state's acts in virtue of *actual* feelings of national identification – in particular, acts that elicit pride or shame on the part of the citizen. The problem with these accounts is that they risk exculpating disaffected or alienated citizens and perhaps threaten unwarrantedly to implicate outsiders who identify with the country in question.

a shared project, would not sustain the normative component of citizenship that grounds responsibility here. Citizenship in some of the states of the United States might well be of this kind. Similarly, individuals who have been granted formal citizenship but are denied inclusion in the joint project of the nation-state would not be subject to the normative pressures that ground responsibility. Think here of Blacks in the Jim Crow South, or Jews in the early years of the Nazi regime, who enjoyed formal citizenship but nonetheless experienced significant political disempowerment. The account advanced here also would not extend to these excluded citizens.

Nonetheless, there is good reason to think that American citizenship is more than sufficiently robust to comprehend the normative elements – in particular, the demand that citizens stand together in judgment – that, I have argued, ground the citizen's responsibility. There are multiple ways in which one could draw out the normative project of the United States. For our purposes, it will suffice to focus on the quasi-spiritual understanding of the nation's mission and the connection to martyrdom that this understanding yields.

At the time of the nation's founding, Americans conceived of themselves as a chosen people[35] and their purpose as a kind of "errand into the wilderness."[36] The image of America as "a city on a hill" – a phrase borrowed from Jesus' Sermon on the Mount – figures in a continuous stream of political speeches, from the earliest Puritan settlers to modern-day political figures as diverse as John F. Kennedy and Ronald Reagan, with riffs on the phrase provided by, among others, George H. W. Bush ("a thousand points of light"), Wesley Clarke ("a beacon of hope and a source of inspiration for people everywhere"), and John Kerry ("we have moved closer to the America we can become – for our own people, for the country, and for the world.").[37] In the wake of the attacks of September 11, 2001, commentators and politicians alike have embraced America's "imperial mission" of delivering the canons of American ideology to the

---

[35] See Rogers M. Smith, *Stories of Peoplehood: The Politics and Morals of Political Membership* (New York: Cambridge, 2003), 7.

[36] For example, Kenneth Karst, *Belonging to America: Equal Citizenship and the Constitution* (New Haven, CT: Yale University Press, 1989), 30.

[37] See generally Kimberly Winston, "From Theological Tenet to Political Password: Three of the Democratic Candidates Have Already Pitched to Their Audiences Some Version of the 'City on a Hill' Speech," *Beliefnet*. Available at http://www.beliefnet.com/News/Politics/2004/02/From-Theological-Tenet-To-Political-Password.aspx.

world at large,[38] a mission toward which "God is not neutral," as former President George W. Bush intoned to the American people.[39]

Religious elements pervade the conception of American citizenship, seen most readily, perhaps, in the steps required of foreigners who wish to become U.S. citizens. The process of Americanization, as the 1997 Jordan Report on naturalization stated, should "cultivate" immigrants in a "*shared commitment* to the American values of liberty, democracy and equal opportunity."[40] Peter Spiro, a noted theorist of citizenship, contends that "in this sense America looks more like a religion, allowing for conversion of belief in the place of any need of lineage."[41]

If the nation was founded in a higher calling, it makes sense that its citizens should be willing to die for its sake, or so political theorists have argued. The original delineation of American citizenship – who was in and who was out – was itself determined with an eye to national security. Membership in the early years of the nation would be conferred to any White person born in the United States as a way of "guarantee[ing] ... the manpower for the nation's defense."[42] Today, military service is the quickest and surest route to naturalization for those not born here: "In times of peace, one year's honorable service in the U.S. armed forces qualifies an alien for naturalization; during periods of military hostilities, including now the post 9/11 period, an alien becomes eligible on enlistment."[43]

Moreover, the connection between military service and citizenship is not just pragmatic. As Paul Kahn argues, for example, the prospect of self-sacrifice is foundational in the American political culture, both in the sense that the United States was born in revolution and that the United States is sustained by the government's continued authority to demand that Americans kill or be killed on its behalf.[44] To make his point, Kahn

---

[38] Fouad Ajami, "Hail the American Imperium," *U.S. News and World Reports* (November 5, 2002): 28. See also W. J. Bennett, *Why We Fight: Moral Clarity and the War on Terrorism* (New York: Doubleday, 2002); Walter Berns, *Making Patriots* (Chicago: University of Chicago Press, 2001); Dinesh D'Souza, *What's So Great about America* (Regnery Publishing, Inc., 2002). See generally Smith, supra n. 35 at 191–210.

[39] George W. Bush, "After September 11" (Speech to Congress, Washington, DC, September 20, 2001). Available at http://www.historyplace.com/speeches/gw-bush-9-11.htm.

[40] Peter Spiro, *Beyond Citizenship: American Identity after Globalization* (New York: Oxford University Press, 2008), 47 (italics added).

[41] Ibid. at 47.   [42] Ibid. at 15.

[43] Ibid. at 38.

[44] Paul W. Kahn, *Sacred Violence: Torture, Terror and Sovereignty* (Ann Arbor: University of Michigan Press, 2008). Although I am foregrounding military service as the central

invites us to consider the naturalization oath of allegiance, which, in requiring individuals seeking American citizenship to pledge that they will "bear arms on behalf of the United States when required by law to do so," conveys, Kahn notes, the "sovereign demand on citizenship as an open-ended willingness to sacrifice."[45] It is not just for immigrants-cum-citizens that the obligation to die for America is made salient; other theorists have noted that, among the duties that all American citizens bear, "[a]bove all others is the duty to bear arms and to face the mortal hazards of the battlefield."[46] Yet the prerogative of the sovereign to demand its citizens' deaths likely only makes sense within a nation-state that claims a commitment of its citizens of the kind at issue here.[47] The notion that Americans should be willing to kill and die for their country is, then, a strong piece of evidence in support of the claim that American citizenship has a normative cast.

To be sure, the prospect of being called to the battlefield is remote for most Americans. Nonetheless, there are moments in Americans'

---

obligation of citizenship, it may be worth noting that jury duty is also indicative of the normative commitment American citizens bear. So important a civic service is jury duty that, in some jurisdictions, sheriffs are empowered to seize individuals eligible to sit on a jury and deliver them to court, where the court finds that it does not have enough people present to empanel a jury (see, e.g., California Code of Civil Procedure Section 211) – a process viewed as kidnapping, by some lights.

Peter Spiro, whose general project is to argue that territorially defined citizenship no longer tracks the affective ties on which citizenship should be grounded, contends that today it makes little sense to restrict jury service to citizens: "[I]f one takes seriously the proposition that criminal defendants are entitled to a jury of their peers, the practice [of excluding resident aliens] looks more like a deprivation of a right rather than an exemption from a duty." Spiro, supra n. 40 at 99. Against Spiro's critique, one might argue that eligibility for jury duty is not about whether the prospective juror counts as a "peer" but instead whether he or she is entitled to stand in judgment – an understanding of the obligation more congenial to the conception of citizenship I advance. On that conception, I argue, citizens are specially placed to hold one another to the laws to which both should be committed and that both should affirm.

[45] Kahn, supra n. 44 at 98.

[46] Spiro, supra n. 40 at 97. See generally George Kateb, *Patriotism and Other Mistakes* (New Haven, CT: Yale University Press, 2006), 7: "How is patriotism most importantly shown? Let us not mince words. The answer is that it is most importantly shown in a readiness, whether reluctant or matter of fact, social or zealous, to die and to kill for one's country."

[47] In this volume, David Luban (chapter 2) offers a critique of the state cast as jealous god, demanding its citizens' lives when its own existence is threatened and fighting wars against other states with near impunity. Although I find his critique compelling, my purpose here is simply to describe, and not evaluate, the cultural phenomenon in question.

lives – moments of "extraordinary politics," as Bruce Ackerman refers to them – when Americans are called on to transcend the pursuit of self-interest in deference to the needs of the country or their compatriots.[48] This transcendence may be less difficult for Americans than others to effect, given that Americans rank higher than any other people on patriotic sentiment.[49] Even those who disagree with U.S. policies can, with the right cast of mind and heart, nonetheless wear the banner of patriotism, for the practice of dissent, far from being taken to rend the fabric of national unity, is reckoned as a paradigmatically American form of enacting one's citizenship and construed as part of the project of national stewardship.[50]

In general, the obligation to act with an eye toward the national interest – whether in times of war or peace – is, in America, a national trope, figuring in presidential addresses ("Ask not what your country can do for you, but what you can do for your country") and patriotic slogans ("I only regret that I have but one life to give my country"). Briefly put, it is hard to imagine an America where commitment to the nation-state is not a feature of the citizen's identity that sits comfortably alongside, and sometimes even transcends, other sources of affinity.[51]

The foregoing provides insight into not only the generic American's responsibility for abuses in Iraq but that of the American opponent of the

---

[48] See Bruce Ackerman, *We The People: Foundations* (Cambridge, MA: Harvard University Press, 1993).

[49] See, for example, Jack Citrin, "Political Culture," in *Understanding America: The Anatomy of an Exceptional Nation*, eds. Peter Schuck and James Q. Wilson (New York: Public Affairs Press, 2009), 154.

[50] Consider, for example, Justice Brandeis's stirring defense of the right to dissent in his concurrence in *Whitney v. California*, 274 U.S. 357 (1927), a case challenging the defendant's conviction for her membership in the Communist Labor Party: "Those who won our independence believed . . . that the greatest menace to freedom is an inert people; that public discussion is a political duty; and that this should be a fundamental principle of the American government. They recognized . . . that the path of safety lies in the opportunity to discuss freely supposed grievances and proposed remedies. . . . Recognizing the occasional tyrannies of governing majorities, they amended the Constitution so that free speech and assembly should be guaranteed." Ibid. at 375 (footnote omitted). Cf. Andrew Mason, "Special Obligations to Compatriots," *Ethics* 107 (April 1997): 444. ("The idea that we have a special obligation to our compatriots to participate fully in public life has been thought to include or entail various specific obligations, such as an obligation . . . to keep a watchful eye on government and speak out when it acts unjustly.")

[51] Cf. Citrin, supra n. 49.

war as well, for the dissident also harbors a commitment to the nation-state. Indeed, it is in virtue of this commitment that dissidents enact their opposition: they believe that the pursuit and conduct of the war in Iraq grossly betray values they take to be fundamental and sacred to their beloved country, and their opposition is intended to restore America to its rightful path (or their conception of it, anyway). Were they not so committed to the United States, they might well have sought to leave it. Having stayed, however, they must accept that its acts redound to them. Just as the nonproducing business partner may not disown the products of his partnership, so the dissident may not disown the acts of the United States.[52]

In short, the commitment inherent in American citizenship grounds Americans' responsibility for the United States' acts, and the expected strength of that commitment determines the magnitude of responsibility they bear through citizenship alone.[53] Four qualifications round out

---

[52] Richard Vernon argues, in his contribution to this volume, that the mere fact that citizens support the project of the nation-state need not entail that they bear responsibility for any acts undertaken in furtherance of that project. In particular, where citizens valiantly oppose the acts in question, Vernon contends, their opposition ought to thwart an attempt to hold them responsible. After all, to will the end is not to will the means, Vernon pithily reminds us. To be clear, then, the ground of responsibility on my account is different from the one that Vernon critiques. For one thing, the dissident would come to bear responsibility for a national wrong on my account even if the wrong proved ineffective at protecting or promoting the nation-state. More generally, dissidents' commitment need bear no relationship – teleological, motivational, or otherwise – to the misdeed of their compatriots for them to merit responsibility for that misdeed. Instead, the ground of dissidents' responsibility follows from an obligation of fidelity that they owe their fellow citizens in virtue of their shared membership in the larger enterprise of the nation-state.

[53] In this volume (Chapter 8), Avia Pasternak advances an account of citizenship as an associative obligation that resonates well with the conception of citizenship articulated here. Nonetheless, I do not agree with Pasternak that her account can justify an equal distribution of burdens among citizens. Instead, it seems to me that the "solidary" nature of citizenship would be disrupted if each citizen were to carry an equal burden independent of the extent of his or her participation in the state transgression in question. Far from fostering solidarity, an insistence on an equal distribution in the face of differential contributions to the wrong might instead prompt friction between citizens, as those who did not participate in the wrong rightfully awaited exoneration – or at least relief from the sharing of burdens – from those who did participate. My account, by contrast, seeks to be sensitive to the different kinds of relationships citizens can have to a transgression of their nation-state and to adjust the magnitude of responsibility accordingly. At the same time, it views citizenship as an inescapable ground of responsibility and in that way may well honor the good of citizenship that Pasternak helpfully and lucidly identifies, without fomenting the resentments to which, I worry, her account may give rise.

this part of the account. First, given that commitment to the nation-state licenses our holding citizens responsible, it is expected only of those individuals who qualify as moral agents. The agency requirement follows from the conditions under which it would be permissible to hold an individual responsible for her *own* acts. Citizens who do not satisfy the criteria for individual responsibility ought not to bear responsibility derived exclusively from their group affiliations.

Second, I assume that it is possible to measure the extent of expected or actual commitment, but I do not offer a methodology for doing so here, leaving that task instead to sociologists and psychologists. Third, I assume further that, in the United States, the expected strength of commitment is the same for all citizens who have reached the age of majority. Thus, the generic American and the U.S. perpetrator of war crimes in Iraq will both bear equal responsibility for these war crimes *in light of their citizenship*. The perpetrator will, in addition to the responsibility she bears *qua* citizen, bear responsibility *qua* perpetrator. We should then expect the perpetrator's responsibility to be significantly greater than that of the generic American. But there is nonetheless some (non-trivial) amount of responsibility appropriately assigned to the generic American citizen.

Finally, I do not venture to spell out the nature of the sanctions appropriate to generic Americans simply in virtue of their citizenship except to say that I assume that the magnitude of their responsibility would be too little to warrant individual punishment. Instead, responsibility of the kind and magnitude entailed by citizenship is much better cashed out in the form of emotional sanctions like resentment and indignation, as we shall see in the next Section. (Indeed, it is for this reason that the American who opposes the war in Iraq likely chooses dissidence over emigration; the costs of uprooting oneself and renouncing one's attachment to one's beloved nation-state are far greater than the sanctions to which, I anticipate, citizenship on its own gives rise.)

Because citizenship grounds the American's responsibility for U.S. transgressions, and because one either is or is not a citizen, Mark Drumbl refers to the account just advanced as "crude,"[54] and he rejects it in favor of what he terms the "crude–careful" way, which delineates the responsible group crudely but allows individual members to escape liability where they can demonstrate, for example, that they sought to prevent the atrocity in question or were themselves victims of their state's crime. This way

[54] Mark Drumbl, "Collective Responsibility and Postconflict Justice." Chapter 1, this volume.

of putting the difference between our accounts is misleading, however, for citizenship is not, on my account, some rough proxy for individual culpability, as it may be on Drumbl's crude-careful account. Citizenship is instead a real basis of individual culpability, although the culpability it yields may be overwhelmed by countervailing sources of moral credit, which include acts undertaken to oppose the atrocity. Indeed, we shall see in the next section that the citizen's dissidence can sometimes, although not always, undercut the warrant for others' resentment or indignation. In short, then, it is not clear that my account is any less careful than Drumbl's; it is just that I attach moral weight to citizenship and Drumbl does not, so that dissident citizens more readily (although not necessarily more deservedly) escape liability on his account than on my own.

On a related note, Drumbl is correct that my account, focused as it is on American wrongdoing in the war in Iraq, does not contemplate situations in which some citizens were themselves victimized by the state transgression for which we seek to assign responsibility. Here, too, however, it is not clear that relying on citizenship, as my account does, produces outcomes that are less just than those of Drumbl's. As I have argued in a different context,[55] requiring formerly oppressed citizens to contribute to programs aimed at rectifying past abuses against them affirms their coequal membership in the nation-state. Further, the compensation amount can be inflated beyond what is owed for the abuses themselves to reimburse the formerly oppressed citizens for their contributions. In this way, victimized citizens' contributions come to have a purely symbolic function: they reinforce the equality that was denied by the oppression by including the victims in the national program of repair, and they do not, in the end, cost the victims anything.

That theorists like Drumbl who appreciate the collective character of atrocity nonetheless deny that blameworthiness can arise independent of individual fault should give us pause. For it turns out that there are deep psychological currents that make an individualist stance difficult to overcome, as we shall now see.

CITIZEN RESPONSIBILITY AND THE REACTIVE ATTITUDES

I noted at the outset that Americans who did not support the war in Iraq might resist the idea that they bear responsibility for abuses committed in

---

[55] Amy J. Sepinwall, "Responsibility for Historic Injustices: Reconceiving the Case for Reparations," *Journal of Law and Politics* 22 (2006): 183–229.

its course. Even were they to encounter the arguments of the last Section, they might nonetheless maintain – with full honesty – that they harbor no guilt over American war crimes committed in Iraq. More specifically, the citizens in question might lack the unpleasant sensation of guilt and might also resist the belief that they have acted wrongly. Their response provides an occasion to assess the relationship between bearing guilt, experiencing guilt, and feeling guilt – or, put more generally, the relationship between responsibility, the reactive attitudes, and their accompanying sensations.

I seek to argue here that although our paradigmatic experience of responsibility involves the blamed individual's felt guilt and acknowledgment of wrongdoing, an assignment of responsibility may well be warranted even where one or both of these pieces are absent. This is not an uncontroversial claim. On some conceptions of responsibility, a judgment of responsibility is believed to be *constituted* by one or more reactive attitudes;[56] further, on some conceptions of the reactive attitudes, emotions are themselves believed to be *constituted* by feeling-sensations.[57] How, then, can we arrive at a justified assignment of responsibility where the citizen – *when presented with the grounds of her responsibility* – neither responds to herself with guilt nor has any kind of guilt sensation? Put differently, how can it at once be appropriate for the Iraqi to resent the American and the American to forswear remorse?

To answer these questions, I begin with the case of the dissident. The dissident need not deny that citizenship is a ground of responsibility, as the last section argues. She may nonetheless maintain that her dissidence functions as a defense. More specifically, the dissident may believe that her acts of resistance more than offset her commitment to the United States, and so exempt her from responsibility. As such, she does not judge herself to have acted wrongly and, accordingly, *feels* no guilt. In the first part of this section, I attempt to make sense of her experience of

---

[56] See, for example, Gary Watson, "Responsibility and the Limits of Evil: Variations on a Strawsonian Theme," in *Responsibility, Character and the Emotions: New Essays in Moral Psychology*, ed. Ferdinand Schoeman (Cambridge: Cambridge University Press, 1987), 257: ("Strawson's radical claim is that these 'reactive attitudes' (as he calls them) are *constitutive* of moral responsibility; to regard oneself or another as responsible just is the proneness to react to them in these kinds of ways under certain conditions."

[57] See, for example, Elisa A. Hurley, "Working Passions: Emotions and Creative Engagement with Value," *Southern Journal of Philosophy* 45 (2007): 83: "Feelings seem to be somehow *essential* to what emotions are, even if they are not necessarily present on every token occasion of emotion"; Morris, supra n. 32 at 102: "When feeling guilty we characteristically suffer pain that is partly constitutive of the feeling."

her relationship to U.S. transgressions in light of resentment that victims of these transgressions might direct toward her.

The generic citizen is situated differently from the dissident. He cannot call on a set of activities that purportedly tempers or eliminates his responsibility to explain his self-asserted innocence. Instead, he invokes the absence of guilt feelings – his own, as well as those of most of his compatriots – as a defense in itself: "Were we who didn't participate morally responsible," this imagined citizen might argue, "at least many of us would feel guilt. But most of us do not feel guilt, so it is doubtful that we are morally responsible." In the second part of this section, I inquire into his response.

Finally, in the last part of this section, I draw out some of the implications of the insights of the first two sections for philosophical thinking about moral responsibility.

Dissidence and Divergent Viewpoints

The dissident believes that her resistance cancels out whatever responsibility she should come to bear in virtue of her commitment to the United States as a whole. She has arrived at this self-judgment because she has synthesized the dimension of her identity that flows from her citizenship and the dimension of her identity that flows from her dissidence and arrived at a coherent conception of herself in which her dissidence is much more definitive of who she is. However, although each of us is empowered to perform this synthesis and arrive at a self-understanding that makes sense of the disparate and sometimes conflicting strands of our identity, none of us is entitled to have others conceive of us as we conceive of ourselves. In particular, the dissident cannot legitimately expect that her self-understanding will govern the Iraqi's conception of her; he is entitled to believe that citizenship looms larger as a constituent element of an American's (or anyone's) identity than do acts opposing the policies or practices of one's government. So long as he does hold this belief, he will harbor resentment toward the American citizen, no matter how valiant her efforts at resistance.

The divergence just described arises from differing conceptions of the relative weights to place on commitment to one's nation-state, on one hand, and resistance to its acts, on the other, in constructing the dissident's individual identity. However, there is a second possible source of separation between the dissident and the Iraqi that arises from a divergence between the conception of America that each harbors. As we have seen, the dissident may undertake opposition to the war in Iraq because she conceives of an America in which the prosecution of the war in Iraq has been distinctly un-American. Indeed, it might be precisely because she harbors a vision of America as different from, and better than, the America of recent times that she is motivated to resist, and thereby restore her beloved nation-state to her imagined conception of it.[58] Yet just as she must recognize that her self-conception is not authoritative for others, so, too, must she recognize that her conception of America must also yield, at least sometimes, to that of outsiders. Thus, an Iraqi might detect a cultural imperialism in the quest to "liberate" his country and an exceptionalism in the potential impunity with which high-ranking U.S. officials have violated the laws of war, that strike him as unmistakably American. Rooted in his perspective on America, the Iraqi might find the dissident's commitment to America all the more reproachable.

Importantly, in each of the sources of resentment just described – the first rooted in divergence over the dissident's identity and the second rooted in divergence over the identity of America – there may be no principled way to adjudicate between the competing conceptions. This is not to say that there cannot be cases in which one or the other party may be mistaken: the dissident could harbor a kind of false consciousness,[59] or the Iraqi might operate with an unduly prejudiced mind-set. In each of these cases, evidence could be invoked to bring the mistaken party to see things differently. Yet, I see no reason to believe that every case is of this kind. Individuals and nations are complex, multifaceted entities, admitting of multiple constructions and narratives, and there may well be several of these that synthesize the constituent elements equally plausibly. In short, there may be an unbridgeable gap between the dissident and the Iraqi, and it is in the face of this gap that resentment may rightfully take hold.

Where there is an insuperable divergence regarding the dissident's blameworthiness, we might well want each party to recognize it and proceed with humility. Thus, we might ask that the dissident resist disclaiming responsibility and the Iraqi withhold contempt, despite the fact that each holds fast to his or her respective beliefs about the dissident's

---

[58] Cf. Dan-Cohen, supra n. 34 at 987–88 ("In this vein, Americans' knowledge that they [would come to bear] responsibility for the Vietnam War in a way that others did not may explain why they were more actively opposed to the war than were, say, the English").

[59] Cf. Karl Jaspers, *The Question of German Guilt*, trans. E. B. Ashton (New York: Fordham University Press, 2001): 97.

relationship to the United States. We might also allow that there are situations in which forbearance is too much to demand. Thus, the Iraqi who lost a family member in the Haditha massacre might, given his loss and also his not completely baseless belief in American prejudice against Muslims of Middle Eastern descent,[60] be permitted his resentment.

Here a kind of cognitive dissonance arises. To inhabit the dissident's perspective on America and on herself, the Iraqi must abandon a stance of righteous anger through which he might seek to vindicate the worth of his lost loved one, or the Iraqi people as a whole. He must instead contend with the notion that he cannot find an outlet in blame for his loss and injury that corresponds sufficiently to their (perceived) magnitude. He would then incur not just the pain of his tragedy but the profound burden of self-restraint in stifling his own sense of the injury and deferring to that of one of his (apparent) injurers. Should we really reproach him for spurning this path? Given the additional pain of forbearance, is he not entitled to presume the legitimacy of his own perspective and proceed with resentment?[61]

Ideally, individuals should be given some latitude in making sense of tragedies that befall them. That latitude ought not to be so great that it permits blaming innocents, but where one possible interpretation is more comforting than another *and the two are equally plausible*, the more comforting interpretation should prevail. Here, then, the Iraqi may legitimately indulge his resentment.[62] This does not, of course, entail

---

[60] See, for example, Chris Hedges and Laila Al-Arian, "The Other War: Iraq Vets Bear Witness," *The Nation* (July 30, 2007), http://www.thenation.com/doc/20070730/hedges: "According to the survey, conducted by the Office of the Surgeon General of the US Army Medical Command, just 47 percent of soldiers and 38 percent of marines agreed that [Iraqi] civilians should be treated with dignity and respect." Laura MacInnis, "U.N. body adopts resolution on religious defamation," *Reuters* (March 26, 2009), http://www.reuters.com/article/idUSTRE52P60220090326, describing a UN Human Rights Council antidefamation resolution that states, among other things, that some Muslims faced prejudice in the aftermath of September 11.

[61] In principle, there may also be cases in which a dissident might be permitted to disclaim, given how violative an ascription of blame for national transgressions is to her vision of her nation-state and herself. I assume here, however, that the transgressions committed against Iraqis are so egregious that it wouldn't be plausible to think that the Iraqi victim's resentment ought to give way to the American dissident's self-conception.

[62] The philosophical literature on resentment contains a debate about whether resentment is, all things considered, a useful emotion or instead one that is self-debasing. Compare Annette Baier, "Hume on Resentment," *Hume Studies* 6 (1980): 133–49, arguing that resentment, for Hume, functioned to call attention, and thereby reduce, imbalances in power; Jeffrie Murphy, "Forgiveness and Resentment," in *Forgiveness and Mercy*, eds. Jeffrie G. Murphy and Jean Hampton (Cambridge: Cambridge University Press, 1988),

that the dissident is compelled to feel guilt – feelings, after all, cannot be compelled. Nor does it entail that she must internalize the Iraqi's assessment of her responsibility. However, although the dissident may inwardly maintain her innocence, she must nonetheless accept that she is an appropriate object of blame. Just as the dissident bears an obligation of loyalty to her fellow members to refrain from disavowing the group act, so, too, she bears an obligation of decency to the victims of her group's transgression to do the same.[63]

The foregoing is intended to suggest that the warrant for resentment need not rest exclusively on an undeniable wrongdoing. It can instead arise where an individual conceives of the harm he suffers as a wrongful injury, and where his understanding of the harm is no less reasonable than is the understanding of the resented party. It follows, then, that resentment can be justified even when the target of resentment cannot recognize her wrongdoing, and this not because she is constitutionally impaired in some way (as the psychopath is) but instead because she rejects the victim's interpretation of her relationship to the wrong. Correspondingly, indignation can be justified even where its target denies wrongdoing, for third parties too might harbor a conception of the injury that implicates someone who does not conceive of herself as culpable, and here too the two conceptions may be equally plausible.

In short, resentment and indignation are meaning-creating emotions, and the circumstances in which they are appropriate are not always clear.

16: "Resentment... is a good thing for it is essentially tied to a non-controversially good thing – self-respect." See, however, Friedrich W. Nietzsche, *On the Genealogy of Morals*, trans. Douglas Smith (New York: Oxford University Press, 1999), 24: "While the noble man lives for himself in trust and openness..., the man of *ressentiment* is neither upright nor naïve in his dealings with others, nor is he honest and open with himself.... he has a perfect understanding of how to keep silent, how not to forget, how to wait, how to make himself provisionally small and submissive." To the extent that I here promote resentment as an important implement in allowing the victim of atrocity to make sense of his or her lot, I align myself with those who defend the usefulness of resentment.

63 Insofar as the argument here permits us to blame, and hence condemn, someone who is not unequivocally culpable, it might be accused of unwarrantedly relying on a retributivist conception of justice. In her contribution to this volume, Erin Kelly exhorts us to abandon retributivist conceptions of justice, where retribution is pursued for its own sake, given the natural and social factors that often undermine human agency. She nonetheless allows that retribution might be permissible for the sake of some other social good. One who is moved by Kelly's rejection of retributive justice for its own sake might nonetheless find no objection with assigning blame to the dissident, given that the assignment may be therapeutic for the victim of the wrong and that the dissident does bear some relationship to the wrong, even if not the relationship that retributive justice ought to require.

Where there is genuine uncertainty about their warrant, it may well be the case that we ought to defer to the interpretation of the injury that confers meaning on the party most in need of making sense of his situation.[64]

Citizen Responsibility and the Emotions

The generic citizen – the one who neither supported nor opposed the war – may insist that he, too, is an inappropriate object of resentment, notwithstanding his commitment to the United States. His defense would proceed not by marshaling considerations intended to rebut or outweigh that commitment, as the dissident's defense does; instead, he may just maintain, without any false consciousness, that the notion that he must accept blame fails to connect emotionally. Underlying his position is the thought that our emotions are presumptive guides to moral truth: contemplating his commitment to the United States, he nonetheless feels no guilt over American war crimes in Iraq; he thus concludes that he bears no responsibility. What might explain his response?

One possibility is that the generic citizen suffers from some kind of psychological or emotional impairment (e.g., depression, narcissism, etc.). This possibility is reasonable, but uninteresting. It is clear that our emotions are not infallible guides to moral truths; we do not always respond to moral wrongs with the appropriate emotions. One citizen's failure to respond to abuses in the war in Iraq portends little for the cogency of the claim that he is nonetheless responsible. By contrast, a widespread absence of guilt – which is characteristic of the American mood these days – is more arresting.[65] It is this mood, personified in the generic citizen here, that invites inquiry. In this section, I explore the implications of the absence of felt guilt for the account of membership responsibility.

---

[64] Compare Bernard Williams, *Shame and Necessity* (Berkeley: University of California Press, 1993), 70, arguing that it may be appropriate for victims of a harm to hold responsible the agent who *unintentionally caused* the harm even though the agent is not a wrongdoer: "Those who have been hurt need a response; simply what has happened to them may give them a right to seek it, and where can they look more appropriately than to you, the cause?"

[65] Compare Ariel Dorfman, "Forward: The Tyranny of Terror: Is Torture Inevitable in Our Century and Beyond?," in *Torture: A Collection*, ed. Sanford Levinson (New York: Oxford University Press, 2004): 8: "[Torture] presupposes, it requires, it craves the abrogation of our capacity to imagine others' suffering, dehumanizing them so much that their pain is not our pain. It demands this of the torturer . . . but also demands of everyone else the same distancing, the same numbness, on the part of those who know and close their eyes, those who do not want to know and close their eyes."

In the next section, I explore the wider metaethical possibilities that arise from the notion that blameworthiness need not be accompanied by an experience of guilt, resentment, or indignation on *anyone's* part.

Others who have contemplated the absence of guilt among members who did not participate in a group transgression have raised the possibility that the responsibility of these members is *not* strictly *moral* responsibility – that is, responsibility understood as appropriate liability to blame; it is instead a highly personal response to a tragedy in which one *chooses* to see one's agency, although one in fact bears no guilt for the wrong. Given that the experience of responsibility is optional on this possibility, the generic citizen who disclaims responsibility is then one who has simply opted not to conceive of his agency in this way.

Karl Jaspers is among the exponents of this possibility. Thus, he argues that the citizen who neither participated nor acquiesced in the Nazi regime bears not moral guilt but *metaphysical guilt* – a kind of guilt that arises although its bearer could not have prevented the wrong. He writes of Germans who survived the war: "We did not go into the streets when our Jewish friends were led away; we did not scream until we too were destroyed. We preferred to stay alive, on the feeble, if logical, ground that our death could not have helped anyone. We are guilty of being alive."[66] Similarly, Larry May, who offers a subtle reconstruction of Jaspers's account, agrees that, if a group member did not participate in the group harm and if she could not have prevented it, "moral responsibility, at least understood on the model of individual moral guilt, would be inappropriate."[67] Finally, Herbert Morris refers to the *nonmoral guilt* the American who visits Hiroshima shortly after World War II might experience – nonmoral because its bearer is, by hypothesis, without fault for the Hiroshima bombings.[68]

Importantly, for each of these theorists, whether the member who did not participate in the group transgression conceives of herself as bearing responsibility for that transgression is a matter over which she alone has authority. For Jaspers, the German citizen's metaphysical guilt is something no one else can "prescribe" or "anticipate";[69] whereas others may

[66] Jaspers, supra n. 59 at 68.

[67] May, *Sharing Responsibility*, supra n. 30 at 152.

[68] Herbert Morris, "Nonmoral Guilt," in *Responsibility, Character and the Emotions: New Essays in Moral Psychology*, ed. Ferdinand Schoeman (Cambridge: Cambridge University Press, 1987), 237–40.

[69] Jaspers, supra n. 59 at 68.

sit in judgment where political or legal guilt is concerned, "[j]urisdiction for [metaphysical guilt] rests with God alone."[70] May also seems to recognize the optional character of metaphysical guilt. Identification with the group is the ground of moral taint for May, and he acknowledges that the degree, or even the presence, of such identification may be up to the individual. Thus, he notes that "for members who are only on the fringe of the community . . . the group identification may be so weak as to not generate feelings of metaphysical guilt."[71] For Morris, nonmoral guilt also rests on identification with the wrongdoer; in particular, he argues that it arises when the individual who is blameless nonetheless identifies with the one who is blameworthy, whether a family member or even just a fellow human being.[72] Reasonably enough, then, he contends that "[w]e may not ask of ourselves or of others that guilt be felt in these situations."[73]

Underlying each of these accounts is the thought that an individual has full discretion about whether she will harbor the identificatory ties on which the experience of responsibility is purportedly predicated. Because, on these theories, these ties may not be mandated from without, neither may the sense of responsibility that they yield.

These theorists may well be right that identification is discretionary in some cases; it is not, however, discretionary in the context of an institutional group like the United States, as I sought to argue in the last section. Instead, as we saw, American citizenship has a normative dimension that compels the citizen to accept blame for U.S. transgressions. To understand the generic citizen's response to the claim that he is responsible, then, we will have to look to something other than theories that entertain discretionary guilt experiences.

An inquiry into the natural history of guilt provides useful insights. Guilt, as Herbert Morris notes, "is a painful state."[74] One can trace the unpleasant sensation accompanying guilt by way of an evolutionary account that looks to the practical effect of our emotional life. On such an account, the unpleasantness of guilt is useful for its power to regulate behavior. We come to associate certain courses of conduct with this pain and refrain from pursuing them to avoid suffering this pain.[75] From an evolutionary standpoint, it makes sense that guilt should have naturally

---

[70] Ibid., 26.
[71] May, supra n. 30 at 153.
[72] For example, Morris, supra n. 68 at 240.
[73] Ibid., 237.
[74] Morris, supra n. 32 at 89.
[75] Compare Joseph Butler, "Sermon VIII: Upon Resentment and Forgiveness of Injuries," in *Fifteen Sermons Preached at the Rolls Chapel*, Leroy Dagg, transcribed 2002, arguing

evolved in connection with wrongs in which we played a causal role, given that the unpleasantness of guilt functions to deter us from future wrongdoing. The natural history of guilt thereby privileges those acts in which our agency is substantially implicated. Correspondingly, for acts in which our causal role is remote or nonexistent, guilt may not be activated.[76]

Importantly, the thought here is not that our relationship to those wrongs of our nation-state in which we did not participate causes us to experience some feeling that we cannot name. Instead, the impoverishment resides in our *emotional* vocabulary: we are bereft of the capacity to *feel* in the face of wrongs in which our agency is not salient. It is perhaps for this reason that Karl Jaspers refers to the German citizen's failure to wage a fruitless opposition against the Nazi regime as *metaphysical guilt*, a species of guilt whose phenomenological component seems utterly mysterious.[77] It is also perhaps for this reason that others who have contemplated the possibility of a sense of responsibility in the absence of wrongdoing have identified shame, rather than guilt, as its attendant emotion.[78]

If guilt does have the natural history just described, then we should not expect cases of wrongdoing that do not fit the paradigm – again, a paradigm in which we bear significant causal responsibility for the wrongs for which we are held responsible[79] – to elicit the feeling of guilt.

that, where virtue fails, individuals may nonetheless be deterred from pursuing wrongdoing by the anticipated unpleasantness of the resentment their wrongdoing would elicit. Available at http://anglicanhistory.org/butler/rolls/o8.html.

[76] Compare Allan Gibbard, *Wise Choices, Apt Feelings: A Theory of Normative Judgment* (Cambridge, MA: Harvard University Press, 1990), 135–38, describing guilt as the experience an individual ought to have in the face of acts that reveal that she is insufficiently motivated to engage in cooperation and reciprocity, and arguing that others' anger in the face of antisocial conduct will tend to induce the guilty party to make amends, thereby restoring faith that she is suitably prepared to cooperate.

[77] Jaspers, supra n. 59 at 68. I do not mean to endorse here the part of Jaspers's account that leaves the experience of metaphysical guilt to the individual's conscience. Nonetheless, the term "metaphysical guilt" may well be apt for cases in which one views oneself as culpable in a wrong for which one is not causally responsible.

[78] See, for example, Morris, supra n. 32 at 137, describing the experience of nonmoral guilt as "a feeling of shame, perhaps before God, because of the evil done by any human being, as if some defect in us were revealed by what any human being did"; May, supra n. 30 at 155 ("moral shame or taint may be the appropriate moral feeling" in instances "when a person's causal agency is not in question, or at least when the causal role one played did not make a difference in the world").

[79] I use the "significant" qualifier because I believe that the citizen does bear a causal relationship to the wrongs of his nation-state, although not one that itself grounds his responsibility. Elsewhere, I have argued that all citizens furnish the nation-state's

Furthermore, without the phenomenological correlates of guilt, the judgment that we are guilty may not be accessible to us through the first-personal experiences on which we typically rely to illuminate the moral character of our acts. However, the impediment to experiencing guilt need not entail that we do not bear a reproachable connection to the wrongdoing. An understanding of guilt's evolutionary role opens up the possibility, then, that our emotional life may track only a subset of the wrongs for which we bear responsibility. This possibility warrants further consideration.

Citizen Responsibility and Licensed Blame

I have argued that resentment may be appropriate even though guilt is not (the case of the dissident) and that one may bear guilt even though the feeling of guilt is universally absent or even universally inaccessible (the case of the generic citizen). As I have characterized them, then, these cases sit uncomfortably alongside several core ideas within philosophical understandings of moral responsibility. In particular, these cases challenge the idea that judgments of moral responsibility are constituted by a particular triad of reactive attitudes, as well as the idea that judgments of responsibility are constituted by reactive attitudes in general. Most fundamentally, these cases challenge the notion that blameworthiness presupposes guilt. I elaborate on each of these implications in turn.

In the literature linking responsibility and reactive attitudes, it is nearly a gospel truth that guilt, resentment, and indignation cotravel.[80] More

capacity to act by sustaining the identity of the nation-state over time, and preserving the rules according to which the acts of some citizens qualify as acts of the nation-state. See Sepinwall, supra n. 55. To that extent, all citizens causally contribute to the nation-state's acts. However, this notion of causality is atypical. In everyday ascriptions of causal responsibility, causality is restricted to instances when one's contribution made a difference to the outcome. Insofar as no individual citizen can be said to have made a difference in furnishing the nation-state's capacity to act, it is not inappropriate to think that the casual contribution flowing from citizenship alone is insufficient to make each and every citizen causally responsible for each and every act of the nation-state. To say that the generic citizen does not bear a significant causal relationship to a transgression of the nation-state is, then, just to say that he did not participate in the transgression in question.

[80] See, for example, Peter Strawson, "Freedom and Resentment," in *Perspectives on Moral Responsibility*, eds. John Martin Fischer and Mark Ravizza (Ithaca, NY: Cornell University Press, 1993), 56–57, referring to resentment and indignation as "kindred" reactive attitudes, and to guilt as the "correlate" of these two; Williams, supra n. 64 at 89: "What arouses guilt in an agent is an act or omission of a sort that typically elicits from other people anger, resentment or indignation." R. Jay Wallace has argued that

specifically, on these accounts – which we may call *Strawsonian* after Peter Strawson's seminal work – one and the same transgression is supposed to induce guilt in the person who carries it out, resentment in its victim, and indignation in third parties who learn of it.[81] However, I have argued that, in the case of the dissident, the supposed triad of guilt, resentment, and indignation dissolves: the dissident may be an appropriate object of resentment and indignation even if she need not conceive of herself as guilty. In other words, there may be asymmetries between the self-reactive attitudes and other-directed reactive attitudes.

The situation for the Strawsonian gets worse when we turn to the reflections on the natural history of guilt marshaled earlier. For the Strawsonian, moral salience is brought to light through the emotions. If I am right that our emotional vocabulary is limited where our causal agency is absent, however, then there may be a whole swath of acts or outcomes for which we bear responsibility and to which we are blind. The blindness becomes troubling when it is not universal – in particular, when victims or third parties assign responsibility to us and we are incapable of experiencing the corresponding self-assessment. It is also possible, however, that our relationship to some wrong will elicit no guilt, no resentment, *and* no indignation. This possibility arises because those who judge us may be no less primed to view responsibility through a causal lens than we are, and so they, too, might overlook the fact that we – now cast as generic members of institutional groups in whose transgressions we have not participated – deserve blame. On this possibility, then, there would be blameworthiness that no emotion could disclose. Yet it is not clear that the interests or status of the individuals affected by the blameworthy act would thereby warrant any less vindication.

Finally, it is not just the Strawsonian understanding of responsibility that occludes judgments of responsibility in cases in which we bear a noncausal relationship to the wrong. It is a commonplace across the literature on responsibility that it is a necessary condition of X's being morally responsible for Y that it be appropriate for X to experience guilt in relation to Y.[82] However, the account of citizen responsibility I have

---

the reactive attitudes should consist *only* of guilt, resentment, and indignation. R. Jay Wallace, "Emotions and Expectations," in *Free Will: Critical Concepts in Philosophy*, ed. John Martin Fischer (New York: Routledge, 2005), 145.

[81] Strawson, supra n. 80 at 57.

[82] See, for example, Gibbard, supra n. 76 at 126: "a person is to blame for something if it would make sense for him to feel guilty for having done it"; Stephen Darwall, *The Second Person Standpoint: Morality, Respect, and Accountability* (Cambridge, MA:

advanced dispenses with the supposedly necessary connection between moral responsibility and the appropriateness of guilt. More specifically, on my account, one need not experience guilt in relation to some wrong to bear moral responsibility for it; sometimes, the fact that others would be licensed in blaming us is enough to ground our moral responsibility.

In sum, then, the account of responsibility advanced here entails not only a dissolution of the guilt–resentment–indignation triad. That account also exposes the implicit primacy accorded to guilt, relative to the other two members of the triad, and it invites us to unseat guilt from its pride of place and replace it with resentment. In the face of legitimate disagreement about the warrant for blame, it is, then, victims, and not wrongdoers, whose perspectives should prevail.

More generally, the account of membership responsibility implies that we may be implicated in wrongs in ways that we do not feel and do not see. Our moral reality may then transcend the scope of our emotional awareness. As such, we ought to be open to the possibility that we bear responsibility for more of the transgressions of our nation-state than we think. Americans, that is, ought to be open to the possibility that they bear responsibility for U.S. war crimes committed in the course of the war in Iraq.

Harvard University Press, 2006), 71: "Guilt feels like the appropriate (second-personal) response to blame: an acknowledgment of one's blameworthiness that recognizes both the grounds of blame and, more importantly for us, the authority to level it (even if only "to God"). To feel guilt, consequently, is to feel as if one has the requisite capacity and standing to be addressed as responsible." Susan Wolf captures the position in question thusly: "guilt is the emotion one feels or should feel in proportion to how much one judges oneself blameworthy." "The Moral of Moral Luck," September 13, 2001. Available at http://www.law.berkeley.edu/centers/kadish/moralluck.pdf.

10

Kicking Bodies and Damning Souls: The Danger of Harming "Innocent" Individuals While Punishing "Delinquent" States

Toni Erskine

The problem with trying to punish an institution that is judged to be "delinquent" – whether a "rogue state," the United Nations (UN), Shell Oil, or the U.S. Army – might be understood as one of responding to an entity that (to invoke Edward, First Baron Thurlow's eighteenth-century account of the corporation) "has no soul to be damned and no body to be kicked."[1] Perhaps this seems a fairly obvious point. After all, even if one can draw some carefully qualified analogies between individual human actors and institutions (as I attempt to do in the first part of this chapter), the two types of entity are different in important ways. One might thereby conclude that the corporeal – and, depending on one's beliefs, even the spiritual – nature of individual human actors renders them vulnerable to forms of punitive harm to which institutions, in the sense of formal organizations, are simply impervious. Alternatively, one might maintain that such an observation has little relevance when we are talking about "delinquent" institutions in international relations. We do not, one might argue, need to be able to anthropomorphize formal organizations to

This argument was first presented at a panel on "Responding to 'Delinquent' Institutions in International Relations" at the International Studies Association Annual Convention in San Diego, California, March 22–25, 2006, and at "No Soul to be Damned, No Body to be Kicked: Responding to 'Delinquent' Institutions in International Relations," the 4th Workshop of the British Academy Network on Ethics, Institutions and International Relations, Aberystwyth University, July 2007. I am grateful to Richard Vernon and Tracy Isaacs for providing me with the opportunity to return to it, and for organizing such a stimulating workshop in London, Ontario, in 2009. I am also grateful to the participants of both workshops for their valuable comments. A version of this chapter was previously published in *Ethics & International Affairs* 24, no. 3 (2010), 261–85.

[1] Quoted in John C. Coffee, Jr., "No Soul to Damn: No Body to Kick: An Unscandalized Inquiry into the Problem of Corporate Punishment," *Michigan Law Review*, 79 (1981): 386–460 (p. 386).

be able to punish them. Indeed, we frequently justify actions toward states, multinational corporations, and intergovernmental organizations in terms of punishment, and these actions often serve successful deterrent, retributive, and even rehabilitative functions.

In this chapter, I want to take a path somewhere between these two responses to the idea of punishing institutions. The distinction between individual human actors and corporations stressed in Baron Thurlow's statement is, indeed, a fairly straightforward one. Nevertheless, it is also a distinction with implications that are largely ignored when we make calls to punish institutions. This distinction does not preclude the possibility of punishment at the level of the institution, but it does point to significant conceptual and practical complexities in how we can coherently respond to formal organizations that are seen to fall foul of their moral responsibilities in international relations.

I have argued elsewhere that institutions – such as states, the UN, and multinational corporations – can be moral agents, and therefore bearers of duties.[2] In negotiating the often controversial step from individual to institutional moral agency, I have asked when (if ever) such a move is appropriate. I have also asked what the practical implications of this step are for confronting ethical issues in international relations. In exploring these questions, I have suggested that identifying both the internal features that allow an institution to qualify as a moral agent and the external conditions that are conducive to its discharging particular duties are critical endeavors. Only then can we consider to which bodies it makes sense to distribute duties in world politics and how blame might be fairly apportioned if these moral responsibilities are unmet.[3] This chapter begins by surveying the terrain of this argument – an argument with which I feel fairly confident, despite its arguably radical bent – and then turns to a proposition that, for me, elicits both hesitation and worry: that we can punish institutions for abrogating their moral responsibilities.

---

[2] Erskine, "Assigning Responsibilities to Institutional Moral Agents: The Case of States and 'Quasi-States,'" *Ethics & International Affairs* 15, no. 2 (2001), reprinted in *Can Institutions Have Responsibilities? Collective Moral Agency and International Relations,* ed. T. Erskine (New York and Basingstoke: Palgrave Macmillan, 2003), 19–40; Erskine, "'Blood on the UN's Hands'? Assigning Duties and Apportioning Blame to an Intergovernmental Organisation," *Global Society* 18, no. 1 (2004), 21–42; and Erskine, "Locating Responsibility: The Problem of Moral Agency in International Relations," *The Oxford Handbook of International Relations,* ed. Christian Reus-Smit and Duncan Snidal (Oxford: Oxford University Press, 2008), 699–707.

[3] I use the terms "moral responsibilities," "duties," and "obligations" interchangeably for the purposes of this chapter.

Even more daunting than determining which institutions in international relations can be assigned responsibilities and burdened with blame (and in what circumstances) is the task of responding to the "delinquent" institution once it has been blamed for a particular act or omission. Especially problematic is judging how (and if) an institution can be "punished" in a way that does not punish its constituents as individuals. The central aims of this chapter are, first, to explain why it makes sense, in the context of certain acts and omissions, to blame an organization at the corporate level for harm or wrongdoing, and, second, to highlight the grave difficulties in turning to punishment as an appropriate response to such institutional delinquency. These difficulties are highlighted by exploring the repercussions for arguably "innocent" individual human constituents when the "delinquent" state is the intended object of punishment.[4]

This chapter is divided into four sections. In the first section, I outline what I will call a "model of institutional moral agency," which not only attempts to define criteria that a collectivity, or group, must meet to qualify as a moral agent but also aims to define those circumstances in which an institutional moral agent can be expected to discharge specific duties. The purpose of this section is to establish why it makes sense, conceptually, to talk about blame and punishment vis-à-vis certain collectivities, even if the attempt to introduce punishment in practice is accompanied by a plethora of difficulties. In the subsequent section, I draw on this model of institutional moral agency to clarify what I mean by a "delinquent" institution. The third section contains a preliminary discussion of problems involved in attempting to punish delinquent institutions. Specifically, I address three types of concern: "guilt by association," "misdirected harm," and "overspill." In the fourth section, I illustrate these problems by turning to the danger of harming "innocent" individuals while ostensibly punishing "delinquent" states through organized violence. To conclude, I offer some points for future development on the following themes: the relative culpability of individual members of delinquent states that have democratic versus nondemocratic decision-making

---

[4] This chapter represents an initial step in extending my examination of institutional moral responsibility and blame to questions of punishment. As such, it seeks to provide an account of some of the problems involved in taking this further step and to preface what will be a more detailed examination of attempts to punish the state (and other institutional agents) by means of extracting reparations, imposing sanctions, and resorting to military intervention. This broader study forms the final section of a monograph titled *Who Is Responsible? Institutional Moral Agency and International Relations* (in progress).

structures; and the logic of nondistributive, as opposed to distributive, forms of punishment in response to delinquent institutions.

A MODEL OF INSTITUTIONAL MORAL AGENCY

In international politics, assertions of moral responsibility are commonplace.[5] These assertions take two forms: claims of prospective moral responsibility, in which *ex ante* judgments are made regarding tasks that an agent ought to perform given certain conditions and (necessarily related) statements of retrospective responsibility, involving *ex post facto* assessments of a particular event or set of circumstances for which an agent's acts or omissions are such that the agent is deemed deserving of moral praise or blame. When confronted with the possibility of crises, whether in the form of famine, genocide, terrorist attacks, or environmental harm, politicians, policy makers, and people on the street speak of duties to avert or mitigate disaster. In the wake of such crises, we demand to know who should have acted but did not or who should have responded more quickly, more efficiently, or more robustly. We point fingers and apportion blame. We frequently also demand that someone – or something – be punished.

The important detail that is often neglected, however, is that any meaningful assertion of moral responsibility (whether prospective or retrospective) requires that those who are called on to uphold duties, and those who are held to account for evading them, must be moral agents – entities that, by definition, possess capacities to contemplate, recognize the significance of, and ultimately execute different courses of action in the first place. Divorcing difficult questions of moral agency from those assertions of moral responsibility regularly voiced in international relations variously results in incoherent policy making, the effective evasion of duties despite nominal calls to action, the creation of "scapegoats," and, perhaps most relevant to the current discussion, the tendency for punishment to be tenuously justified and carelessly directed.

We understand specifically *moral* agency first and foremost in the context of individual human beings. Extending this designation to groups is both complex and contested. Indeed, some critics would maintain that any allusion to groups bearing duties or being apportioned blame can only

---

[5] In this section, I summarize arguments that I have made in the following places: "Assigning Responsibilities to Institutional Moral Agents," in *Can Institutions Have Responsibilities?*, pp. 21–26, and "'Blood on the UN's Hands'?" 23–27.

be shorthand for referring to the actions of individual human beings. For these "individualists," collectivities can be considered neither agents nor moral agents.[6] According to this position, (misguided) accounts of group action are always reducible to descriptions of the actions of their individual human constituents. Prescriptions and evaluations of action must therefore refer to these fundamental moral units. This rejection of the idea that groups might be moral agents leaves certain concerns unaddressed, however. Just as formal organizations arguably possess the capacity to address injustices and respond to crises in ways that individuals on their own cannot and might thereby be assigned responsibilities that could not be borne by individual human actors, formal organizations might also be blamed for wrongdoing, misjudgment, neglect, or harm that is not attributable on the same scale to particular individuals within the organization. Of course, this proposed move from individual to institutional accounts of obligation and blame must be carefully and critically examined.

Can institutions qualify as moral agents? Because the concept of moral agency tends to be invoked with respect to individual human beings, this seems a logical place to start in asking what it would mean to speak of an institution as a moral agent.[7] Although philosophers rely on quite different standards to identify those specific features of individual human beings that define them as moral agents, they agree, in general terms, that to qualify as such, the individual must possess capacities both for understanding and reflecting on moral requirements and for acting in such a way as to conform to these requirements. Importantly, for the individual then to *exercise* moral agency and to be able to discharge specific duties, an additional condition must be satisfied. He or she must possess not only the capacity to act in response to moral requirements but also the freedom to do so. In other words, the exercise of moral agency

---

[6] "Individualism" is a label that is used for a number of theoretical positions. Here, I am referring to both "methodological individualism," according to which all social facts must be explained exhaustively in terms of the actions, beliefs, and desires of individual human beings, and "ontological individualism," according to which only human beings are "real" and, therefore, possible agents.

[7] The approach of drawing on parallels between individual human capacities and those of institutions is taken by Onora O'Neill, in "Who Can Endeavour Peace?," *Canadian Journal of Philosophy,* suppl. 12, *Nuclear Weapons, Deterrence, and Disarmament,* ed. David Copp (1986): pp. 41–73, to establish an account of "institutional agents" able to respond to ethical reasoning and nuclear dangers. This article, and discussions with its author, have greatly influenced my position here.

requires that one enjoy some degree of independence from other agents and forces.[8]

The question of when – if ever – a group is a moral agent has been largely neglected by theorists of International Relations. It is necessary, therefore, to look outside that discipline to find an example of how one might extend moral agency beyond the individual. Writing in the area of business ethics, Peter French challenges what he identifies as an "anthropocentric bias" in our moral reasoning and aims to illustrate that the corporation can be a moral person.[9] In this pursuit, he identifies features of what he labels "conglomerate collectivities," or those groups that he suggests are "full-fledged members of the moral community." A brief overview of some of these features provides the starting point for identifying criteria that can be usefully invoked in explaining whether certain institutions in world politics – such as states – qualify as moral agents.

"A conglomerate collectivity," French maintains, "is not exhausted by the conjunction of the identities of the persons in the organization." Put simply, it is more than the sum of its constituents; it has what might be called a "corporate" identity. Another characteristic of French's conglomerate collectivities is that they have "internal organizations and/or decision procedures."[10] The idea that his corporate moral person must have a central decision-making function is important for two reasons. First, it stipulates that the group be able to deliberate, a requisite feature of moral agency outlined earlier. Second, it entails a degree of decision-making unity that would allow the group in question to arrive at a predetermined goal, rather than simply displaying the spontaneous convergence of individual interests that one might experience in a crowd or a mob, for example.

A feature that French does not mention but that seems fundamental to any group that would qualify as a moral agent is an executive function linked to this decision-making capacity. It is not enough for a group to be able to consider moral guidelines and weigh the consequences of different courses of action; the group must be able effectively to translate decisions into action. Structures must be in place to allow decisions to be realized. Decision-making procedures and structures for carrying out the

---

[8] O'Neill sets out this position in "Who Can Endeavour Peace,?" p. 51.
[9] Peter French, *Collective and Corporate Responsibility* (New York: Columbia University Press, 1984), p. 46.
[10] Ibid., p. 13.

resulting resolutions come together to ensure that a group has a capacity for purposive action.

Outside his discussion of conglomerate collectivities, French observes that "persons" are generally understood to have an identity over time. They are considered to be "project-making things that can 'conceive of themselves as having a past accessible to experience-memory and a future accessible to intention.'"[11] Those that qualify as members of the moral community must have continuity. This is a feature that would seem to apply equally to groups. Another related criterion, implicit in the way that French describes persons as being able to "conceive of themselves" as having an identity over time, might be added to this list: to be a candidate for moral agency, groups must be self-asserting. This is not meant to demand that they be self-aware or "conscious." Rather, this criterion requires that they not be merely externally defined, thereby disqualifying groups that do not see themselves as units.

Adding to and elaborating on French's account of conglomerate collectivities, I propose that a group qualifies as a moral agent if it possesses the following: an identity that is more than the sum of identities of its constitutive parts, a decision-making structure, an executive function linked to this decision-making structure that allows policies to be implemented, an identity over time, and a conception of itself as a unit. I refer to groups that have these characteristics as "institutional moral agents." On the basis of these criteria, the following collectivities might reasonably be understood to qualify as institutional moral agents: Hamas, Amnesty International, Microsoft, the Catholic Church, Harvard University, and the World Bank. Moreover, the state, which is central to the subsequent analysis of punishment, would also qualify as an institutional moral agent.[12]

The terminology here is significant. The label "institution" can, of course, mean different things, and I use it here in a particular way: in the sense of a formal organization, or what might be called a "structured institution."[13] Yet even while I am focusing on formal organizations,

---

[11] Ibid., p. 85. French is quoting from David Wiggens, "Locke, Butler and the Stream of Consciousness: And Men as a Natural Kind," in *The Identities of Persons*, ed. Amelie Oksenberg Rorty (Berkeley: University of California Press, 1976), p. 161.

[12] I go through each of the stated criteria with specific reference to the state in Erskine, "The Case of States and Quasi-states," in *Can Institutions Have Responsibilities?*, 27–28.

[13] The label "structured institution" is used by inter alia K. A. Shepsle in "Rational Choice Institutionalism," in the *Oxford Handbook of Political Institutions*, ed. R. A. W. Rhodes, S. A. Binder, and B. A. Rockman (Oxford: Oxford University Press, 2006), 23–38 (p. 27).

another connotation of the term – which highlights the norms, rules, procedures, practices, and cultures that frame and channel the decisions and actions of individual human actors within these organizations – is also useful. The label *institutional* moral agent thereby provides important clues as to why certain types of collectivity reach decisions and act in ways that I argue cannot be described in terms of the aggregate decisions and actions of their individual members.

Three points of clarification should be offered here to avoid misunderstanding about the proposal that institutions can be moral agents. The first responds to the criticism that I am ascribing to institutions features of the individual human actor that one could not realistically expect an institution to possess. I am *not* suggesting that institutions are the same as individuals. Indeed, one of the starting points of this chapter is that they differ in significant ways that have a direct bearing on discussions of punishment. I am simply suggesting that institutions share with individual human actors certain capacities that allow both to be considered moral agents. I do not assume that institutions can be the perfectly unitary, rational, and independent entities that individuals are sometimes, problematically, portrayed to be. Rather, by acknowledging that institutions cannot be accurately portrayed as such but can nonetheless be moral agents, I am, in effect, challenging an idealized conception of the moral agent that is often tied to the individual human being.

The second point is simply that the moral agency of institutions in no way precludes or undermines the moral agency of those individual human actors, and subgroups, that comprise them. Moral agency is understood here to exist simultaneously at different levels. This means that the assignment of duty or the apportioning of blame at the level of the state, for example, does not allow those multifarious agents within it (such as individual citizens, a particular government or administration, the state leader, or its military organizations) to evade either moral expectations or censure for those discrete actions that are ascribable separately to them. Rather, moral agents at all levels can be responsible for concurrent, complementary, or even coordinated acts and omissions.

Finally, the model of institutional moral agency offered earlier says nothing about the substance of the moral demands to which formal organizations might be expected to conform. There is no attempt being made to adjudicate between different sources of obligation, codes of conduct, and, indeed, accounts of morality in international relations. This must, I think, be a separate project, and one on which the current endeavor need not rest. Claims are frequently made that institutions in international relations are morally responsible for certain failures. Institutions are variously held to account, blamed, and, indeed, made targets of attempts at punishment. The value of a model of institutional moral agency is to address the coherence of such charges – and of particular responses to alleged institutional delinquency – given the proposed objects of condemnation and sanction. Without making assertions about the source, nature, or force of perceived duties in international relations, one can nevertheless ask who – or what – can respond to certain calls to action and who – or what – can be held to account for breaches of what we understand to be moral imperatives.

Having made this final point, it is not the case that we are left without any moorings in discussions of duty. On questions of obligation in international relations, it is possible to point to principles that represent areas of near-universal agreement. Following Mervyn Frost, one might refer to these principles as "settled norms," defined not by their universal observance, but, more soberly, by the perceived need to provide special justification for any attempt to either deny or override them.[14] The principle of noncombatant immunity, according to which noncombatants are illegitimate intended targets of organized violence, is a good example of such a norm.[15] Furthermore, in cases in which states, for example, sign on to codes of conduct, such as the 1948 Genocide Convention or the 1984 Convention against Torture, certain acts (such as the abuse of prisoners at Abu Ghraib) and omissions (such as the failure to intervene in the Rwandan genocide) would seem to provide uncontentious examples of derelictions of duty.[16] Of course, identifying the appropriate objects of blame in cases in which there is widespread agreement that a particular moral responsibility has been abrogated, and deciding how best to respond to this culpable body, remain complex issues. It is to these issues that this chapter now turns.

[14] Mervyn Frost, *Ethics in International Relations: A Constitutive Theory* (Cambridge: Cambridge University Press, 1996), 105.

[15] I discuss the strength of this norm, despite prominent derogations from it, in Erskine, *Embedded Cosmopolitanism: Duties to Strangers and Enemies in a World of "Dislocated Communities"* (Oxford: Oxford University Press, 2008), 188–90.

[16] Kirsten Ainley highlights the important point that responsibilities are not only assigned to institutions in international relations but are also incurred and assumed by them. See her "The Social Practice of Institutional Responsibility," in *How Can We Respond to Delinquent Institutions? Blaming, Punishing, and Rehabilitating Collective Moral Agents in International Relations*, ed. T. Erskine (forthcoming).

DEFINING DELINQUENCY AMONG INSTITUTIONAL
MORAL AGENTS

When can an institutional moral agent be blamed for a particular act or omission? In other words, when can an institutional moral agent reasonably be labeled "delinquent"? Perhaps the best place to begin in answering this question is to identify cases in which institutional moral agents do not respond to what are understood to be moral imperatives, and, yet, *cannot* coherently be blamed for their apparent transgressions. From there it will be possible to move on to cases in which institutional moral agents that do not discharge particular duties can reasonably be held to account.

When Duties Cannot be Discharged: "Weak"
and "Constrained" Institutions

Importantly, fulfilling the criteria for institutional moral agency is not enough to determine that a particular body can be blamed for failing to respond to a moral imperative in a specific set of circumstances. Even those entities that we can call moral agents cannot be expected to discharge duties for which they are unable to perform requisite actions. As with individual moral agents, institutional moral agents might be prevented from responding to particular ethical demands for two sets of reasons, both of which are extremely important to how I go on to define institutional delinquency.

First, the group in question might possess capacities for deliberation and action that are limited in some respects. The suggestion that these capacities can be apparent but limited leads one to ask whether the attribution of moral agency to institutions is necessarily an "all-or-nothing" exercise. I suggest that it is not. Rather, each of the criteria posed earlier for determining which groups qualify as moral agents can be met in degrees. This qualification can be illustrated if one applies the criteria for institutional moral agency to states. Although "quasi-states," or states that lack positive sovereignty, tend to have, for example, weak decision-making structures, they can nevertheless satisfy the criteria for moral agency and be held accountable for *some* actions at the corporate level of the state. (A "failed state," conversely, cannot meet the criteria for institutional moral agency; any evaluation of accountability must be redirected toward the myriad individuals and groups that can be said to be acting.)[17] In other words, a group may possess capacities for deliberation and action that allow it to qualify as a moral agent, even when it faces internal impediments that render these capacities limited or unreliable in a way that prevents the group from discharging some duties that it would otherwise be understood to bear. I label such an entity a "weak institution."

Second, an actor might face external limits to discharging particular duties. *Perfect* freedom from other actors and influences is neither achievable nor necessary for exercising moral agency.[18] However, to be considered vulnerable to the apportioning of blame if particular duties are abrogated, institutional moral agents must be able to pursue their own objectives relatively free from external impediments. Some obstacles faced by institutions in international relations are disenabling: states are constrained by the financial demands (and imposed policies) of foreign creditors; certain intergovernmental organizations are designed to perform functions and are delegated responsibilities accordingly, but are not provided with the resources necessary to fulfill them. That such external factors can undermine an institution's ability to exercise moral agency in particular cases, and thereby render unreasonable expectations that certain duties be discharged, follows from the understanding of individual moral agency offered earlier. I label a formal organization thus restricted a "constrained institution."

Both categories of institutional moral agent are crucial to the discussion of holding collectivities to account for moral transgressions in international relations. Although collectivities that meet the criteria for institutional moral agency are able to discharge specific responsibilities and can be blamed for their acts and omissions in certain circumstances, an actor – whether individual or institution – cannot coherently be blamed, held to account, or punished for abrogating a duty that he, she, or it was unable to discharge in the first place.

"Delinquent" Institutions

The considerations of, first, whether an institution possesses the sophisticated, integrated capacities for deliberation and action that would allow

---

[17] Erskine, "The Case of States and Quasi-States," in *Can Institutions Have Responsibilities?*, 28–31.

[18] Here, again, I am following O'Neill. See her "Who Can Endeavour Peace?," 65.

it to qualify as a moral agent and, second, whether, as an institutional moral agent, it is either weak (due to internal limitations) or constrained (as a result of external circumstance) in ways that would prevent it from discharging duties in the context of specific actions are fundamental to discussions of moral responsibility in world politics. These steps do not lead to an account of whether certain groups are somehow inherently moral or immoral and on their own cannot determine whether these groups deserve praise or condemnation. Asking whether a group is a moral agent – and then examining the degree to which it is able to act in specific circumstances – are necessarily prior questions to determining whether it is vulnerable to assignments of duty and ascriptions of blame in the context of specific actions. In other words, an analysis of an organization's internal capacities and external conditions must come before any attempt to evaluate the degree to which it can be said to have breached its obligations and thereby be vulnerable to condemnation – and possibly sanction.

In cases in which an institutional moral agent enjoys both the capacities and enabling conditions to discharge specific duties but fails to do so, blaming that institution for the consequences of its failure is a coherent response. I refer to institutions in these circumstances as "delinquent institutions." Delinquent institutions in this sense might be understood to include Union Carbide in Bhopal, India; the UN in the context of Rwanda, Srebrenica, and Darfur; France in Rwanda; the U.S. military with respect to both civilian deaths and prisoner abuse in Iraq; and, possibly, BP in relation to the 2010 oil spill in the Gulf of Mexico.[19]

---

[19] For the example of Union Carbide as a delinquent institution warranting a response, see Lynn Dobson, "Plural Views, Common Purpose: On How to Address Moral Failure by International Political Organisations," *Journal of International Political Theory* 4, no. 1 (April 2008), 34–54. For examples of the UN's alleged derogations from duty in Rwanda, Srebrenica, and Darfur, see, respectively, Erskine, "'Blood on the UN's Hands'?"; Anthony Lang, Jr., "The United Nations and the Fall of Srebrenica: Meaningful Responsibility and International Society," in *Can Institutions Have Responsibilities?*, pp. 183–203; and Howard Adelman, "Blaming the United Nations," *Journal of International Political Theory* 4, no. 1 (April 2008), 9–33. For the delinquency of France in Rwanda, see Daniela Kroslak, "The Responsibility of Collective External Bystanders in Cases of Genocide: The French in Rwanda," in *Can Institutions Have Responsibilities?*, 159–82. For a discussion of the delinquent institutional agents that might be held to account for civilian deaths and the abuse of prisoners in Iraq, see Neta Crawford, "Individual and Collective Responsibility for Systemic Military Atrocity," *The Journal of Political Philosophy* (2007) and the respective contributions by Crawford and Kateri Carmola in *How Can We Respond to Delinquent Institutions?* Finally, I ask whether BP's catastrophe in the Gulf of Mexico represents another case of institutional delinquency in *Who Is Responsible?*

THE PROBLEMS WITH PUNISHING
DELINQUENT INSTITUTIONS

I have suggested that institutional moral agents – such as states, intergovernmental organizations, and multinational corporations – are capable of addressing injustices and responding to crises in ways that individuals on their own cannot. Concomitantly, they might be deemed to have similar scope for causing harm and perpetuating injustices. Given these capacities, it makes intuitive sense to argue that such bodies can be blamed and held to account for their acts and omissions *as institutions.* Yet does it make sense to talk about punishing them as institutions, or is this a step too far?

It is important to note here that punishment is not the only possible response to institutional delinquency. Other types of response include forgiveness, reconciliation, rehabilitation, and compensation. Each of these also deserves attention. My central purpose in trying to construct a model of institutional moral agency as part of a broader project on institutional responsibility is not to defend or most appropriately apportion punishment in specific cases. This might be one possible application of this model, but it is not a necessary end product. Making assertions and raising questions of responsibility in international relations need not be understood to lead either logically or inevitably to assertions and questions of punishment.[20] Punishment is, however, a significant concern – and justification for action – in international relations. For this reason it makes sense to address it in the context of the model of institutional moral agency that I have offered.

Even if a compelling case can be made for addressing the issue of punishment in response to institutional delinquency, how to conceptualize an institution being punished is a challenge. Although an institutional moral agent is characterized, in part, by an identity that is greater than the sum of identities of its constituent parts, it is, nevertheless, made up of individual human actors. Punishing the entity that these individuals together help to form without punishing them each *as individuals* is incredibly difficult. A colorful depiction of this conundrum can be found in an unlikely place. In *A Christmas Carol,* Charles Dickens offers an

---

[20] For a similar point, see O'Neill, "Who Can Endeavour Peace?," 58, fn. 13. Anthony F. Lang, Jr., has taken a radically different position on the centrality of punishment to questions of moral responsibility. See, for example, his *Punishment, Justice and International Relations: Ethics and Order after the Cold War* (London and New York: Routledge, 2008).

imperfect image of what it would look like to punish an institution (and, in doing so, rises to the challenge set by Baron Thurlow of responding to a delinquent corporation when it lacks a "soul to be damned"). Beginning a journey of self-reflection, Dickens's protagonist, Scrooge, is forced to witness an unsettling scene of suffering spirits and damned souls who are being punished for failing to lead ethical lives. Upon hearing "incoherent sounds of lamentation and regret; wailings inexpressibly sorrowful and self-accusatory," Scrooge, to his horror, observed that

> [t]he air was filled with phantoms, wandering hither and thither in restless haste, and moaning as they went. Every one of them wore chains . . . some few [they might be guilty governments] were linked together.[21]

In this portrayal, the purported punishment of guilty governments entails no more than the suffering of individual human actors. In other words, punishment might be described as distributive. Whether we consider a fictional purgatory (and the ghosts of governments) or real-life sanctions imposed on concrete regimes, Dickens's image points to a crucial problem. Can we effectively punish an institution while remaining faithful to the understanding of responsibility as nondistributive that the model of institutional moral agency supports?

In what follows, I want to touch on three concerns that I have with the attempt to punish institutions. I do not mean to suggest that these pose necessarily insurmountable obstacles to the viability of institutional punishment. They do, however, represent problems that must be raised and addressed in any preliminary exploration of the subject. The first, which I address under the heading of guilt by association, deals with the danger of punishing all of the members of a group for the misdeeds, or failures to act, of certain constituents of that group. The second concern is over the possibility of misdirected harm, which would include the punishment of individuals *as individuals* in response to institutional delinquency. The third and final apprehension is about the harmful side effects of institutional punishment for, among others, "innocent" individual human actors (as well as individual human actors who are less culpable than the institution, the wrongdoing of which provides the basis for punishment). Drawing on an article by John C. Coffee, the title of which invokes the

---

[21] Charles Dickens, *A Christmas Carol and Other Stories* (London: Odhams Press), p. 28.

statement by Baron Thurlow that I cite at the beginning of this chapter, I refer to this final concern as the "overspill problem."[22]

Guilt by Association

One serious concern with the proposal to punish institutions is that such a move might rely on guilt by association.[23] According to this objection, we unfairly blame, and punish, the many for the misdeeds of the few. This is a very real problem, but one that I want to suggest flows from a conception of moral responsibility that departs radically from the notion of institutional moral agency that I have proposed.

The alternative understanding of group responsibility that generates this apprehension is referred to by the frequently invoked and much maligned phrase "collective responsibility," and is no stranger to discussions of justice and reparation, guilt and apology, and retribution and reprisal in international politics. According to this conception, a degree of solidarity within a group, or a shared aspect of identity, allows those who are not party to a specific action to be morally praised or blamed for the action of an agent or agents within the same group.[24] Responsibility in this sense has been addressed in the specific sense of exploring the degree to which individual citizens must bear and retain guilt for the past deeds of their governments. It has garnered particular attention with regard to the issue of whether the German people are "collectively responsible" for the Holocaust.[25] By this account, membership within the group in question, and therefore the distribution of responsibility among

[22] Coffee, "No Soul to Damn," 387, fn. 4. It is important to note that Coffee is specifically addressing fines imposed on corporations.

[23] Elsewhere, and in a previous draft of this chapter, I used the label "vicarious responsibility" synonymously with "guilt by association." I am grateful to Larry May for pointing out another way in which the notion of "vicarious responsibility" is often employed in the literature on collective responsibility and, to avoid confusion, use only "guilt by association" here.

[24] Daniel Warner provides a valuable analysis of the bearing that this notion has on theorizing about international relations in *An Ethic of Responsibility in International Relations* (Boulder and London: Lynne Rienner, 1991).

[25] See, among others, K. Jaspers, *The Question of German Guilt*, trans. E. B. Ashton (New York: Fordham University Press, 1947/2000). Jaspers, it should be noted, is careful to distinguish between different types of responsibility. He adamantly rejects any suggestion that all Germans took part in criminal activity and, therefore, were criminally guilty. Nevertheless, his notion of "political guilt" comes close to the notion of "guilt by association" to which I am referring. For Jaspers, all Germans were to some extent politically guilty, or answerable for the acts of the regime to which they belonged,

its members, may even be understood to extend transgenerationally –
and, in another variation on this position, to extend universally so that
the relevant group is conceived of as humanity as a whole.²⁶ Aversion to
this notion of responsibility – and any call to punishment that might arise
from it – is not difficult to explain. It runs counter to the understanding
that one cannot be blamed for the wrongdoing of another. This conception of group responsibility diverges significantly from what I introduced
earlier in the chapter. An implication of the model of institutional moral
agency that I outlined cannot be that all members of a group are responsible for the actions of discrete members within that group. Institutional
responsibility is simply not distributive in this way. The group itself is
the moral agent. If the group is also the proposed object of punishment
(in response to acts that cannot be described in a way reducible to its
constituents), then the fear that punitive action is being directed against
individuals who are being unfairly held to account is unwarranted.

This particular concern is based on the conceptual difficulties of talking about blaming and punishing a formal organization. These difficulties
can be overcome by rejecting the equation of institutional blame with
guilt by association and reserving the apportioning of responsibility to
institutions for instances in which the relevant action is one that can
genuinely be described at the corporate level. The subsequent two concerns, however, relate to the *practical* difficulties of actually punishing an
institution, even after we have established that it is the institution itself
that deserves blame. The following concern appears to be particularly
intractable.

Misdirected Harm

In cases in which we are responding to acts or omissions that cannot be
reduced to the agents that constitute the group – and we can, therefore,
coherently talk about *institutional* responsibility – punishing the institution, as an institution, makes sense, at least in theory. One problem

---

even if they could be accused of neither supporting nor cooperating with this regime
(pp. 43–44).

²⁶ In *The Guilt of Nations* (New York and London: W. W. Norton, 2000), Elazar Barkan
explores cases of restitution for historical injustices that often find the descendants of
both victims and perpetrators embroiled in questions of guilt, responsibility, and compensation. For the proposal that collective responsibility extend to all of humanity, see
Hannah Arendt, "Organized Guilt and Universal Responsibility," in *Collective Responsibility: Five Decades of Debate in Theoretical and Applied Ethics*, ed. L. May and S.
Hoffman (Savage, MD: Rowman and Littlefield, 1991), pp. 273–83.

that remains, however, is that it is not apparent how one goes about "punishing an institution as an institution." Here we are back to Baron Thurlow's observation that an institution "has no soul to be damned and no body to be kicked." So how do you punish it? Perhaps more to the point of my immediate concern here is the question of how to punish the institution at the corporate level (at which blame has been apportioned) rather than inflicting punishment on the aggregate of its individual human constituents (who *do* have bodies to be kicked and souls to be damned). In other words, if my previous concern might be referred to as the danger of misdirected responsibility, then this concern is one of misdirected harm.

Overspill

The final concern also relates to the danger of harming individuals in the attempt to punish the institutions. However, in this case, such harm is the indirect consequence of effectively punishing the institution. If we can assume that it is possible to get past the previous sources of concern by first appropriately identifying the relevant institutional agent as an object of blame in the context of a specific action, and second arriving at a means of punishment that targets this agent at the corporate level, this third problem remains. Even punishment that is directed at the corporate level of the institution risks *indirectly* harming individuals – both those who are constituents of the institution and those who benefit from the services provided by the institution. As Coffee quips, "when the corporation catches a cold, someone else sneezes."[27] He goes on to observe that overspill from a penalty levied against a corporation occurs at various levels.[28] Individuals benefit from the functions performed, and, indeed, the duties discharged, by an institution. Although one might argue that the long-term deterrent or rehabilitative effect of punishing an institution could result in the institution in question better fulfilling its functions and discharging its duties – to the ultimate benefit of the individuals

---

[27] Coffee, "Corporate Punishment," 401.

[28] Note, again, that Coffee is referring to financial penalties. Those that he maintains are adversely affected by the overspill resulting from such penalties are the following: stockholders, who suffer from the diminished value of their securities; bondholders and other creditors, who also find that the value of their securities has been reduced (due to "the increased riskiness of the enterprise"); the workforce ("lower echelon employees") who face layoffs if the corporation is hit hard enough by the fine; and the consumer, if the corporation responds to the fine by setting higher prices. See Coffee, "Corporate Punishment," 401–2.

that it serves – in the short term, these individuals might nonetheless suffer.[29]

In the subsequent section I aim to illustrate each concern in the context of attempts to apportion punishment through military means. Specifically, I touch on examples taken from the recent wars in Afghanistan and Iraq. I am not accepting either state as a delinquent institution, but, rather, using these cases of *alleged delinquency* to interrogate the logic of justifying military action in response. Particularly useful in the current context are the discrepancies that these cases entail between the purported objects and the actual victims of punitive harm.

KICKING BODIES AND DAMNING SOULS: "INNOCENTS" AND THE PROBLEM OF PUNISHING THE STATE

Talk of punishment is nothing new to discussions of the ethics of war. Indeed, a just cause for engaging in organized violence was traditionally seen to include punishment of wrongdoing. Although accepted justifications for war have narrowed to self-defense in most contemporary articulations of the Just War tradition, punishment as a reason for war has not disappeared – and, arguably, has experienced a reemergence.[30] This is apparent in both academic and political commentary on the so-called War on Terror. For example, in response to the 2001 attacks on the World Trade Center and the Pentagon, Jean Elshtain maintained that "a carefully worked out and unprovoked act of terror against non-combatants of one's own country is an injury – an act of war – that demands a response. That response is just *punishment*."[31] President Bush, defending wars against both Afghanistan and Iraq, also spoke passionately of "bringing justice to the enemies."[32] Punishment has been unmistakably present as an underlying justification for military action in the War on

---

[29] Dobson makes the point that individuals who depend on institutions suffer if these institutions are prevented from performing their functions in "Plural Views, Common Purpose."

[30] Cian O'Driscoll addresses this theme in *Negotiating the Just War Tradition: The Right to War in the Twenty-First Century* (New York: Palgrave Macmillan, 2008).

[31] Jean Bethke Elshtain, "How to Fight a Just War," in *Worlds in Collision: Terror and the Future of Global Order*, ed. Ken Booth and Tim Dunne (Basingstoke: Palgrave, 2002), 263–69 (p. 264), emphasis mine. See also Jean Bethke Elshtain, *Just War against Terror: The Burden of American Power in a Violent World* (New York: Basic Books, 2003).

[32] "Remarks by the President at Michigan Rally," Jerome-Duncan Theatre at Freedom Hall, Sterling Heights, Michigan, May 3, 2004. Available at: http://www.whitehouse .gov/news/releases/2004/05/20040504.html.

Terror – even though it has not been the only, or, indeed, in the case of Iraq, the predominant (explicit) justification for engaging in war. Analyzing the idea of war as punishment by appealing to the idea of institutional moral agency, then, serves as more than a mere conceptual puzzle. It is an endeavor that reveals far-reaching and important implications pertaining to how we understand, and respond to, purported cases of institutional delinquency in international politics. These implications are addressed by revisiting the three categories of concern generated by the idea of punishing institutions.

Narrowing the Enemy: The Specter of Guilt by Association

The perceived danger of relying on guilt by association in ostensibly punishing a delinquent state is apparent in the context of the War on Terror. This perceived danger is revealed in dedicated attempts to avoid it – through explicit endeavors to narrow the purported objects of punishment. Breaking with the conventional understanding of "the enemy" in war as the collective body against which one is fighting, there have been recent moves, particularly with respect to the war in Iraq, to limit significantly who is described as falling within this category. "Enemy," it seems, has taken on the connotation of those who are "guilty" – and who are, therefore, deemed to be legitimate targets. President Bush, for example, declared at the start of the war that "our *enemy* in this war is the Iraqi regime, not the people who have suffered under it."[33] Expressing a similar sentiment, Prime Minister Tony Blair assured the Iraqi people that "our enemy is not you but your barbarous rulers."[34] Drawing this nominal distinction might be perceived as particularly important because of the underlying justification of war as punishment. Punishment implies a guilty party, yet, in many cases, there is a dissonance between treating the state (as a corporate entity) as the object of organized violence (and therefore, implicitly, as the object of punishment) and accurately portraying the party whose delinquency has provoked a military response. In the case of Iraq, eliding punishment with other just-cause arguments required an overt denial that all members of the Iraqi state were being held collectively responsible for the wrongdoing of a corrupt few. Falling into the

---

[33] President Bush, "President Rallies Troops at MacDill USAF Base," March 26, 2003, emphasis mine.

[34] Prime Minister Blair, "Blair Calls for Unity," BBC News, March 21, 2003. Cited by Alex J. Bellamy, "Is the War on Terror Just?," *International Relations* 19, no. 3 (September 2005), 275–96 (p. 277).

trap of assuming guilt by association was seen to be a real danger. Of course, narrowing the category of those labeled "guilty" and thus justifiably vulnerable to punitive action is more straightforward than effectively limiting those who ultimately become targets of attack. Indeed, the apparent attempt to avoid the charge of apportioning guilt by association in this case raises the question of whether war *can* be an appropriate means of punishment when culpability is thought to lie only with certain individuals – or a subgroup – within a state. This question brings us back to the separate problem of misdirected harm.

Individual and Innocent Deaths: The Reality of Misdirected Harm

Misdirected harm, as described earlier, occurs when the objects of a punitive response are distinct from the entity whose delinquency is invoked to justify the punishment in the first place. Even if one avoids the charge of bringing notions of guilt by association into justifications for punishing the state – by, for example, making the sorts of statements offered by Bush and Blair in the context of the war in Iraq – the danger of misdirecting punishment remains a concern. I want to suggest that there are two ways in which this problem is manifest when punishment is directed against the state through military means. The first brings us back to the difficulty of punishing the state as a corporate entity (in a way that does not effectively target its individual constituents) when it is the corporate entity that is being held to account for some wrong. The second introduces the problem of whether one can coherently use war as an instrument of punishment against a state if it is not the state as a whole that is deemed to be delinquent, but, rather, a subgroup within the state. I address each in turn.

The Just War tradition has a long-established and complex means of limiting legitimate human targets in war: the principle of noncombatant immunity. Accounts of this principle describe noncombatants as deriving their immunity from their "innocence" – a term variously used to connote their lack of moral guilt or, more commonly in contemporary arguments, the fact that they are "not harming."[35] Of course, killing in war is never completely delimited and discriminate. Noncombatants are

---

[35] Attention to its etymology uncovers "innocent" as the negative form of *nocentes,* meaning "harming." See the following: Norman, *Ethics, Killing and War*, p. 168; McMahan, "Innocence, Self-Defense and Killing in War," *The Journal of Political Philosophy* 2 (1994), 193–221 (p. 193); and Anthony Kenny, *The Logic of Deterrence* (London: Firethorn Press, 1985), p. 10. Drawing on this notion of "material" rather than "moral"

regularly killed. When this is "unintended," they are designated "collateral damage."[36] When this distinction between permissible and prohibited human targets is drawn, why it is morally significant, and which individual and institutional actors are to be blamed when noncombatants become victims of attack (intentionally, disproportionately, or due to insufficient efforts to safeguard them) are difficult and important questions. They are not, however, addressed here. Arguably, these dilemmas fade into the background if war is portrayed as a means of punishing a particular state. This is because killing noncombatants and soldiers alike becomes problematic if we are talking about responding to institutional wrongdoing. Indeed, even accounts of combatant vulnerability that rest either implicitly or explicitly on notions of the "guilty" soldier sit uneasily with justifications for war that rely on the notion of institutional (rather than individual) culpability.[37] Punitive harm is *misdirected* toward individual human beings when it is the state that is being blamed for an alleged delinquency.

There is at least one conceivable retort to the claim that harm is misdirected in this case. As I argued earlier in this chapter, institutional responsibility does not preclude concomitant individual responsibility. One might invoke this point to argue that war can legitimately achieve the aim of punishing both the state at the corporate level *and* those individual citizens who are understood to be either directly or indirectly responsible for the policies of the state. This is an argument that warrants serious consideration. Yet even if one were to defend this extreme position, it must be conceded that, in some cases, it is particularly difficult to point the finger of blame at individual citizens for contributing – to whatever

innocence, the vulnerability of combatants is explained by analogy to the domestic notion of self-defense: we can target those who pose a direct threat to us.

[36] The appeal to civilian deaths as "unintended consequences" of military actions (otherwise known as "collateral damage") is rooted in the doctrine of double effect. According to this doctrine, it is possible to distinguish between two types of foreseeable consequences of an act: those that are either military goals or means to achieving military goals (intended consequences) and those that are merely the side effect of the act (or unintended consequences). According to the Just War tradition, deaths of noncombatants can never, morally, be the intended consequences of a military attack.

[37] I have argued in the following two papers that the moral relevance of the principle of noncombatant immunity within Just War arguments is (problematically) based on either explicit or implicit assumptions of the combatant's culpability: "Justifying Prohibited and Permissible Human Targets: Concepts of Blame, Punishment and Collective Moral Agency in the Ethics of War," paper presented at the 42nd Annual Convention, Chicago, Illinois, February 20–24, 2001 and "'Soldiers Are Made to be Killed?' The Principle of Combatant Vulnerability," paper presented at the 44th Annual International Studies Association Convention, Portland, Oregon, February 25–March 1, 2003.

degree – to the delinquency of the state to which they belong. Indeed, such an argument is stretched to breaking point when membership within a nondemocratic state means that individual citizens play no part in its decision-making process (and, perhaps, risk having any opposition to the ruling government or attempt to introduce democratic reform brutally oppressed). It is exactly this scenario that leads to the second possible manifestation of misdirected harm.

Misdirected harm also occurs when the state is the proposed object of punishment, yet delinquency is so narrowly associated with a specific group within the state that it becomes impossible to talk about delinquency at the corporate level of the state at all. To defend punishing the state in such a case would involve either embracing the idea of guilt by association and treating many as collectively responsible for the misdeeds of a few or eschewing this idea of transferred guilt and succumbing to the equally serious misdemeanor of misdirected harm. This second variation on misdirected harm is exemplified in the recent wars against Afghanistan and Iraq to the extent that attempts were made to justify them in terms of punishment even while explicitly asserting that the delinquent parties did not include those citizens who were inevitably placed under attack.

Earlier in the chapter, I described attempts by President Bush and Prime Minister Blair to make explicit that they were not holding the Iraqi people collectively responsible for what they presented as the grievous misdeeds of their "barbarous rulers." Perhaps the sharp distinction between the overwhelming majority of members of this "rogue state" who bore no responsibility for its alleged delinquency and the culpable minority in power served to intensify the perceived need to make clear that civilians would be protected. Prime Minister Blair announced in the context of the attack on Afghanistan that "[t]his military plan has been put together mindful of our determination to do all we can to avoid civilian casualties"; President Bush stated at the start of the Iraq war that, "[p]rotecting innocent civilians is a central commitment of our war plan."[38] Of course, noncombatants were killed. The way in which this represents a case of misdirected harm resulting from the state being punished is subtly different from that just addressed. Whereas in the previous manifestation of misdirected harm, the problem was identified as one of effectively punishing individuals *as individuals* in the attempt to punish the institutions

---

[38] Prime Minister Blair, "Statement on Military Action in Afghanistan," October 7, 2001; President Bush, "President Rallies Troops at MacDill USAF Base," March 26, 2003.

to which they belong, in this case harm is directed outside the corporate entity (whether this be the Taliban or Saddam Hussein's regime), the delinquency of which is invoked as a justification for engaging in punitive action. Even somehow successfully punishing the state at the corporate level would, in this case, nevertheless entail misdirected harm because the state as a whole is not being assigned responsibility for the alleged delinquency. Alternatively, apportioning punishment that affects individuals as individuals in such a case (which I have argued is the necessary, if unintended, outcome of trying to punish the state through war) would result in *compounded* misdirected harm. One of the reasons that the people of Afghanistan and Iraq provide such deeply problematic recipients of punitive harm is that they are not the perpetrators (nor, one might add, are they in any way the beneficiaries) of the delinquent deeds with reference to which punishment is being justified.

Indirect Harm: The Problem of Overspill

The problem of overspill brings us back to the indirect harm with which both individuals and groups might be afflicted when an institution is punished and is no longer able to perform certain functions toward either its members or those outside the institution who depend on it. In the case of punitive military action against the state, overspill might take the form of suffering caused by destruction of the state's infrastructure, disruption to health services, and population displacement (each leading, for example, to the spread of infectious diseases and malnutrition), as well as the erosion of the rule of law. Moreover, environmental damage might affect those within and without the state. Finally, military action might place burdens on neighboring states in terms of refugee flows and on external institutions with respect to rebuilding the affected region. Examples of overspill can be identified in the ongoing problems associated with the occupation of Iraq.

Overspill is significantly different from misdirected harm. Misdirected harm represents a disjuncture between the objects of blame and the direct objects of punishment. Overspill does not involve such a disjuncture. Rather, overspill involves the indirect, and unintended, harm of those who are neither held morally responsible for an alleged delinquency nor targeted in the ensuing punishment. To be defined as overspill as I have presented it here, the harm generated must be no more than a side effect of the punitive act. Overspill is likely to be unavoidable to some degree in all cases of punishment (whether individual or institutional).[39] It is a problem that should be carefully considered in the context of determining what constitutes legitimate and effective institutional punishment. Yet, unlike the problem of misdirected harm, I do not think that overspill undermines the logic of a particular form of punishment for institutional delinquency. For overspill to be acceptable, there must be concerted efforts to avoid it, and this indirect harm must be proportionate to the overall good achieved by the resort to institutional punishment.

CONCLUSION

This chapter has addressed some of the conceptual and practical difficulties that threaten to render morally incoherent those attempts to punish formal organizations that are deemed to be institutionally delinquent. Although some acts and omissions are best described at the corporate level of an institution, and moral responsibility for these cases of harm and neglect should be correspondingly located, attempts to punish institutions are fraught with difficulties. There is reason for grave concern that trying to punish an institution will, in fact, unfairly harm its individual human constituents. This concern can be tied to three specific potential problems, which I have labeled guilt by association, misdirected harm, and overspill. These problems have been explored through endeavors to punish the state as a delinquent institution by means of organized violence, with particular attention to the disjuncture between the punitive justifications for engaging in violence and the ultimate objects of harm in the recent wars in Afghanistan and Iraq.

I have argued that punishment cannot represent a morally coherent response to culpability that is located at the corporate level of an institution if the individual human members of the institution are, in fact, targeted. This can happen either because they are assumed to be guilty by association (so that attributions of moral responsibility are effectively

---

[39] The comparison between individual and institutional punishment is interesting here. Incarcerating the family members of a convicted murderer either because of their relationship to the criminal (despite their innocence) or to punish the criminal through the family members would be widely understood as unacceptable. Conversely, incarcerating the criminal knowing that this would indirectly affect his or her dependent family members could reasonably be presented as a foreseen harm that is proportionate and acceptable as a side effect of the criminal's punishment. The two variations on the first example are analogous to what I have called, respectively, guilt by association and misdirected harm in the case of attempts at institutional punishment. The second example is analogous to what I have called overspill.

misdirected) or because the punishment directly affects those whose culpability is not invoked to justify the punitive response in the first place (and harm is thereby misdirected). In other words, where present, the problems of guilt by association and misdirected harm undermine any attempt to justify punishment at the institutional level. Overspill, however, or indirect harm to actors that is a consequence of punishing an institution, is contingently acceptable – if the harm caused is proportionate and attempts are made to minimize it. In coming to these conclusions, two themes have arisen that deserve attention in future attempts to explore different forms of punishment levied against institutional actors. I touch on these briefly in the specific context of the state, which has been the focus of this chapter, before reiterating the broader points that we can – and cannot – take from the discussion to this point.

The first theme that warrants further attention is that of democratic versus nondemocratic decision making and the extent to which this should affect our considerations of how to respond to a delinquent state. Barry Buzan's provocative analysis of whom we may bomb – an analysis tied to the degree to which a people *deserves* their government – might be instructive here.[40] To what degree are citizens of a democracy responsible for the foreign policy of their state (in a way that citizens in repressive regimes with no say in such decision making are not)? A classically ambiguous statement by President Bush is interesting in this context: "I want each and every American to know for certain that I am responsible for the decisions that I make and each of you are as well."[41] To what extent can we take this literally? To what extent does taking this literally render unnecessary any distinction between holding a government to account for its policies, practices, and delinquencies and holding the citizens of a state to account for their individual actions? To what extent – and this is a separate question – does taking literally the statement that each and every citizen is responsible for the policies of the state make the idea of punishing the state as an institutional moral agent, through organized violence, more coherent – and more palatable? Each of these questions requires careful consideration of how culpability (both of the individual and of the state as a corporate entity) is affected by the degree to which citizens contribute to the state's decision-making process.

---

[40] Barry Buzan, "Who May We Bomb,?" in *World in Collision: Terror and the Future of Global Order*, ed. Ken Booth and Tim Dunne (New York: Palgrave Macmillan, 2002).
[41] George W. Bush, "Live with Regis," September 20, 2000.

A second theme that follows on from this is that of distributive versus nondistributive blame and punishment. If culpability is established at the corporate level of the state, then one might argue that an appropriate response must be one that is nondistributive (in other words, one that is directed at the institution). Only if one is responding to an aggregate of individuals who are individually deemed responsible for a harmful act or omission should blame and punishment be distributive (or directed at the individuals themselves).

In identifying some problems that I think need to be addressed in broaching the possibility of institutional punishment, it is, perhaps, important to end by clarifying the things that I am *not* arguing. First, *I am not suggesting that institutional punishment is necessarily unviable.* There are a variety of possible means of punishing formal organizations – including dismantlement, boycott, and "naming and shaming" – and a variety of types of organization against which some form of punishment might be deemed appropriate. Organized violence against a state is only one – admittedly extreme – example of punishment that one might attempt to justify on the basis of institutional culpability. Other forms of punishment might be more effective in punishing an institution *as an institution* in a way that avoids, or minimizes, punishing its constituents as individuals. Second, *I am not proposing that punishment is necessarily an incoherent basis on which to engage in military action.* There are a plethora of issues regarding the legality, and indeed prudence, of justifying war in terms of punishment that deserve attention and have not been addressed here. In the context of this discussion of institutional moral agency and responsibility, the focus of concern has been on whether it makes sense to justify military actions toward a state in terms of culpability *at the corporate level.* My point here is that war waged against the state represents a form of punishment that is necessarily distributive (in that it directly harms those within the group *as individuals*) and can only represent a coherent response when responsibility for the acts or omissions that have motivated the punitive action is also judged to be distributive (in that blame is clearly reducible to the constituents of the state). To return to Baron Thurlow, one might observe that the state has many bodies to kick and many souls to damn, but engaging in either practice fails to respond coherently, and proportionately, to institutional delinquency.

Punishing Collectives: States or Nations?

Richard Vernon

The idea of collective liability comes into play because it seems right to attribute acts to collectives that cannot plausibly be seen as acts of their members, or even as a simple aggregation of their members' actions. To the extent that liability can be individually assigned, or to the extent that some or all members contributed personally to some portion of a blamable action, individual liability (selective or across the board) is all we need. However, as all of the chapters in this book have argued, individual liability often fails to match reality. As several chapters have noted, that point was perhaps most strikingly made by Arendt's "banality of evil" construct: not all or even most of those whose complicity is essential to evil acts are themselves essentially evil. If they were, the right retributive response would be to try them, one by one, for their deeds, if one could. (If the number of offenders is high, the problem, although severe, is practical, not conceptual.) The reason for not doing so is that collectives have features that their members do not have: first, individual behavior is profoundly conditioned by the collective context; second, collective action has consequences that are not the intended consequences of many of those who contribute to it. Both causes and effects are latent, as it were, in the agents' social and political context. Thus, we need to ask, it would seem, if collectives are punished and the effects of punishment distribute downward, becoming costly for members, hasn't an injustice been done?

Yet, if we want to punish collectives only on account of those things for which their members are *not* individually blamable, we confront a dilemma. Whatever else it is, a punishment is necessarily consequential. It is the deliberate imposition of a loss (of life, liberty, goods), and losses can be experienced only by sentient beings. Abstractions, fictive entities, or collective nouns cannot suffer losses; something counts as a loss only if a sentient being suffers it, for nonsentient beings lack souls to damn or bodies to kick. How, though, can we reconcile this with the point just made – that the idea of punishing collectives makes sense just because, or to the extent that, what is blamable in their acts is not properly attributable to their members' sentient purposes? If only persons have punishable features, can it make any sense at all to speak of punishing a collective?

I believe we can approach this dilemma only by exploring the respects in which costs imposed on a collective can justly distribute downward to its members – thus counting as punishments – and that we can explore that question only by way of the character of their membership. Whether individuals can be made to suffer on account of what their collective has done depends on how they are connected to it; that in turn depends on how the collective is (relevantly) characterized. Specifically, this chapter asks: is it as a state or as a nation that a political entity is held accountable? Alternatively put: is it as cocitizens or as conationals that its members can justly be made to bear a personal share of punishment, by virtue of their membership alone? To avoid prejudging this question, I refer to the constituent territorial units that make up the world as sociopolitical entities (SPEs). We could of course simply call them "nations" or "states." (Sometimes they are called "nation-states," although that matches reality only if we relax the term "nation" quite a bit, so that the term "nation-state" embraces multinational states.) I want to avoid the terms "state" or "nation" at this basic level, however, because I want to address an issue that brings into question the moral relevance of both of the ideas of community to which they may be taken to refer.

The practical point of that question could at once be challenged on the (true) grounds that sanctions, or many of them, have the same effect regardless of how, exactly, we conceptualize their target. Suppose, for example, we impose a financial penalty ("reparations"), take away territory, or impose constitutional limitations, such as forbidding the SPE to develop certain kinds of military resources: these amount to constraints on the SPE whether we think of it as *essentially* a politically organized entity ("state") or *essentially* as a historically abiding entity that survives changes of regime ("nation"). When, for example, division was imposed on Germany after the end of World War II, we could describe that division – if we regard it as a kind of punishment, as the context surely allows – as a sanction directed at the (previous) German state, or else as one aimed at eliminating (previous) German national identity. However, there would surely be a point, all the same, if it were to turn out that the way in which the SPE is characterized were to govern the way in which its punishment could justly distribute downward, and hence the kind of collective sanction that could justly be imposed. I argue that this intuition is supported.

The argument of this chapter proceeds in three stages. First, the idea of an SPE's collective liability in general is explored, and a case is made that it is as a state, rather than as a nation, that its liability is best secured. It is acknowledged, however, that this case is an on-balance one rather than decisive (the first two sections). To reinforce the case, the question is then approached from the other end, that is, in terms of liability *for punishment*, and what is additionally required for that (third and fourth sections). Finally, if we are to conclude that, as argued, it is as states that SPEs may be punished – and that punishment may justifiably distribute down to members by virtue of cocitizenship, rather than shared nationality – what could their punishment be like (concluding section)?

THE QUESTION OF CONTINUITY

An important feature of the state-centered approach is the claim that it identifies a continuous agent, to which responsibility can be attached. Chandran Kukathas, for example, in his discussion of the topic of restitution, rejects the idea of attributing responsibility to "society as a whole" and argues that we should look instead to entities that have "structures of *authority* that are thus able to make collective decisions and that "endure over time."[1] Janna Thompson, also in connection with the topic of restitution, rejects the "moral collectivism" that attributes guilt to suprapersonal entities, and builds an argument on the necessity of transgenerational commitments by states.[2] Toni Erskine, in a seminal article, argues for attributing responsibility only to those groups that have deliberative and decision-making capacity, and that, like states, "have an identity over time."[3]

Very interestingly, however, it is precisely the topic of continuity that grounds one of David Miller's three objections to the state-centered

---

[1] Chandran Kukathas, "Responsibility for Past Injustice: How to Shift the Burden," *Politics, Philosophy and Economics* 2 (2003), 165–90, pp. 180–83.

[2] Janna Thompson, "Collective Responsibility for Historic Injustices," in *Shared Intentions and Collective Responsibility*, eds. Peter A. French and Howard K. Wettstein (Boston: Blackwell, 2006).

[3] Toni Erskine, "Assigning Responsibility to Collective Agents," *Ethics and International Affairs* 15 (2001): 67–85, p. 71.

approach and, hence, his own argued preference for taking nations as the subject. "We may want to hold nations responsible for actions performed by states that no longer exist," he writes, citing the case of Germany after the end of the Nazi regime.[4] This objection is double-edged and gives rise to competing considerations. On one hand, of course, the point suggests that states, in the case of regime change, are *not* continuous entities and, thus, as Miller suggests, that one of the important reasons for the state-centered view fails. On the other hand, punishing state leaders may be intended as a way to defuse *national* responsibility – I take it that exactly this was part of the justification of the Nuremberg Trials, which we may regard as a practical expression of the view that nations are not properly seen as the responsible entities, at least in those cases in which their political character has been fundamentally altered.[5]

Yet, should we accept the view that the continuity of states does not survive regime change? That question has the distinction of being among the oldest questions in political science, having been raised by Aristotle himself. His answer, although magisterial, is unhelpful. We may think of a polis in terms of a territory or population, he says, or in terms of an association formed in a particular (constitutional) way; given his views about constitutions, it is no surprise that he opts for the latter, and thus for the view that when the constitution changes, the very identity of the polis changes – it is no longer the same thing.[6]

That view, however, is at once rendered indecisive, in two ways. First, it applies (he says) only to a polis, not to states that have the dimensions of a "people" (*ethnos*), a view that surely reflects his focus on forms of intense political association in which political arrangements mold the whole character of relations among people, and even (he says) the character of the people themselves, so that it is plausible to think of constitutions as defining collective identity. Second, he distinguishes the question of identity from the question of obligation: whether or not a polis is the same after regime change, it is, he says, a distinct question from whether its previous obligations survive. In an appendix to his edition of the *Politics*, the political theorist Ernest Barker drew attention to the Athenian democracy's view that it should honor the war debts incurred by the thirty oligarchs whom it had overthrown, a view that

[4] David Miller, "Holding Nations Responsible," *Ethics* 114 (2004): 240–68, p. 244.
[5] See Gary Jonathan Bass, *Stay the Hand of Vengeance: The Politics of War Crimes Tribunals* (Princeton, NJ: Princeton University Press, 2000), chap. 5.
[6] Aristotle, *The Politics*, Book III, chap. 3.

may well have suggested the practical qualification that Aristotle makes to his main, deductive argument.[7]

Even if the modern SPE were like a polis, then, so that we could suppose regime change altered its very identity, it would not follow, on Aristotle's view, that its obligations were altered. Of course the modern SPE is not much like a polis (nor even a "people," the alternative term in Aristotle's vocabulary). According to modern international law, "A state comes into existence when the community involved acquires the basic characteristics associated with the concept of a state: a defined territory, an operating and effective government, and independence from outside control," the international lawyer Gerhard von Glahn writes (adding "etc.").[8] No doubt there are complex questions about when it is appropriate to recognize a government as "operating and effective," especially when its claim is contested, but those questions are about which of the competing claimants to recognize, not about whether the state whose government awaits recognition exists. When a regime changes, even if the new rulers dissociate themselves root and branch from their predecessors – perhaps even to the extent of renaming the SPE or renumbering the calendar years so that their predecessors are expunged from history – they do not feel obliged to justify, starting from nothing, the physical extent of the state's jurisdiction. The *in rem* right survives, implying strongly that the *res* does, too.

So for these reasons it seems that, adopting Anthony Lang's suggestion,[9] we should distinguish states from regimes. We should see states as politically organized populations occupying definite territories, and hence as subsisting even when their mode of political organization changes. This allows us, conceptually, to introduce a collective entity that meets the continuity requirement, without at once resorting to nationhood. It also meets the difficulty that punishing "regimes" appears, on the face of it, to be collective punishment only in a marginal sense, for the penalties (such as lustration) fall directly on individuals, by virtue of their own agency. True, the penalties may be imposed on categories of persons, such as officeholders above a certain level of responsibility, and this may involve some significant legal creativity, but from a moral

[7] *The Politics of Aristotle*, ed. Ernest Barker (London: Oxford University Press, 1972), 381n.

[8] Gerhard von Glahn, *Law among Nations*, 7th ed. (New York: Longman, 1995), 68.

[9] Anthony F. Lang, Jr., "Crime and Punishment: Holding States Accountable," *Ethics and International Affairs* 21 (2007): 239–57, p. 253.

point of view it is no great stretch of the idea of "agency" to include in it the holding of an office. (One could have exercised agency by leaving it.) Without an idea of statehood that is distinct from regime, then, we may lack a concept that allows some dimensions of collective responsibility to be grasped.

CAN WE DISTINGUISH STATES FROM NATIONS?

The problem with this provisional conclusion, however, is that states thus conceived of become difficult to distinguish from "nations," to the extent that these are regarded not as Aristotle's *ethnoi* but as civic entities. They are defined, in part, by the desire for political recognition and self-organization (although this need not go so far as statehood). Consider, too, the civic-nationalist idea of a "shared public culture" as a constituent of nationality.[10] It is "a set of ideas about the character of the community," "to some extent the product of political debate," and modifiable (although not easily so) by further political debate.[11] "Public culture" looks like a more restrictive requirement than mere population-plus-territory, as indeed it is; to have a public culture is more than to share space, it is to share space on broadly agreed terms, and it is that agreement that is, we may suppose, at the heart of nationality in the relevant sense. However, several considerations press the notion toward an almost-pure idea of citizenship in which the distinctively national element is somewhat attenuated. Consider, for one example, the case of multinational states, a topic that, understandably, is bracketed in Miller's discussion here.[12] If SPEs are to be held accountable on the basis of nationality, we have to bring into play an idea of nationhood that encompasses multinational states, or else we exempt several once-powerful states (Britain, the Soviet Union) from responsibility for what they did; and the conception of "nationality" that is usable here picks out what is for the most part a political identity that is consistent with the stronger and more ethically or culturally comprehensive subnationalities within. It is at one possibly quite large remove from what would seem to be the most basic constituents of identity. With at least one significant difference that will be explored in a moment, this conception may not be at a great distance from shared statehood.

---

[10] Miller, "Holding Nations Responsible," 243.
[11] David Miller, *On Nationality* (Oxford: Clarendon, 1995), 68–69.
[12] Miller, "Holding Nations Responsible," 244n.

For a second example, consider the topic of change in the shared public culture. It is certainly arguable that some changes in public culture are more fundamental than some regime changes. The public culture of the province of Quebec is generally thought to have evolved radically, during what is termed the "Quiet Revolution" in the 1960s, from a Catholic and conservative nature to a secular and progressive one. This was, as surely one might judge, a greater change than (say) France experienced in the transition from the Fourth to the Fifth Republic. Because its objective is to show that nations are more continuous than states, the nationalist argument must presumably absorb the point by claiming that a public culture subsists despite change, in a way in which states do not subsist through regime change. Why, when it changes, is it the same public culture?

Here we may seem to return to Aristotle, this time, however, to the famous metaphor of the ship[13] that is entirely replaced piece-by-piece while remaining the same ship; or, alternatively, to Michael Oakeshott's metaphor of "Sir John Cutler's famous stockings, so continuously darned with wool that they became wholly transformed, not one particle of silk remaining."[14] Is continuous identity secured by a chain of continuous links, such that even though nothing intrinsically links A to N, if there are links from A to B and from B to C and so forth all the way to N, then A and N are continuous? That model, although perhaps solving some problems, does not seem to make the decisive difference that is sought, in this context at least (because there are equivalent links, of an institutional kind, from the Fourth French Republic to the Fifth). I do not think we should be content with the incremental model, however, for the examples invite us to examine a further question. There are two importantly distinct ways of thinking about continuity that they force us to consider.

First, unlike ships or stockings, human communities work on themselves. They are not the products of another's workmanship but of self-creation, and so, we may say, what underwrites their endurance is not a causal sequence but continuous agency. The province of Quebec was transformed from A to N: what makes it the same entity is not that A led

---

[13] But for doubts about whether the example is Aristotle's, see "The Importance of Ships in Greek Philosophy" on Barry Stocker's blog: http://web.mac.com/barrystocker.

[14] Michael Oakeshott, *On History* (Oxford: Blackwell, 1983), 114. Actually – perhaps because of classist assumptions? – Oakeshott gets the example wrong. Sir John's stockings were originally worsted and were darned with silk. The reference is to Alexander Pope, *Memoirs of the Extraordinary Life, Works and Discoveries of Martinus Scriblerus* (Dublin: Faulkner, 1741), 96–97.

to B which led to C and so forth, but that the process was undertaken by a self-identifying collective agent. The difference between self-induced change and externally imposed change is rightly stressed by theorists of multiculturalism: what multiculturalist policy seeks, they say, is not that cultures should be preserved in their present form, like museum exhibits, but that they should be in secure possession of a "structure" that enables them to determine their own path of development.[15] Further, their claim to possession of that is normatively compelling in a way that a blindly conservative preservationist ethic, focused on cultural content, would not be. If we accept that view, then, we will want to find a normative place for the self-determining capacity of SPEs that have a sufficiently strong sense of their political identity (either as states or as subunits enjoying recognition within states). This recognizes the important truth in the view that continuity requires something other than a "state" in the sense of a regime – there is some enduring entity behind the regime, seeking agency through it. However, the way in which that truth has been acknowledged here emphasizes that what lies behind the regime is a society identified by its political character.

The distinction between continuity as preservation and continuity through self-determination is important. However, is it clear that we can do without preservation altogether? Let us (fancifully) suppose, for example, that the province of Quebec, exploiting its self-determining power within the Canadian federation, decided to abandon the French language, as a commercial and political impediment in the globalized world. Would we really be quite so sure that Quebec was "the same"? To be sure, it can remain "the same" while abandoning some identity-markers, such as Catholicism and political conservatism, but would it be the same if it gave up the last continuous marker, its language? That question invites a return to the metaphors. Aristotle's ship remained a ship, after all, whereas another series of modifications could perhaps have turned it into a large toboggan or an elaborate garden shed. Sir John Cutler's stockings continued to be stockings, as opposed to being made into dusters for his servants' use; as Oakeshott notes, there are "unchanged items in the situation, namely the shape and so on which identifies the stockings as stockings, which survives and is not composed by the differences."[16] This invites a rather different response.

---

[15] Will Kymlicka, *Liberalism, Community and Culture* (Oxford: Clarendon, 1989), chap. 8.
[16] *On History*, 115n.

On the former view, the continuity of an SPE is established by the continuity of its internal political process. It is enough, on this view, that there should be a civic process, regardless of where that process may lead. On that view, I have suggested, the line between state membership and nationality may be hard to draw with any confidence. On the latter view, however, there must be an abiding "shape" that underwrites continuity despite change. This, because we are setting ethnic nationalism aside, can only be provided by the values contained within a nation's public culture. So, I believe, we are led to a choice. Are people to be held responsible on the basis of their membership in a political community or on the basis of their adherence to a set of shared national values?

There is a basic objection to the latter view. The objection is that practical conclusions do not follow immediately from values. It is not true that, if one is committed to value *A*, one is more closely bound to act *a* – one justified in *A*'s name – than anyone committed to value *B* is, for mediating considerations come into play. Christians with conservative views on, say, extramarital sex or abortion have more in common with many Muslims, in that respect, than they do with many Christians, despite the fact that their theological starting point is closer to that of any Christian than to that of any Muslim. If people can be held responsible for anything, it must be for something that is *done*, and what is to be *done* cannot be read off one's fundamental beliefs in such a way as to imply complicity in what others take their practical requirements to be. Furthermore, here the confusing potential of the ends–means distinction comes to light. Whatever the merits of that distinction, it cannot mean that we first settle on ends and then and only then begin to think about means, for what we ought to think about ends should involve thinking about the means that are necessary to their realization. If means have consequences that outweigh the value of the end sought, the end should not be sought in the first place. We have to choose sequences of ends and means together, and it has to be that it is for the sequence that we choose that we are held accountable – not for our endorsement of the end alone. For despite our endorsement of the end, we may come to believe its value to be outweighed by the moral costs of the means adopted.

Those who plotted (at terrible cost) to assassinate Hitler were German patriots. So was Werner Heisenberg, who, speculation suggests, surreptitiously undermined the Nazi nuclear bomb project by dragging his feet and exaggerating the likely costs.[17] Neither unpatriotically wanted

---

[17] See John Cornwell, *Hitler's Scientists* (New York: Viking, 2003), chap. 23.

their country to lose the war. Shostakovich was a Russian patriot who loathed and feared Stalin but also feared a German victory. Bishop Bell was a British patriot who bravely denounced the bombing of Dresden. They all emphatically endorsed some *A* while refusing some *a*. I do not think we should take them to be accountable for their endorsement of *A* absent some heroic costs for their rejection of *a*. The Hitler assassins *were* heroic. Heisenberg could excusably have avoided heroism, given the world-destroying risks of a Nazi bomb. Shostakovich was cryptically evasive and ironic. Bishop Bell lost preferment. The price that they had to pay was contextually determined. Given the distinction that I have tried to draw thus far, however, I do not believe their responsibility should be determined on that basis, for to will the end is not to will the means, and we need not be excused for something that we have never willed in the first place.[18] The manner in which values are politically mediated is decisive, and when the means adopted – specific policies of aggression or atrocity – are criminal, their criminality cannot be seen as immediately implicating those who hold the national values in question.

COLLECTIVE RESPONSIBILITY?

The foregoing does not claim to be decisive. There is, clearly, too much overlap between the nationalist and statist views, the one positing a nation with a political culture behind the state, the other requiring only a political society – somewhat resembling (conceptually) the "civil society" that Locke interposed between the state of nature and the creation of a political regime, perhaps. There is obviously room for contestation, furthermore, over what should and should not be immediately attributable to a nation's values. In real-world cases, continuity will normally involve elements of both the self-determination model and the value-stability model, so that even if an analytic distinction could be made it would have little or no application. All the same, however, the distinction is one that demands to be pursued in one context at least: that of collective liability to punishment, for that specific liability calls for a specific justification.

In *The Question of German Guilt*, effectively the beginning of the modern discussion of the topic, Karl Jaspers unfortunately conflates the issues of general liability and liability to punishment, in the following way. His book famously distinguishes between four kinds of guilt, introducing the category of "political guilt" for what is incurred by membership in

---

[18] But see Amy Sepinwall's chapter in this volume.

an SPE that has committed crimes. As others have pointed out, "guilt" is a poor term for what he has in mind, which might better be called "liability," for its implications are entirely a matter of what can be done to members of a criminal SPE when it has been defeated.[19] Unlike "guilt" properly so-called – something incurred only by what someone has done – liability is a forward-looking concept. It is about what may befall you. If your SPE commits aggression and atrocity and is defeated in war, you should expect to suffer whatever the consequences turn out to be. Terminology aside, after defining the concept, Jaspers immediately goes on to announce two propositions: "Everybody is co-responsible for the way he is governed," and "Jurisdiction rests with the power and will of the victor." These two propositions cover at least three possible scenarios, which may provoke quite different moral responses.

There are, first, what we may term the natural consequences of waging aggressive war. Obviously the term "natural" is only approximately right, for what happens to either side in a war results in large part from voluntary decisions by its adversary. We can hardly say that the destruction of Dresden was a natural consequence of the bombing raids on Coventry, mediated as it was by Air Marshal Arthur Harris's vengeful response.[20] However, something, involving some degree of severe physical damage obviously not statable in advance, would almost certainly have been the consequence. Other consequences of war include economic dislocation, shortage of vital resources, loss of population, military occupation, and perhaps forced migration when disputed territory is lost. Such things are rightly describable as "the consequences of the deeds of the state whose power governs me and under whose order I live."[21] We may extend those consequences to embrace another case, too. Let us suppose that one side or other, after the conflict, must bear certain costs, and that it is within the discretion of the victor to decide to whom they should fall. Those on the losing side would have to accept, as "consequences of the deeds of [their] state," that if resources are scarce the populations of victorious states, or of states victimized by the aggression, will be given higher priority, or that if capital for reconstruction is in short supply, then reconstruction in the territory of the aggressor state will be given low priority. I think that both of these cases demonstrate the force, but also the limits, of

[19] On the distinction between guilt and responsibility, see especially Hannah Arendt, *Responsibility and Judgment* (New York: Schocken, 2003), 147–58.
[20] See Randall Hansen, *Fire and Fury: The Allied Bombing of Germany 1942–45* (Toronto: Doubleday Canada, 2008).
[21] Jaspers, *Question*, 31.

Tony Honoré's notion of "outcome responsibility," that type of responsibility that we appeal to in deciding where the benefits and burdens resulting from an action should fall. As Miller explains the notion, it is distinct from both causal responsibility – we might be causally responsible for remote or improbable consequences that we should not suffer for – and moral responsibility – it may not arise from moral fault.[22] This certainly seems a good idea of responsibility to employ when we are looking for something more than mere causation and something less than moral guilt, but it takes for granted that there is some *given* set of benefits and burdens to be distributed, somehow, and so cannot justify our creating *new* or additional burdens on the basis of an attribution of guilt.[23] It would be one thing to feed civilian refugees before feeding captured prisoners of war from an aggressor state, if one had to make that hard choice. It would be something else deliberately to withhold available food from the latter.[24]

This brings us to the third case, that of punishment. Jaspers maintains that it is a matter of absolute discretion on the part of the victor. "The victor can, if he will, bring the consequences into a form of right, and thus of moderation."[25] This idea apparently comes out of nowhere in Jaspers's book. There is perhaps a Nietzschean echo in the implication that "right" is not a constraint on the strong but something that the strong may optionally "will" if, exercising discretion, they choose "moderation." However, it is hard to find mooring for the idea in either political theory or international law; in neither do we find good arguments, or any argument at all in fact, for the idea that anyone's power should be unrestrained by anything. It is simply not a good idea. Nor is it even barely consistent with any developed idea of "punishment," which standardly entails a degree of proportionality between offence and sanction, something that is of course entirely inconsistent with the so-called punisher's absolute discretion.[26]

---

[22] Miller, "Holding Nations Responsible," 245–46.

[23] I follow Anthony Lang ("Crime and Punishment," 247) in maintaining that "the *infliction* of harm in response to a violation of a norm" (emphasis added) is essential to the idea of punishment, and I assume that this means that the infliction is justified *as* such a response and not as an element of some other purpose (such as military victory). I also follow Lang (ibid., 248) in excising the requirement that punishment be inflicted by states, thus rejecting Kant (*Metaphysics of Morals* 6.331), whose view implies that states and their rulers cannot be "punished."

[24] For a relevant controversy, see S. P. MacKenzie "On the *Other Losses* Debate," *International History Review* 14 (1992): 661–80.

[25] Jaspers, *Question*, 36.

[26] This is so even if we take a relaxed view of the proportionality requirement: see Jon Elster, "Retribution," in *Retribution and Reparation in the Transition to Democracy*, ed. Jon Elster (New York: Cambridge University Press, 2006), 39–40.

If we reject Jaspers's proposal, however, we are left with no clear basis, among his categories, for the justification of collective punishment. His category of "metaphysical guilt," it is true, is often taken to implicate all conationals, but on Jaspers's account, it is actually presented as universal[27] – although it is somehow intensified by conationals' proximity and association, it is everyone's, and as Jaspers describes it would presumably attach in some degree to appeasing nations who failed to obstruct the rise of Nazism. "Criminal guilt" and "moral guilt" rest on attributions of individual agency and cannot tell us what should happen to collectives. It is this that forces us to confront hard choices about what the collective is. For whereas the collective, whatever it is, will indeed suffer certain necessary consequences, we cannot deliberately impose further consequences without a more compelling account of the capacity in which it is to be made to suffer them.

COMPLICITY, RISK, AND LIABILITY

To be a member of an SPE is to share in a complex and unpredictable mix of advantages and risks. Although both advantages and risks are important from a normative point of view, it is the former that have most commonly been emphasized in political thought. The receipt of benefits has often been taken to be one of the most important grounds of political obligation, requiring (it has been argued) a contribution of service or obedience in return. The case for national liability may be made in the same way. Miller, for example, relies on it as an alternative (or supplement) to the argument from shared values. Setting "like-mindedness" aside, members of a group are engaged in cooperative relations that make them "beneficiaries of a common practice" and so liable for "their share of the costs," such as external costs imposed by their group on other groups.[28]

In its more narrowly political form, where it is often called the "fair-play" thesis, the argument from the receipt of benefits has been repeatedly and effectively criticized. One kind of critique, given a famous formulation by Robert Nozick and developed in detail by A. John Simmons, contends that the receipt of benefits is morally inconclusive. You may not have wanted the benefits, or what you are called on to do in return for

---

[27] Jaspers, *Question*, 32; but see Erin Kelly's contribution to this volume (Chapter 7) for a different view.

[28] Miller, "Holding Nations Responsible," 253.

them exceeds their value to you. There may be cases in which people have voluntarily chosen to receive benefits, but there are probably not enough such cases to sustain a theory of obligation that entitles states to general obedience.[29] Another kind of critique, developed by Robert Goodin, points out that the respective scopes of receiving and giving do not map on to each other: we give protection to various categories of vulnerable people without expecting to receive anything from them in return.[30] A third kind of critique, aimed particularly at Rawls's view of civic reciprocity and the (limited) internationalism that he derived from it, refers to facts of interdependence in a globalized world, in which networks of beneficial exchange do not coincide with, but far exceed, the boundaries of SPEs.[31] I believe that the same or similarly serious obstacles stand in the way of the nationalist version. The considerations that obstruct the benefits-received case for political obligation also make it hard to accept the parallel case for requiring conationals to bear responsibility for the external costs imposed by their nation's actions.

Elsewhere I have argued, however, that the risks entailed in association are more normatively powerful than the benefits produced by it.[32] That one is part of an association that generates risks for others generates a special reason for concern about its actions. That is true regardless of where one's account stands in an audit of benefits and costs. What makes the individual liable is not an individual accounting but participation in a general scheme. What *justifies* that scheme, or makes it morally defensible, is indeed the hope of net benefit, as the social contract tradition maintained. What *legitimates* it,[33] however, or entitles it to claim your support, is that it systematically presents everyone with the possibility of loss, so that all participants are bound to do what they can to diminish its riskiness. The moral intuition here is a basic one: individuals are especially liable for what they contribute to, and the most ordinary acts of members of an SPE amount, in effect, to contributions to its support. The risks that it imposes are many. Some arise from the fact that, by collectivizing

---

[29] See Robert Nozick, *Anarchy, State and Utopia* (Oxford: Blackwell, 1974), 90–95; A. John Simmons, *Moral Principles and Political Obligation*, chap. 5.

[30] Robert Goodin, "What Is So Special about Our Fellow-Countrymen?" *Ethics* 98 (1988): 663–86.

[31] See, for example, Joshua Cohen and Charles Sabel, "Extra Rempublicam Nulla Justitia?" *Philosophy and Public Affairs* 34 (2006): 147–75.

[32] Richard Vernon, "States of Risk: Should Cosmopolitans Favor Their Compatriots?" *Ethics and International Affairs* 21 (2007), 451–69. The view is developed in *Cosmopolitan Regard* (Cambridge: Cambridge University Press, 2010), chap. 2.

[33] The distinction is made by Simmons, *Moral Principles*, chap. 1.

security arrangements, SPEs diminish personal capacity (the capacity of Mill's "savage" to "shift for himself," because "civilization," as he says in his essay with that title, makes us codependent). Some arise from the fact that by promoting intense forms of interdependence, they increase each member's vulnerability to others. Some arise from the fact that minorities inevitably expose themselves to majority tastes and preferences from which they cannot and perhaps even should not be wholly protected. Some arise from the pervasiveness of political demands on us. Some arise from the fact that SPEs acquire, through the compliance of their members, enormous coercive force.

It is, of course, with the last of these that we are concerned here – the internal support that enables SPEs to deploy external violence. The topic of collective punishment is triggered when the coercive resources of an SPE are deployed against members of other SPEs in ways that rise to the level of international crime. Such crime is possible only because of the organized resources of an SPE, and members of the SPE are related to it by virtue of their participation as citizens in a structure of arrangements that make possible the deployment of physical force on a massive scale and in an effective way. That, I think, remains true even when we insist that an SPE is not only a political structure, that it also embodies a set of shared beliefs, for the fact remains that, whatever the relation between those beliefs and criminal state acts, it is the political structure that enables one practical intention, as distinct from other potential practical intentions (sustainable by those beliefs) even to be formed, and the intended acts then to be executed.

Why, though, is it proper for the members of an SPE to be made to suffer punishment for what their collective, in its political aspect, does? In the final section of this chapter, I argue that in fact many forms of punishment are improper, but we need a reason why *any* might be proper. It is of course a standard feature of theories of collective responsibility that responsibility is collective just to the extent that it does not reduce to responsibility on the part of the collective's members. Members may also have individual responsibility, of course, by virtue of what they have personally done, and that responsibility will be graded (as international law seeks to do) on the basis of what they did. That simple membership should incur responsibility, however, is another matter. Nor do I think we can settle that matter by invoking a domestic equivalent of the "double-effect" doctrine in military ethics. Invoking that, we might say: sometimes visiting costs on the innocent is a sad but unfortunate ("collateral") effect of punishing the guilty, but one that we must accept if the guilty are not to go unpunished. That argument proceeds against the secure background of a theory of retribution that has already established that punishment is deserved, however, and is not available at a point at which we are trying to decide about punishability in the first place. Members of an SPE are not "collateral" to it, they comprise it, and are the very people on whom, under a certain description, punishment is to fall.

It is the special nature of political membership that may provide at least the outline of an answer here. Being a member of a social group does not necessarily entail responsibility for what it does. Consider David Miller's example of a crowd on a rampage, different members of it contributing differentially to its destructiveness.[34] Although not all of the crowd's members intended its most destructive acts, and some may indeed regret them, it is still the case that the whole group can be held responsible for the damage done and that all its members can be made liable for repairing it. That seems true, but only within certain limits. Suppose, to modify the example, a group of workers go on (legal) strike and take their turns maintaining a picket line. Some pickets lose their cool and overturn a vehicle that tries to cross the line. Is the whole group responsible? If we think not, then in the case of social groups, it seems, we draw some kind of a line – no doubt always in need of contextual interpretation – between a group's essential aims and what is extrinsic to them. If militant philatelists were to get together and demonstrate in favor of some philatelically relevant cause, and one among them were to be convicted of an opportunistic crime (shoplifting, let us say), we would surely not hold all philatelists collectively responsible for the offence, or hold philately itself to be morally tainted by larceny.

Political society is different, however, in that what we let ourselves in for, by virtue of our membership in it, is *inherently* open-ended. In the case of social groups, exit is normally possible, sometimes even easy. In the case of social groups, moreover, the ends are normally transparent. In the case of SPEs, neither condition applies; exit is costly, and the ends to be adopted are opaque in the sense that what they will turn out to be escapes any one person's control. An SPE in which neither of those conditions applied would not have the features that made the existence of SPEs possible or even desirable. If exit were easy – as easy as exit from a typical social group – it would have to be the case that an SPE offered only the minimal advantages that could automatically be replicated elsewhere, not the basis for any sort of continuous identity. On the other hand, an SPE that guaranteed to any of its members that its future decision stream would conform reliably to their values would have to be a closed society, precommitted to a collective identity in ways that foreclosed future politics.

Political liberals are strongly wedded to the idea that responsibility attaches only to individual agents and are likely to resist the claim that anything but one's own agency can lead to commitment.[35] Yet, even if we hold, at the level of moral principle, the view that people should be held responsible only for their own decisions, we must recognize that in supporting a state we effectively lend our support to unknown future policies. This is true even in the case of liberal states that impose constitutional side constraints on the choice of possible future policies, for that only reduces the range of uncertainty, albeit significantly, without eliminating it. To be part of a state of any kind is to be exposed, by way of the most ordinary activities of citizenship, to acute moral risk. The risk is that of complicity in policies of which one may strongly disapprove. This may seem to depend on an overly generous notion of complicity, one that makes the individual complicit in decisions that others have made without his or her approval. For reasons stated by Locke himself, however, unless this is so, there can be no political society, for the very idea of a political society depends on the general adoption of binding decision-rules that exclude personal consent.[36] That adoption is simply inseparable from the functional capacity that grounds the justification of states. It is this forward-looking element, an implication of future, as-yet-unknown commitment, that enables us to say that state membership creates liability in a way in which shared national values do not. It is part of being a citizen that one should recognize that the political power that one supports will be put to as-yet-unknown use; it is not similarly part of being a member of a nation that one should be implicated in as-yet-unknown constructions of the values that one recognizes. When others (in my judgment) misconstrue the values that I share with them, I can unilaterally dissociate myself from their views; I cannot in the same way unilaterally dissociate myself from the practical support that I have given to a political system that, as it happens, adopts policies that I detest.

In Mark Drumbl's terms, the attribution proposed here is "crude," in passing over moral differentiations and excuses.[37] That view, as Drumbl rightly notes, is immediately objectionable, for its reach is indiscriminate.

[35] Ibid., 242.
[36] Locke, *Second Treatise*, s. 98.
[37] Mark Drumbl, *Atrocity, Punishment and International Law* (New York: Cambridge University Press, 2007), 197. For a defense of crude attributions, see Amy Sepinwall, Chapter 9, this volume.

Those who object to the reach of the view, for liberal (or perhaps other) reasons, may be somewhat reconciled to it by the following section, which briefly sets out reasons for limiting the consequences of political liability. Accepting the crude characterization, I propose that the crudeness of attribution demands restraint in punishment, as the final section of the chapter suggests.

POLITICAL PUNISHMENT?

To recapitulate, this chapter rejects Jaspers's view of political "guilt" as absolute: such a view would effectively obliterate any distinction between collective and individual liability, because the victor and "punisher" could impose unlimited sanctions on collective and individual alike, or, if nominally on the collective alone, without regard for how collective sanctions distributed to individuals. The view advanced here is different, in specifying that sanctions must fall on the collective in its political aspect, so that their (foreseeable) distribution to individuals should respect the distinction between their political identity and their other identities. The view advanced here is also different, however, from Tracy Isaacs's category of "membership responsibility," a category that imputes responsibility that is defeasible by an individual's resistance to, or protest against, the acts of her collective. I agree with Isaacs that this is identical to personal moral responsibility and, being *basically* distributive, not properly a species of collective liability at all.[38] Political liability, as defended here, is collective and indefeasible. However, unlike Jaspers's "political guilt," it is not unlimited.

What might it mean, though, to punish a collective "in its political aspect"? It could of course mean extinguishing its political identity altogether (thus exemplifying Rousseau's dictum that "It is possible to destroy a state without destroying any of its members"[39]). This could be done by incorporating it within a larger state or by dividing it into several pieces. Or it could mean imposing regime change upon it. (MacArthur's Japan is the notable example, perhaps only formally marred, as an example, by the retention of the emperor as the state's embodiment.) Moving down a level, punishment could mean imposing strict limits on a state's political capacity, particularly its military capacity: the limits imposed

---

[38] Tracy Isaacs, *Moral Responsibility in Collective Contexts* (New York: Oxford University Press, forthcoming).

[39] Rousseau, *Social Contract*, I.4.

at Versailles on German rearmament, and Article 9 of the post-1945 Japanese constitution (forbidding offensive military capability) are examples. Moving down another level, we can imagine more minor restrictions on sovereignty, such as enforced no-fly zones, monitored guarantees to minorities, or international inspection regimes, as, potentially, forms of punishment, although to my knowledge, such things have never been imposed as punishments but by UN peace-and-security decision or by treaty.

All these are measures that, by striking at political capacity, can be discriminated as political punishments, and thus as valid forms of collective punishment, according to the foregoing argument. A particularly difficult issue is posed, however, by reparations, which are among the oldest forms of penalty imposed by victors. For here the argument points in two directions. On the one hand, assuming that reparations will be paid from tax revenue, imposing reparations will amount to a political penalty as described earlier, because it is the raising of revenue that constitutes an essential feature of states and the spending of revenue that constitutes one of the principal modes of political independence. Requiring an SPE to pay reparations inhibits or replaces other potential uses of its revenue, thus striking fundamentally at its political capacity. On the other hand, given the fungible nature of money, reparations amount to replacements of other uses to which taxpayers might put their resources, individually or collectively, thus striking at them not (only) as citizens but in a generic capacity as consumers of private or public goods. Should we regard this, reverting to an idea from military ethics mentioned earlier, as an instance of "collateral damage," the penalty to consumers being inseparable from the penalty to citizens, and thus legitimate?

The objection to that approach may be formed in terms of yet another borrowing from military ethics. Suppose there is some resource that is essential to both military and other purposes: the electricity grid, let us say, that powers not only radar stations and missile batteries but also hospitals and homes: can that be targeted, on the grounds that the damage to hospitals and homes is "collateral" to the destruction of military assets? Henry Shue argues persuasively that it cannot.[40] Although we may justifiably regard a munitions factory as primarily a military target even though civilians work in it and will die if we bomb it, we cannot regard

---

[40] Henry Shue, "Bombing to Rescue? NATO's 1999 Bombing of Serbia," in *Ethics and Foreign Intervention*, eds. Deen K. Chatterjee and Don E. Scheid (Cambridge: Cambridge University Press, 2003).

general purpose infrastructure as "primarily" anything (or it would not be *general* purpose). Taking that consideration back to the case in hand, money is, surely, the most general purpose of all goods, in fact, the one example of a good that is a good only because it *is* general purpose – as Marx vividly explained in the *1844 Manuscripts*. Thus the argument that prohibits attacks on general purpose infrastructure would seem to rule out forced reparations as well.

What might tip the argument the other way, however, is another consideration mentioned earlier. A distinction was made between what could (with reservations) be called the natural consequences of a decision, punishment for making a decision, and, between the two, the issue of allocating burdens when allocations must be made between the guilty and innocent parties. If damage from conflict reaches the point at which what is left cannot save both parties from severe deprivation, it would seem legitimate for the innocents to put their needs first. The situation in which this dilemma arises is rare, however. The decision to prefer the innocent would arise not from any theory of punishment but from two principles: that the victims of injustice should not be made to suffer further and that the agents of justice should not be penalized. Even in the extreme case, then, the argument here supports only political punishment (properly so-called), for political membership, not for national identity. Political membership, I have argued, invites liability in a way that national identity does not but, correspondingly, what it invites – in terms of punishment – is quite restricted. The strongest reason for collective sanctions weakens their modality.

Index